Fig 5. 1782 portrait of Elizabeth Raffald

SAUCE LABELS
1750 – 1950

BY JOHN SALTER

The Wine Label Circle, 2002

Published 2002 by
Antique Collectors' Club
5 Church Street, Woodbridge, Suffolk
in association with
The Wine Label Circle
Website http://mindlink.net/circom

ISBN 1 85149 431 6

© John Salter, 2002

This publication is protected by International Copyright Law and the right of John Salter to be identified as author of this work has been asserted by him in accordance with the Copyright, Designs and Patents Act, 1988..
All rights reserved. No part of this publication may be reproduced, stored in a retrieval system, or transmitted in any form or by an means, electronic, mechanical, photocopying, recording or otherwise, and whether or not transiently or incidentally to some other use of this publication, without the prior written permission of the copyright owner.

British Library Cataloguing in Publication Data is available from the British Library

Salter, J.R. (John R.), 1932-
Sauce Labels

Includes bibliographical references, list of illustrations and index

Design and photography by John Bloxham

Printed and bound in England by Saffron Media Ltd

Set in Stone Serif typeface

SAUCE LABELS
1750 – 1950

BY JOHN SALTER
M.A., F.C.M.I., F.C.I.W.M., F.R.G.S., F.R.S.A., A.C.I.Arb.

President 1986 – 1987 and Honorary Solicitor
Of The Wine Label Circle

In celebration of its Golden Jubilee

Antique Collectors' Club
in association with
The Wine Label Circle, 2002

Fig 1. The Circle's Presidential Badge was designed by Mark Fitzpatrick, a student who won an open competition, and produced by CJ Vander Ltd.

PREFACE

BY THE PRESIDENT OF THE WINE LABEL CIRCLE

THE YEAR 2002 sees not only the 50th Anniversary of the Reign of Our Gracious Queen Elizabeth II but also of the founding of the Wine Label Circle, of which I have the honour of being its first Lady President, by the late Edward J. Pratt for the stimulation and encouragement of research into the history and development of labels for use on decanters, whether containing wine or vinegar, spirit or essence, cordial or condiment.

This book reflects the lively interest in sauce labels of several long-standing active members of the Wine Label Circle. The sauce label and the wine label are closely related in form, utility and craftsmanship, whether made of gold, silver, enamel, porcelain, mother-of-pearl or other materials. It is only to be expected that many people interested in investigating the wine label would bring the same talent to bear on an exhaustive study of the sauce label and it is therefore appropriate that this volume should appear under the aegis of the Wine Label Circle.

It is therefore with particular pleasure that I commend to the reader this publication by a former Chairman of The Silver Society and a former President of this Society on a subject which will give pleasure not just to the silver and glass enthusiast but also to the cook, the gastronome and the antiquarian. It will indeed serve as an hors d'oeuvre to the long awaited new book on wine labels to be published shortly as a companion volume to this publication by the Society and we are indeed fortunate to have it edited by Professor Salter. I would also like to thank the Book Committee under the Chairmanship of Patrick Gaskell-Taylor for their sterling work and support given to our publishing ventures.

MARGARET PULLAN

Fig 2. Rare Silver-Gilt Soy frame complete with all six original labels by Robert Piercy, London, 1775

FOREWORD

THIS BOOK explores two different aspects of antiquarian interest: those of the collector of silver and of glass, because of the inter-relation of sauce labels and bottle frames made of silver and the various types of glass bottles, decanters and vessels that the labels once adorned.

It is Professor Salter's ambition to mount an exhibition, perhaps in London, which will demonstrate this relationship clearly. In the meantime, this book provides an insight into the eating customs and habits of our forefathers, and of their gastronomic excesses if the recipes and bills of fare are anything to go by.

Such research into the history of glass has been undertaken recently, and this has raised awareness of a fascinating subject. This book on sauce labels takes matters further, but there is still much work to be done on the relationships between the suppliers of glass bottles and the silversmiths.

There is an awakening of interest in the use of sauces. Frames and their bottles can still be bought for use on the dining table, often in conjunction with flavoured vinegars purchased at the supermarket and then decanted. The labels are still useful as well as being decorative, adding to the presentation of a meal. This book will help in experimentation. As Master of a City of London Livery Company I am happy to commend this book.

Kenneth F Bacon
Master, The Worshipful Company of Glass Sellers of London
2001 - 2002

PREFACE.

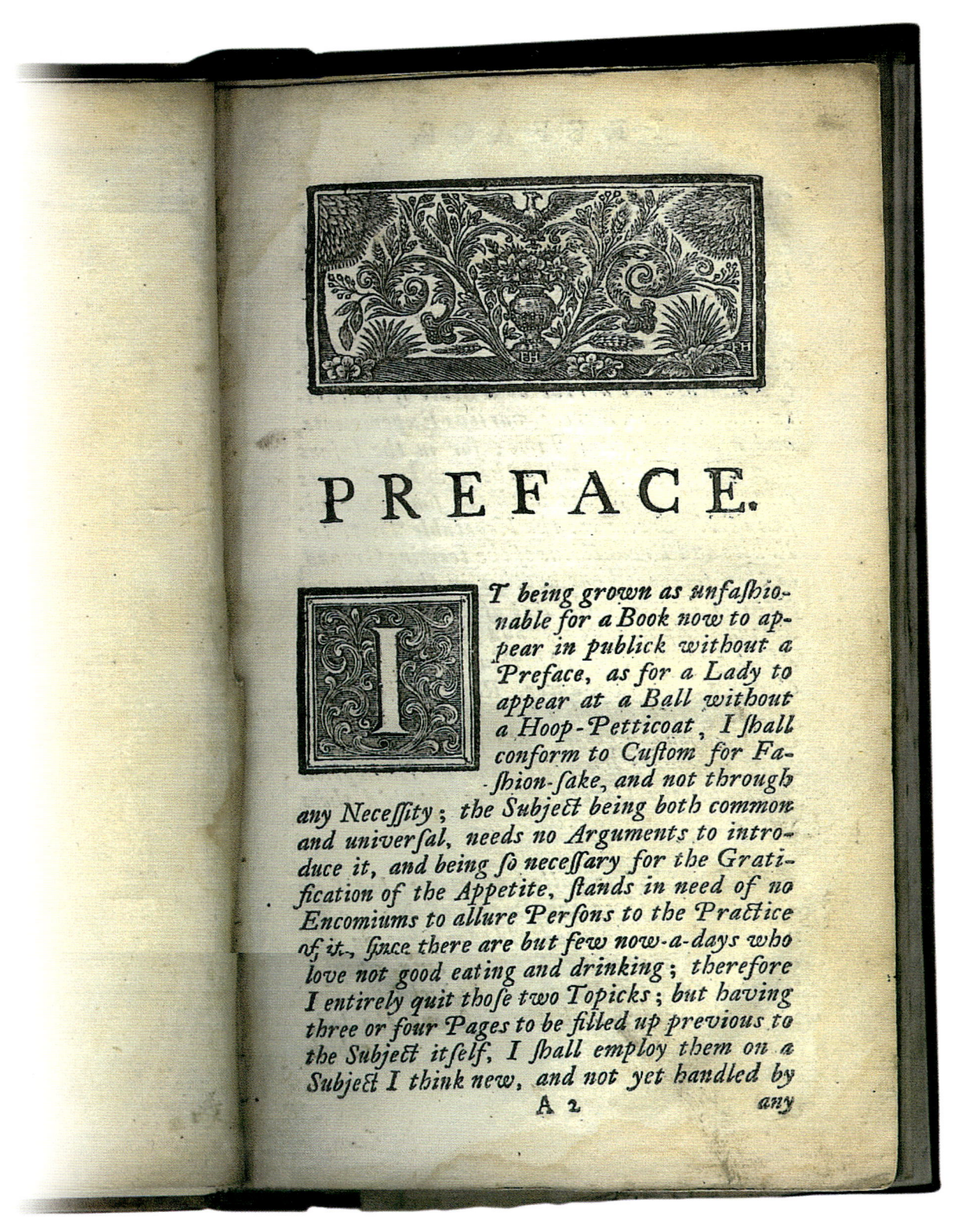

I*T being grown as unfashionable for a Book now to appear in publick without a Preface, as for a Lady to appear at a Ball without a Hoop-Petticoat, I shall conform to Custom for Fashion-sake, and not through any Necessity; the Subject being both common and universal, needs no Arguments to introduce it, and being so necessary for the Gratification of the Appetite, stands in need of no Encomiums to allure Persons to the Practice of it, since there are but few now-a-days who love not good eating and drinking; therefore I entirely quit those two Topicks; but having three or four Pages to be filled up previous to the Subject itself, I shall employ them on a Subject I think new, and not yet handled by*

A 2   any

Fig 3. Part of Elizabeth Smith's preface of 1737. Clinging muslin dresses from France replaced the huge hoops and wide skirts, which were confined to Court occasions at St James's Palace from 1790 until Queen Charlotte's death in 1818.

CONTENTS

DEDICATION

To my wife

CITATIONS

The Journal of The Wine Label Circle is cited as follows:

Volume No, WLJ, Page No.

For example 10 WLJ 15 means page 15 of the tenth volume

Citations of 1 WLJ and 2 WLJ refer to pagination contained in the Second Edition of 1 WLJ and 2 WLJ

Where Sauce Titles listed in Chapter 3 appear in the text they are shown by the use of Roman Capitals, for example ANCHOVY.

SG, used in Chapter 5, stands for Silver – Gilt and G stands for Gold

ACKNOWLEDGEMENTS

The author is grateful to the Wine Label Circle for permitting materials previously published in the Journal to be reproduced in this book, to Baldwin's numismatists for drawing the Author's attention to Diderot's Encyclopedia, to the Circle's President for photographs 1, 67 and 68, to Mr Andrew Gilmour for the photograph in fig. 112 and photographs 3, 36, 48, 50 and 73, to Mr Brian H. Watson for the photograph in fig. 112, to Mr Theo Deelder of Eloy Foundation for photograph 72 and to Messrs. Garwood and Voight for the print in fig. 117.

PREFACE By the President of the Wine Label Circle	V
FOREWORD By the Master Glass Seller	VII
DEDICATION	IX
CITATIONS	IX
ACKNOWLEDGEMENTS	IX
REFERENCES	XI
1. THE INTRODUCTION	1
2. THE SAUCES	23
3. THE TITLES	35
4. THE RECIPES	41
5. THE LABELS	67
6. THE MAKERS	89
7. THE DESIGNS	119
8. THE ARMORIALS	143
9. THE GOLD AND SILVER-GILT	149
10. THE NON-SILVER	155
11. THE MARKS AND SETS	157
12. THE BOTTLES, CHAINS AND FRAMES	163
ILLUSTRATIONS	174
INDEX	176

Fig 7. Extracts from Mrs Beeton's well-used Cookery Book, 1910 Edition.

REFERENCES

1. De Re Coquineria (on cookery). Marcus Apicius. Circa 400 AD. The original ninth century transcription is held by the New York Academy of Medicine. A second edition (by Blasius Lanciloti) was published in Venice around 1500 AD. English translation by John Edwards, The Roman Cookery of Apicius. 1984 (APICIUS)

2. Royal Cookery of the Complete Court-Cook containing the Choicest Receipts in all the particular branches of Cookery now in use in the Queen's Palaces. Patrick Lamb. 1710 (LAMB)

3. The Cook's Dictionary. John Nott. 1726 (NOTT)

4. The Country Housewife and Lady's Director. Richard Bradley. 1727, 6th Edition 1736 (BRADLEY)

5. The Compleat City and Country Cook. Charles Carter. 1730 (CARTER)

6. The Compleat Housewife or Accomplished Gentlewoman's Companion. Elizabeth (Eliza) Smith. 8th Edition 1737 (SMITH)

7. Diaries of a Country Parson. James Woodforde. 1758 – 1802 (WOODFORDE)

8. Cookbook. Martha Curtis. Presented by Taylor Wine Company. 1759 (CURTIS)

9. Cook's Paradise – a Complete System of Cookery. William Verral. 1759 (VERRAL)

10. The Art of Cookery made Plain and Easy. Hannah Glasse. 1747, 7th Edition 1774 (GLASSE)

11. The English Art of Cookery. Richard Briggs. 1st Edition 1788 (BRIGGS)

12. The Housekeeper's Instructor, or Universal Family Cook. William Henderson. 7th Edition circa 1797 (HENDERSON)

13. The Experienced English Housekeeper. Elizabeth Raffald. 1769, 12th Edition 1799 (RAFFALD)

14. The London Art of Cookery and Housekeeper's Complete Assistant. John Farley. 10th Edition 1804 (FARLEY)

15. The Cook's Oracle. Dr. William Kitchener. 1817, 4th Edition 1822 (KITCHENER)

16. The New Female Instructor or Young Woman's Companion and Guide to Domestic Happiness. Perhaps by Elizabeth Insull. 1st Edition 1824 (INSULL)

17. The House Book or Family Chronicle of Useful Knowledge and Cottage Physician. Dr. William Scott. 1st Edition 1826 (SCOTT)

18. The Cook's Dictionary. Richard Dolby (of the Thatched House Tavern, St. James's Street, London). 1836 (DOLBY)

19. The Lady's Own Cookery Book and New Dinner-Table Directory. Lady Charlotte Bury. 3rd Edition 1844 (BURY)

20. The Wife's Own Book of Cookery. Frederick Bishop. 1st Edition 1855 (BISHOP)

21. The Housewife's Reason Why. Robert Philp. 1st Edition 1857 (PHILP)

22. The Book of Household Management. Isabella Beeton. 1st Edition combining the monthly supplements published between 1859 and 1861 in the Englishwoman's Domestic Magazine. 1861 (BEETON)

23. Family Fare or The Young Housewife's Daily Assistant. Cre-Fydd. 2nd Edition 1864 (CRE-FYDD)

24. The Englishwoman's Cookery Book. Isabella Beeton. Known as Mrs Beeton's Shilling Cookery Book. 1870 (BEETON SHILLING)

25. Liebig Company's Recipe Book. Justus von Liebig and H. M. Young. Warrington. 1885 (LIEBIG)

26. Mrs Beeton's Cookery Book. Isabella Beeton. 1910 (BEETON COOKERY)

Fig 8. Oil and Vinegar Frame by William Darker, London, 1720, with labels circa 1750 probably by Richard Binley.

CHAPTER 1

THE INTRODUCTION

1.1 Lady Pembroke wrote in 1779: "There being a fashion for antiques now in England is quite a mistake. They are admired according to their desert as usual by those who understand them." The object of this book is to aid the understanding and to help to prevent mistakes concerning the humble sauce label on the 250th anniversary approximately of its arrival on the English scene. In the most recent publication by the Victoria and Albert Museum on four hundred years of dining in style "Elegant Eating" edited by Philippa Glanville and Hilary Young there is hardly a mention of sauce labels and the important part they played in society and in the dining room in particular. Silver bottle labels for OIL and VINEGAR (generally called "sauce labels") first made their appearance in the 1750s to adorn oil and vinegar bottles either in a two bottle stand or frame or in the five item Warwick cruet. Illustrated is a frame by William Darker, London 1720 (Fig. 8), showing two of the earliest known sauce labels, copying as they did in the 1750s in terms of size and style the wine label which was in use at that date. At the time that the Battersea enamellers of 1753-56 were working there was no wide demand or need for sauce labels and none were made or advertised by them. Whilst there are entries in Volume One of the Wakelin Ledgers for "small bottle tickets" in 1748 and 1750 there is no evidence that these entries related to sauce labels and the weights stated of between 4 and 5.5 dwt per label suggest that they were probably too heavy for the purpose. On the other hand early sauce labels like those illustrated were on the large side because they were used on vinegar bottles and not on soy bottles. Crescent shaped labels were sold by Edward Wakelin in the 1750s and early sauce labels were of this shape. Illustrated is a diamond-cut vinegar decanter of around 1760 with pull off silver cap, displaying an unmarked well-decorated crescent label for HARVEY, a pair with WORCESTER (Fig. 9). It is recorded that in

Fig 9. Single Diamond Cut Vinegar Bottle circa 1760, with pull off cap and label for Harvey, one of a pair with Worcester

1

THE INTRODUCTION

1757 Wakelin's firm made six "half-moon" bottle tickets out of two ounces of silver at a cost of six shillings. The feathered decoration on the OIL and VINEGAR labels illustrated is typical of the work of Richard Binley who ceased production in 1764. The curvature of the labels matches exactly the curvature of the bottles. Early labels can be detected even if unmarked by the size of the lettering. So attributable to the late 1760s are the plain crescents for SOY and KYAN unmarked (1) and for CAYON PEPPER and PEPR VINEGAR by Margaret Binley (2), who from 1767 is recorded as having made sauce labels for Edward Wakelin and John Parker.

1.2 To understand the demand for use at table of condiments in the period 1750 – 1770 we must first delve into some history. In the 17th Century sugar, pepper and mustard were dispensed from castors or lidded vases, salt from secondary salts (such as bell salts) and trenchers (top table had a rather special container), spices from a "box" and pickles from "saucers" using pickle spoons like those illustrated (Fig. 10). In the late 17th Century frames starting being made for pickle jars which needed large labels with long chains to go around the jars. The Earl of Bedford paid seventeen shillings in 1689 for a stand for all sorts of pickle. Saucers developed handles in the 1690s. Pickles and relishes were highly flavoured and very spicy and designed to be taken in small quantities. In the 17th Century castors were made in sets of three without stands or frames. They came in two sizes, a large dredger for sugar and two smaller castors for black pepper and dry mustard or red pepper, like the set illustrated by Thomas Bamford (Fig. 11). They were often made by specialist silversmiths who tried to maintain their use for as long as possible because it was good for business. Small castors or muffineers were also used for pepper and dry mustard but not on the grand dining table. The silver frame was introduced in the 18th Century to keep condiments together and make it easier at that time for servants to deliver condiments at table, clearly labelled to assist in identification. Makers of opaque glass bottles which were attractively labelled followed this concept in the 1770s. The glass bottles were put on various kinds of stands made of various materials. Salt for perhaps historical reasons was kept separate from the cruet frame. It was served using a clean knife and later on salt spoons from trenchers, salt boxes and circular cellars, all with gilt insides. Illustrated are a pair of circular salt cellars by Ebenezer Oliphant of Edinburgh made in 1742 (Fig. 12). Only one label for SALT has consequently been recorded and that probably related to a SALT sauce. In grand homes the salt container on top table was a work of art performing a traditional function as an aid to seating arrangements from the time of the hour glass salt in the late 15th Century followed by the rock crystal salt, the drum salt, the clock salt and the steeple or obelisk salt, until the mid 17th Century when the use of prime and secondary salts faded away, leaving only originally the trencher salt and then the circular salt (Fig. 12) at table. So during the course of the 17th Century the prime salt lost its importance – perhaps these salts went into the melting pot to help pay for the civil war – and was replaced by the centre-piece reflecting the change in dining room seating and habits. Salt continued to be taken from the trencher or cellar with a knife until the shovel and then the salt spoon was

Fig 10. A pair of rat-tailed Pickle Spoons by Isaac Davenport, London, 1698.

Fig 11. Set of Casters by Thomas Bamford I, London, 1720.

Fig 12. Pair of Salt Cellars by Ebenezer Oliphant, 1742.

THE INTRODUCTION

Fig 13. Mustard Pots by Thomas Daniel, London, 1776 (with spoon) and William Carr Hutton, Sheffield 1894 (in silver gilt).

introduced at the end of the 17th Century. The shovel seems to have been a scaled down model of the pickle spoon (Fig. 10). Salt remained separate from the cruet until the late 19th Century with the introduction of the salt pot. Wet mustard on the other hand was included in the larger usually eight bottle 1780s onwards frame served from silver pots with glass liners using mustard spoons. Dry mustard was served from a castor comprised in the Warwick cruet frame. However self standing mustard pots with spoons and glass liners are frequently found from the 1760s onwards. Illustrated (Fig. 13) are pots by Thomas Daniel in 1776 and William Carr Hutton in 1894.

1.3 In 1674 George Ravenscroft was granted a patent for a "particular sort of Chrystaline Glasse resembling Rock Crystall". On many occasions Ravenscroft described certain of his new glass products as "crewets". Thus, for example, the Earl of Bedford bought from him in 1682 a "large water crewet" for two shillings and six pence. Oil and vinegar frames with glass bottles, which were larger than the small essence or soy bottles, date back to the 1690s. Could the contents be easily distinguished without the need for labels? It would appear so until the introduction of choice in flavoured vinegars in the 1750s. The cutting of the glass, into diamond shapes for example, did cloud vision and it became necessary to distinguish by labelling between oil and vinegar bottles before that date. The Warwick cruet was probably introduced by Benjamin Pyne around 1706, although it has been said to have been invented and made by Anthony Nelme for the Earl of Warwick in 1715. It combined the three self standing silver castors with the two bottle oil and vinegar set into a five condiment single frame. The glass was blown thin at this time and was decorated with hollows or simple fluting which would not have obstructed a clear view of the contents. However with the introduction of complicated patterns exquisitely cut into thicker glass oil could easily be mistaken for vinegar and labelling was the easiest solution introduced in the 1750s following wine labelling practice. An advertisement of 1752 encouraged the purchase of diamond cut glass vinegar decanters. These

THE INTRODUCTION

would have been placed on stands holding three or four vinegar decanters, as satellites to the central epergne until around 1780 when the use of the epergne started to decline.

1.4 The silver wine label first made its appearance(3) felt among the richer families, it seems, in the 1730s for use on dark green shaft and globe-decanter bottles and on the cut flint glass decanter. At this time imbibers were becoming concerned to know what the contents were because of the increasing variety of imported wines being made available. The prohibition on the sale of bottled wines was lifted in 1735 and about this time the decanter-bottle began to give way to the globe decanter which had a string collar over which a wine label could be hung (4). Also at this time decanters were being blown sufficiently thickly to enable them to be diamond cut, as advertised, for example, by Jerome Johnson in 1742. The Victoria and Albert Museum has a cylindrical oil or vinegar decanter made of English glass cut all over with hollow diamonds, making it very difficult to see through, with a pull-off silver cap hallmarked in Amsterdam for 1743, fitting a frame likewise hallmarked with the maker's mark of Anthony de Rooy.

1.5 It was, however, the introduction in the 1750s of two new styles of cruet bottles for use with a cruet frame, namely a cylindrical bottle with a tapering neck for flavoured vinegars (like ELDER VINEGAR, TARRAGON VINEGAR, CHILI VINEGAR, GARLIC VINEGAR, CAMP VINEGAR, CAYENNE VINEGAR, CUCUMBER VINEGAR, PEPPER VINEGAR, PINK VINEGAR, and RED VINEGAR to name a few), and an urn shaped small bottle mounted on a spreading foot for soy and essences (like SOY, LEMON and KETCHUP), which were usually fluted on the body with additionally two or more grooves cut around the middle for form horizontal prisms, that led to a need to identify their contents by labelling. The frame for vinegars was known as a vinegar decanter and the frame for three, four, five, six, or eight little "sauce" bottles was known as a soy frame. The soy frame may well have been introduced by Jabez Daniel (or Daniell) in 1750 for Viscount Powerscourt (see below, para. 12.3). Thomas Daniel was a skilled maker of sauce labels in sets of four for his exquisite circular frames. Elizabeth Aldridge was also a maker of early circular soy frames. In 1767 she made a superb silver gilt circular soy frame. Each of the five soy bottles had pull off silver gilt caps. One bottle with large holes in its cap was presumably for black pepper. One cap had numerous small holes. None had a cayenne spoon. Unfortunately the silver gilt labels were missing(5). Robert Piercy made six bottle circular frames in 1765 and 1775 (see Fig. 2).

1.6 For centuries every mansion and substantial house was dependent on stored, dried and salted food with the exception of fish and game caught on the estate locally. Even the game was hung for some time to make it tender. As transport facilities improved less reliance was placed on highly flavoured sauces to make food palatable. Flavourings were supplied from the long established traditional herb garden. Ginger, cloves, cinnamon, peppers and many other spices were imported, especially from the then colonies, the Dutch East India Company and overseas territories controlled by Great Britain.

Fig 14. Spice Box, with three compartments and nutmeg grater, by André Martin, Marseilles. 1758-63.

THE INTRODUCTION

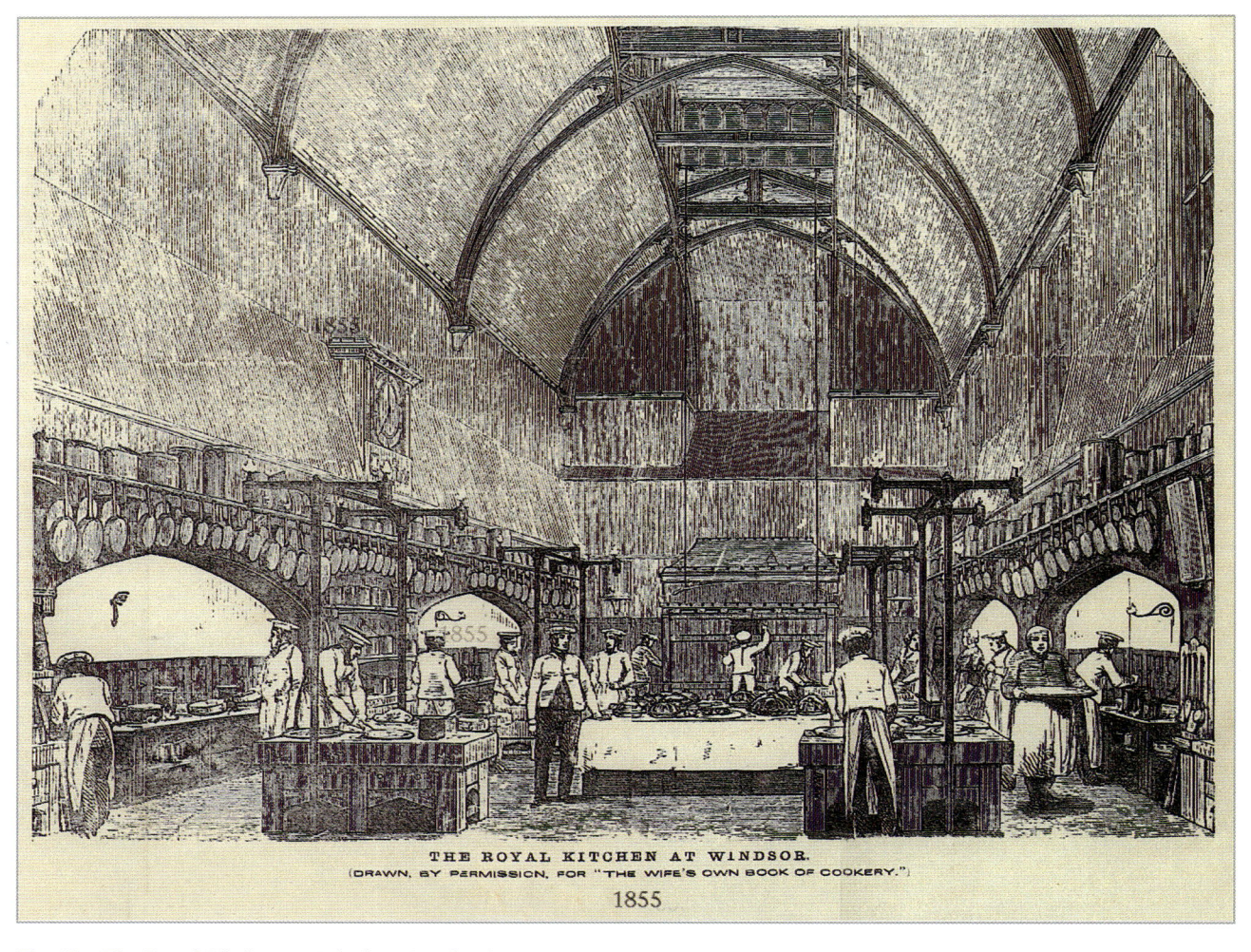

Fig 15. The Royal Kitchen at Windsor Castle, circa 1855

Ginger, nutmeg and cinnamon were often kept in and served from a silver spice box(6). A three-compartmented box of circa 1760 is illustrated (Fig. 14).

1.7 What gravy-type sauces were available for the dining table in the 1730s, before the fashion for French cuisine in England demanding a large variety of sauces got underway, were distributed by means of the silver sauce boat, which had been introduced around 1698. This was not suitable for labelling and the open nature of the sauce boat enabled its liquid contents to be easily recognised. In the 1760s however the silversmith had to compete with the enormous output of porcelain sauce boats coming from Chelsea, Derby, Longton Hall and Worcester. The production of the sauce tureen, being covered, was the silversmith's answer to the need to keep sauces piping hot which the porcelain makers could not guarantee. The silver Argyle was also used to keep gravy-type sauces hot. Towards the end of the Century with improved transport facilities there was more fresh food available and this required a light butter sauce which would not hide its flavour and ceramic sauce boats were the best vessels for this purpose. In any event the silversmiths' promotion of the silver frame for various purposes, in original designs, was without doubt successful and should be viewed in the light of this competitive background.

1.8 It was the introduction of the wider range of flavoured vinegars as mentioned above in the 1750s dispensed from the vinegar frame and of a wider variety of choice of flavourings and essences dispensed from the soy frame for use on their own or in combination, or by application to suitable stock sauces, that gave an impetus to labelling. The wonders of India were talked

THE INTRODUCTION

about at home and a number of spicy Indian sauces prepared. Sauce frames with labelled bottles were needed at each end and also in the centre of longer tables as in the case of New College Oxford. So frames were made in pairs or triples. Popular condiments in the 1760s were KARACHI, BLACK PEPPER, SOY, MUSHROOM KETCHUP, WALNUT KETCHUP, LEMON ESSENCE and ANCHOVY ESSENCE. The makers of "Bristol" blue or white opaque sauce bottles from 1760, which were contained in soy or "Warwick" cruet type frames, or self standing, in sets of three, four, five or six bottles, found it necessary to label the bottles to distinguish the contents. The five bottle "Bristol" cruet set in the Yorkshire Museum presented by Lord Bolton is labelled, like a Warwick cruet, for OIL and VINEGAR and for SUGAR, PEPPER and MUSTARD. The "Bristol" blue soy sets usually include ANCHOVY and LEMON, a popular pair.

1.9 Dining at the time of the Restoration involved service by servants from a buffet. On the table were salts and self standing sets of three castors containing pepper, dry mustard and sugar. These were required to enjoy a menu typically comprising a stew (ragout), a roast and/or fish, pies, salad, dessert and coffee. As dining à la française developed, with the encouragement of the Court of Charles II, servants laid out dishes from the buffet in prescribed geometric patterns and distributed condiments as required. Then came the development of courses. There were too many dishes for the hostess to cope with and so diners had to help themselves. At the turn of the Seventeenth Century the central tureen, ragout, stew or soup dish dominated the start of the first course, but the guests were left to help

Fig 16. Mrs Beeton's sweetmeats and displays of fresh fruits, 1910.

THE INTRODUCTION

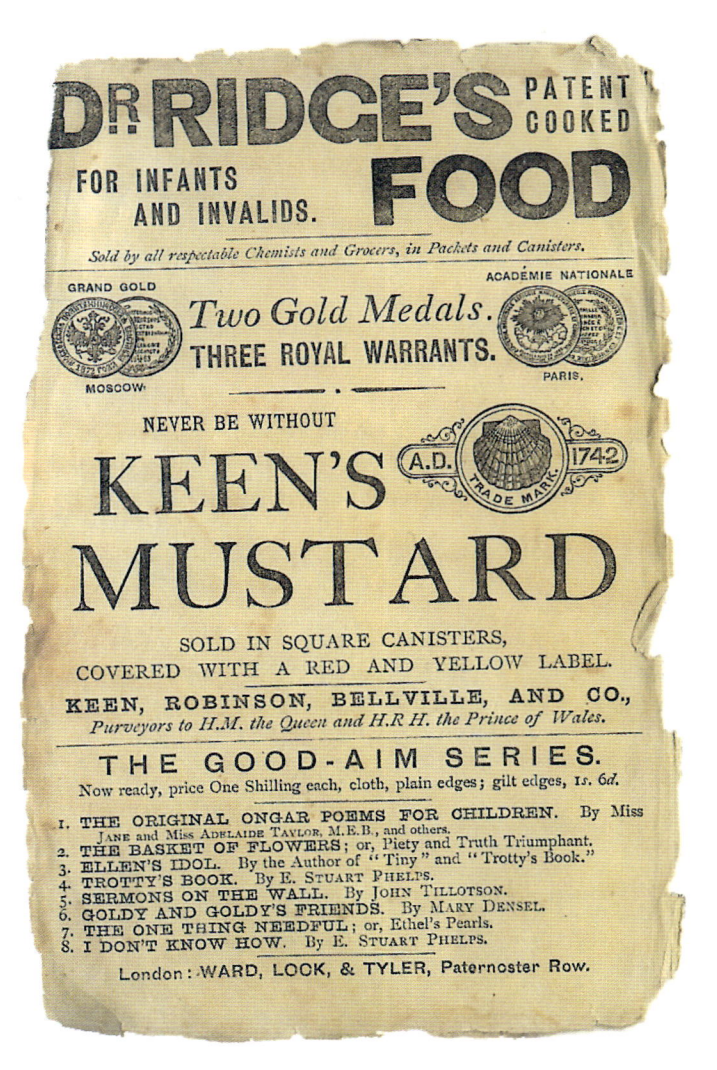

Fig 17. Advertisement for Mr Keen's Mustard, 1870.

themselves to various meats and fish. The second course involved other meats, game, puddings and tarts. The third course comprised the dessert with fruits being an important element. By the 1730s all the condiments were placed on the table and then handed round. They were refilled by servants at the sideboard which by the middle of the Eighteenth Century had replaced the buffet. Lamb, the Master Cook at four Royal Palaces (St James', Kensington, Hampton Court and Windsor) in 1710 sets out thirty-five different up-market bills of fare including "hash'd carps, bisque of pigeons, lumber-pye, sucking rabbets, butter'd crab with smelts fry'd and rock of snow and sullebubs." These dishes were however adopted by Elizabeth Smith in 1737 as can be seen from her Bills of Fare in Figure 36. There was plenty of room to manoeuvre in a Royal kitchen as can be seen

from the 1855 illustration of Windsor Castle's hive of activity (Fig. 15). Also on the dining table was a central epergne or tazza for distributing fruit and ice-cream. Sauceboats, sauce tureens and pickle dishes were all brought to the table at the start of each course. The table would normally have been covered by a white linen cloth until the final stage in dining was reached. Big spreads were laid out on the table, instead of on the buffet or sideboard, with service by servants offering chosen dishes. Layouts were suggested in cookery books. An ornate silver centrepiece could contain two soy frames, two sets of castors and two oil and vinegar frames. Food was served in courses and layouts devised for each course. Each course consisted of from three to nine main dishes with an equal number of side dishes. After these courses the cloth would be removed and the dessert served, which usually consisted of baskets of fresh and candied fruits, ornamental pastries, ice cream and jellies, sweetmeats and syllabubs (see Fig. 16). The gentlemen would be given their wine glasses and, after the introduction in the late eighteenth century of formal mixed dining whereby men and women sat alternately, as shown in Rowlandson's "Miseries of Social Life" published in 1807, in what has been called "a new promiscuous mode of seating"(7), the ladies would withdraw. Rowlandson writes that after dinner with a favourite party when the cloth has been removed the wine of conversation as well as the bottle just begin to brighten. Conversation is as free as it can be, wrote François de la Rochefoucauld visiting England in 1784, and everyone expresses his political opinions with much frankness. The meal started at any time between 3 and 7 pm and lasted for several hours. At the turn of the eighteenth century the fashionable hour for dining was 7pm. Rochefoucauld was concerned by the length of time spent at table. "Dinner is one of the most wearisome of English experiences, lasting as it does four or five hours"(8). There was plenty of time to savour flavourings. Sugar was dispensed from the sifter and then from elegant sugar bowls. Dry mustard from the caster was replaced by wet mustard served from the mustard pot. From 1742 Keen sold mustard in square canisters (Fig. 17). Sauces which needed to be kept warm

THE INTRODUCTION

Fig 18. Elizabeth Smith's Preface. It took her a long time to collect all her recipes

Fig 19. Elizabeth Smith's Kitchen in 1737.

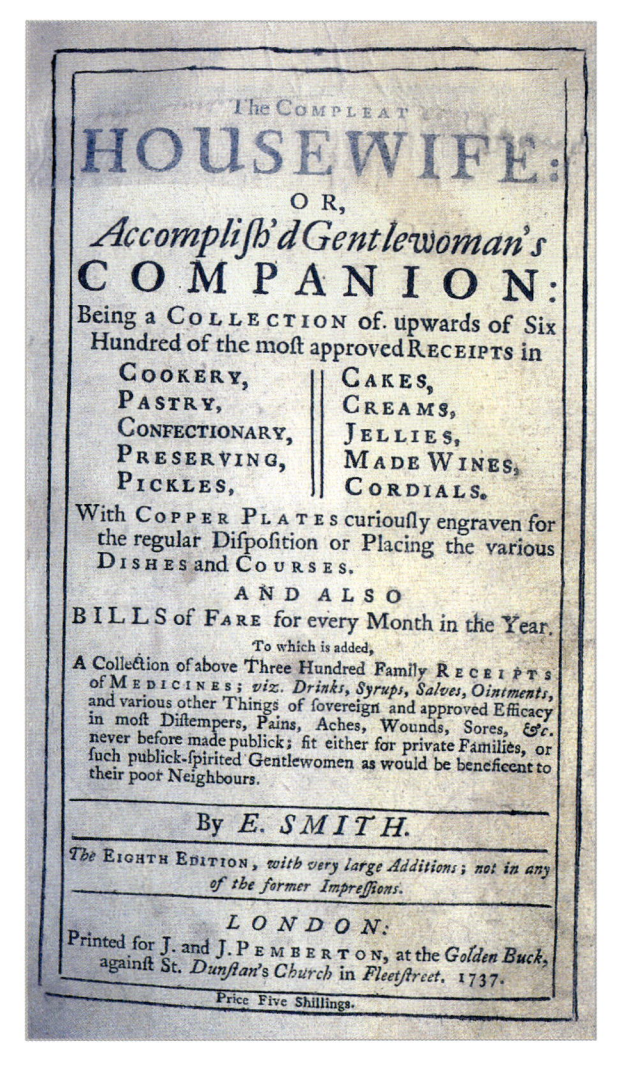

Fig 20. Elizabeth Smith's Title Page in 1737.

were served from Argyles or from sauce tureens placed on dish-crosses which prevented the table from being marked by heat through the cloth.

1.10 It took Eliza Smith thirty years to collect her recipes (Fig. 18). So in 1737 the eighth edition of Eliza Smith's "The compleat housewife" (Fig. 20) shows preparations in the kitchen as a frontspiece (Fig. 19) and laid out on the buffet an arrangement for supper (Fig. 21) showing where to put the dishes for pickles and anchovies, and an arrangement for a two course supper comprising a First Course (Fig. 22) and an arrangement for a specially grand dessert with a pyramid centrepiece (Fig. 23) as a Second Course. Contrast this with the seventh edition of William Henderson's "The Housekeeper's Instructor" circa 1797 (Fig. 24), which likewise shows preparations in the kitchen as a frontispiece (Fig. 25), designed and engraved by Collinger, and sets out on a table a two course dinner for a small company (Fig. 26) and for a larger company a first course of 25 dishes (Fig. 27) and a second course of 25 dishes (Fig. 28), all in accordance with the instructions given on

THE INTRODUCTION

Fig 21.   Elizabeth Smith's Buffet layout for Supper 1737.

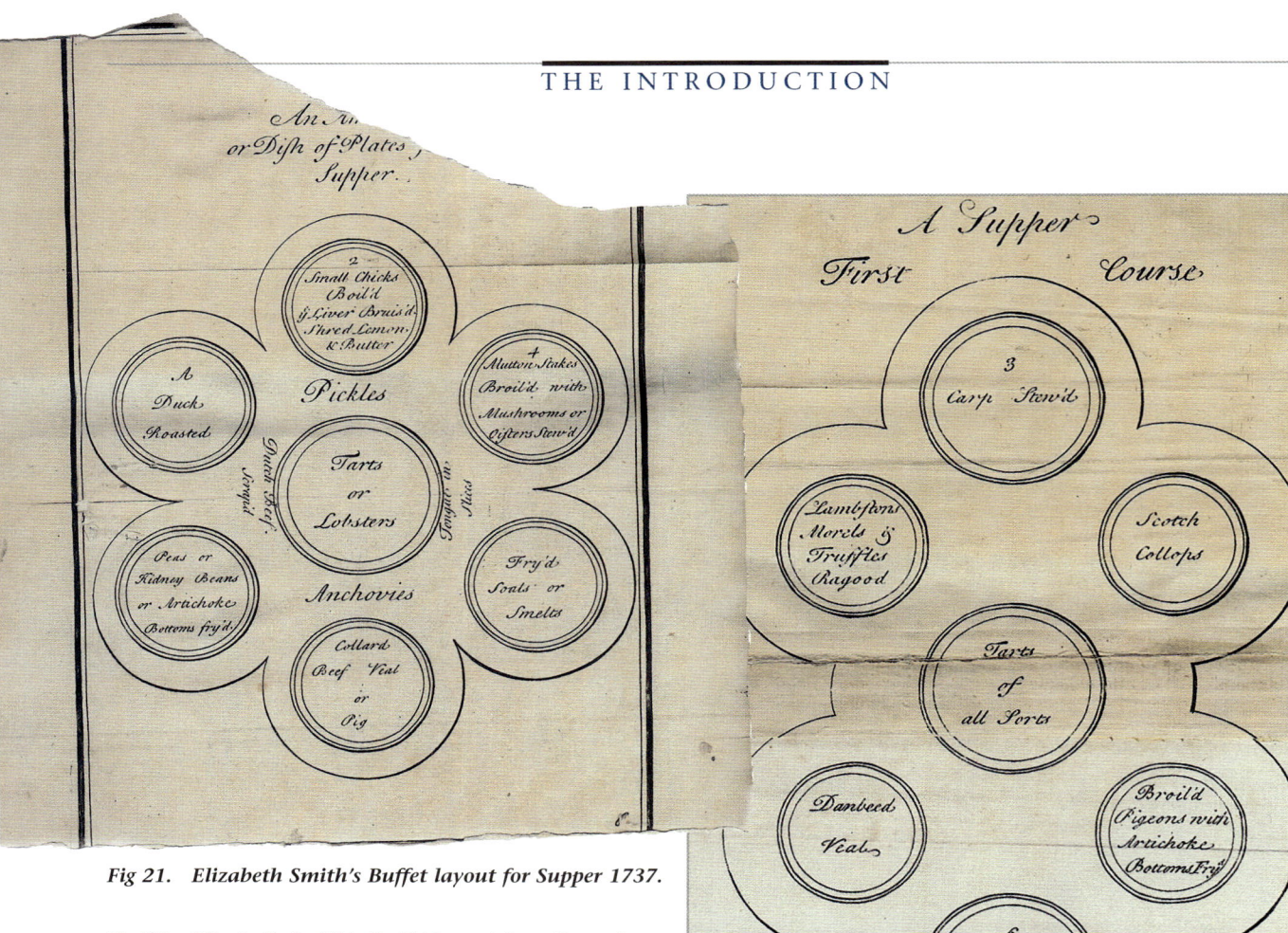

Fig 23.   Elizabeth Smith's Buffet layout for a Second Course 1737.

Fig 22.   Elizabeth Smith's Buffet layout for a First Course 1737.

page 382 (Fig. 29).

1.11 Hannah Glasse in her "Art of Cookery" in 1774 (Fig. 30) gives 12 bills of fare for January through to December each of 3 courses of 9 dishes each! Parson Woodforde recalls in his diary (Volume II) for 18th August 1783 that at his dinner with Mr. Townshend there were two courses of nine dishes each but most of the things were spoiled by being so "Frenchified in dressing". This reflects the great interest in a variety of flavourings in the 1780s. William Henderson in c.1797 gives 12 arrangements of the table displayed in two different courses for each month of the year comprising 11 dishes in each course. He instructs that "all your sauce in boats or basons" should be placed "to answer each other at the corners"(9). Elizabeth Raffald in her English Housekeeper in 1799 (Fig. 4) advised

THE INTRODUCTION

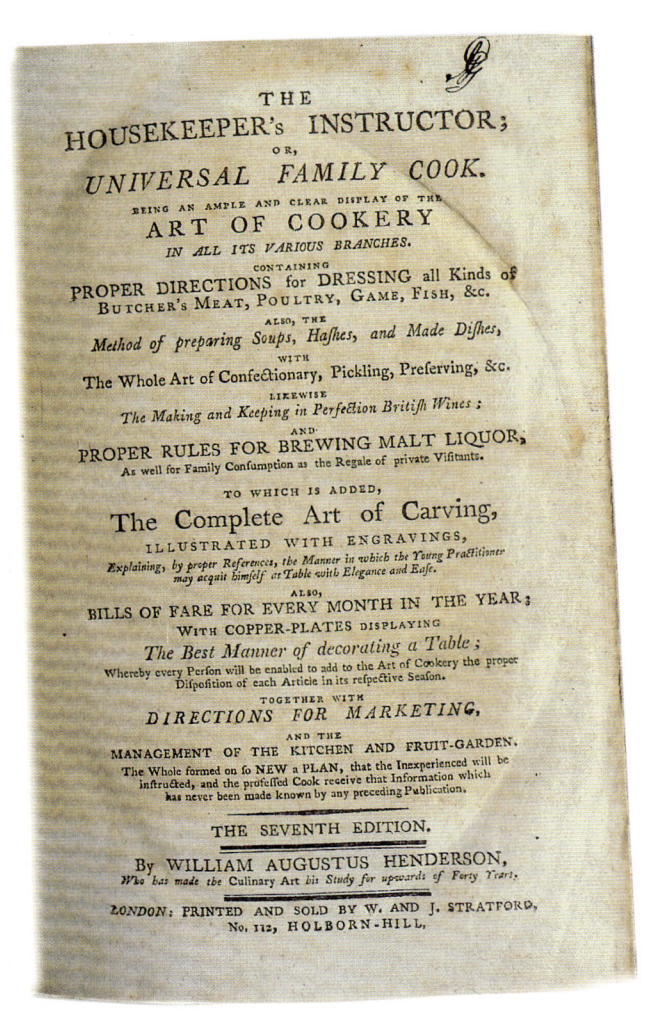

Fig 24. William Henderson's Title Page in c. 1797

Fig 25. William Henderson's Kitchen in c. 1797

complicated layouts for First (Fig. 31) and Second (Fig. 32) Courses. John Farley (Fig. 33) in "The London Art of Cookery" in 1804 (Fig. 34) gives 12 bills of fare for January to December each of two courses of 10 dishes each. His Bills of Fare for August and September are illustrated (Fig. 35). These make interesting comparisons with Elizabeth Smith's Bills of Fare for April until September (Fig. 36). Farley provides for a "salmagundy" and Smith for wonderful second course dishes. A study of contemporary cook books helps to explain the rapid development and range of sauce labels.

1.12 The changes in fashionable dining took time to be implemented. Sets of three individual castors apparently not dispensed from a frame were still in use in the 1770s. Illustrated in Chapter 12 is a set by Andrew Fogelberg of Church Street, Soho, made in 1774 (Fig. 103) in what Arthur Grimwade has called a style of "elegant restrained classicism"(10) for use presumably in giving a reflection or memory of earlier dining habits. The dry mustard castor is blind. So although during the 18th Century new forms of silver vessels evolved, such as sauce boats, sauce tureens and sauce frames, all this took time: there were no sudden or great changes. Matthew Boulton writing in 1772 explains the reason why: "Ye present age distinguishes itself by adopting the most Elegant ornaments of the most refined Grecian artists; I am satisfy'd in conforming thereto, and humbly copying their style, and making new combinations of old ornaments without presuming to invent new ones".

1.13 During the early Nineteenth Century a new style of dining, said to have been derived from the Russian Court and known as à la russe, gradually took over (there was some reluctance) from the

11

THE INTRODUCTION

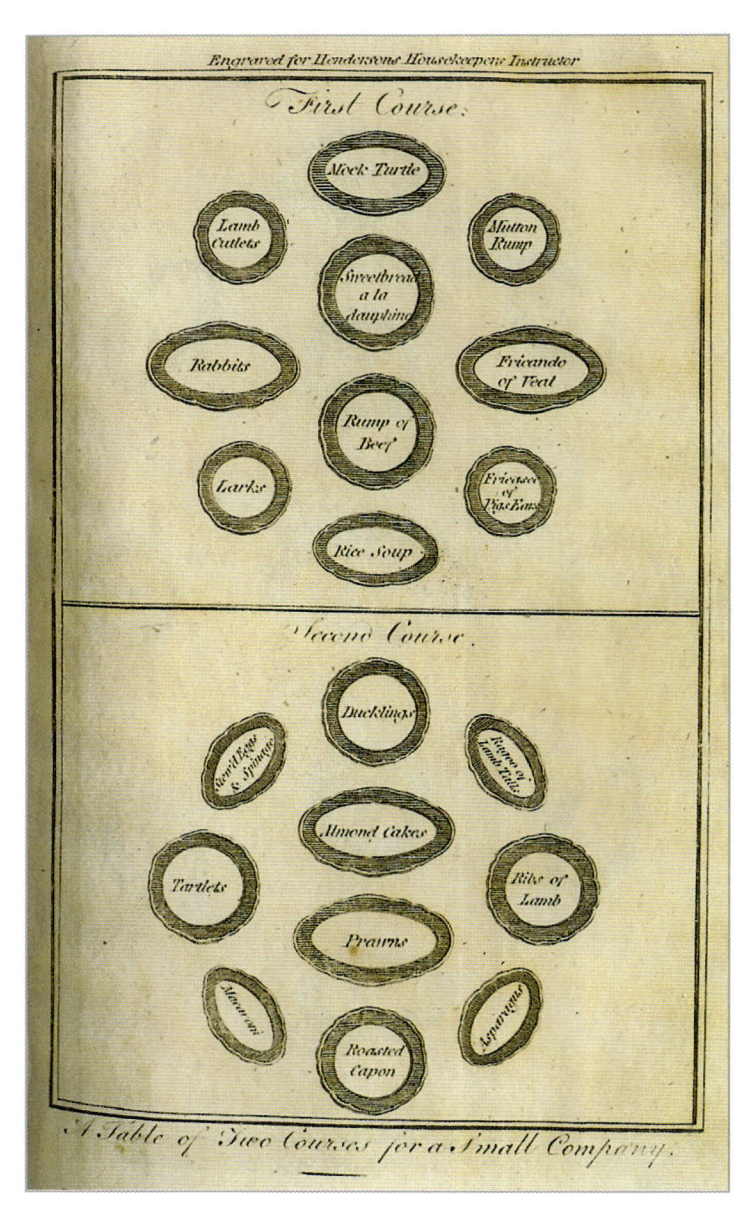

Fig 26. William Henderson's Table Plans for a Small Company in c. 1797

old style, said to have been derived from the French Court and known as à la française. Instead of helping themselves during the first and second courses from dishes already laid out on the dining table, guests had to wait to be served individually by servants. The host carved the joints at the sideboard in full view of the assembled company. Hence the need for cookery books to set out careful advice on this important subject. The guests' attention to dining could not be diverted by a study of displayed dishes. However, decorative arrangements had an effect. With the demise of the epergne as a centrepiece and space left in the centre for the soup tureen or ragout bowl, something had to take their place. By the 1850s dining tables were dominated by floral arrangements – even single bottle wine coolers were appropriated for floral displays. In the 1880s it was the turn of the pickle jar to adorn the table to house the delights of MABYN'S PICKLE or CAPTAIN WHITE'S and there was a revival of interest in silver-labelled sauce bottles. Thus Edward Hutton made in 1890, hall-marked in London, three "eared" enclosed crescents for CHILI, TAROGON and WORCESTER to match two unmarked 1770s labels of this style for HARVEY and SALAD-OIL, all fitted with silver neck-ring attachments (the 1770s HARVEY and 1890 TAROGON are illustrated in Fig. 37). The five labels are displayed on bottles with silver mounts (with one exception) dated 1879 contained in an Edward Hutton cruet of 1879 in the dining room of Brighton's Preston Manor. The two 1770s labels have wider circles, more interesting shapes and better lettering than the 1890 reproductions. Oil and vinegar labels were used on cruets in the Edwardian period. Illustrated is an art nouveau crescent VINEGAR label with distinctive lettering and made of silver gilt in 1901. Thus the silver sauce label is perhaps a unique barometer of taste from the 1750s to the 1900s.

1.14 Documentary evidence relating to the origin of sauce labels should be weighed with caution. The expression commonly used in ledgers is "bottle-ticket". This can also refer to a wine decanter label as well as to a toilet bottle label. The weight if given is a good guide to size. But some spirit, ratafia and cordial labels are of small size. Just because a label is of small size does not mean that it must be a sauce label. Soy tickets are recorded in Wakelin Workmens Ledgers. The earliest entry is possibly that of 10 June 1748 which refers to 14 large and 12 small bottle tickets. Twelve tickets could adorn two frames of six bottles or three frames of four bottles. Subsequent entries disclose that on 14 July 1748 20 small and 18 large bottle tickets were supplied – possibly allowing four four frames of five-; on 27 April 1750 12 small bottle tickets – a significant number-; on 24 November 1750 10 small bottle tickets – possibly for two frames of

THE INTRODUCTION

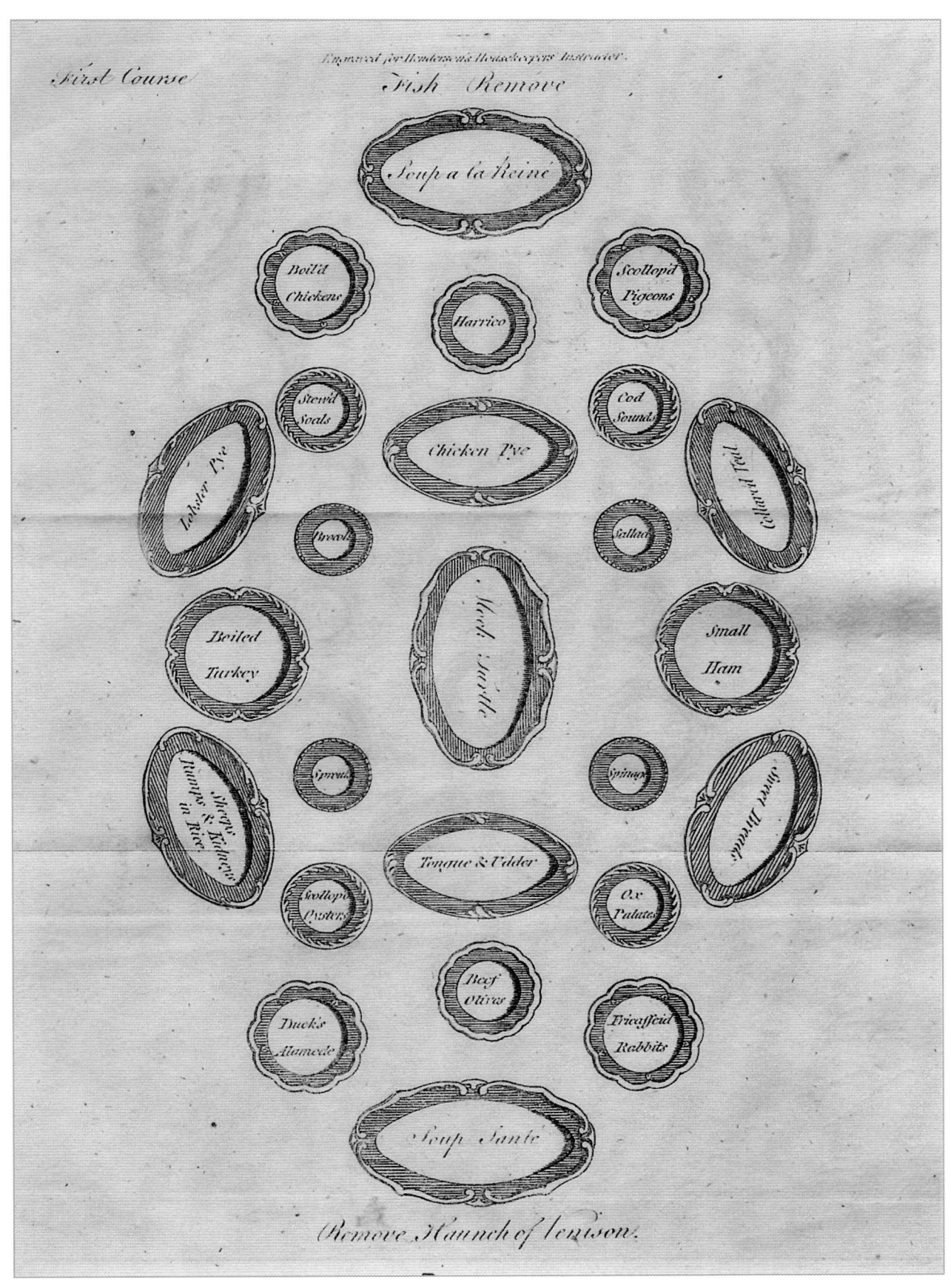

Fig 27. William Henderson's First Course for a Dinner Party in c. 1797

THE INTRODUCTION

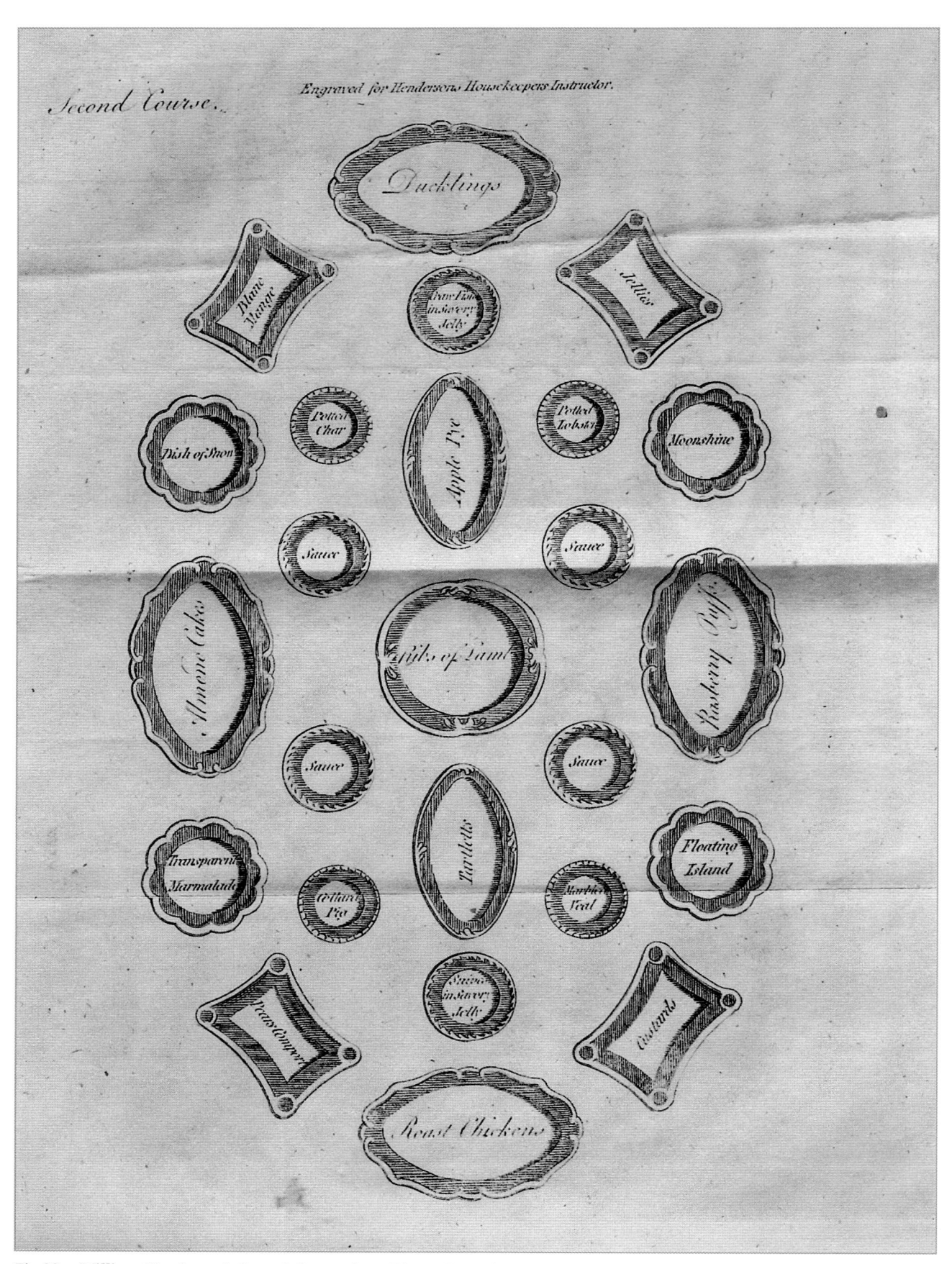

Fig 28. William Henderson's Second Course for a Dinner Party in c. 1797

THE INTRODUCTION

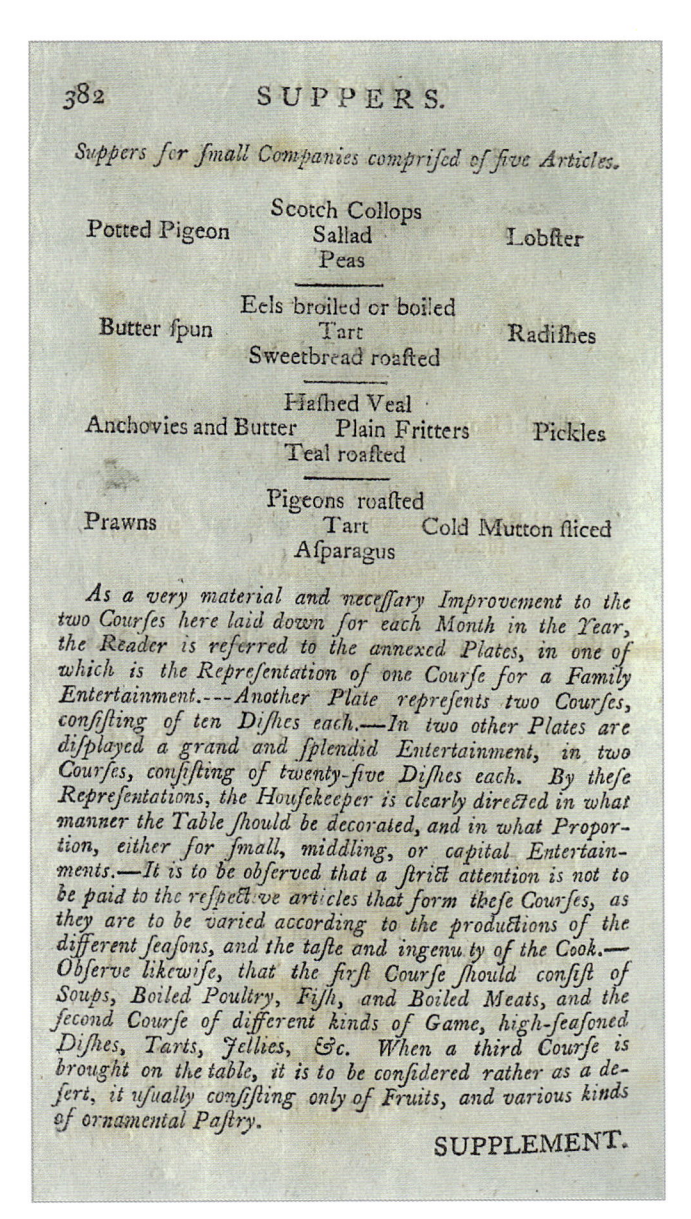

Fig 29. William Henderson's Instructions for Supper in c. 1797

five-; on 4 May 1752 6 small bottle tickets – again a significant number-; and on 27 December 1755 2 small bottle tickets – perhaps for an oil and vinegar frame. In 1758 there is an entry for October 15 "to 3 dozen large and 3 dozen small bottle tickets". All the above is somewhat speculative. Thirteen small square bottle tickets were made for the Earl of Stratford in 1766. Some of the earliest soy frame (not vinegar frame) labels seem to be squarish in shape as made, for example, by Thomas Daniel in London in 1774.

1.15 The earliest entry noted in Volume III of Edward Wakelin's ledgers undoubtedly relating to a sauce label not being a small label or a half-moon bottle ticket is for 6 small crescent soy cruet labels supplied by James Ansill and Stephen Gilbert (who once had worked in Wakelin's workshop having been apprenticed to him in 1752), utilising 9dwts of silver, for Mr. Letheutier, the customer, on 22 November 1766. A further 6 were supplied for sale in the shop in March 1767. They weighed 1.5 dwt each respectively. The cost price in each case was 3 shillings or 6 pence per label. Two sets of six were supplied for Hammick's and Buller in 1768, one set of five for Bellasize in 1769 and a set of six in 1770 for Bourchier who added an extra label two months later and another seven months later. It is believed that Bourchier kept adding to his cruets new titles to keep up to date with his dining friends. In 1770 there is also mention of the making of a set of six for Hopkins, for Williams and for Ruby and a set of five for Tongue. There is mention of a set of four in 1771 for Scourfield and a set of five in 1772 for Bennett. Later on there are mentioned sets of eight: for example the Hon. Henry Fane paid £2 3s 6d for eight "soy ticketts for an epergne" on 15 February 1779. Six-bottle soy frames were supplied in 1774 to John Fane, the Earl of Louth and Mrs. Armisted, in 1775 to Richard Benyon and in 1776 to the Earl of Lincoln and William Barker Baniel.

1.16 Pictorial evidence is uncommon. James Gillray's "Voluptary under the Horrors of Digestion", drawn in 1792, depicts a table in the Prince Regent's Carlton House on which stands a gilded castor labelled CHAIN for cayenne pepper (see Fig. 38). Gillray's "Germans eating sour-kraut" of 1803 shows a bottle labelled VINEGAR. No doubt this was needed to aid digestion of the meal, which was taking place at a well-known German eating-house in London. In France in the 1760s ketchup and flavoured vinegars were still being dispensed from the butler's table, as shown in an oil painting(11) by Jean-Baptiste-Simeon Chardin (1699-1779), thought to have been painted in 1763. Two vinegar decanters are illustrated, with pull-off caps, standing in a dispenser on his table.

15

THE INTRODUCTION

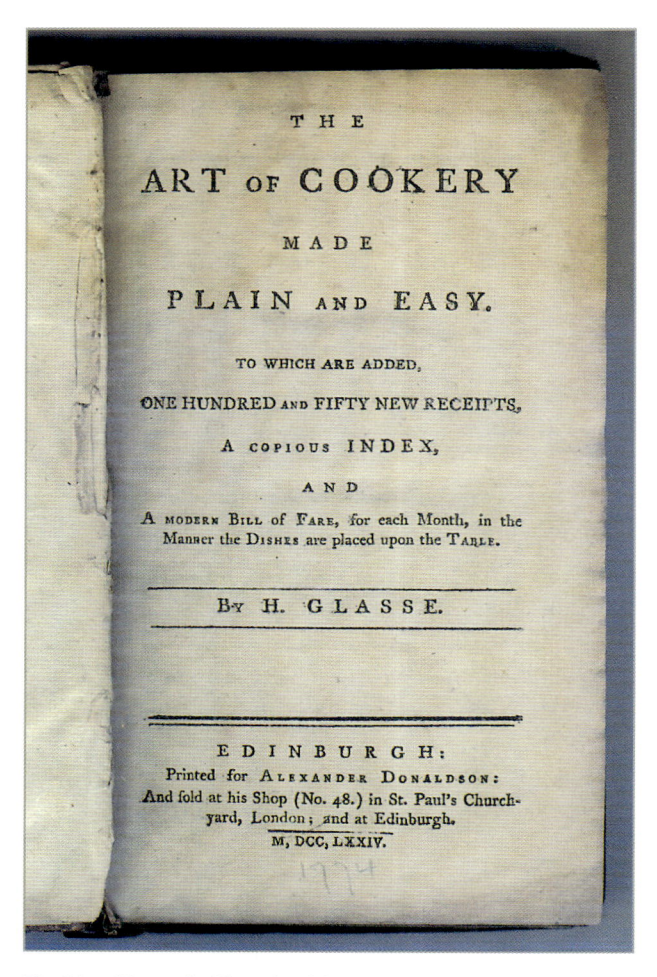

Fig 30. Hannah Glasse's Title Page, 1774

1.17 Interesting evidence also comes from notebooks kept by collectors such as Mr. Weed and Mrs. Marshall. The Alice and George Burrows so-called set of 13 labels of 1805 formerly in the Weed collection are in reality two sets, one of 5 and one of 8. This is made clear by Mr Weed's notes written onboard the RMS Laconia in 1927 (see Chapter 11). The actual labels are illustrated as is also a close up of the famous ZOOBDITTY MATCH. ZOOBDITTY, a spicy Indian fish sauce, was the title of a label supplied to the Earl of Chesterfield in 1778. It was advertised as being for sale by John Burgess in the 1780s.

1.18 The most popular size of soy frame seems to have been the six-bottle followed by the four-bottle and then the eight-bottle. On nine of the sixteen occasions when orders were placed by Wakelin from Margaret Binley or from Ansill and Gilbert to buy in labels as disclosed in the Workmens' Ledgers the order was for a set of six labels. The Gentlemen's Ledgers show that the highest number of purchasing occasions (11 out of 29) were for sets of six labels. The six-bottle frame seemed to be appropriate for the grand occasion judged by the number made in silver gilt.

1.19 By the late 1760s everything was so disguised by sauces that nothing appeared in its "native properties". It is not surprising that in the best selling recipe book of the time, Mrs. Hannah Glasse's "The Art of Cookery" (sixth edition 1760), there were more than thirty recipes for sauces – including her famous stock ANCHOVY sauce which was supposed to keep for a whole year. In 1765 Robert Piercy produced a six-bottle silver soy frame weighing 28ozs 12 dwts, accommodating six glass bottles with unmarked silver caps engraved for TARRAGON, ELDER, GARLICK, SOY, LEMON and CAYENNE(12). These titles are entirely consistent with this early date. In 1775 he made the silver-gilt soy frame illustrated in Fig. 2. It bears an armorial. The frame has six bottles with unmarked very stylish silver-gilt labels for TARRAGON, ELDER, SOY, ANCHOVY, KETCHUP and KYAN.

1.20 Edward Wakelin's Workmens Ledgers show that he bought in from Margaret Binley and Ansill and Gilbert a total of 76 sauce labels between 1776 and 1772 at a cost of £1.15s. 8d. His Gentlemens Ledgers show that he sold retail 83 labels between 1770 and 1779 at a cost of £16 9s. 8d. and 68 sauce labels between 1780 and 1785 at a cost of £11.13s.4d. The number of sauce labels increased as the range of titles grew and grew. John Burgess in the 1760s was advertising only the availability for sale of ESSENCE OF ANCHOVIES, TARRAGON PICKLE and TARRAGON SAUCE. By 1779 he had introduced his new FISH SAUCE, LEMON PICKLE, his general UNIVERSAL SAUCE and MUSHROOM KETCHUP. In the 1780s he was advertising SALAD OIL, CAMP VINEGAR, ELDER VINEGAR DEVONSHIRE SAUCE and the famous ZOOBDITTY. At the same time silver sauce labels were being made for WORCESTER SAUCE (not to be confused with WORCESTERSHIRE SAUCE introduced by Lea and Perrins around 1835),

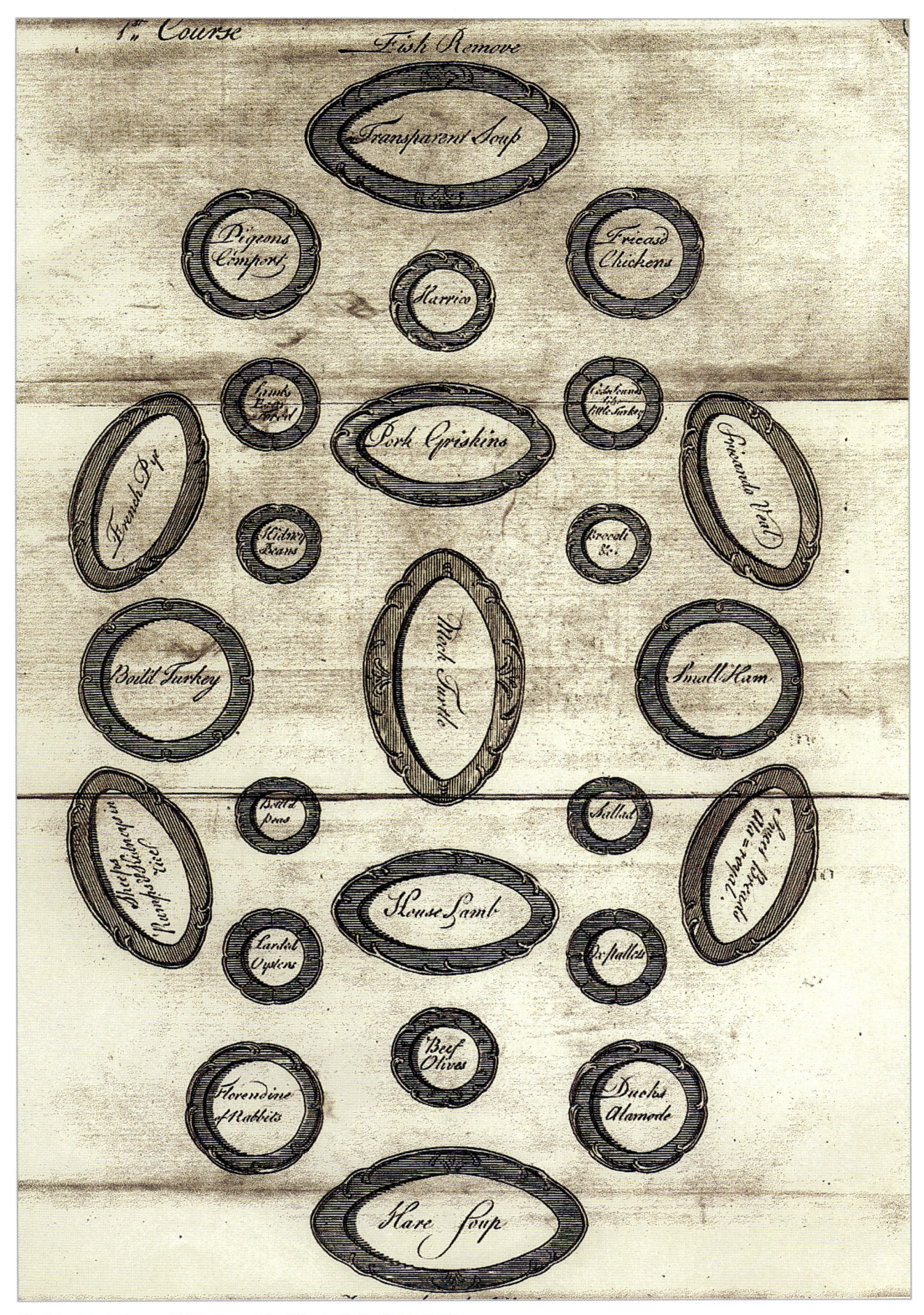

Fig 31. First Course Table layout by Elizabeth Raffald, 1799.

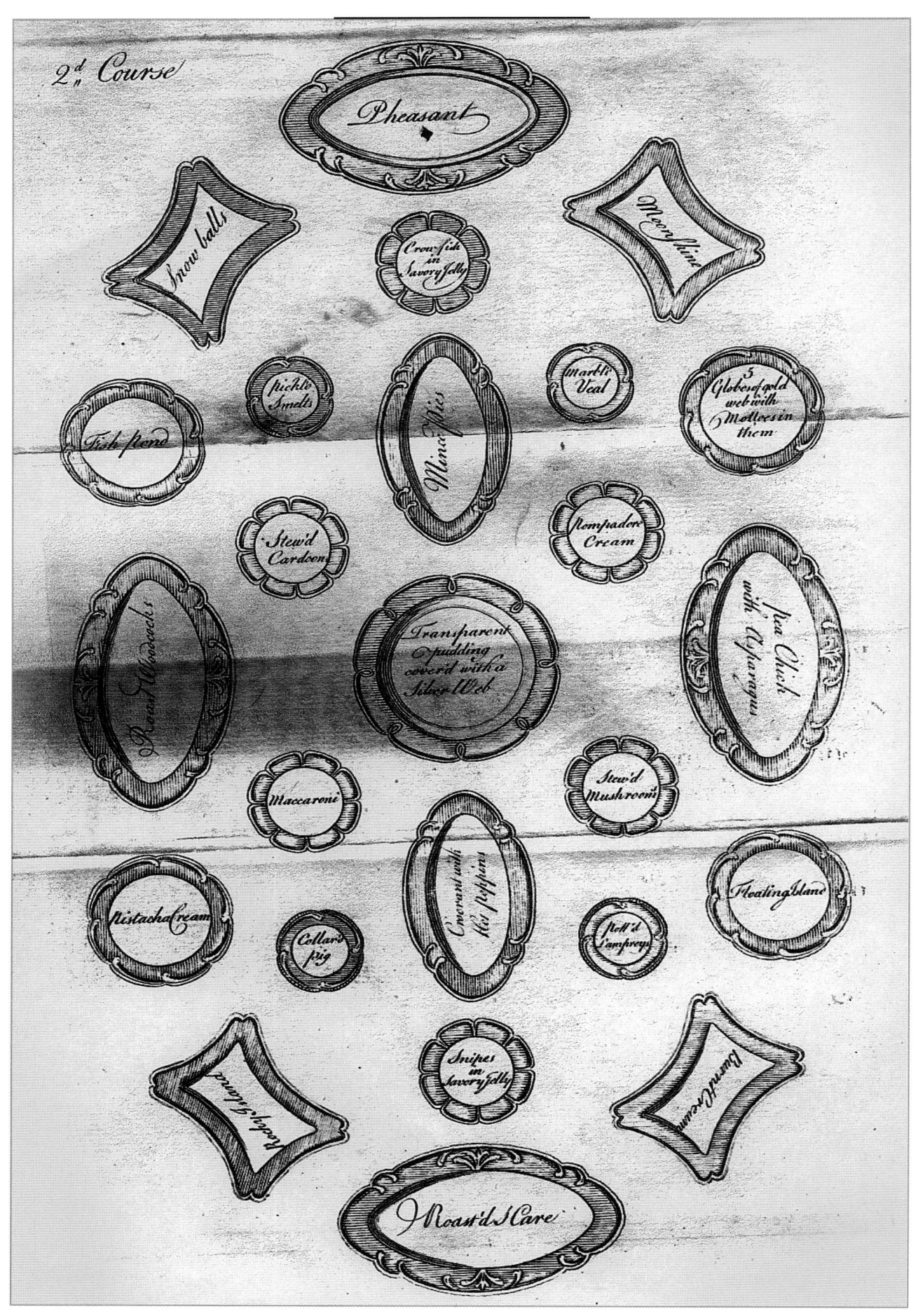

Fig 32. Second Course Table layout by Elizabeth Raffald, 1799.

THE INTRODUCTION

Fig 33. Portrait of John Farley, 1804.

SAUCE ROYAL, READING SAUCE, QUIN'S SAUCE and HARVEY'S FISH SAUCE.

1.21 From 1780 for some sixty odd years the demand for a wide range of sauces was incessant. In the early 1790s labels were being made for even more flavoured vinegars such as WHITE VINEGAR, RED VINEGAR, CAYENNE VINEGAR, CAMP VINEGAR, CHILLI VINEGAR, CUCUMBER VINEGAR, PEPPER VINEGAR and LEMON VINEGAR. French "pickles" were popular such as WALNUT PICKLE and QUIN'S PICKLE. New sauce titles included CAMP, BERNIS (for Bearnaise sauce) and QUEEN'S. In the 1800s ESSENCE OF TOMATO, LIME JUICE and CAVICE (for Esceavechi) were added to the frame. PINK, RASPBERRY and SHALOT VINEGARS appeared. In Scotland LOBSTER SAUCE seemed to be very much appreciated.

1.22 Sauce labels, unlike the general run of wine labels, vary considerably in size according to use. Ginger jars and pickle jars tend to be fat requiring larger labels with long chains. Stock bottles were on the large size. Vinegar bottles were very much bigger than the tiny soy bottles.

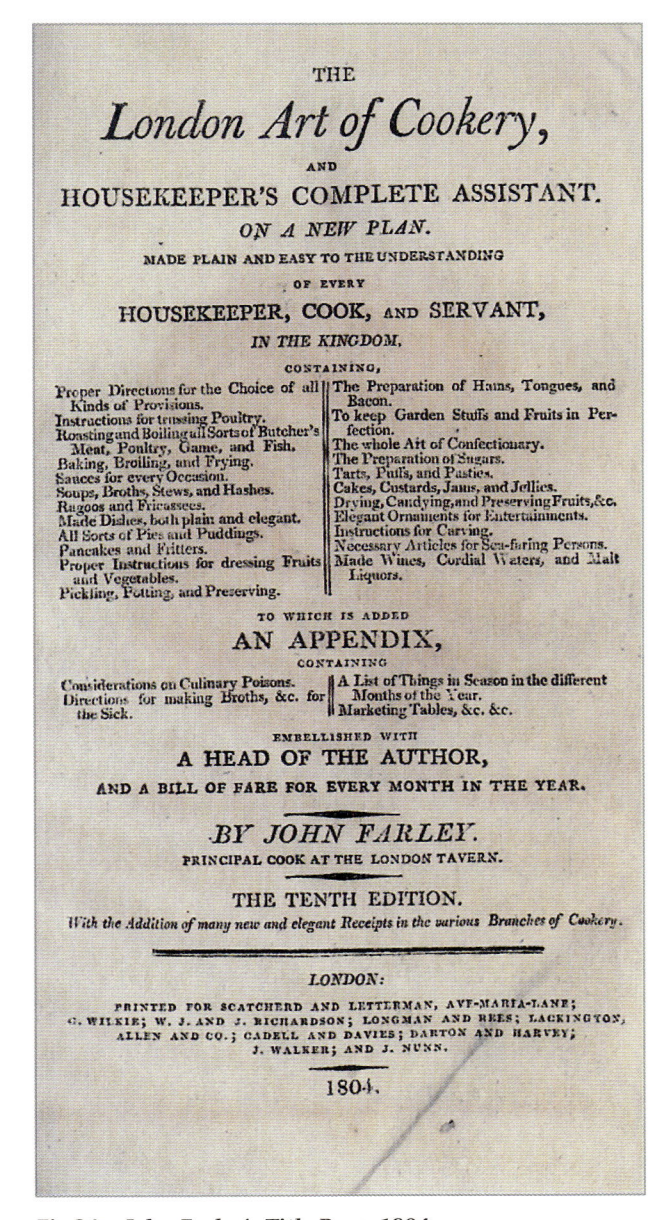

Fig 34. John Farley's Title Page, 1804.

Epergne labels were delicately hung. Illustrated is a pickle frame (Fig. 39) with cut glass jars labelled for CHUTNEE by Edward Hutton and WALNUT by William Carr Hutton. The labels are on the large side and have long chains.

1.23 The sauce title can often be a good guide to dating. WORCESTERSHIRE, for example, does not appear before 1835. CAYON or KAYON were only used during the period 1760 – 1780. CORATCH and its variants were only used after 1790. CARRISH was only used during the 1770s. CARRACHE and its variants were only used in

19

THE INTRODUCTION

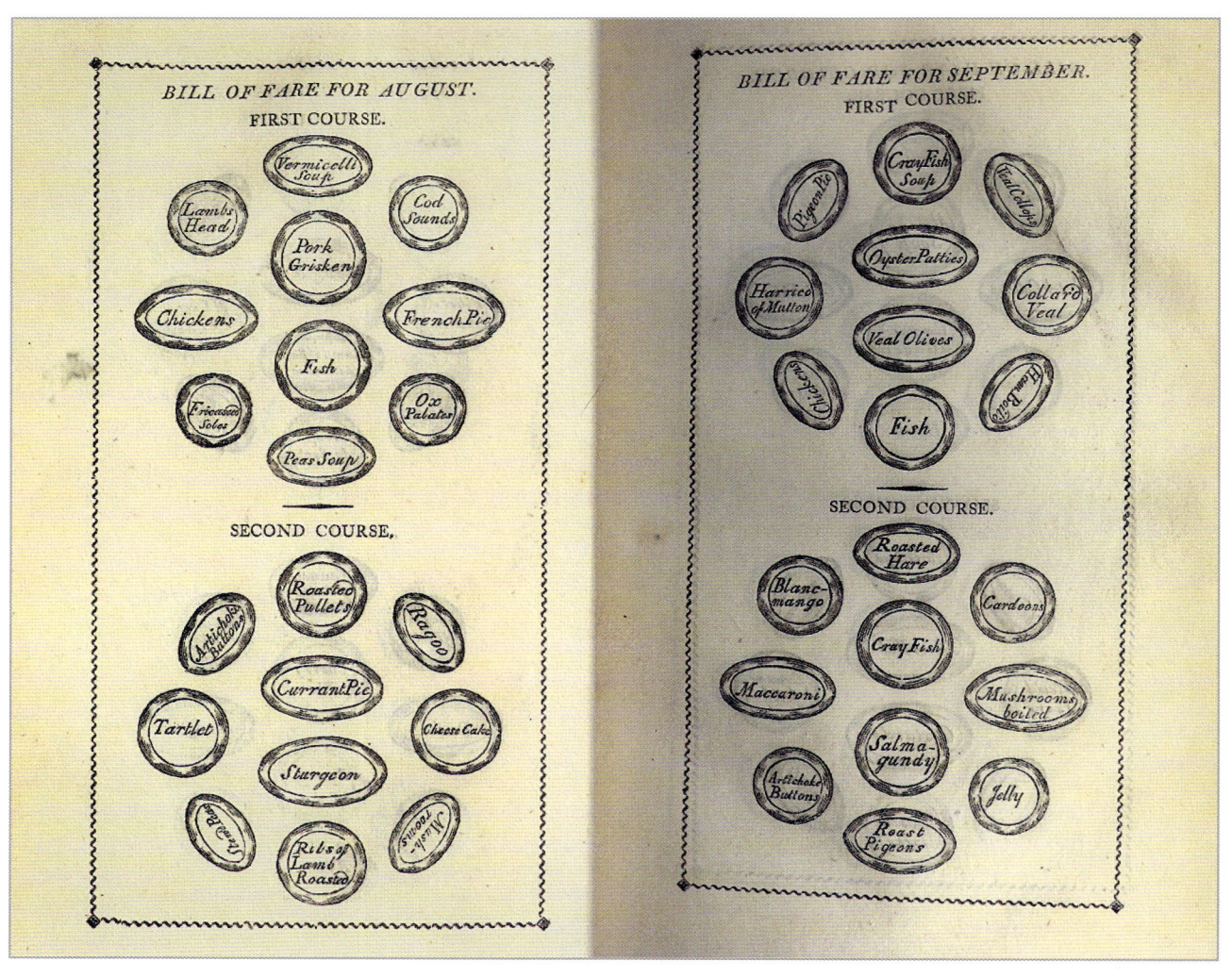

Fig 35. John Farley's Bills of Fare for August and September.

the 1760s and 1770s. One cannot be too precise. These are only guidelines but nonetheless may be helpful.

1.24 Later Victorian cruets, for salt, pepper and mustard, did not need labelling. A rather splendid example of 1878, made by C.F. in Sheffield, at Trinity House in London, consists of a skiff salt, buoy mustard and lighthouse pepper pot, with a dolphin handle on a stormy sea. ■

Fig 37. Old and new crescent soy labels for HARVEY and TAROGON displayed at Preston Manor, Brighton.

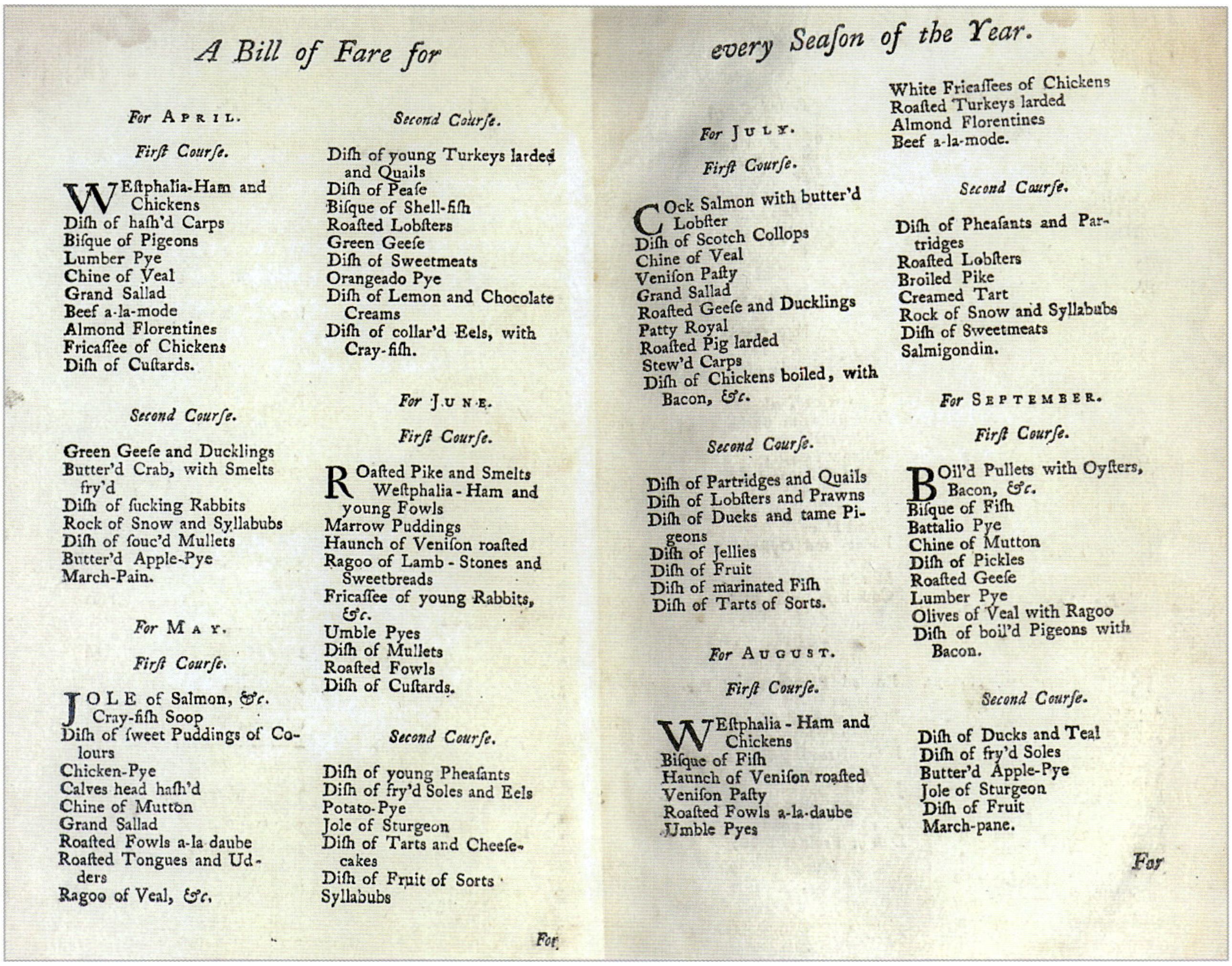

THE INTRODUCTION

A Bill of Fare for every Season of the Year.

For APRIL.
First Course.
Westphalia-Ham and Chickens
Dish of hash'd Carps
Bisque of Pigeons
Lumber Pye
Chine of Veal
Grand Sallad
Beef a-la-mode
Almond Florentines
Fricassee of Chickens
Dish of Custards.

Second Course.
Dish of young Turkeys larded and Quails
Dish of Pease
Bisque of Shell-fish
Roasted Lobsters
Green Geese
Dish of Sweetmeats
Orangeado Pye
Dish of Lemon and Chocolate Creams
Dish of collar'd Eels, with Cray-fish.

For MAY.
First Course.
Jole of Salmon, &c.
Cray-fish Soop
Dish of sweet Puddings of Colours
Chicken-Pye
Calves head hash'd
Chine of Mutton
Grand Sallad
Roasted Fowls a-la-daube
Roasted Tongues and Udders
Ragoo of Veal, &c.

Second Course.
Green Geese and Ducklings
Butter'd Crab, with Smelts fry'd
Dish of sucking Rabbits
Rock of Snow and Syllabubs
Dish of souc'd Mullets
Butter'd Apple-Pye
March-Pain.

For JUNE.
First Course.
Roasted Pike and Smelts
Westphalia-Ham and young Fowls
Marrow Puddings
Haunch of Venison roasted
Ragoo of Lamb-Stones and Sweetbreads
Fricassee of young Rabbits, &c.
Umble Pyes
Dish of Mullets
Roasted Fowls
Dish of Custards.

Second Course.
Dish of young Pheasants
Dish of fry'd Soles and Eels
Potato-Pye
Jole of Sturgeon
Dish of Tarts and Cheesecakes
Dish of Fruit of Sorts
Syllabubs

For JULY.
First Course.
Cock Salmon with butter'd Lobster
Dish of Scotch Collops
Chine of Veal
Venison Pasty
Grand Sallad
Roasted Geese and Ducklings
Patty Royal
Roasted Pig larded
Stew'd Carps
Dish of Chickens boiled, with Bacon, &c.

Second Course.
Dish of Partridges and Quails
Dish of Lobsters and Prawns
Dish of Ducks and tame Pigeons
Dish of Jellies
Dish of Fruit
Dish of marinated Fish
Dish of Tarts of Sorts.

For AUGUST.
First Course.
Westphalia-Ham and Chickens
Bisque of Fish
Haunch of Venison roasted
Venison Pasty
Roasted Fowls a-la-daube
Umble Pyes
White Fricassees of Chickens
Roasted Turkeys larded
Almond Florentines
Beef a-la-mode.

Second Course.
Dish of Pheasants and Partridges
Roasted Lobsters
Broiled Pike
Creamed Tart
Rock of Snow and Syllabubs
Dish of Sweetmeats
Salmigondin.

For SEPTEMBER.
First Course.
Boil'd Pullets with Oysters, Bacon, &c.
Bisque of Fish
Battalio Pye
Chine of Mutton
Dish of Pickles
Roasted Geese
Lumber Pye
Olives of Veal with Ragoo
Dish of boil'd Pigeons with Bacon.

Second Course.
Dish of Ducks and Teal
Dish of fry'd Soles
Butter'd Apple-Pye
Jole of Sturgeon
Dish of Fruit
March-pane.

Fig 36. Elizabeth Smith's Bills of Fare from April until September.

NOTES

(1) Lot 176A, Bonham and Brooks, sale number 28750, held on 9.10.2001.

(2) Lot 161, ibid., illustrated. The chains were missing.

(3) In the 1640s white tin-glazed delftware pottery bottle-shaped wine decanters had applied wine names in blue lettering: for example, for "Whit", "Sack" or "Claret".

(4) See further Andy McConnell, The British Decanter, Antique Collecting, May 1999, p.44.

(5) Exhibited by Paul Bennett at Claridge's Antique Fair, held on 5.4.2001.

(6) A spice box made by William Jamieson (1806-1841) is illustrated on p.122 of James' "Goldsmiths of Aberdeen". The three sections or compartments were inscribed respectively GINGER, NUTMEG and CINNAMON. Trinity House in London has an 1880 copy by Robert Garrard of the original 1690s silver Eddystone Lighthouse (erected by Winstanley around 1696) in the ownership of his descendants, which served as a combined ceremonial salt, pepper and spice box. The top (the light) pulls off for cayenne pepper. The next section (the gallery) pulls off for salt. The next section (the entrance door) pulls off probably for ginger or nutmeg. The next section (the staircase) pulls of probably for cinnamon or other spices. It was too early for labelling.

(7) Margaret Willes, Scenes from Georgian Life, pp38-39, reviewing caricatures and cartoons from Calke Abbey in Derbysire.

(8) Ibid., p38.

(9) HENDERSON, p.380. footnote.

(10) "London Goldsmiths", First Edition 1976, p.511.

(11) Oil on canvas, Musee du Louvre, Paris (M.I. 1040), called "The Butler's Table".

(12) Sold at Sotheby's on Thursday 25.10.62, lot 44.

Fig 38. Gillray's view of a user of SAUCE ROYAL and CHIAN pepper.

CHAPTER 2

THE SAUCES

2.1 On the use of sauces in English cooking, De Re Coquinaria, by Marcus Apicius of the early Fifth Century AD contains many references to PEPPER, CINNAMON, GINGER, NUTMEG, CLOVES, cardamon, spikenard and costum. Many of these spices and herbs were imported from India and the Far East. PEPPER was the most important seasoning for Apicius. It was in most cases the first ingredient in his sauces. LOVAGE ranked second in importance. Apicius used its seeds, roots and leaves. In small quantities he used RUE (a green herb), an uncommon seasoning, in his sauces. His meat sauce consisted of PEPPER, LOVAGE, wine, stock, OLIVE OIL and green herbs. The meat was then often served in a second sauce of VINEGAR and HONEY with reduced stock from the first sauce. As well as RUE, other uncommon seasonings he used were laser, colewort, elecampane and his own recipe for fish-pickle. His recipes, being classical in content, were derived from Greek and Roman cooking experience. He describes some 174 different sauces which have been reviewed by John Edwards in his Roman Cookery of Apicius of 1984.

2.2 However much the recipes of Apicius took root in Roman Britain, the cooking experience did not survive the Dark Ages, unlike on the continent. So in the eighth edition of a standard cookery book by Elizabeth Smith in the Eighteenth Century there is reference to only two sauces, although there are a number of references to pickles and flavourings. In her Preface of 1737 – it being, she explained, as fashionable for a book not to have a Preface as it would be for a lady to appear at a ball without a hoop petticoat – she noted that in earlier times mankind had no need of any additions to food or sauces beyond APPLES, nuts and HERBS. But when men began to pass from a vegetable to an animal diet seasonings became necessary. The Preface is reproduced (in part) in Fig. 3.

2.3 In her book a bill of fare is given for each month of the year listing in each case some seven first courses and some seven second courses. The first 78 pages are given over to descriptions of how to cook certain dishes. 22

Fig 39. Pickle Frame with jars labelled for CHUTNEE by Edward Hutton and WALNUT by William Carr Hutton.

23

THE SAUCES

Fig 40. Elizabeth' Smith's first recipe of 1737.

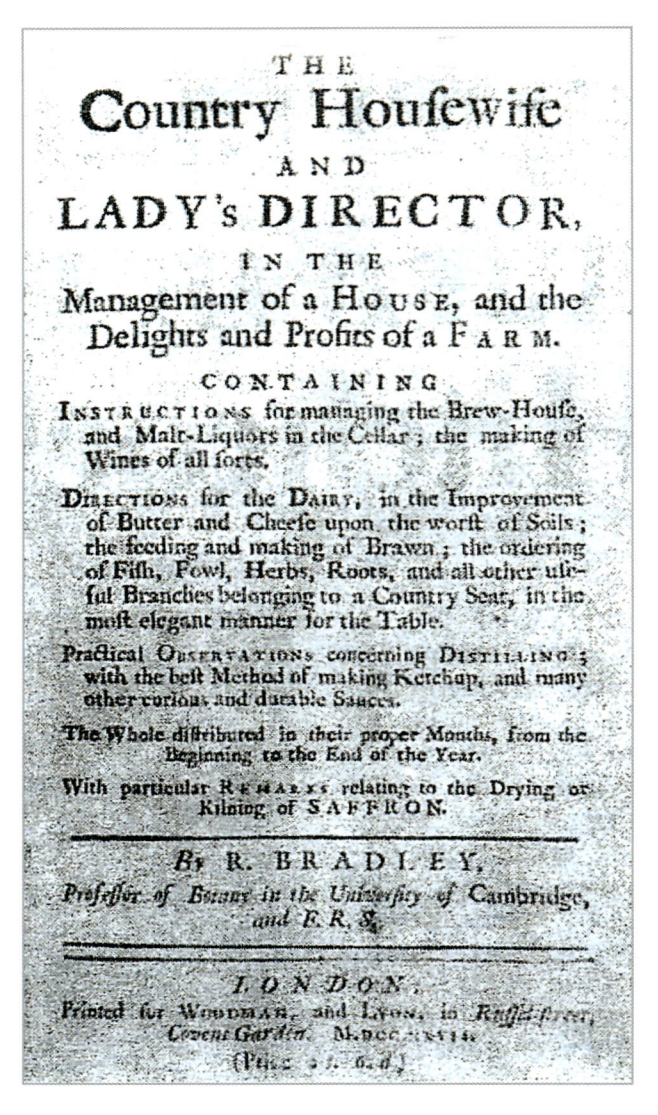

Fig 41. Richard Bradley's Title Page, 1727.

pages are devoted to recipes (she collected these over a period of thirty years – see Fig. 18 – and her first recipe of 1737 is reproduced in Fig. 40) for five different types of MUSHROOM PICKLE, six different types of WALNUT PICKLE, one version of CUCUMBER PICKLE, an explanation of how to make KATCHUP and a recipe for GOOSEBERRY VINEGAR, being a flavoured vinegar. GOOSEBERRY can thus be a wine or a sauce title. It is difficult to be precise but size of label is often a good guide as to whether a label went on a wine decanter or on a vinegar decanter. The two sauces described, which would probably be served from sauceboats, were a sauce for fish and a CUCUMBER sauce for mutton and for woodcock. The sauce for fish was based on ANCHOVIES. This stock sauce perhaps gave rise

to the "bon mot" about England having sixty different religions but only one sauce, attributed by the Oxford Dictionary of Quotations to the Marquis Domenico Caracciola 1715 – 1789 replacing Prince Francesco Carracioli 1732 – 1799. Elizabeth Smith attached six plans to her book showing how dishes were to be laid out (Figs. 21-23), and the place settings for pickles and anchovies were noted (Fig. 21). Pickles were still very much in vogue at this time, dispensed from saucers placed in the positions noted. Sauces hardly featured. Some seventy years later, when pickles were being passed round the table, a glass pickle dish was used set in a silver handled frame. An example is illustrated (Fig. 107) made by John Reily in London in 1801. He was a noted maker of sauce labels.

THE SAUCES

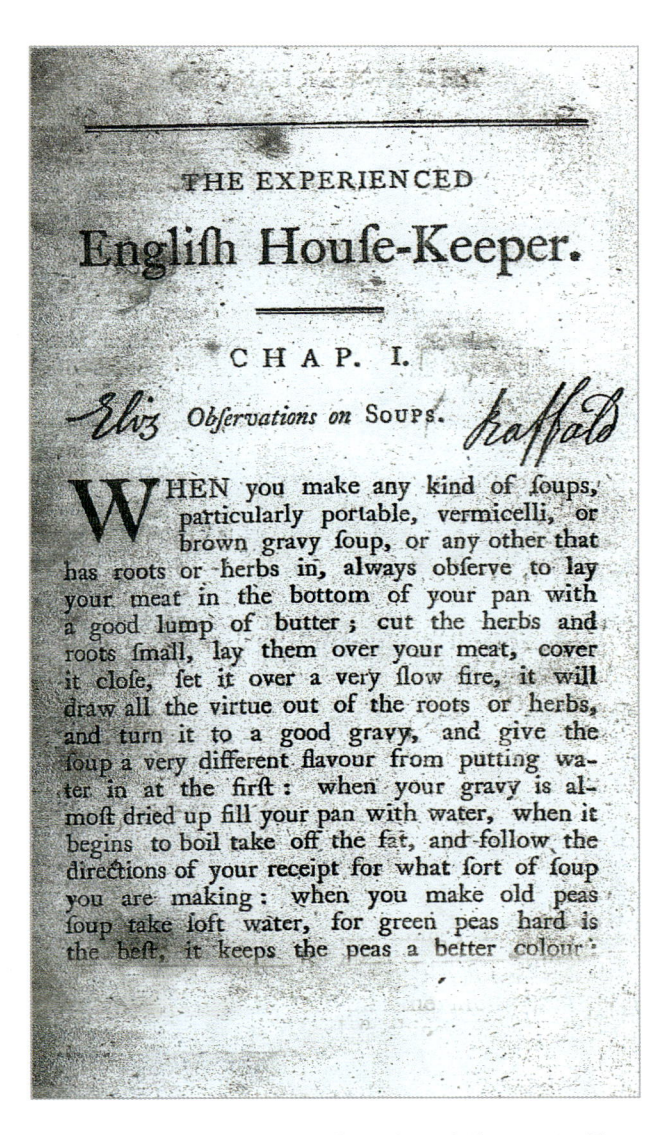

Fig 42. Raffald's autographed opening of Chapter 1 of her 1799 edition.

Fig 43. Farley's autographed conclusion of his Preface in 1804

2.4 A similar situation can be gleaned from the pages of John Nott's "The Cook's Dictionary" of 1726, Carter's "The Compleat City and Country Cook" of 1736 and Richard Bradley's "Country Housewife and Lady's Director", sixth edition, 1736. The latter was first published in 1727 and was an immediate success. This may have been due to the fact that the author was a Professor of Botany at Cambridge University and a Fellow of the Royal Society with a keen interest in collecting recipes. From the Devil Tavern in Fleet Street he acquired a recipe for Stewed Cucumbers, from the Spring Gardens at Vauxhall a recipe for Stewed Beefsteaks and from a Mr. Shepherd of Windmill Street a luncheon recipe for Potato Pudding (1). Most interestingly he obtained from a Mrs L. a recipe for peppermint water which makes clear that a label with this title was meant for the liqueur decanter. He describes it as "an incomparable pleasant Dram tasting like Ice, or Snow, in the Mouth, but creates a fine warmth in the Stomach and yields a refreshing Flavour"(2). His FISH SAUCE, said to combine "several quite vigorous flavours"(3), included beef consomme, light red wine, LEMON PEEL, 3 chopped ANCHOVIES or 2 teaspoonfuls of ANCHOVY ESSENCE (showing the strength of an ESSENCE), ONION, butter, 2 bouquet garni, SALT, PEPPER, CLOVES, mace and NUTMEG(4). He set out the "best method of making KETCHUP, and many other curious and durable sauces", as can be seen from his Title page in 1727 (Fig. 41).

2.5 In the 1750s interest in French food was on the increase in England. It was beginning to cause concern as it represented, according to Campbell in 1747, a "depraved Taste of spoiling wholesome Dyet, by costly and pernicious Sauces and absurd mixtures"(5). By the 1770s the position had changed dramatically. In 1774 Hannah Glasse published the seventh edition of her "Art of Cookery Made Plain and Easy" (Fig. 30). Her Preface was very practical. Concern was expressed. about the excessive dressing up of food "so much a blind folly of this age that they would rather be imposed upon by a French booby than give encouragement to a good English cook". She continues "if gentlemen will have French cooks, they must pay for French

THE SAUCES

Fig 44. William Scott's Title Page of 1826.

Fig 45. Mrs Scott at work in 1826.

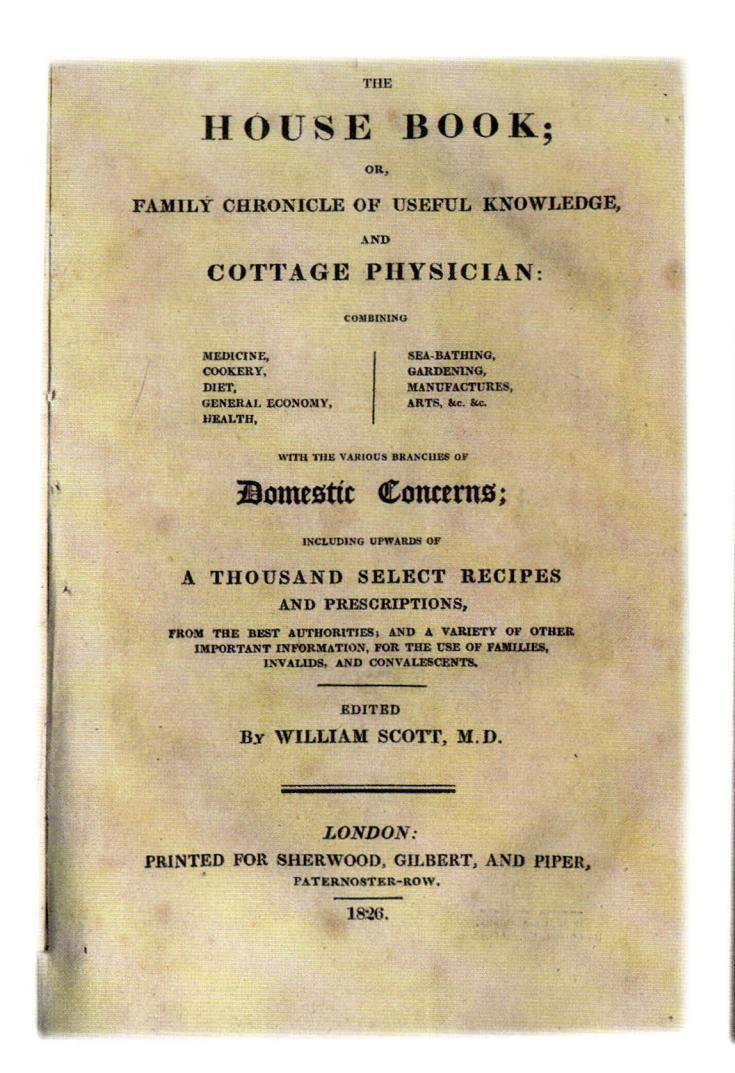

tricks". The use of some of the French language was becoming fashionable, as in VINAIGRE ORDINAIRE, so she explains "I have indeed given some of my dishes French names to distinguish them, because they are known by those names".

2.6 In Chapter 1 of Hannah Glasse's book, which deals with roasting and boiling, sauces are prescribed for roast geese, roast turkeys, fowls, roast ducks, pheasants, partridges, larks, boiled turkeys, boiled geese, boiled ducks and boiled rabbits. Chapter 2 deals with made up dishes. Chapter 3 deals with sauces. It contains the rubric "read this chapter and you will find how expensive a French cooked sauce is". Chapter 5 deals with dressing fish and gives recipes for LOBSTER SAUCE, SHRIMP sauce, oyster sauce and the standard ANCHOVY sauce. A table of dishes for each month of the year for first and second courses is included in the usual way. The first course often contained soups and many "made" savouries. The second course contained roasts and desserts. A comprehensive index gives references on how to make sauces, directions concerning the most appropriate sauce for steak and venison, recipes for MUSHROOM SAUCE for all sorts of white fowls, a recipe for CELERY sauce for roasted or boiled fowls, turkeys, partridges or any other game, a recipe for brown CELERY sauce as an alternative to CELERY sauce, and recipes for EGGS sauce for roast chicken, chalot (SHALOT) sauce for roasted fowls and for boiled mutton, MUSHROOM sauce to dress livers, LEMON sauce for boiled fowls and the standard stock fish sauce (ANCHOVY) to keep the whole year.

THE SAUCES

Fig 46. Frederick Bishop's Frontispiece showing a kitchen in 1855.
Fig 47. Bishop's Title Page of 1855

2.7 Spices had to be kept ready to hand to give that extra touch to exotic desserts. CINNAMON, NUTMEG and ground mace were sprinkled over Eighteenth Century quaking puddings. ANCHOVIES, PICKLES, LEMON and VINEGARS were the "sharp" flavourings for giving interest to a salomon-grundy, the bits and pieces remnants put together as a kind of hors d'oeuvre(6).

2.8 For those who went in for pub meals William Verral, who was the landlord of the White Hart in Lewes in Sussex, came up with some good recipes such as for spinach with cream and eggs and peach fritters with Rhenish wine(7). In his 1759 introduction to a recipe for a rich chilled soup for supper he says "this may seem to be a simple thing to place among these high matters;

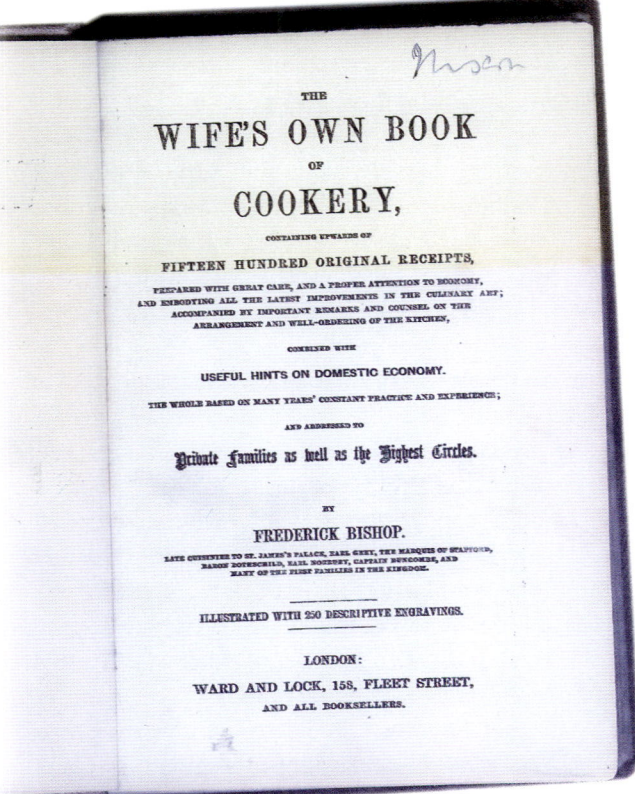

THE SAUCES

Fig 48. *Bishop's view of the art of carving in 1855.*

Fig 49. *Insull's joints, 1824*

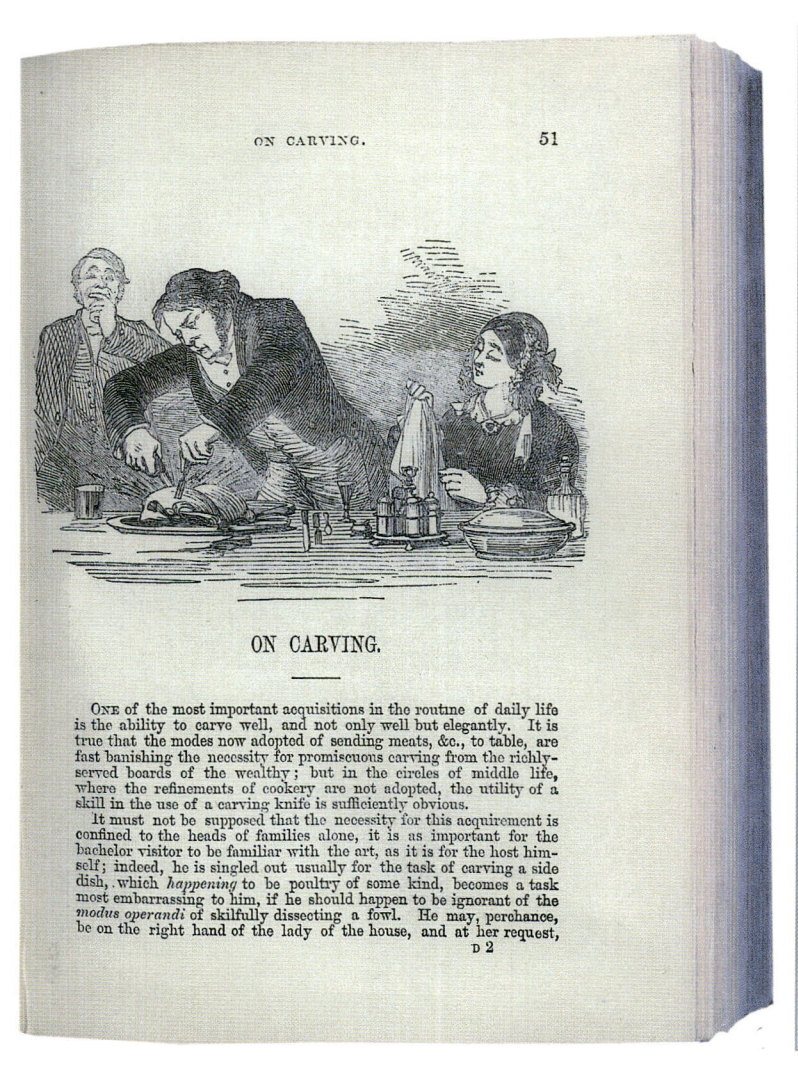

but I never see it come from table without a terrible wound in it. If it has the approbation of a few it will pay very well for the room it takes up here". It is made clear in his "Complete System of Cooking" that he had acquired his skill from "the celebrated Mr. De St. Clouet, sometime since cook to His Grace the Duke of Newcastle". So in the French manner he used vegetables as a base to some of his sauces, such as his magnificent White Onion Sauce — labelled ONIONS perhaps — which contained orange juice making its colour more golden then white – perhaps GOLDEN TRASSER – for use on French beans(8).

2.9 Sauce titles exist other than those listed in Chapter 3 which are related to silver or silver-plated objects. Many are on glass objects. Some are documentary as in the case of Dr Kitchiner's Sauce Box. He records 28 titles in 1822 in his "Cook's Oracle" for use as part of a travelling store chest or in connection with a table centrepiece upon which he comments as follows: "This is a convenient auxiliary to the Cook. It may be arranged as a pyramidical epergne for the centre of the table or as a travelling store chest. The following sketch will enable anyone to fit up an assortment of flavouring materials according to their own fancy and palate, and, we presume, will furnish sufficient variety for the amusement of the gustatory nerves of a thorough-bred Grand Gourmand of the first magnitude, if CAYENNE and GARLICK have not completely consumed the sensibility of his palate". The so-called "Sauce Box" thus described contained four eight

THE SAUCES

ounce bottles, sixteen four ounce bottles and eight two ounce bottles, with these titles: BRANDY, CAYENNE, CURACOA, CURRY POWDER, ESHALLOT WINE (SHALLOT), ESSENCE OF ANCHOVY, ESSENCE OF CELERY (CELERY), LEMON JUICE (LEMON), LEMON PEEL, MUSHROOM CATSUP, MUSTARD OIL, pew powder, PEPPER, PICKLES, POWDERED MINT (MINT), pudding, catsup, ragout powder, salad sauce, SALT, sauce superlative, soup-herb powder, SOY, sweet herbs, SYRUP, VINEGAR, WALNUT PICKLE and ZEST. Sauce titles in lower case lettering have not (as yet) been recorded in silver. The list well illustrates some of the problems which arise. For example BRANDY is also found as a spirit label but also as part of a set of sauce labels. CURACAO is also found as a liqueur label but clearly was part of the Sauce Box. ESHALLOT WINE is not a wine label. GOOSEBERRY was a wine, a flavoured vinegar and a chutney. BERGAMOT is recorded as a flavouring but was also used as a flavoured toilet water along with frangipani.

Fig 50. Insull's cuts, 1824.

Fig 51. Insull's instructions on carving, 1824.

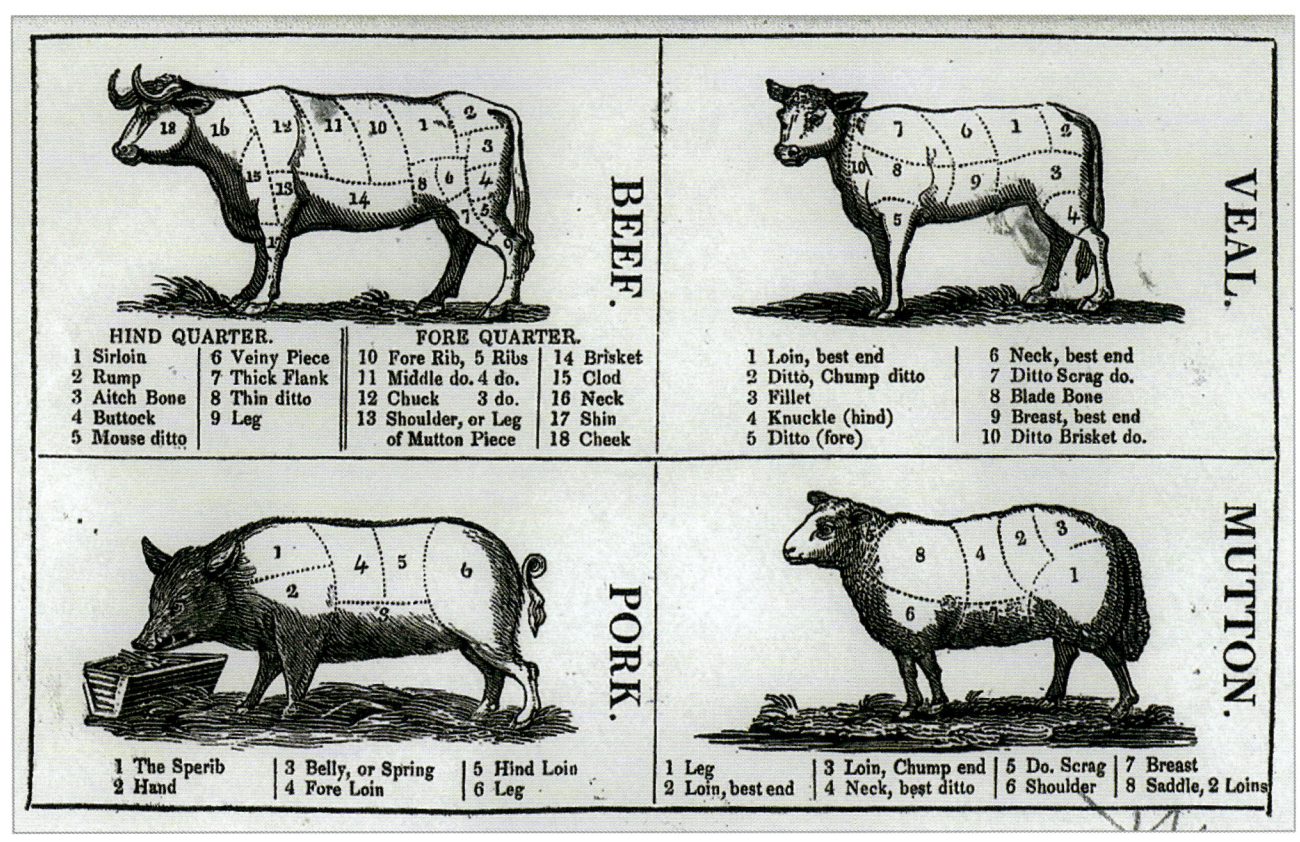

496   THE NEW FEMALE INSTRUCTOR

CARVING.—PLATE 1.

A Cod's Head.—Fish in general requires very little carving, the fleshy parts being those principally esteemed. A cod's head and shoulders, when in season, and properly boiled, is a very genteel and handsome dish. When cut, it should be done with a fish-trowel, and the parts about the back-bone on the shoulders are the most firm and the best. Take off a piece quite down to the bone, in the direction, *a, b, c, d,* putting in the spoon at *a, c,* and with each slice of fish give a piece of the sound, which lies underneath the back bone and lines it, the meat of which is thin and a little darker coloured than the body of the fish itself: this may be got by passing a knife or spoon underneath, in the direction *d, f.* About the head are many delicate parts, and a great deal of the jelly kind. The jelly part lies about the jaw-bones, and the firm parts within the head. Some are fond of the palate, and others the tongue, which likewise may be got by putting a spoon into the mouth.

Aitch-bone of Beef.—Cut off a slice an inch thick all the length from *a* to *b*, in the figure opposite, and then help. The soft fat which resembles marrow, lies at the back of the bone, below *c*; the firm fat must be cut in horizontal slices at the edge of the meat *d*. It is proper to ask which is preferred, as tastes differ. The skewer that keeps the meat properly together when boiling is here shown at *a*. This should be drawn out before it is served up; or, if it is necessary to leave the skewer in, put a silver one.

Sirloin of Beef may be begun either at the end, or by cutting into the middle. It is usual to inquire whether the outside or the inside is preferred. For the outside the slice should be cut down to the bones: and the same with every following helping. Slice the inside likewise, and give with each piece some of the soft fat.

The inside done as follows eats excellently: Have ready some shalot-vinegar boiling hot: mince the meat large, and a good deal of the fat; sprinkle it with salt, and pour the shalot-vinegar and the gravy on it. Help with a spoon, as quickly as possible, on hot plates.

BEEF.

HIND QUARTER.
1 Sirloin
2 Rump
3 Aitch Bone
4 Buttock
5 Mouse ditto
6 Veiny Piece
7 Thick Flank
8 Thin ditto
9 Leg

FORE QUARTER.
10 Fore Rib, 5 Ribs
11 Middle do. 4 do.
12 Chuck 3 do.
13 Shoulder, or Leg of Mutton Piece
14 Brisket
15 Clod
16 Neck
17 Shin
18 Cheek

VEAL.
1 Loin, best end
2 Ditto, Chump ditto
3 Fillet
4 Knuckle (hind)
5 Ditto (fore)
6 Neck, best end
7 Ditto Scrag do.
8 Blade Bone
9 Breast, best end
10 Ditto Brisket do.

PORK.
1 The Sperib
2 Hand
3 Belly, or Spring
4 Fore Loin
5 Hind Loin
6 Leg

MUTTON.
1 Leg
2 Loin, best end
3 Loin, Chump end
4 Neck, best ditto
5 Do. Scrag
6 Shoulder
7 Breast
8 Saddle, 2 Loins

29

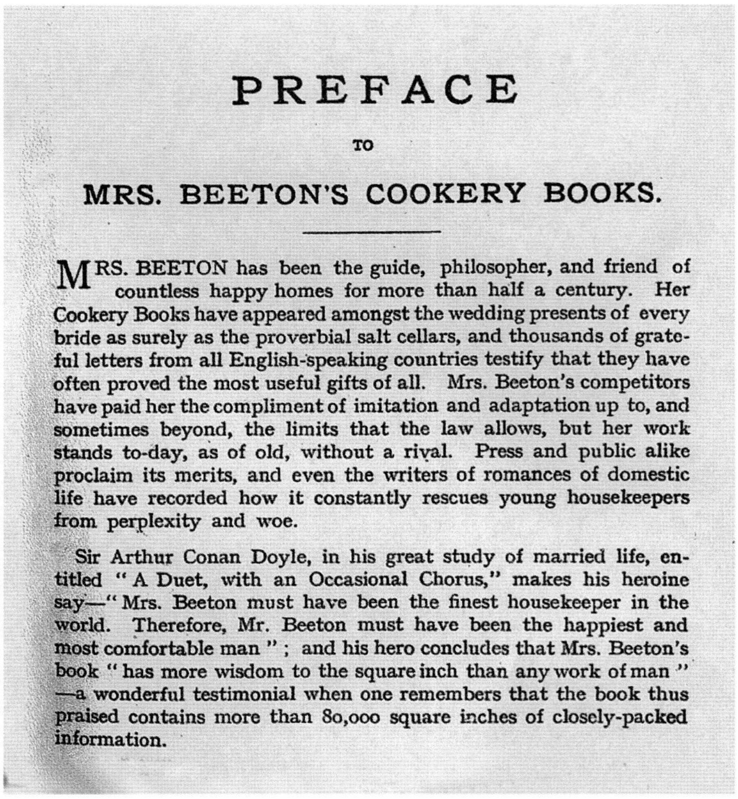

THE SAUCES

> # PREFACE
> ## TO
> ## MRS. BEETON'S COOKERY BOOKS.
>
> MRS. BEETON has been the guide, philosopher, and friend of countless happy homes for more than half a century. Her Cookery Books have appeared amongst the wedding presents of every bride as surely as the proverbial salt cellars, and thousands of grateful letters from all English-speaking countries testify that they have often proved the most useful gifts of all. Mrs. Beeton's competitors have paid her the compliment of imitation and adaptation up to, and sometimes beyond, the limits that the law allows, but her work stands to-day, as of old, without a rival. Press and public alike proclaim its merits, and even the writers of romances of domestic life have recorded how it constantly rescues young housekeepers from perplexity and woe.
>
> Sir Arthur Conan Doyle, in his great study of married life, entitled "A Duet, with an Occasional Chorus," makes his heroine say—"Mrs. Beeton must have been the finest housekeeper in the world. Therefore, Mr. Beeton must have been the happiest and most comfortable man"; and his hero concludes that Mrs. Beeton's book "has more wisdom to the square inch than any work of man"—a wonderful testimonial when one remembers that the book thus praised contains more than 80,000 square inches of closely-packed information.

Fig 52. 1910 Preface to Mrs Beeton's Cookery Books.

2.10 In the Nineteenth Century herbs and spices in powder form were no longer dispensed from glass bottles but from cool earthenware spice jars. Mrs Beeton records row upon row of tempting flavours in carefully labelled jars in her description of a Victorian kitchen in her well-known "Book of Household Management" first published as monthly supplements between 1859 and 1861 in the Englishwoman's Domestic Magazine. She mentions twenty-two herbs and spices: NUTMEG, including mace the outside shell, GARLIC, oregano, GINGER, sage, MINT, CAYENNE (or RED PEPPER), thyme, chives, bay leaves, rosemary, marjoram, BLACK PEPPER, CLOVES, CHILLI, coriander, paprika, parsley, caraway, turmeric (or curcuma), TARRAGON and basil. She could well have added a number of seeds such as mustard seed, cardamon seed, fennel seed, cumin seed and aniseed. Sometimes herbs and spices were mixed to save time in preparation giving rise to "mixed spices" and "mixed herbs" and the silver label for MIXT.

2.11 At the turn of the Eighteenth Century elegant ornaments were produced for grand entertainments. These included such concoctions as a floating island, a Chinese Temple, an obelisk, a desert island, a moonshine arrangement and a dish of snow! The naming of sauces by the use of silver labels fitted in with such grand designs. GINGER, CLOVES, NUTMEG, CINNAMON and SUGAR were all used in the displays for use at the appropriate time. In 1769 Elizabeth Raffald (Fig. 5) first published "The Experienced English Housekeeper". In the twelfth edition published in 1799 (Fig. 4) instructions are given for the assembly of Chinese Temples and obelisks as well as for Solomon's Temple in flummery and for the spinning of silver webs to cover sweetmeats. She was born in Doncaster. Not only was she a caterer, owner of a confectioner's shop in Manchester, owner of an Agency for domestic staff in Manchester and then the keeper of three different inns in succession but also she found time to present to her husband no less than thirteen daughters! She was therefore well versed in looking after a big family which was quite the norm. Her book was dedicated to the Hon. Lady Elizabeth Warburton (Fig. 6) in whose kitchen she received her training, becoming her Housekeeper. She also had published the very first Manchester Directory. Her recipes can easily be used to-day as has been shown in the case of recipes for mackerel, veal, seed cake, chocolate puffs, sweetmeat and lemonade white wine (9). She gives excellent recipes for TARRAGON, ELDER flower, GOOSEBERRY and SUGAR VINEGARS(10). Her recipes for sauces include Carp, White Fish, FISH, LOBSTER, CAVEACH, Pig, ONION, Goose, Oyster, Turkey, EGG, LEMON PICKLE and CELERY. Her book makes it quite clear that labels for WALNUT CATSUP and MUSHROOM CATSUP were related to sauces. Chapter XV contains her observations on wines, catsups and vinegars. Catsups were made to be kept. When matured WALNUT CATSUP was said to be "good in fish sauce". Her very firm signature is reproduced from an autographed copy of Chapter 1 of her book (Fig. 42).

2.12 Many recipe books were published in the Nineteenth Century. Mr John Farley, whose

THE SAUCES

Fig 53. Frontispiece to Mrs Beeton's 1910 edition.

Fig 54. Pickles and Vinegar advertisement, 1910

portrait is reproduced in Fig. 33, was Principal Cook at the London Tavern. In his book published in 1804 (Fig. 34) he gave hints on potting, salting and sousing. The sauces he mentioned in his Chapter XII included SICILIAN, Ham, APPLE, MINT SAUCE, Robert, WHITE SAUCE, Bechamel Sauce, ONION, LOBSTER, EGG, SHRIMP, ANCHOVY, Oyster, CELERY and MUSHROOM. The conclusion of his Preface is illustrated in Fig. 42 together with his signature. In 1822 Dr William Kitchener had published his first edition of his Cook's Oracle, which is mentioned above as giving particulars of an elaborate Sauce Box.

2.13 In 1824 "The Female Instructor or Young Woman's Companion and Guide to Domestic Happiness" was published – its frontispiece is reproduced in Fig. 59 – "being an epitome of all the acquirements necessary to form the

THE SAUCES

female character in every class of life with examples of illustrious women". Added in were "advice to servants", a "complete art of cookery" and "plain directions for carving". It contains fairly standard recipes for EGG SAUCE, bread sauce, ANCHOVY SAUCE, SHRIMP SAUCE, oyster sauce, GOOSEBERRY SAUCE, fennel sauce, caper sauce, LEMON SAUCE, MINT SAUCE and parsley sauce.

2.14 In 1826 Dr William Scott published "The House Book" (Fig. 44). He wrote in his introduction that "in the science of the stomach, the great secret consisted in rendering food acceptable to the palate, without unnecessary expense to the pocket; nourishing without being inflammatory and savoury without surfeiting; constantly endeavouring to maintain that salutary equilibrium which ought to distinguish economy from parsimony, epicurism from coarseness, and which constitutes the golden mean, the real philosopher's stone, the true panacea of human happiness, namely health and longevity". He gave five recipes for the flavoured vinegars so popular at that time: for common WHITE wine vinegar, common VINEGAR or VINAIGRE ORDINAIRE, SUGAR vinegar, GOOSEBERRY vinegar and RAISIN vinegar(11). He advised that salmon should be served with SHRIMP, ANCHOVY or LOBSTER sauce in one terrine and fennel with butter sauce in another terrine. If, however, you had ESSENCE OF ANCHOVY to hand he advised that you should send plain melted butter to table with it. This indicates how essences were applied and used. His Frontispiece (Fig. 45) shows the family hard at work.

2.15 Possibly written by Lady Charlotte Bury is the "Lady's Own Cookery Book", first edition 1832, second edition 1835 and third edition 1844. About a hundred sauces are described in the 1844 edition including Sultana, Spanish, Richmond, RAVIGOTTE, QUEENS, FISH SAUCE (for which no less than eighteen recipes are given), PIQUANTE, LEMON, HARVEY'S, DEVONSHIRE, WALNUT KETCHUP (for which five recipes are given), TOMATA SAUCE (for which three recipes are given), TOMATO KETCHUP and CAVECHI (for which three

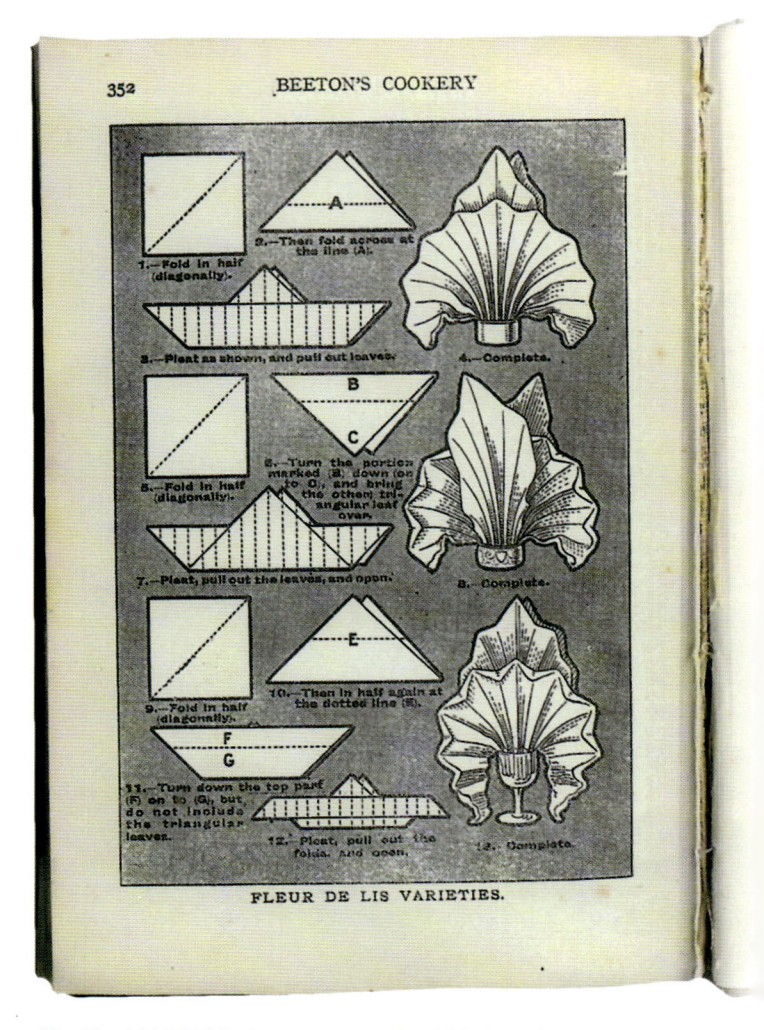

Fig 55. 1910 Table Arrangements for folded napkins.

recipes are given). Frederick Bishop writing in the 1850s (Fig. 47) took the view that in the circles of middle life the refinements of cookery were not adopted. The Wife's Own Book of Cookery had 250 engravings (Fig. 46). The head of the household however had to be good at carving (Fig. 48). Insull in 1824 very helpfully illustrated the ten most popular joints (Fig. 49) with carving instructions (Fig. 51) and the cuts of beef, veal, mutton and pork (Fig. 50).

2.16 Robert Kemp Philp in 1857 produced the "Housewife's Reason Why" attempting to answer some 1,500 questions. The excessive use of spices is warned against because they are said to impair the nervous irritability of the stomach and weaken its digestive powers. By "nervous irritability" he meant that healthy excitability which sets it in action whenever food is taken. His advice was not heeded by Isabella Beeton

32

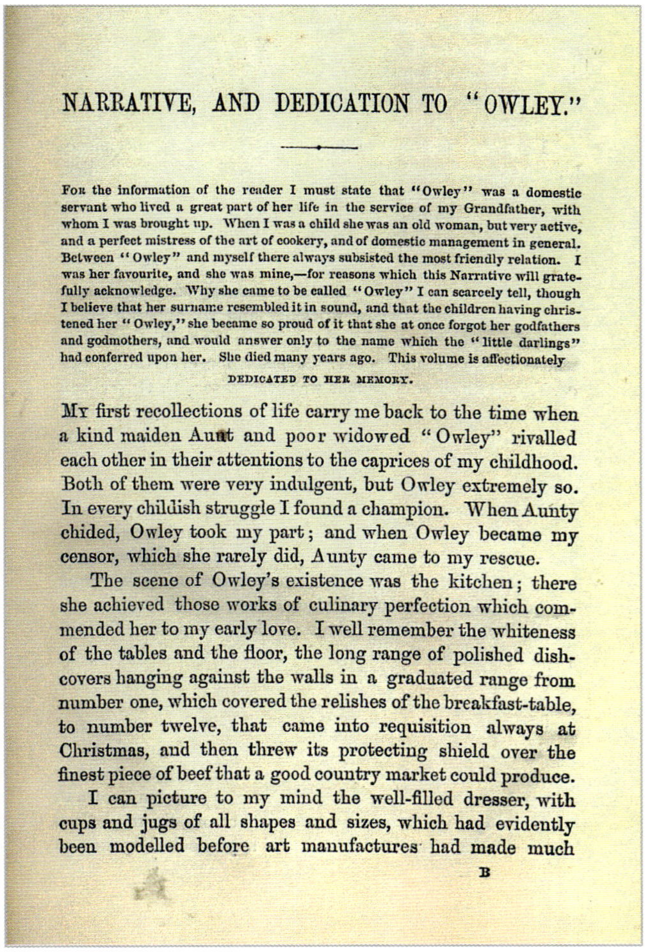

THE SAUCES

Fig 56. Robert Kemp Philp's inspiration for his recipes.

writing from 1859 onwards. Mr Philp explains why PICKLES should not be kept in metal vessels and why meat should be kept for some time before it is salted.

2.17 Published in 1864 by an "authoress" whose name is not given, Cre-Fydd's Family Fare or The Young Housewife's Daily Assistant gives a bill of family fare for each day of the year. Shrove Tuesday and Ash Wednesday are noted but not Christmas Day. Mr. J.B. Westrup, a chemist, manufactured in 1864 using the authoress' recipes three "Cre-Fydd condiment sauces". These were Casureep for brown soups, gravies and "made" dishes of either meat, fish or game; PIQUANTE condiment for stewed eels, rump steak, mutton cutlets and hashes; and Gialla Sauce for veal or pork cutlets, fried eels, broiled mackerel, fresh herrings, curries or cold meat(12). Under the heading Condiment and Other Sauces recipes are given for TOMATO SAUCE, PIQUANT SAUCE, CHUTNEY SAUCE, WHITE SAUCE, MUSHROOM KETCHUP, WALNUT KETCHUP, Pickled Walnuts, Pickled Onions, Pickled Cabbage, Pickled Beetroot, Pickled Shallots, Pickled Pears, Curry Powder, mixed sweet herbs and mixed spice, It is interesting to see how many old favourites of the 1760s remained favourites in the 1860s and even longer.

2.18 First published in 1861 Isabella Beeton's Book of Household Management "stands to-day, as of old, without a rival" in 1910 (see Fig. 52) Her "books have been tried and tested, and not found wanting, by generations". The new edition of 1910 (Fig. 53) contained sauce recipes, advertisements for PICKLE and VINEGAR (Fig. 54) and CATSUP and CHUTNEY (Fig 57) and advice on producing fleur de lis varieties of folded napkins (Fig. 55) and on table arrangements generally (13). ∎

NOTES

(1) See BERRIEDALE for details of these recipes with modern interpretation.
(2) See BERRIEDALE page 138 for details.
(3) BERRIEDALE, at page 126.
(4) The full recipe is given in modern format in BERRIEDALE at page 126.
(5) Robert Campbell, "London Tradesman", 1747, cited by Stancliffe in "Bottle Tickets" at page 11.
(6) Raffald gives two versions of a solomon-grundy on page 280 (1799 edition).
(7) See BERRIEDALE page 132 for details.
(8) An up-to-date versions is given by BERRIEDALE on page 131 (6 servings).
(9) All in BERRIEDALE.
(10) RAFFALD, pages 340 and 341.
(11) SCOTT, page 384.
(12) CRE-FYDD, page 341.
(13) BEETON'S COOKERY, page 353 and following.

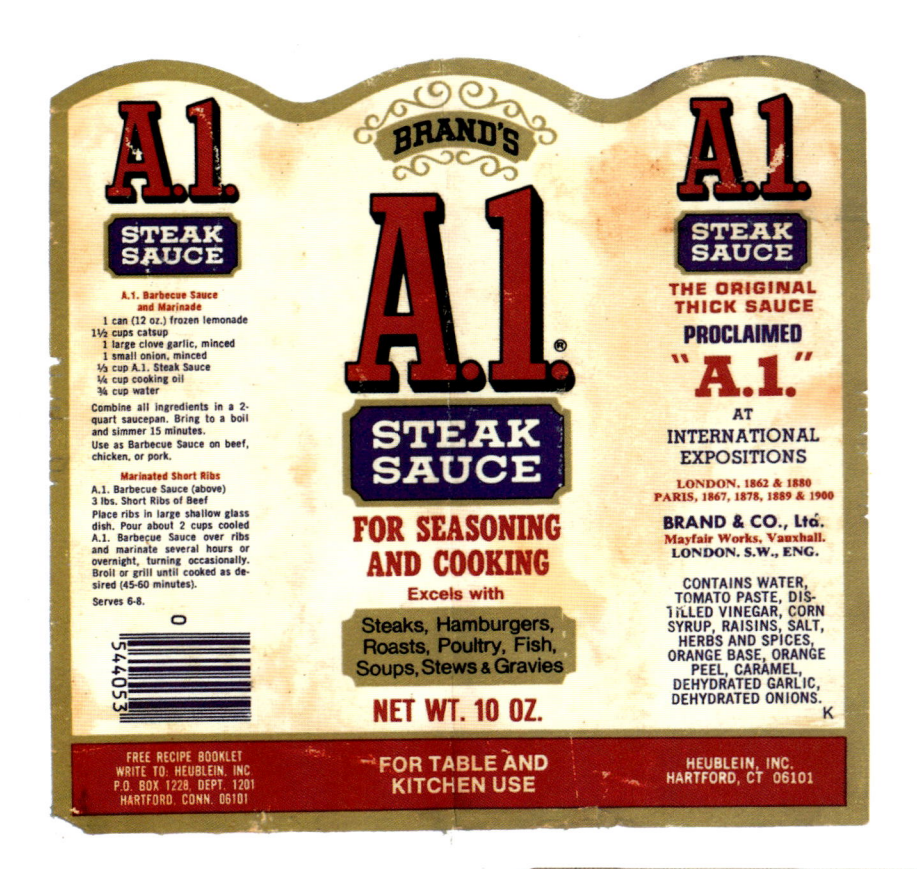

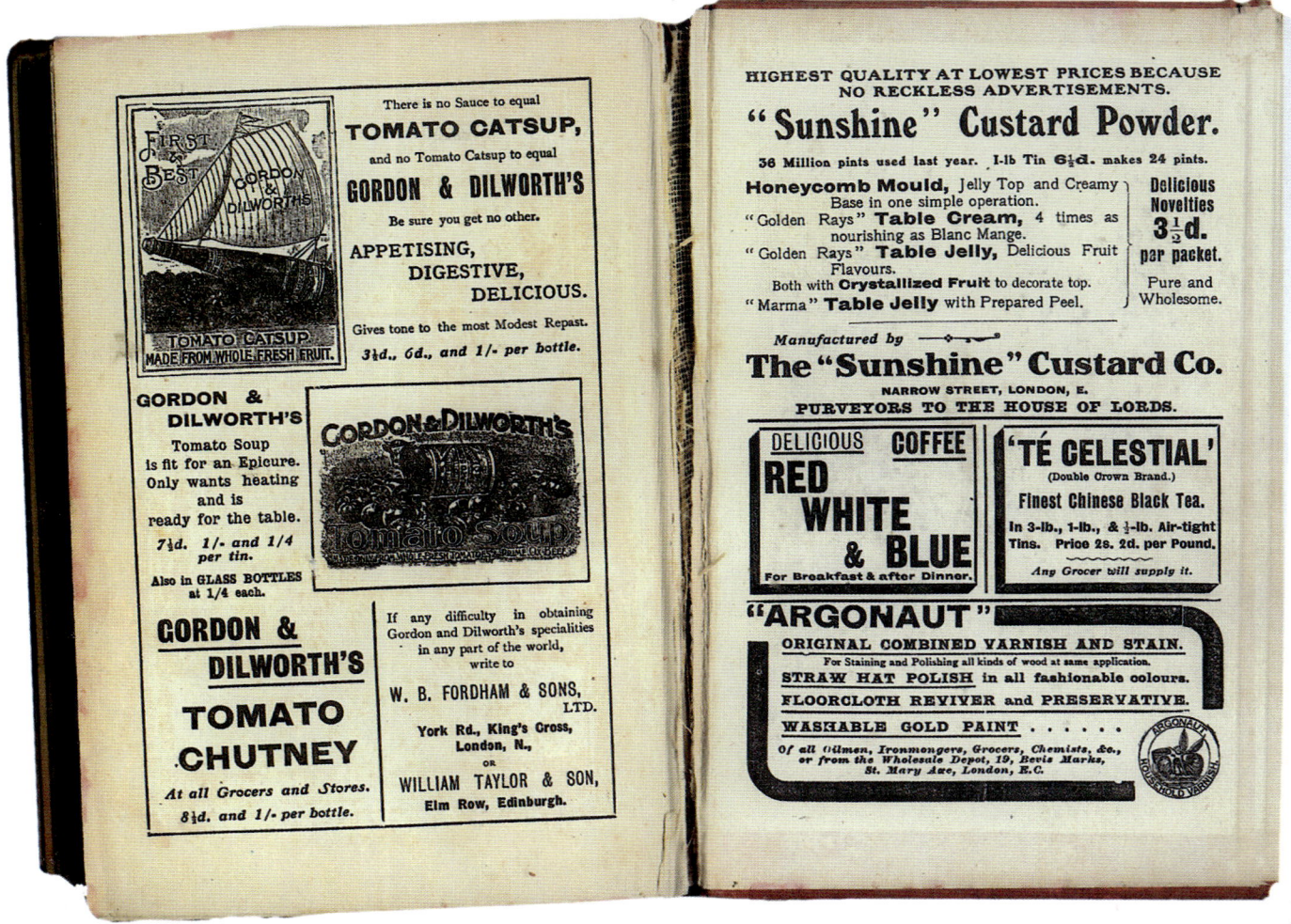

Fig 57. A.1., Tomato Catsup and Tomato Chutney advertisements

CHAPTER 3

THE TITLES

CONDIMENT OR "SAUCE" LABELS are used on various types of bottles and on rare occasions hung on epergnes. The bottles can be cruets, soy bottles, jars, vinegar bottles, and decanters. The labels can be hung by chains, hung by neck rings, engraved on bottle collars, engraved on mounts, or engraved on bottle stoppers. The names can be in respect of sauces, flavourings, essences, condiments, herbs, spices, extracts, pastes, liquids, fruits, jams, seasonings, dressings, oils, vinegars, catsups, sauce wines, sauce spirits, sauce liqueurs, and pickles. Not included in the list of titles are soft drinks, non-sauce liqueurs, non-sauce spirits, non-sauce wines and cordials and labels used for medicinal or toiletry purposes.

Listed below in alphabetical order are names appearing on gold, silver-gilt, silver, silver-plated and similar labels noted by the author over a period of some thirty-years. Variant names are inset, and these are placed in very approximate historical development order as a guide to assist in dating.

Roman capital letters are for the most part used on sauce labels. The use of lower case lettering in the list indicates that the title is not pierced or engraved in capital letters, as is the norm, but is engraved in lower case, script, gothic or decorative lettering. Script titles have been noted for Anchovy, Elf Anchovies, Cayenne, Chilli Vin, Fish Sauce, Soy, Vinegar, Walnut Pickle and Worcester. Sometime fancy lettering is used, such as the Puginesque style used on an Art Nouveau label for VINEGAR. Script lettering is favoured by makers from Denmark and Sweden. As in the case of wine labels, single cut-out initial letters are sometimes found, such as "K" for KYAN. The list of titles is by no means exhaustive. It is indicative of the range of titles used. American, Danish, Dutch, French and Swedish sauce label titles are included. Some titles used on non-silver labels are recorded in Chapter 10 with labels made in or titles engraved upon materials other than silver.

1.	A1	20.	Black	39.	CAMP VINR
2.	A LA RUSSE	21.	BLOATERS	40.	CAMP-VINR
3.	ANCHOVY SAUCE	22.	BRANDY	41.	CAMP.VIN
4.	ANCHOVIES	23.	BRIGHTON	42.	CAMP VIN
5.	ANCHOVIEE SE	24.	BROWN	43.	CAMP VIN:
6.	Anchovie	25.	BROWN'S	44.	CAMP V.
7.	ANCHOVIE	26.	BUDOCK	45.	CAPSICUM
8.	ANCHOVES	27.	BURGESS.S FISH SAUCE	46.	CAPTAIN WHITE'S
9.	ANCHOVEY	28.	BURGESS SAUCE	47.	CARRACHI
10.	Anchovy	29.	BUR.s S.ce	48.	CARRACHE
11.	ANCHOVY	30.	BURGESS	49.	CARACHA
12.	Elf Anchovies	31.	B	50.	CORRACHE
13.	APPETISSANTE	32.	BURGUNDY	51.	CORACK
14.	APPLE	33.	BURMAN SAUCE	52.	KORAC
15.	AZIJN (vinegar, Dutch)	34.	CABBAGE	53.	CARRACHIO
16.	BEEF	35.	CAMP SAUCE	54.	CARATCH
17.	BERGAMOT	36.	CAMP	55.	CORATCH
18.	BERNIS	37.	CAMP – SAU^E	56.	CORRATCH
19.	BLACK PEPPER	38.	CAMP VINEGAR	57.	CORRACKE

35

THE TITLES

58.	CORACHA	108.	CHERRY	158.	DEVONSHIRE
59.	CORACH	109.	CHETNA	159.	DEVON
60.	CORRASH	110.	CHILLI	160.	EAU DE MIEL
61.	CARRACK	111.	CHILI	161.	EGGS
62.	CARRACH	112.	CHILLY	162.	ELDER
63.	GARRACH	113.	CHILIA	163.	ELDER-VINEGAR
64.	CEORATCH	114.	CHILLIA	164.	ELDER VINEGAR
65.	CARRISH	115.	C	165.	ELDER-VINr
66.	CATSUP	116.	CHILLI VINEGAR	166.	ELDER VINr
67.	KATSUP	117.	CHILLIE VINEGAR	167.	ELDER VIN
68.	Cayenne	118.	CHILE VIN	168.	ELDER Vr
69.	CAYENNE	119.	CHILI VINEGAR	169.	ESCAVECHI
70.	CAYAN	129.	CHILLY VINEGAR	170.	CAVICHE
71.	KYAN	121.	CHILLE-VINr	171.	CAVEZA
72.	CYAN	122.	CHILI VINr	172.	CAVEACH
73.	CAYENN	123.	CHILLY VINr	173.	Caveace
74.	CAYON	124.	CHILLI VIN	174.	CAVEACE
75.	KAYON	125.	CHILLI-VIN	175.	CAVICE
76.	CAION	126.	Chilli Vin	176.	CAVIC SAUCE
77.	CAON	127.	CHILLI.VIN	177.	ES
78.	KIAN	128.	CHILI VIN	178.	ESSENCE
79.	KAEN	129.	CHILI. VIN	179.	ESSENCE ANCHOVIES
80.	CHIAN	130.	CHILI VING^R	180.	ESSENCE OF ANCHOVY
81.	CHAON	131.	CHILLY VIN		
82.	CIAN	132.	CHILLI. VINr.	181.	ESSENCE OF ANCHOVIES
83.	CYENNE	133.	CHILLI V		
84.	KAYENNE	134.	CHILI V.	182.	E.A.
85.	CAYENE	135.	C. VINEGAR	183.	ESSENCE OF CHILI
86.	CAYENE. Sc.	136.	CH. VINEGAR	184.	ESSENCE OF CHILLI
87.	KAYAN	137.	C.V.	185.	ESSENCE OF GINGER
88.	KAYEN	138.	CHUTNEE	186.	ESSENCE GINGER
89.	KAYANNE	139.	CHUTNEY	187.	ESS: GINGER
90.	CAYANNE	140.	CHATNEY	188.	ESSENCE-OF-KAYAN
91.	K	141.	CINNAMON	189.	ESSENCE OF LEMON
92.	CAYENNE PEPPER	142.	CINAMON	190.	FANCY
93.	CAYON PEPPER	143.	CITRONELLE	191.	FINE HERBS
94.	CAYENNE PEPr	144.	CITRON	192.	FINES HERBES
95.	CYAN PEPPER	145.	CLOVE	193.	FISH SAUCE
96.	CAYENNE VINr	146.	CLOVES	194.	Fish Sauce
97.	CAYENNE VIN	147.	CLOAVES	195.	FISH-SAUCE
98.	CAY. VINr	148.	CREOLE	196.	FISH.S
99.	CHYAN VINEGAR	149.	CROWN SAUCE	197.	FISH. SAUCE
100.	CELERIE	150.	CROWN	198.	FISH. Sae.
101.	CELERY	151.	CUCUMBER	199.	F. SAUCE
102.	CHEROKEE SAUCE	152.	CUCUMBER V.	200.	Fh SAUCE
103.	CHER SAUCE	153.	CUCUMBER VIN	201.	Fh. SAUCE
104.	CHERKE SAUCE	154.	CURACOA	202.	Fh, SAUCE
105.	CHERe SAUCE	155.	CUROCOA	203.	FISH
106.	CHEROKEE	156.	CORACAO	204.	F
107.	CHEREKEY	157.	CURRY	205.	FLORe

36

THE TITLES

206.	FOWL	256.	IRISH	306.	MIXT
207.	FRENCH	257.	JAM VINEGAR	307.	MOGUL SAUCE
208.	FRENCH VINEGAR	258.	JAPAN SOY	308.	MOGUL
209.	FRUIT	259.	JESSAMINE	309.	MUSHROOM KETCHUP
210.	GAME	260.	JUNIPER	310.	Mushroom Ketchup
211.	GARLICK	261.	KETCHUP	311.	MUSHm KETCHUP
212.	GARLIC	262.	KETCHIP	312.	MUSHROOM KETp
213.	G	263.	KETSHUP	313.	MUSHROOM CATCHUP
214.	GARLICK VINEGAR	264.	KETSCHUP	314.	M. KETCHUP
215.	GK VINEGAR	265.	KECHUP	315.	M. CATCHUP
216.	GARLICK.VIN	266.	KETSUP	316.	MUSHROOM
217.	GARLICK–VINEGAR	267.	KATCHUP	317.	M
218.	GARLICK VINEG^R	268.	KATSHUP	318.	MUSHROOM CATSUP
219.	GARLICK VING	269.	CATCHUP	319.	MUSTARD
220.	GARLICK VING^R	270.	LEMON	320.	NEPAUL
221.	GAR. VINr.	271.	LEMMON	321.	N. SAUCE
222.	GARLIC VINEGAR	272.	LEMON PEEL	322.	NIG
223.	GINGER	273.	LEMON P.	323.	NUTMEG
224.	GOLDEN TRASSER	274.	LEMON PICKLE	324.	OIL
225.	GOOSEBERRY	275.	LEMMON-PICKLE	325.	OLIVE OIL
226.	GOOSE-BERRY	276.	LEMON-PICKLE	326.	ONIONS
227.	GRAY SAUCE	277.	LEMON.PICle	327.	ORANGE
228.	HARVEY SAUCE	278.	LEMON PICK	328.	ORDINAIRE
229.	HARVEYS SAUCE	279.	LEMON-PICK	329.	OUDE SAUCE
230.	HARVEY'S SAUCE	280.	LEMON.PICk	330.	OUDE
231.	HARVEY,S SAUCE	281.	LEMON. PIC	331.	OUDE'S SAUCE
232.	Harvey's fish sauce	282.	LEMON PIC^{LE}	332.	KING OF OUDE
233.	HARVEYS	283.	LEMON PICL	333.	PACKE
234.	HERVEY SAUCE	284.	LEMON-PICl	334.	PARAGON
235.	HERVEY.S	285.	LEMON Pkle	335.	PATE SAVONNEUSE
236.	HERVEY	286.	LEMON PICKE	336.	PEACH
237.	HERVY	287.	LEMON PICE	337.	PEPPAR (Pepper, Swedish)
238.	HERVE	288.	LEM. PICKLE	338.	PEPPER
239.	H. SAUCE	289.	LEM PICKle	339.	PEPPERMINT
240.	Hy. SAUCE	290.	LEM. PICK	340.	PEPPERMENT
241.	H	291.	L. PICKLE	341.	P'MINT
242.	HARVEY	292.	LEMON V.	342.	PEPPER VINEGAR
243.	HARVY SAUCE	293.	LIME JUICE	343.	PEPR VINEGAR
244.	HARVy. SAUCE	294.	L. JUICE	344.	PEPPER V
245.	HARVEY.S	295.	LIMOSIN	345.	PEPr VIN
246.	HARVEY'S	296.	LOBSTER SAUCE	346.	PEPr VINr
247.	HENRY	297.	LOBSTER	347.	PEPr VIN:
248.	HINOJO	298.	LOVAGE	348.	PICKLES
249.	HOT VINEGAR	299.	MADEIRA	349.	PICKLE
250.	HOT	300.	MADRAS FLAME	350.	PICKLE PEPPER
251.	HUILE (Oil, French)	301.	MALVERN WATER	351.	PINK VINEGAR
252.	HUILLE	302.	MAPLE SYRUP	352.	P. VINEGAR
253.	IMPERIAL	303.	MARMALADE	353.	PINK
254.	INDIA	304.	MAYBN'S PICKLE	354.	PINK VINEG
255.	INGEFARA (Ginger, Swedish)	305.	MINT		

THE TITLES

#		#		#	
355.	PITT SAUCE	405.	SAUCE-ROY	455.	TOMATO
356.	PITTS	406.	SAUCE R^L	456.	TAMATA S.
357.	PORT	407.	SAUCE Rl	457.	TOMATA
358.	PORT SAUCE	408.	SAUCE R	458.	UNIVERSAL SAUCE
359.	POUVRADE	409.	ROYAL	459.	VALE OF AYLESBURY
360.	POUVERADE	410.	SCYRUP	460.	VEAL & HAM
361.	PRESERVED CHERRIES	411.	SHALLOT	461.	VINEGAR
362.	QUEEN'S SAUCE	412.	SHALOT	462.	Vinegar
363.	QUIN	413.	ESCHALOTTE	463.	VINIGAR
364.	QUIN SAUCE	414.	SHALLOT VINEGAR	464.	VINAIGRE (Vinegar, French)
365.	QN. SAUCE	415.	SHALOT-V	465.	VINAIGRE ORDINAIRE
366.	QUIN-SAUCE	416.	SHERRY	466.	V
367.	QUIN'S SAUCE	417.	SHRIMP	467.	WALNUT
368.	QUINCE	418.	SHROPSHIRE	468.	WALLNUT
369.	QNS PICKLE	419.	SICILIAN	469.	WALNUt
370.	RAISIN	420.	SIROP DE GROSEILLE	470.	WALNt
371.	RASPBERRY VINEGAR	421.	SIROP DE VINAIGRE	471.	WALNUT PICKLE
372.	RASBERRY VINEGAR	422.	SOHO	472.	WALT PICKLE
373.	RASBERRY	423.	SOURING	473.	Walnut Pickle
374.	RASPBERRY	424.	SOY	474.	WALNUT KETCHUP
375.	RP BERRY	425.	Soy.	475.	WALNUT KETCH
376.	Rp. BERRY	426.	INDIAN SOY	476.	WALNUT CATCHUP
377.	RAVIGOTTE	427.	INDIA SOY	477.	WALNt KETc
378.	RAVIGITTE	428.	INDIA	478.	WAL^T KET^C
379.	READING SAUCE	429.	S	479.	W. KETCHUP
380.	READING'S	430.	SOYER	480.	WALNUT CATSUP
381.	READING	431.	SOYE	481.	WALNUT CAT.SUP
382.	R	432.	SOYA	482.	WHITE PEPPER
383.	RED VINEGAR	433.	STRAWBERRY	483.	WHITE VINEGAR
384.	R. VINEGAR	434.	SUGAR	484.	WHITE
385.	REGENT	435.	TARRAGON	485.	Wm IV
386.	RIEN QUI MANQUE	436.	TARGON	486.	WOODS SAUCE
387.	RUE	437.	TARRAGAN	487.	WOODS FISH SAUCE
388.	RUW	438.	TARRAGONA	488.	WOOD
389.	SALAD OIL	439.	TARREGON	489.	WOODS
390.	SALAD-OIL	440.	TARAGON	490.	WORCESTER SAUCE
391.	SALT	441.	TERRAGON	491.	WORCESTER
392.	SALT SAUCE	442.	TERAGON	492.	Worcester
393.	S. PIQUANTE	443.	TAROGON	493.	WORCESR.
394.	PICQUANTE	444.	T	494.	WORCESTERSHIRE
395.	PIQUANTE	445.	TARRAGON VINEGAR	495.	YORKSHIRE RELISH
396.	PIQUANT	446.	TARAGON VINEGAR	496.	YORKSHIRE
397.	SAUCE	447.	TARRIN VIN	497.	ZEST
398.	SAUCE A LA MILITAIRE	448.	TARR.n VIN	498.	ZOOBDITTY MATCH
399.	SAUCE A LA SUISSE	449.	TARRAGON VIN	499.	ZOOBDITTY
400.	SAUCE BLANCHE	450.	TERRAGON VIN	500.	ZOOBy MATCH
401.	SAUCE ROYAL	451.	TERAGON VIN	501.	ZOOBY MATCH
402.	SAUCE ROYl	452.	TARRAGn VINEGAR	502.	ZOOB.y MATCH ■
403.	SAUce: ROYl:	453.	TARRAGON V		
404.	SAUCE ROY	454.	TOBASCO		

PREFACE.

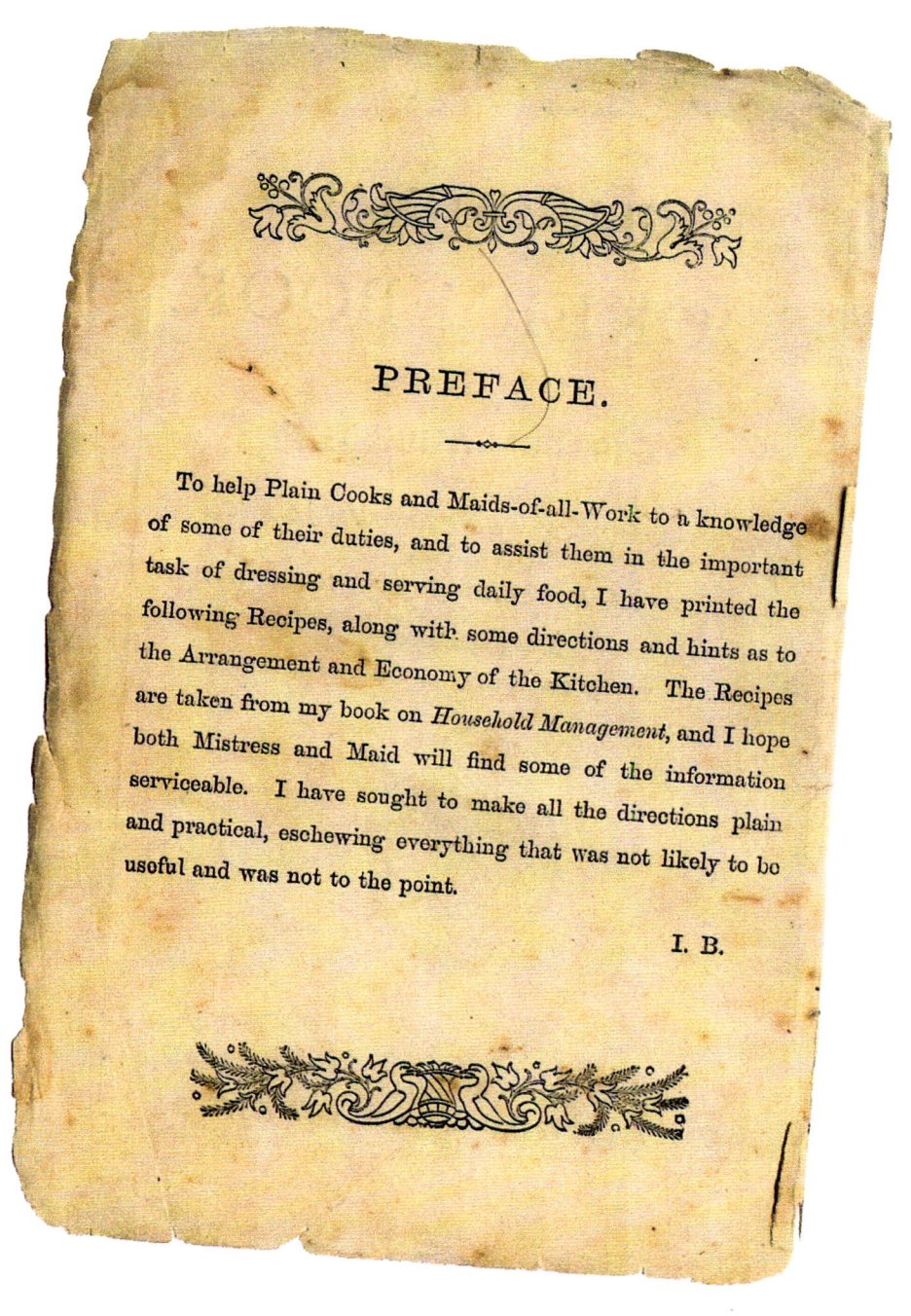

To help Plain Cooks and Maids-of-all-Work to a knowledge of some of their duties, and to assist them in the important task of dressing and serving daily food, I have printed the following Recipes, along with some directions and hints as to the Arrangement and Economy of the Kitchen. The Recipes are taken from my book on *Household Management*, and I hope both Mistress and Maid will find some of the information serviceable. I have sought to make all the directions plain and practical, eschewing everything that was not likely to be useful and was not to the point.

I. B.

Fig 58. Preface to Mrs Isabella Mary Beeton's "The Englishwoman's Cookery Book". She married, at the age of 20, Samuel Orchard Beeton, a junior partner in publishers Charles H. Clarke & Co. Her book on Household Management sold 60,000 copies in its first year. She died in 1865. aged 28, following the birth of her fourth child. By 1968 her book had sold 2 million copies.

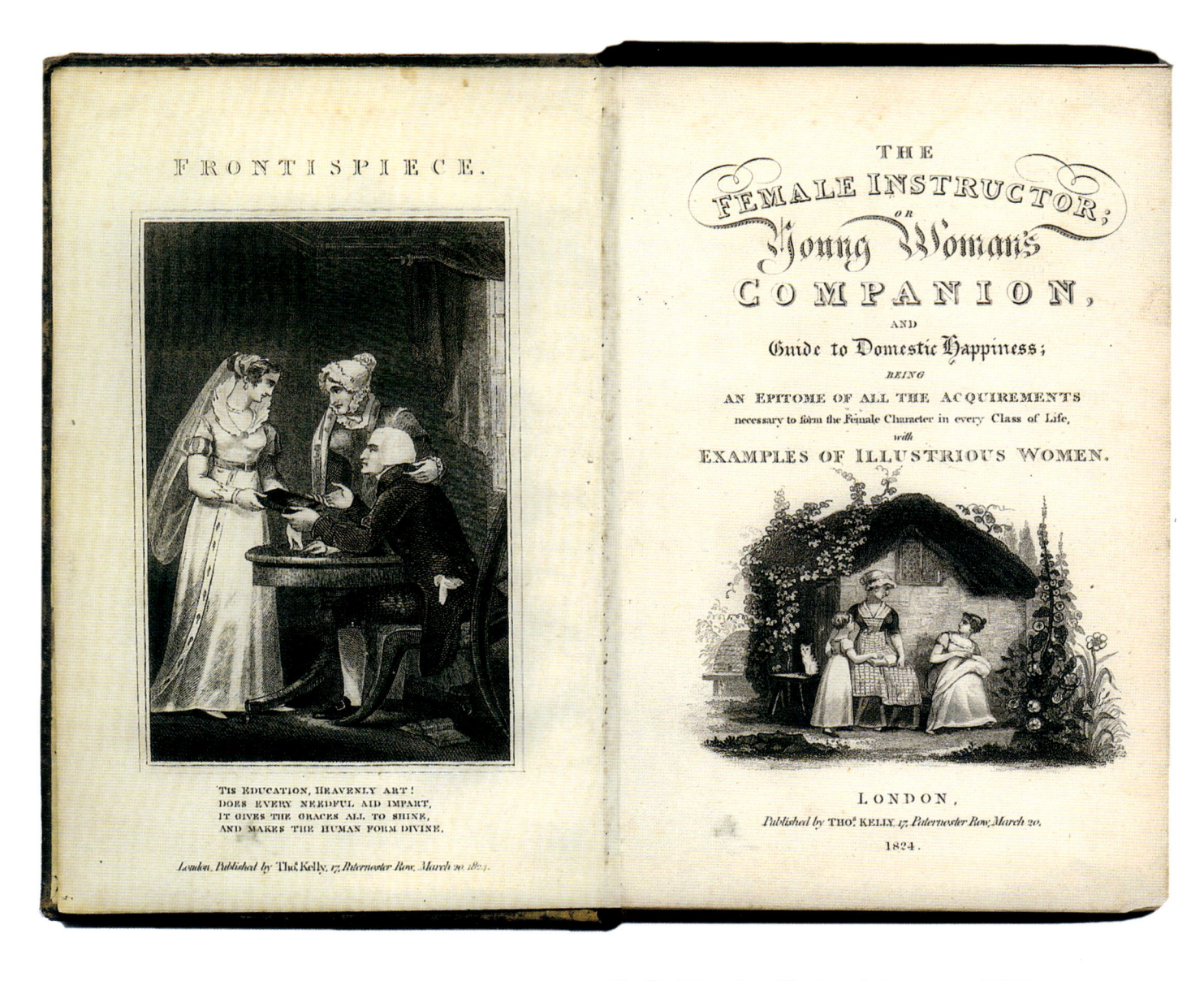

Fig 59. Taken from The Female Instructor of 1824.

CHAPTER 4

THE RECIPES

IN THIS CHAPTER we comment on some of the sauces mentioned in Chapter 3. Owley was Robert Kemp Philp's mentor as explained in his Dedication (Fig. 56). Parents were supposed to bring up their daughters well educated in the art of housekeeping. The Frontspiece to Insull's "Female Instructor" of 1824 shows the young bride being given her copy of essential recipes (Fig. 59). Bishop gives a useful instruction for a Bridal Breakfast à la Fourchette (Fig. 60), which can be adapted for a christening.

1. A1.
This title is rare because the sauce was usually served in late Victorian times straight from the tall narrow-necked bottle containing this proprietary brand of meat sauce (see Fig. 57).

2. A LA RUSSE
This title refers to a sauce of this name containing tarragon, chervil or parsley in béchamel sauce to go with the new style of dining (1).

3. APPETISSANTE
French for appetizing, relishing, delicious, stimulating the appetite and exciting a desire.

4. ANCHOVY
Anchovies like pickles were used to give relish at the supper table. Layout plans often prescribed a place for them. Anchovy sauce was a standard stock sauce to go with fish. A cookery book records that Dr. QUIN (the epicure and not the actor who is said to have had a sauce named after him) used to declare that "of all the Banns of Marriage I ever heard, none gave me half as much pleasure as the Union of delicate ANN CHOVY with good JOHN DORY". An 1870 recipe for preparing this fish is shown in Fig. 61. ANCHOVY was strong in ESSENCE form. William Scott gives a recipe at page 385 for this concentration. Take anchovies, he says, from two pounds to four and a half pounds, pulp through a fine hair sieve, boil the bones with seven ounces of SALT in six pints of water and strain. Add seven ounces of flour and the pulp of the fish: boil and pass the whole through the sieve and colour with Venetian red to your fancy. This, he says, should

Fig 60. Bishop's Bridal Breakfast à la fourchette.

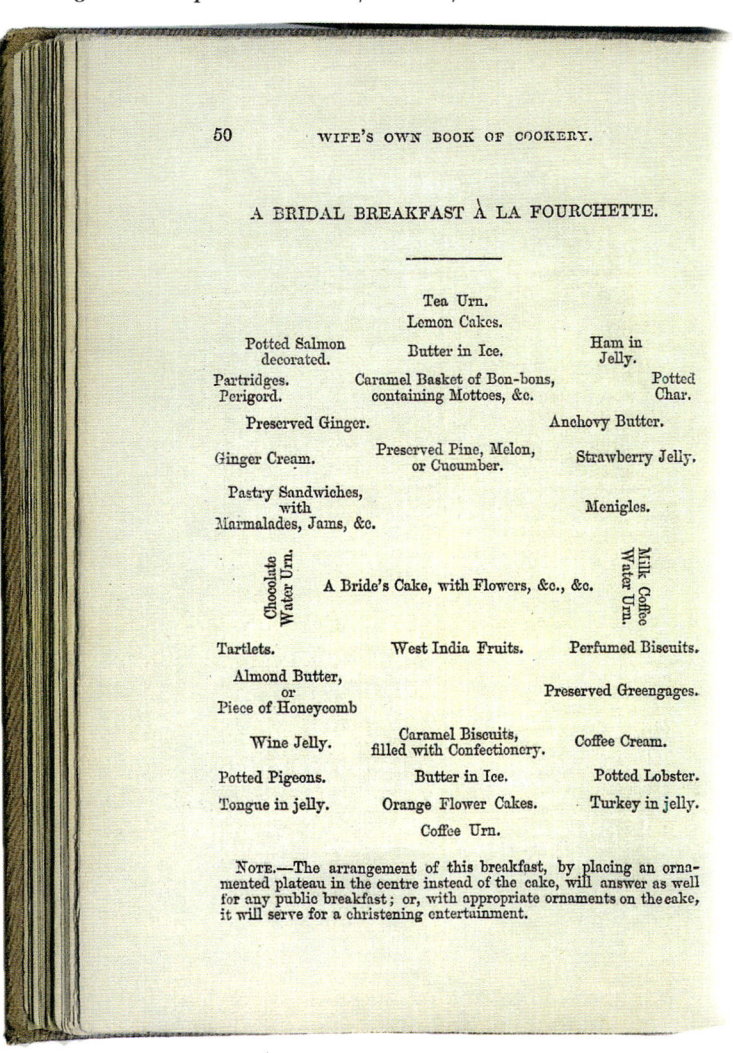

THE RECIPES

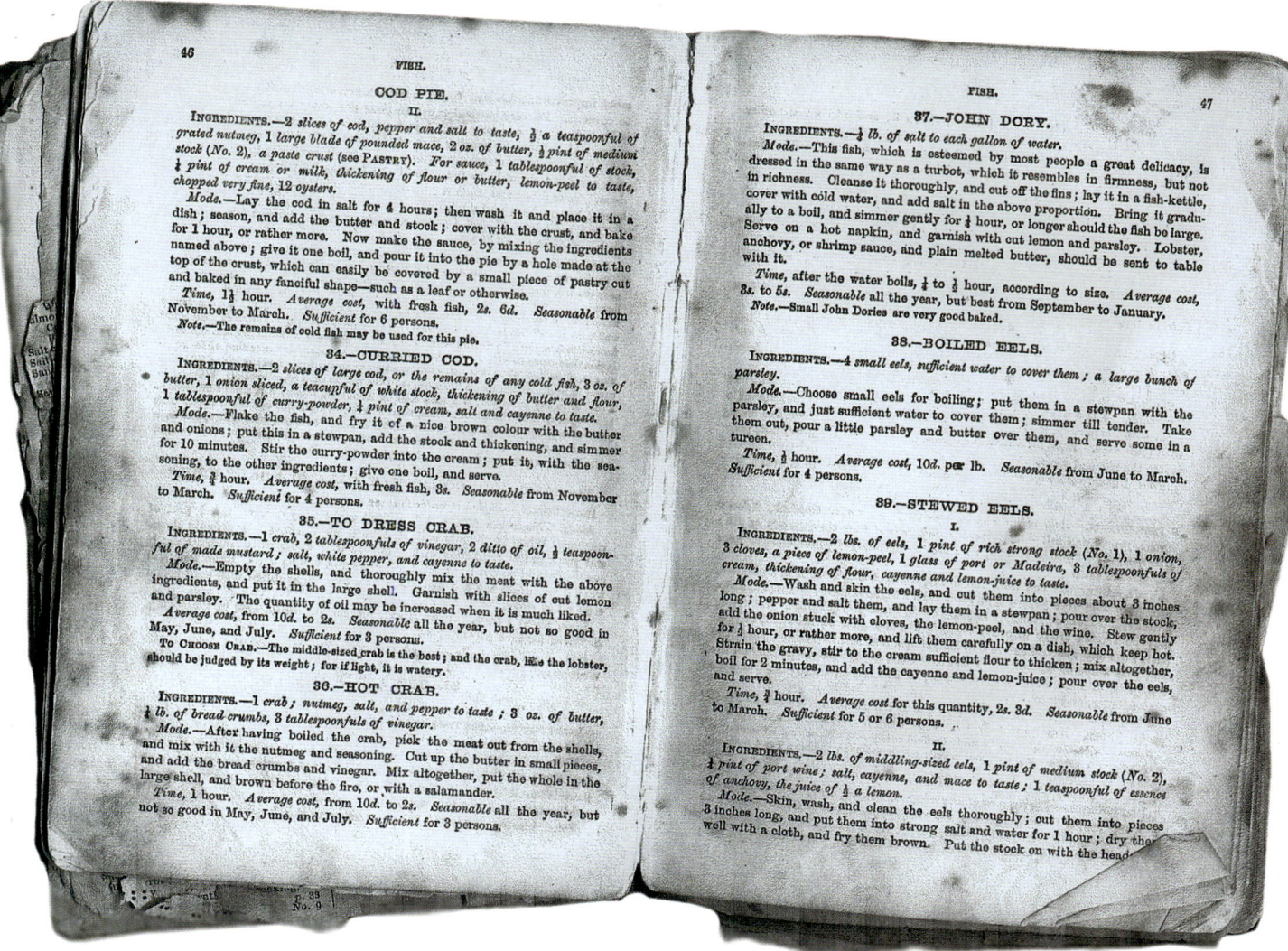

Fig 61. Recipe for preparing John Dory with ANCHOVY, 1870.

Fig 62. Poetical recipe from Sydney Smith (1741-1845).

> To make this condiment, your poet begs
> The pounded yellow of two hard-boiled eggs;
> Two boiled potatoes, passed through kitchen sieve,
> Smoothness and softness to the salad give;
> Let onion atoms lurk within the bowl,
> And, half suspected animate the whole.
> Of mordant mustard add a single spoon,
> Distrust the condiment that bites so soon;
> But deem it not, though man of herbs, a fault
> To add double quantity of salt.
> And lastly, o'er the flavoured compound toss
> A magic soupspoon of anchovy sauce.
> Oh, green and glorious! Oh herbaceous treat!
> 'T would tempt the dying anchorite to eat;
> Back to the world he'd turn his fleeting soul,
> And plunge his fingers in the salad bowl!
> Serenely full, the epicure would say,
> Fate cannot harm me, I have dined today
>
> Sydney Smith (1741-1845)

produce one gallon. William Scott's recipe for ANCHOVY SAUCE in 1826 required the pounding of three anchovies in a mortar with a small portion of butter. Then rub it through a double hair sieve with the back of a wooden spoon. Alternatively stir a tablespoon of ESSENCE OF ANCHOVY into half a pound of melted butter. To the above Scott says many cooks add LEMON JUICE and CAYAN. "Foreigners", writes Scott at page 280, "make this sauce with good brown sauce, or white sauce, instead of melted butter, and add to it CATSUP, SOY and some flavoured vinegars, such as ELDER or TARRAGON, PEPPER and fine spice, sweet herbs, capers & SHALLOTS etc. They serve it with most roasted meats". The best known retailer of ANCHOVY ESSENCE was John Burgess. His firm kept to the tried and tested recipe. However "Old John Burgess' son gave strict instructions that in the

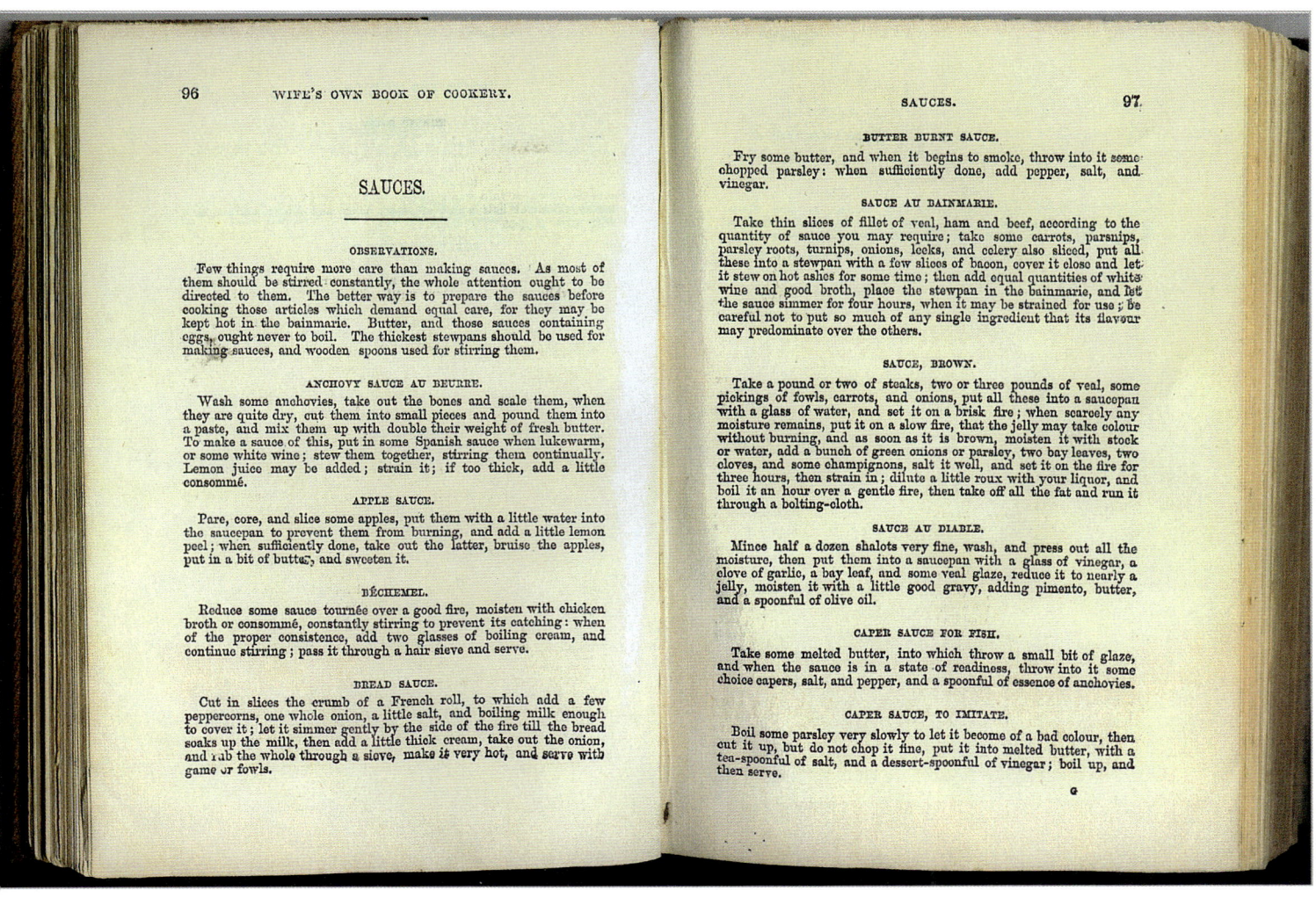

Fig 63. The opening pages of Bishop on Sauces, 1855.

making of ANCHOVY ESSENCE the only alteration allowed to speed production would be the substitution of twelve days' pounding by two men to six days' by four"(2). Cre-Fydd at page 34 recommends pounding anchovies into a smooth paste mixed with CAYENNE, LEMON and water. The mixture was then boiled up and strained. Sydney Smith's salads were spiced up with "a magic soupspoon of ANCHOVY SAUCE" in his recipe for a condiment (Fig. 62).

5. APPLE
This Hester Bateman off-cut was perhaps designed to hang on an epergne. In such a position it would defy close scrutiny.

6. AZIJN
This label proves that in The Netherlands oil and vinegar labels were used, AZIJN being Dutch for VINEGAR (see also Photo. 72).

7. BEEF
This suggests a gravy type sauce using BEEF stock.

8. BERGAMOT
Used for flavouring, this herb label could adorn a spice jar. Alternatively, and confusingly, it could also adorn a toilet-box bottle to describe its perfumed contents. The name is derived from the citrus bergamia.

9. BERNIS
From its size and appearance this label in the M.V. Brown collection in the London Museum looks like a sauce label although Dr Penzer in his Book of the Wine Label speculated that it would be for a wine of similar

THE RECIPES

To make MUM CATSUP.

TO a quart of old mum put four ounces of anchovies, of mace and nutmegs sliced one ounce, of cloves and black pepper half an ounce, boil it till it is reduced one third; when cold bottle it for use.

To make a CATSUP to keep seven Years.

TAKE two quarts of the oldest strong beer you can get, put to it one quart of red wine, three quarters of a pound of anchovies, three ounces of shalots peeled, half an ounce of mace, the same of nutmegs; a quarter of an ounce of cloves, three large races of ginger cut in slices, boil all together over a moderate fire, till one third is wasted, the next day bottle it for use; it will carry to the East-Indies.

To make MUSHROOM CATSUP.

TAKE the full grown flaps of mushrooms, crush them with your hands, throw a handful of salt into every peck of mushrooms, and let them stand all night, then put them into stew-pans, and set them in a quick oven for twelve hours, and strain them through a hair sieve; to every gallon of liquor, put of cloves, Jamaica, black pepper, and ginger, one ounce each, and half a pound of common salt, set it on a slow fire, and let it boil till half the liquor is wasted away; then put it in a clean pot, when cold bottle it for use.

Fig 64. Recipes for CATSUP from Raffald's Experienced English Housekeeper, p339.

Fig 65. Cherokee Chiefs bring their sauce to England.

name. In fact it surely must stand for Sauce Bearnaise. Spelling was not the silversmith's strongpoint and after all he was usually given verbal instructions which led to so many varieties in the spelling of sauce titles.

10. BLACK

This stood for BLACK PEPPER, a favourite item in recipes.

11. BLOATERS

This fish paste was dispensed like VEAL & HAM paste from a jar. Like most labels for jars they were plated. Presumably stock and storage jars never left the kitchen, although jam and ginger jars being of finer quality glass did. These jar labels were fairly large, often rectangular in shape. The label for BLOATERS had however a leafy edge design with a flower in the centre of each of its four sides.

12. BRANDY

Usually a spirit decanter label, BRANDY did appear in the soy frame as a flavouring.

13. BRIGHTON

A brown sauce, as is known from recipe books at Attingham Park, a National Trust property in Shropshire, built in 1785 for the first Lord Berwick with magnificent Regency interiors, which suggest that there may be a connection with the Prince Regent and his sojourning at Brighton Pavilion. A BRIGHTON sauce label is in the Marshall Collection in the Ashmolean at Oxford.

14. BROWN S

Another brown sauce which is known from the time of Roman Britain. It was strong and pungent and known by the Romans as "garum". It was produced in large salting pans about three feet deep and eighteen inches wide, wherein fish were left to rot in salted water. In Victorian times a completely different Brown Sauce was popular for which Frederick Bishop provided a recipe in 1855 (Fig. 63). Modern BROWN sauce has as ingredients apples, spirit VINEGAR, molasses, sugar, cornflour, acetic acid, tomato puree, salt, rye flour, spice extracts,

THE RECIPES

> **Cavechi, an Indian Pickle. No. 1.**
> This is excellent for sauce. Into a pint of vinegar put two cloves of garlic, two spoonfuls of red pepper, two large spoonfuls of India soy, and four of walnut pickle, with as much cochineal as will colour it, two dozen large anchovies boned and dissolved in the juice of three lemons, and one spoonful of mustard. Use it as an addition to fish and other sauce, or in any other way, according to your palate.
>
> **Cavechi. No. 2.**
> Take three cloves, four scruples of coriander seed, bruised ginger, and saffron, of each ten grains, three cloves of garlic, and one pint of white wine vinegar. Infuse all together by the fireside for a fortnight. Shake it every day; strain off the liquor, and bottle it for use. You may add to it a pinch of cayenne.
>
> **Cavechi. No. 3.**
> One pint of vinegar, half an ounce of cayenne, two tablespoonfuls of soy, two of walnut pickle, two of ketchup, four cloves of garlic, and three shalots cut small; mix them well together.

Fig 66. Lady Charlotte Bury's 1844 recipes for CAVECHI.

wheat flour, onion, garlic, mustard and colouring.

15. BUDOCK
Flavourings like burdock were used at table and they were also used in the making of country wines.

16. BURGESS
In full this stood for BURGESS FISH SAUCE which was retailed by John Burgess & Son, best known for their ANCHOVY sauce and also for "very curious new French Olives, LEMON PICKLE, CAMP VINEGAR, ELDER VINEGAR, DEVONSHIRE sauce, ZOOBDITTY MUTCH, with a great variety of rich sauces for Fish, Beefsteaks, and etc" according to John Burgess & Co.'s advertisement in the first issue of the Times in 1788.

17. BURGUNDY
There was also a well-liked BURGUNDY sauce. BURGUNDY was one of a set of four sauce labels acquired by Mr. Weed from Maurice Freeman of Clerkenwell in 1927. He also bought a PORT label from a collection of four larger size wine labels. These labels by John Mortimer and John Samuel Hunt of 1840 had the "heaviest modelling" Mr. Weed had "ever seen". A highly rococo effect had been achieved by the use of the concave side of the tridacna. HARVEY was in the same set as BURGUNDY. The hall marks are on the face of the labels in the manner of Paul Storr.

18. BURMAN
Presumably this refers to a hot spicy sauce from Burma.

19. CABBAGE
Possibly finely chopped raw cabbage was used as a seasoning.

20. CAMP
This is a ketchup containing tomatoes, vinegar and spices according to a recipe in Law's "Grocers Manual" (at page 82). It was also retailed by John Burgess in 1788 in a more liquid form as CAMP VINEGAR. It remained popular well into Edwardian times.

21. CAPSICUM
This refers to the genus of tropical plants producing PEPPER and CHILLI such as Guinea Pepper (capsicum annuum) and Spur Pepper (capsicum frutescens) and their fruit in the form of berries, particularly CAYENNE PEPPER.

22. CAPTAIN WHITE'S
Served from a jar, it was a kind of curried paste supplied by the Army and Navy Stores in late Victorian times. It is listed in their catalogue for 1907 as a curry powder and a curry paste; so it could have been dispensed in powder form. It was priced at 1s 10d per bottle.

23. CARRACHI
With many alternative spellings such as CARRACHIO, CARATCH, CARACHA, CARRACHE, CORACH, CORATCH, CARRISH and CHARAC, CARRACHI was an Indian sauce supposedly coming from Karachi, the capital city of Sind Province, and, as Penzer has pointed out, an important seaport of the Indus delta. John Timbs in "Lady Bountiful's Legacy" published in 1868 gives (at page 228) a recipe: take two SHALLOTS, a sliced CLOVE of GARLIC, an ounce of CHILIES, a wine-glassful of SOY and a wine-glassful of WALNUT liquor; put into a pint of VINEGAR; infuse for three weeks; and then filter for use. It may be kept for two to three years. In Victorian times it was retailed in bottles which according to their labels indicated that their contents included red PEPPERS, GARLIC, PICKLED WALNUTS, MUSHROOM KETCHUP and cochineal, all in VINEGAR.

24. CATSUP
WALNUT CATSUP (see Fig. 92) and MUSHROOM

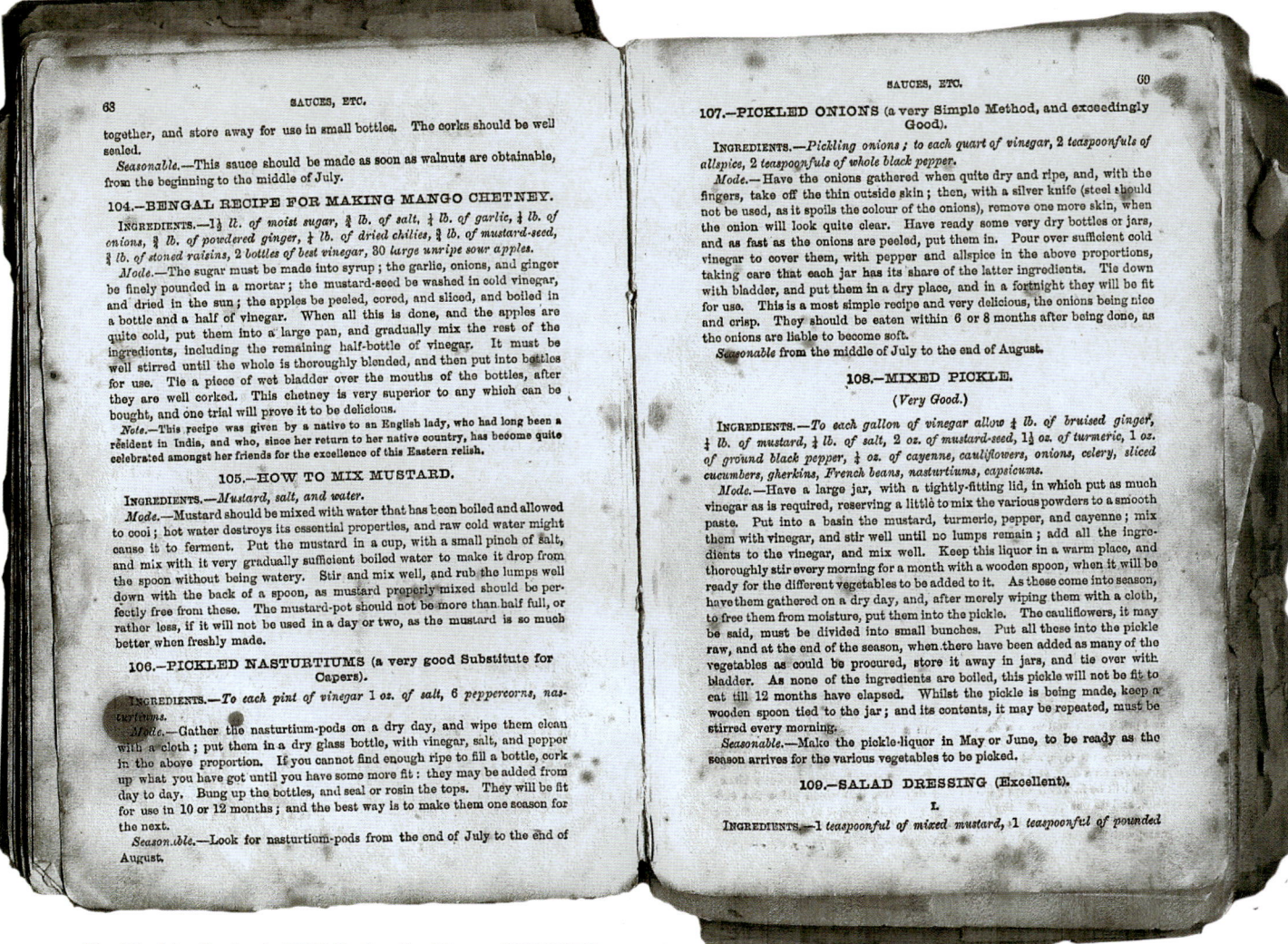

Fig 67. Mrs Beeton's 1870 Recipe for Mango CHETNEY.

CATSUP were the essential ingredients of QUIN SAUCE. CATSUP was also used in ANCHOVY SAUCE. It was therefore a bottled stock sauce and very popular in the United States in America. In fact it is said that the world's largest CATSUP bottle stands alongside Route 159, just South of downtown Collinsville, Illinois. It was designed for use as a water tower and built in 1949 by The Caldwell Company for the G.S. Suppiger CATSUP bottling plant. Mrs Beeton's 1910 Edition included an advertisement for TOMATO catsup (Fig. 57). Elizabeth Raffald's original recipe for a CATSUP to keep for seven years is reproduced (Fig. 64), said indeed to be strong enough to carry to the East Indies presumably to be exchanged for spices or to help the crew's digestion of shipboard fare along the way. Her recipes for MUM CATSUP and MUSHROOM CATSUP are also reproduced (Fig. 64) taken from page 339 of the English Housekeeper.

25. CAVEACH

Known also as ESCAVECHI, CAVEOCH, CAVECHI, CAVICE and ESCABECHE, there being other alternative spellings, CAVEACH is an Indian conserve of pickled mackerel for use with fish. According to Henderson at page 271 (1780) and Farley (1792) one takes half a dozen fine large mackerel and cuts them into round pieces; then take an ounce of beaten PEPPER, three large NUTMEGS, a little mace and a handful of SALT. Mix your SALT and beaten SPICE together, then make two or three holes in each piece with your finger; thrust the seasoning into the holes; wrap the pieces all over with seasoning; fry them brown in OIL and let them stand until they are cold;

then put them into VINEGAR and cover them with OIL. If well covered they will keep a considerable time and are most delicious eating. This is the classic recipe. However three further alternative recipes were given by Lady Charlotte Bury in 1844. Into a pint of VINEGAR she suggests one puts two CLOVES of GARLIC, two spoonfuls of red PEPPER, two large spoonfuls of INDIA SOY and four of WALNUT PICKLE, with as much cochineal as will colour it, two dozen large ANCHOVIES boned and dissolved in the juice of three LEMONS, and one spoonful of MUSTARD. Use it she says, at page 188, as an addition to fish and other sauces, or in any other way according to your palate. The second recipe advises one to take three cloves, four scruples of coriander seed, bruised GINGER, and saffron, of each ten grains, three CLOVES of GARLIC and one pint of white wine VINEGAR. Infuse all together by the fireside for a fortnight. Shake it every day, strain off the liquid and bottle it for use. You may add it to a pinch of CAYENNE. Her third recipe suggests taking one pint of VINEGAR, half an ounce of CAYENNE, two tablespoons of SOY, two of WALNUT PICKLE, two of KETCHUP, four CLOVES of GARLIC and three shallots cut small. One is then told to mix them well together. Lady Charlotte Bury's three recipes for CAVECHI are reproduced in Fig. 66.

26. CAYENNE

CAYENNE is a pepper brightish red in appearance made from crushed capcisum berries. Grown in America, it was imported under this name. Grown in Africa it was called Guinea pepper according to Farley. Scott's advice on preparation is, at page 454, to "take CAPSICUM berries and common salt, of each, one pound; grind together, and colour with vermilion; some use red lead, but this is injurious". It was dispensed from the soy bottle with the aid of a silver-gilt spoon built into the bottle stopper. This is the bottle on which to hang a KYAN label. There are a considerable number of variant spellings. It was also used to make a flavoured VINEGAR. In concentrated form it was prepared as the powerful ESSENCE OF KAYAN.

27. CELERY

This was a stock sauce kept in a large bottle needing a large label. Frederick Bishop, lately cuisenaire to St. James' Palace, in 1855 suggests, at page 98, cutting three heads (Mrs. Raffald says ten heads) of fine white celery into two inch lengths. Keep them so, or shred them down as straws; then boil them for a few minutes. Strain them off, return the celery into the stew pan, and add some brown or white stock, boiling until tender. If there is too much liquor, then reduce

Fig 68. Premier Household Recipe Book's recipes for pickles and CHUTNEY (1930s).

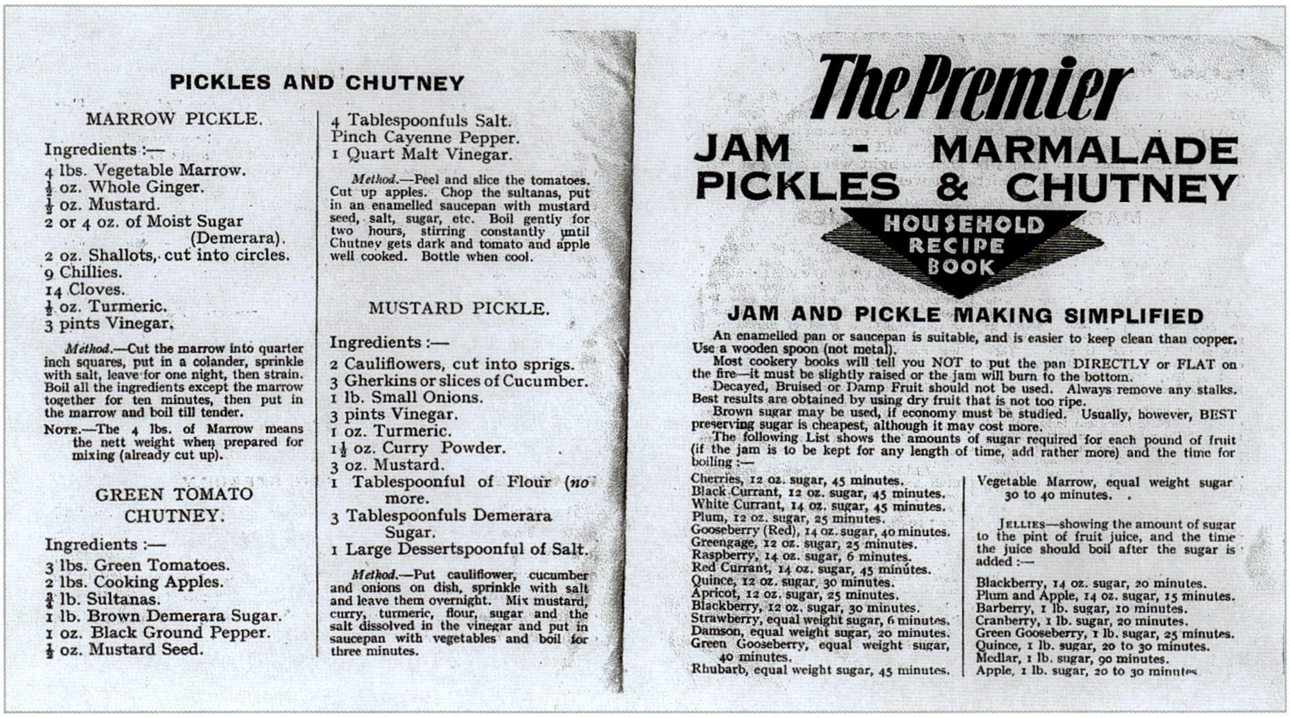

PICKLES AND CHUTNEY

MARROW PICKLE.

Ingredients :—
4 lbs. Vegetable Marrow.
½ oz. Whole Ginger.
½ oz. Mustard.
2 or 4 oz. of Moist Sugar (Demerara).
2 oz. Shallots, cut into circles.
9 Chillies.
14 Cloves.
½ oz. Turmeric.
3 pints Vinegar.

Method.—Cut the marrow into quarter inch squares, put in a colander, sprinkle with salt, leave for one night, then strain. Boil all the ingredients except the marrow together for ten minutes, then put in the marrow and boil till tender.

NOTE.—The 4 lbs. of Marrow means the nett weight when prepared for mixing (already cut up).

GREEN TOMATO CHUTNEY.

Ingredients :—
3 lbs. Green Tomatoes.
2 lbs. Cooking Apples.
¾ lb. Sultanas.
1 lb. Brown Demerara Sugar.
1 oz. Black Ground Pepper.
½ oz. Mustard Seed.
4 Tablespoonfuls Salt.
Pinch Cayenne Pepper.
1 Quart Malt Vinegar.

Method.—Peel and slice the tomatoes. Cut up apples. Chop the sultanas, put in an enamelled saucepan with mustard seed, salt, sugar, etc. Boil gently for two hours, stirring constantly until Chutney gets dark and tomato and apple well cooked. Bottle when cool.

MUSTARD PICKLE.

Ingredients :—
2 Cauliflowers, cut into sprigs.
3 Gherkins or slices of Cucumber.
1 lb. Small Onions.
3 pints Vinegar.
1 oz. Turmeric.
1½ oz. Curry Powder.
3 oz. Mustard.
1 Tablespoonful of Flour (*no* more.
3 Tablespoonfuls Demerara Sugar.
1 Large Dessertspoonful of Salt.

Method.—Put cauliflower, cucumber and onions on dish, sprinkle with salt and leave them overnight. Mix mustard, curry, turmeric, flour, sugar and the salt dissolved in the vinegar and put in saucepan with vegetables and boil for three minutes.

The Premier
JAM - MARMALADE
PICKLES & CHUTNEY
HOUSEHOLD RECIPE BOOK

JAM AND PICKLE MAKING SIMPLIFIED

An enamelled pan or saucepan is suitable, and is easier to keep clean than copper. Use a wooden spoon (not metal).

Most cookery books will tell you NOT to put the pan DIRECTLY or FLAT on the fire—it must be slightly raised or the jam will burn to the bottom.

Decayed, Bruised or Damp Fruit should not be used. Always remove any stalks. Best results are obtained by using dry fruit that is not too ripe.

Brown sugar may be used, if economy must be studied. Usually, however, BEST preserving sugar is cheapest, although it may cost more.

The following List shows the amounts of sugar required for each pound of fruit (if the jam is to be kept for any length of time, add rather more) and the time for boiling :—

Cherries, 12 oz. sugar, 45 minutes.
Black Currant, 12 oz. sugar, 45 minutes.
White Currant, 14 oz. sugar, 45 minutes.
Plum, 12 oz. sugar, 25 minutes.
Gooseberry (Red), 14 oz. sugar, 40 minutes.
Greengage, 12 oz. sugar, 25 minutes.
Raspberry, 14 oz. sugar, 6 minutes.
Red Currant, 14 oz. sugar, 45 minutes.
Quince, 12 oz. sugar, 30 minutes.
Apricot, 12 oz. sugar, 25 minutes.
Blackberry, 12 oz. sugar, 30 minutes.
Strawberry, equal weight sugar, 6 minutes.
Damson, equal weight sugar, 20 minutes.
Green Gooseberry, equal weight sugar, 40 minutes.
Rhubarb, equal weight sugar, 45 minutes.
Vegetable Marrow, equal weight sugar 30 to 40 minutes.

JELLIES—showing the amount of sugar to the pint of fruit juice, and the time the juice should boil after the sugar is added :—

Blackberry, 14 oz. sugar, 20 minutes.
Plum and Apple, 14 oz. sugar, 15 minutes.
Barberry, 1 lb. sugar, 10 minutes.
Cranberry, 1 lb. sugar, 20 minutes.
Green Gooseberry, 1 lb. sugar, 25 minutes.
Quince, 1 lb. sugar, 20 to 30 minutes.
Medlar, 1 lb. sugar, 90 minutes.
Apple, 1 lb. sugar, 20 to 30 minutes

THE RECIPES

it by boiling, and add either white or brown sauce to it. Season it with SUGAR, CAYENNE PEPPER and SALT. It was therefore used as a stock sauce below stairs and kept in a storage jar enhanced by the use of a large plated label, an example of which is in the Marshall Collection in Oxford, Drawer IV number 34, measuring 5.2cm by 2.7cm, a pair with CLOVES having the same measurements and provenance.

28. CHEROKEE

The introduction of this sauce into England perhaps dates from the visit of three Cherokee Indian Chiefs (shown in the illustration (Fig. 65) with their interpreter on the left) from the Carolinas and Georgia in the United States of America to London in 1762. They were somewhat unusual ambassadors seeking to restore the peace between the English and

Fig 69. Lady Charlotte Bury's Preface and recipe for DEVONSHIRE sauce (1844).

PREFACE.

The Receipts composing the Volume here submitted to the Public have been collected under peculiarly favourable circumstances by a Lady of distinction, whose productions in the lighter department of literature entitle her to a place among the most successful writers of the present day. Moving in the first circles of rank and fashion, her associations have qualified her to furnish directions adapted to the manners and taste of the most refined Luxury; whilst long and attentive observation, and the communications of an extensive acquaintance, have enabled her equally to accommodate them to the use of persons of less ample means and of simpler and more economical habits.

---

192 SAUCES.

whole boil together till it is of a fine rich consistency; pass it through the sieve; then give it another turn over the fire, and serve it up hot.

Devonshire Sauce.
Cut any quantity of young walnuts into small pieces; sprinkle a little salt on them; next day, pound them in a mortar and squeeze the juice through a coarse thin cloth, such as is used for cheese. To a pint of juice add a pound of anchovies, and boil them slowly till the anchovies are dissolved. Strain it; add half a pint of white wine vinegar, half an ounce of mace, half an ounce of cloves, and forty peppercorns; boil it a quarter of an hour, and, when cold, rack it off and bottle it. A quarter of a pint of vinegar put to the dregs that have been strained off, and well boiled up, makes an excellent seasoning for the cook's use in hashes, fish sauce, &c.

Sauce for Ducks.
Stew the giblets till the goodness is extracted, with a small piece of lean bacon, either dressed or not, a little sprig of lemon-thyme, some parsley, three or four sage leaves, a small onion quartered, a few peppercorns, and plenty of lemon-peel. Stew all these well together; strain and put in a large spoonful of port wine, a little cayenne pepper and butter, and flour it to thicken.

Dutch Sauce.
Put into a saucepan some vinegar and water with a piece of butter; thicken it with the yolks of two eggs; squeeze into it the juice of a lemon, and strain it through a sieve.

Dutch Sauce for Fish.
Slice a little horseradish, and put it into a quarter of a pint of water, with five or six anchovies, half a handful of white peppercorns, a small onion, half a bay-leaf, and a very little lemon peel, cut as thin as possible. Let it boil a quarter of an hour; then strain and thicken with flour and butter and the yolk of an egg. Add a little elder vinegar, and then squeeze it through a tamis. It must not boil after being strained, or it will curdle.

Dutch Sauce for Meat or Fish.
Put two or three table-spoonfuls of water, as many of vinegar, and as many of broth, into a saucepan, with a piece of butter; thicken it with the yolks of two eggs. If for fish, add four anchovies; if not, leave them out. Squeeze into it the juice of a lemon, and strain it through a sieve.

SAUCES. 193

Dutch Sauce for Trout.
Put into a stewpan a tea-spoonful of flour, four of vinegar, a quarter of a pound of butter, the yolks of five eggs, and a little salt. Set it on the fire, and keep continually stirring. When thick enough, work it well that you may refine it; pass it through a sieve; season with a little cayenne pepper, and serve up.

Egg Sauce.
Take two or three eggs, or more if you like, and boil them hard; chop the whites first and then the yolks with them, and put them into melted butter.

The Exquisite.
Put a little cullis into a stewpan, with a piece of butter the size of a walnut rolled in twice as much flour, salt, and large pepper, the yolks of two eggs, three or four shalots cut small, and thicken it over the fire. This sauce, which should be very thick, is to be spread over meat or fish, which is afterwards covered with finely grated bread, and browned with a hot salamander.

Fish Sauce. No. 1.
One pound of anchovies, stripped from the salt, and rinsed in a little port wine, a quarter of an ounce of mace, twelve cloves, two races of ginger sliced, a small onion or shalot, a small sprig of thyme, and winter savory, put into a quart of port wine, and half a pint of vinegar. Stew them over a slow fire covered close; strain the liquor through a hair sieve, cover it till cold, and put it in dry bottles. By adding a pint of port wine and the wine strained that the anchovies were rinsed in you may make an inferior sort. When used, shake it up: take two spoonfuls to a quarter of pound of butter; if not thick enough add a little flour.

Fish Sauce. No. 2.
Take a pint of red wine, twelve anchovies, one onion, four cloves, a nutmeg sliced, as much beaten pepper as will lie upon a half-crown, a bit of horseradish sliced, a little thyme, and parsley, a blade of mace, a gill of vinegar, two bay-leaves. Simmer these all together until the anchovies are dissolved; then strain it off, and, when cold, bottle it up close. Shake the bottle up when you use it; take two table-spoonfuls to a quarter of a pound of butter, without flour and water, and let it boil.

Fish Sauce. No. 3.
Take chili pods, bruise them well in a marble mortar, strain off the juice. To a pint bottle of juice add a table-spoonful of

K

the Indians which had been greatly impaired due to the actions of lawless frontiersmen in respect of which the Indians had exacted reprisals. A Treaty of Friendship was signed about a year after their visit. The sauce probably included at that time scrapings from the bark of the sassafrass tree which are the basis of the condiment known in the Southern States of the USA as "file". It is believed that file powder was used by the Chiefs during their London visit(3) and that this unusual flavouring was quickly noted and admired. A recipe for this sauce is given in Mrs Beeton's "All About Cooking", 1890 edition. It was said to be a store sauce. You take half an ounce of CAYENNE PEPPER, five CLOVES of GARLIC, two tablespoonfuls of SOY, one tablespoonful of WALNUT KETCHUP and one pint of VINEGAR; boil gently for

Fig 70. Lady Charlotte Bury's General Rules for a Good Dinner in 1844.

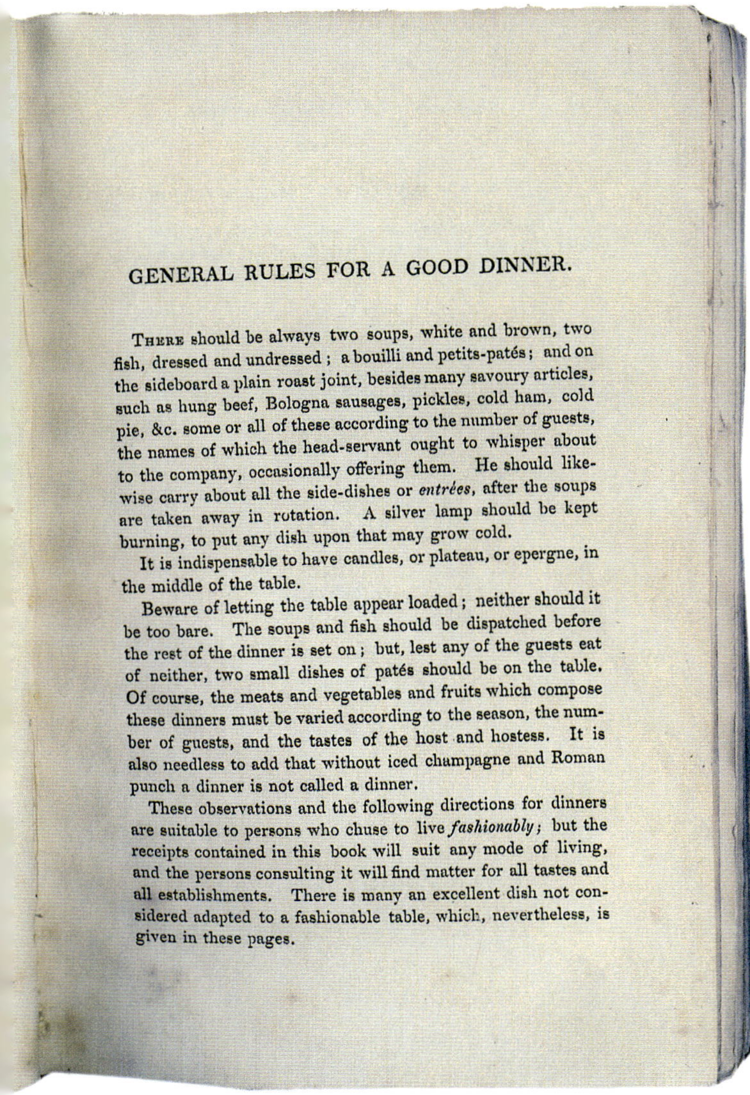

GENERAL RULES FOR A GOOD DINNER.

There should be always two soups, white and brown, two fish, dressed and undressed; a bouilli and petits-patés; and on the sideboard a plain roast joint, besides many savoury articles, such as hung beef, Bologna sausages, pickles, cold ham, cold pie, &c. some or all of these according to the number of guests, the names of which the head-servant ought to whisper about to the company, occasionally offering them. He should likewise carry about all the side-dishes or *entrées*, after the soups are taken away in rotation. A silver lamp should be kept burning, to put any dish upon that may grow cold.

It is indispensable to have candles, or plateau, or epergne, in the middle of the table.

Beware of letting the table appear loaded; neither should it be too bare. The soups and fish should be dispatched before the rest of the dinner is set on; but, lest any of the guests eat of neither, two small dishes of patés should be on the table. Of course, the meats and vegetables and fruits which compose these dinners must be varied according to the season, the number of guests, and the tastes of the host and hostess. It is also needless to add that without iced champagne and Roman punch a dinner is not called a dinner.

These observations and the following directions for dinners are suitable to persons who chuse to live *fashionably*; but the receipts contained in this book will suit any mode of living, and the persons consulting it will find matter for all tastes and all establishments. There is many an excellent dish not considered adapted to a fashionable table, which, nevertheless, is given in these pages.

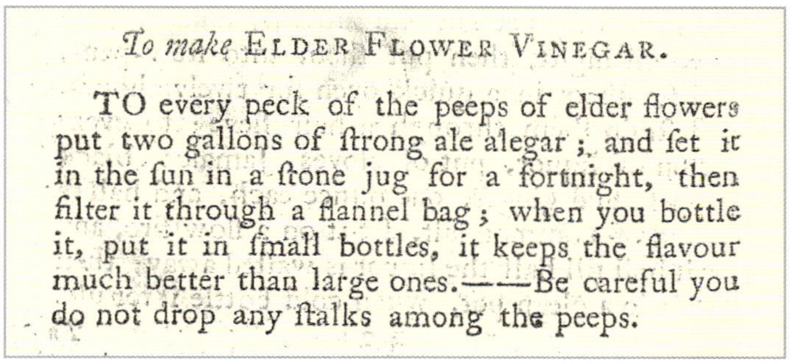

To make ELDER FLOWER VINEGAR.

TO every peck of the peeps of elder flowers put two gallons of ſtrong ale alegar; and ſet it in the ſun in a ſtone jug for a fortnight, then filter it through a flannel bag; when you bottle it, put it in ſmall bottles, it keeps the flavour much better than large ones.——Be careful you do not drop any ſtalks among the peeps.

Fig 71. Elizabeth Raffald's recipe for ELDER Flower Vinegar (1799).

about half-an-hour; strain and bottle. On the basis of this recipe it was really a flavoured VINEGAR.

29. CHERRY

Like other fruits such as STRAWBERRY, RASPBERRY and GOOSEBERRY, cherries were used to make a flavoured VINEGAR. Preserved fruits could be taken as a relish.

30. CHETNA

Probably a misspelling of Chatna, this title was engraved on a neck-ring label dated 1829(4). It was a sauce made with coconut, LIME JUICE, GARLIC and CHILLIES according to Forbes' Oriental Memoirs which were published in 1813(5). An unmarked silver label with this title is in the Marshall Collection (Drawer XIX number 337) in a set with FLORe and WALNt. It could have been a misspelling of Chetney (see Mrs Beeton's recipe reproduced in Fig. 67).

31. CHILLI

This is the dried pod of a species of CAPSICUM being a reddish coloured PEPPER. It was also used to make a flavoured VINEGAR and a strong ESSENCE OF CHILI.

32. CHUTNEY

Cre-fydd says at page 283 take a pound of new raisins, stoned, a pound of tamarinds, stoned, three ounces of GARLIC, peeled, and mince all these to a fineness; add three pounds of sour apples, peeled and cored, a pound of coarse brown sugar, two quarts of VINEGAR, a quarter pound of SALT, a quarter ounce of CAYENNE, two ounces of ground GINGER, and three ounces of pounded yellow MUSTARD seed. Boil up, cool, and keep for six months. See below for GRAY'S CHUTNEY. Mrs Beeton has an interesting

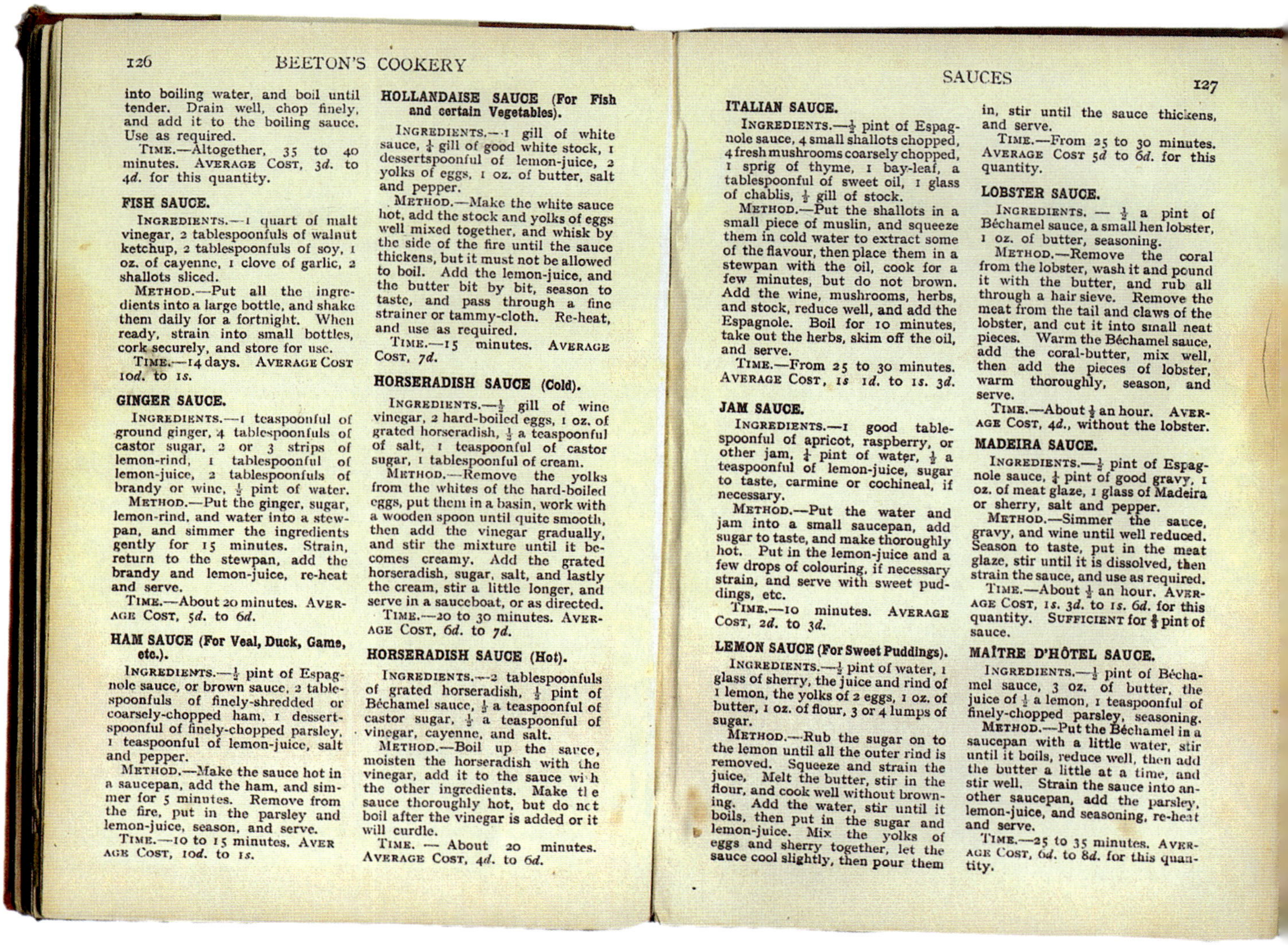

126 BEETON'S COOKERY

into boiling water, and boil until tender. Drain well, chop finely, and add it to the boiling sauce. Use as required.

TIME.—Altogether, 35 to 40 minutes. AVERAGE COST, 3*d*. to 4*d*. for this quantity.

FISH SAUCE.

INGREDIENTS.—1 quart of malt vinegar, 2 tablespoonfuls of walnut ketchup, 2 tablespoonfuls of soy, 1 oz. of cayenne, 1 clove of garlic, 2 shallots sliced.

METHOD.—Put all the ingredients into a large bottle, and shake them daily for a fortnight. When ready, strain into small bottles, cork securely, and store for use.

TIME.—14 days. AVERAGE COST 10*d*. to 1*s*.

GINGER SAUCE.

INGREDIENTS.—1 teaspoonful of ground ginger, 4 tablespoonfuls of castor sugar, 2 or 3 strips of lemon-rind, 1 tablespoonful of lemon-juice, 2 tablespoonfuls of brandy or wine, $\frac{1}{2}$ pint of water.

METHOD.—Put the ginger, sugar, lemon-rind, and water into a stewpan, and simmer the ingredients gently for 15 minutes. Strain, return to the stewpan, add the brandy and lemon-juice, re-heat and serve.

TIME.—About 20 minutes. AVERAGE COST, 5*d*. to 6*d*.

HAM SAUCE (For Veal, Duck, Game, etc.).

INGREDIENTS.—$\frac{1}{2}$ pint of Espagnole sauce, or brown sauce, 2 tablespoonfuls of finely-shredded or coarsely-chopped ham, 1 dessertspoonful of finely-chopped parsley, 1 teaspoonful of lemon-juice, salt and pepper.

METHOD.—Make the sauce hot in a saucepan, add the ham, and simmer for 5 minutes. Remove from the fire, put in the parsley and lemon-juice, season, and serve.

TIME.—10 to 15 minutes. AVERAGE COST, 10*d*. to 1*s*.

HOLLANDAISE SAUCE (For Fish and certain Vegetables).

INGREDIENTS.—1 gill of white sauce, $\frac{1}{4}$ gill of good white stock, 1 dessertspoonful of lemon-juice, 2 yolks of eggs, 1 oz. of butter, salt and pepper.

METHOD.—Make the white sauce hot, add the stock and yolks of eggs well mixed together, and whisk by the side of the fire until the sauce thickens, but it must not be allowed to boil. Add the lemon-juice, and the butter bit by bit, season to taste, and pass through a fine strainer or tammy-cloth. Re-heat, and use as required.

TIME.—15 minutes. AVERAGE COST, 7*d*.

HORSERADISH SAUCE (Cold).

INGREDIENTS.—$\frac{1}{2}$ gill of wine vinegar, 2 hard-boiled eggs, 1 oz. of grated horseradish, $\frac{1}{2}$ a teaspoonful of salt, 1 teaspoonful of castor sugar, 1 tablespoonful of cream.

METHOD.—Remove the yolks from the whites of the hard-boiled eggs, put them in a basin, work with a wooden spoon until quite smooth, then add the vinegar gradually, and stir the mixture until it becomes creamy. Add the grated horseradish, sugar, salt, and lastly the cream, stir a little longer, and serve in a sauceboat, or as directed.

TIME.—20 to 30 minutes. AVERAGE COST, 6*d*. to 7*d*.

HORSERADISH SAUCE (Hot).

INGREDIENTS.—2 tablespoonfuls of grated horseradish, $\frac{1}{2}$ pint of Béchamel sauce, $\frac{1}{2}$ a teaspoonful of castor sugar, $\frac{1}{2}$ a teaspoonful of vinegar, cayenne, and salt.

METHOD.—Boil up the sauce, moisten the horseradish with the vinegar, add it to the sauce with the other ingredients. Make the sauce thoroughly hot, but do not boil after the vinegar is added or it will curdle.

TIME. — About 20 minutes. AVERAGE COST, 4*d*. to 6*d*.

SAUCES 127

ITALIAN SAUCE.

INGREDIENTS.—$\frac{1}{2}$ pint of Espagnole sauce, 4 small shallots chopped, 4 fresh mushrooms coarsely chopped, 1 sprig of thyme, 1 bay-leaf, a tablespoonful of sweet oil, 1 glass of chablis, $\frac{1}{2}$ gill of stock.

METHOD.—Put the shallots in a small piece of muslin, and squeeze them in cold water to extract some of the flavour, then place them in a stewpan with the oil, cook for a few minutes, but do not brown. Add the wine, mushrooms, herbs, and stock, reduce well, and add the Espagnole. Boil for 10 minutes, take out the herbs, skim off the oil, and serve.

TIME.—From 25 to 30 minutes. AVERAGE COST, 1*s* 1*d*. to 1*s*. 3*d*.

JAM SAUCE.

INGREDIENTS.—1 good tablespoonful of apricot, raspberry, or other jam, $\frac{1}{4}$ pint of water, $\frac{1}{2}$ a teaspoonful of lemon-juice, sugar to taste, carmine or cochineal, if necessary.

METHOD.—Put the water and jam into a small saucepan, add sugar to taste, and make thoroughly hot. Put in the lemon-juice and a few drops of colouring, if necessary strain, and serve with sweet puddings, etc.

TIME.—10 minutes. AVERAGE COST, 2*d*. to 3*d*.

LEMON SAUCE (For Sweet Puddings).

INGREDIENTS.—$\frac{1}{2}$ pint of water, 1 glass of sherry, the juice and rind of 1 lemon, the yolks of 2 eggs, 1 oz. of butter, 1 oz. of flour, 3 or 4 lumps of sugar.

METHOD.—Rub the sugar on to the lemon until all the outer rind is removed. Squeeze and strain the juice, Melt the butter, stir in the flour, and cook well without browning. Add the water, stir until it boils, then put in the sugar and lemon-juice. Mix the yolks of eggs and sherry together, let the sauce cool slightly, then pour them in, stir until the sauce thickens, and serve.

TIME.—From 25 to 30 minutes. AVERAGE COST 5*d* to 6*d*. for this quantity.

LOBSTER SAUCE.

INGREDIENTS. — $\frac{1}{2}$ a pint of Béchamel sauce, a small hen lobster, 1 oz. of butter, seasoning.

METHOD.—Remove the coral from the lobster, wash it and pound it with the butter, and rub all through a hair sieve. Remove the meat from the tail and claws of the lobster, and cut it into small neat pieces. Warm the Béchamel sauce, add the coral-butter, mix well, then add the pieces of lobster, warm thoroughly, season, and serve.

TIME.—About $\frac{1}{2}$ an hour. AVERAGE COST, 4*d*., without the lobster.

MADEIRA SAUCE.

INGREDIENTS.—$\frac{1}{2}$ pint of Espagnole sauce, $\frac{1}{4}$ pint of good gravy, 1 oz. of meat glaze, 1 glass of Madeira or sherry, salt and pepper.

METHOD.—Simmer the sauce, gravy, and wine until well reduced. Season to taste, put in the meat glaze, stir until it is dissolved, then strain the sauce, and use as required.

TIME.—About $\frac{1}{2}$ an hour. AVERAGE COST, 1*s*. 3*d*. to 1*s*. 6*d*. for this quantity. SUFFICIENT for $\frac{5}{8}$ pint of sauce.

MAÎTRE D'HÔTEL SAUCE.

INGREDIENTS.—$\frac{1}{2}$ pint of Béchamel sauce, 3 oz. of butter, the juice of $\frac{1}{2}$ a lemon, 1 teaspoonful of finely-chopped parsley, seasoning.

METHOD.—Put the Béchamel in a saucepan with a little water, stir until it boils, reduce well, then add the butter a little at a time, and stir well. Strain the sauce into another saucepan, add the parsley, lemon-juice, and seasoning, re-heat and serve.

TIME.—25 to 35 minutes. AVERAGE COST, 6*d*. to 8*d*. for this quantity.

Fig 72. Mrs Beeton's 1910 recipe for GINGER sauce.

Bengal recipe for making mango CHUTNEY (Fig. 67). The Premier Household Recipe Book of the 1930s contained recipes for pickles and CHUTNEY (Fig. 68).

33. CINNAMON

This was dispensed from a large spice jar which explains the size of the label illustrated in the Journal(6) and of enamel labels for Canelle.

34. CITRON

Citron or Citronelle is a lemon flavoured essence made using a herb known as balm gentle. It was also used to flavour a drink known as Citronelle Ratafia, a recipe for which has been given by Richard Dolby in 1836. It was also used in the toilet-box. There was a hair oil known as Citronella and it was also used as a perfume. A fourteen bottle set has survived, complete with shagreen case. It contains eight splayed hoop collars or rings of unusual design datable to 1800 with titles engraved for CITRON, CLOVES, Lavender, MINT, Rosemary, Woodbine, Attar of Roses and BERGAMOT(7).

35. CLOVES

Cloves were kept in a kitchen jar handy for use by the cook. This could be enhanced by the use of a large silver-plated label, an example of which is in the Marshall Collection (Drawer IV number 40), measuring 5cm by 2.7cm, a pair with CELERY. This title on a very small label would probably be for the medicine chest or the toilet-box as CLOVES were a handy cure for toothache.

36. CREOLE

This was indeed a hot sauce to go with West Indian style cooking. It included peppers, spices and strong seasoning. It was dispensed out of a jar which explains the size of these labels. An enamel label with

THE RECIPES

Fig 73. Raffald's recipe for GOOSEBERRY vinegar.

this title was one of a set of three enamels designed to decorate the jars on a pickle frame (8).

37. CROWN
This title was sometimes used to denote a certain quality or brand of a product.

Fig 74. Family Recipe for GOOSEBERRIE Chutney.

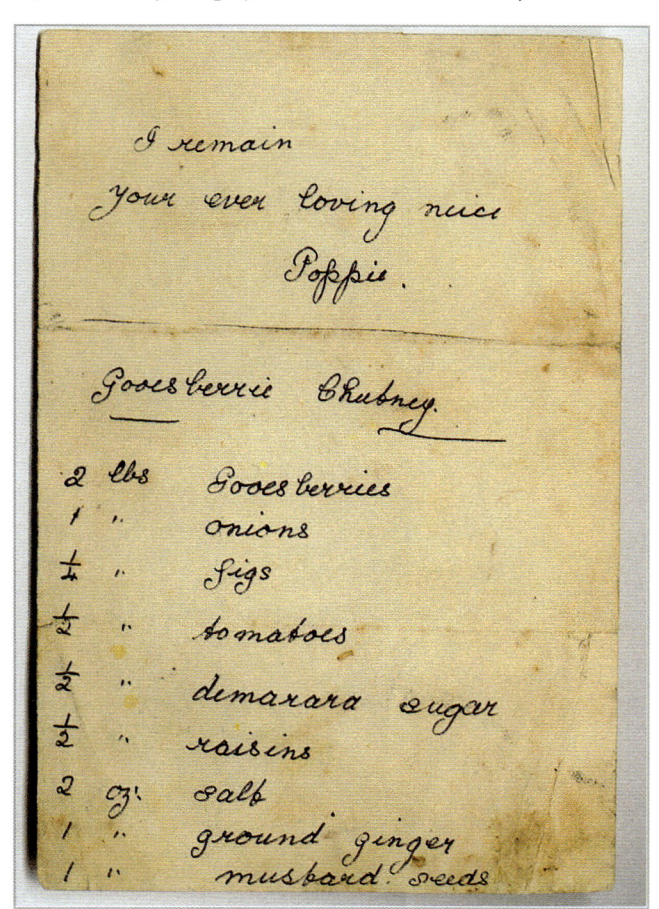

38. CUCUMBER
For this sauce Bishop says, at page 99, slice up two large cucumbers, put them in a basin, let them lie a quarter of an hour, take them out, put them into a stew pan with one onion and a little good brown stock, boil it all until nearly dry, and then put a few spoonfuls of brown sauce into it, the juice of a lemon, a teaspoonful of VINEGAR, and a little SUGAR, PEPPER and SALT. This was then used to make the flavoured CUCUMBER VINEGAR.

39. CURACAO
It was sometimes used as a flavouring, like BRANDY for example. This title was included significantly in Dr Kitchiner's Sauce-Box of 1822.

40. CURRY
CURRY powder was used as a flavouring. Its use reflected the enthusiasm in the 1780s for all things Indian, as encouraged by the Prince Regent with the building of Brighton Pavillion modelled on Indian Palaces. In 1809 Sake Dean Mahomed with his Irish

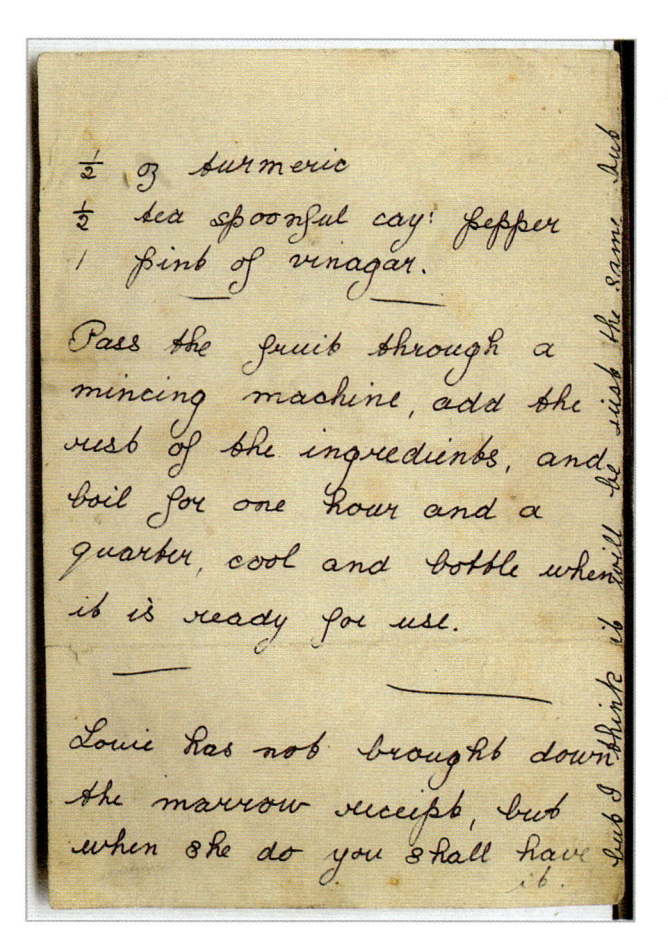

THE RECIPES

Fig 75. 1831 cartoon published by H Gans showing the Prime Minister's cronies enjoying the fine rich soup in the State Sauce Pan to the detriment of John Bull, a figure invented in 1712 to represent all that could be regarded as basically British.

wife opened an Indian Coffee House in George Street (off Portman Square) as curry house. He was a favourite of the Prince of Wales in Brighton.

41. DEVONSHIRE

According to Lady Charlotte Bury (at page 192) one should cut a quantity of young walnuts into small pieces and then sprinkle a little salt on them (see Fig. 69). Next day, pound them in a mortar and squeeze the juice through a coarse thin cloth such as is used for cheese. To a pint of juice add a pound of ANCHOVIES, and boil them slowly until the ANCHOVIES are dissolved. Strain it, add half-a-pint of white wine VINEGAR, half an ounce of mace, half an ounce of CLOVES and four peppercorns. Boil it for a quarter of an hour and when cold rack it off and bottle it. A quarter of a pint of VINEGAR put to the dregs that have been strained off when well boiled up makes an excellent seasoning for the cook's use in hashes, FISH SAUCE etc. This sauce was popular enough for John Burgess to retail it in 1788. Lady

Charlotte's general rules for a good dinner are illustrated (Fig. 70).

42. EAU DE MIEL

Whilst this label is probably for use for perfumery, miel or honey was used as a sauce in liquid form to add sweetness and so it could be a sauce label.

43. EGGS

Bishop's recipe at page 100 is to boil three eggs hard, cut them into small squares and them mix them up with a good butter sauce. Make it very hot and squeeze into some LEMON JUICE before serving. Henderson says much the same at page 116 in his book. EGGS has been noted on a large label and also was engraved on a small silver crescent label (9).

44. ELDER

ELDER was a flavoured VINEGAR. Farley at page 200 recommends that two gallons of strong ale "allegar" (presumably vinegar) to a peck (the fourth part of a

52

Description of the PLATE.

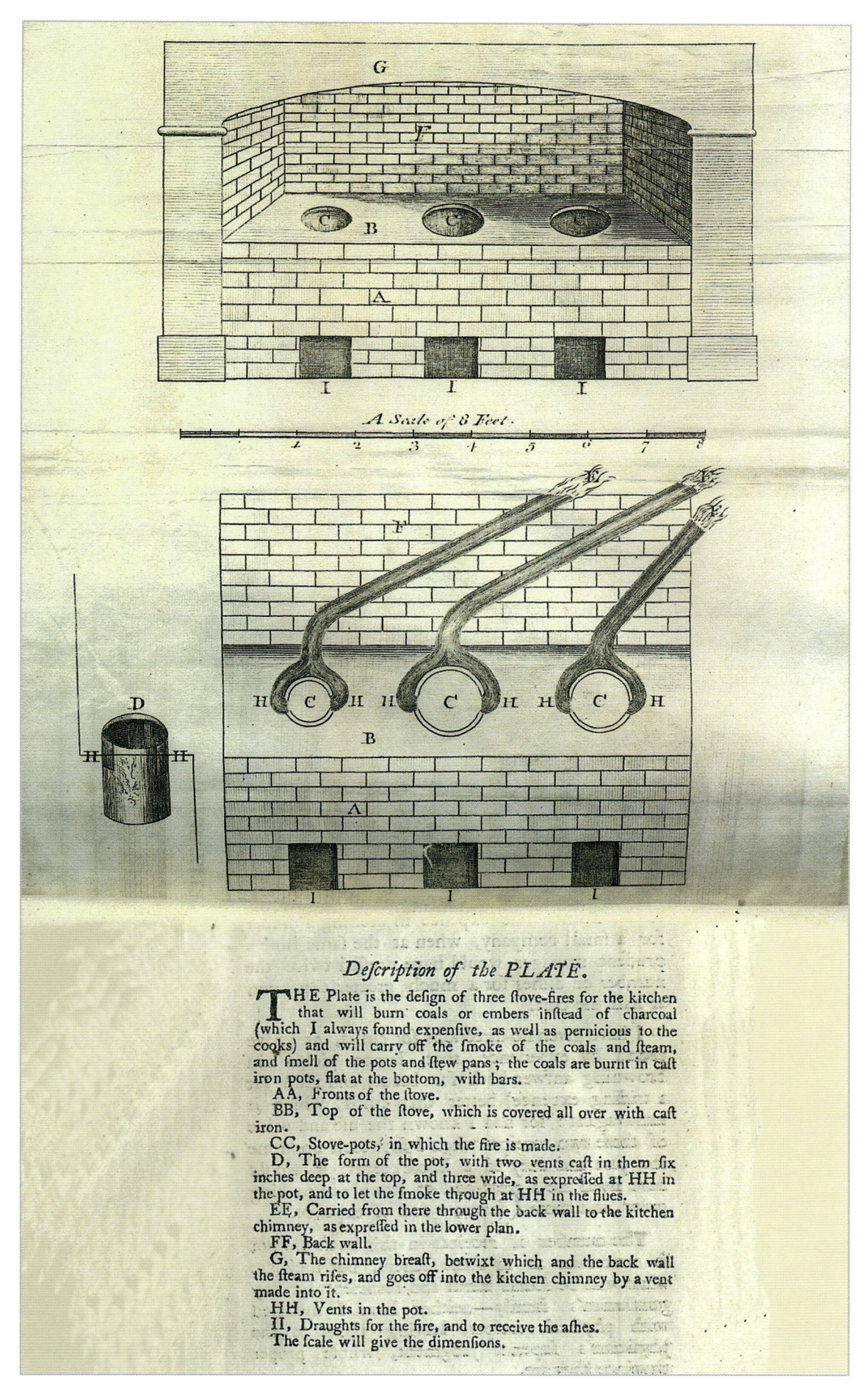

THE Plate is the design of three stove-fires for the kitchen that will burn coals or embers instead of charcoal (which I always found expensive, as well as pernicious to the cooks) and will carry off the smoke of the coals and steam, and smell of the pots and stew pans; the coals are burnt in cast iron pots, flat at the bottom, with bars.

AA, Fronts of the stove.

BB, Top of the stove, which is covered all over with cast iron.

CC, Stove-pots, in which the fire is made.

D, The form of the pot, with two vents cast in them six inches deep at the top, and three wide, as expressed at HH in the pot, and to let the smoke through at HH in the flues.

EE, Carried from there through the back wall to the kitchen chimney, as expressed in the lower plan.

FF, Back wall.

G, The chimney breast, betwixt which and the back wall the steam rises, and goes off into the kitchen chimney by a vent made into it.

HH, Vents in the pot.

II, Draughts for the fire, and to receive the ashes.

The scale will give the dimensions.

Fig 76. The new fangled stove of 1799 used for the preparation of sauces taken from Raffald.

THE RECIPES

bushel or more simply "a lot") of elder flowers be placed in the sun in a stone jar for a fortnight and then filtered through a flannel bag. To add to the confusion ELDER can also be a home-made wine and a perfume distilled from elder flowers. John Burgess retailed ELDER VINEGAR in 1788. It was heavily used from the 1760s onwards. Raffald's recipe is shown at Fig. 71.

45. FANCY
This is a bit of a mystery. It could be a house title for a popular condiment in the mansion.

46. FINE HERBS
These are very much in use today as always.

47. FISH
Sauces for FISH were in great demand. There was considerable variety and some FISH SAUCES were given special names when following a particular recipe.

48. FLORe
This could be an abbreviation for Florentine or more likely Florence which was a superior kind of olive oil but this would be pure speculation. The engraver could not get the full title on the label for the letter "E" was reduced in size to indicate that there were letters omitted. That the label was a sauce label is confirmed by its provenance being one of a trio with WALNt, also abbreviated for WALNUT and CHETNA.

49. FOWL
Probably for a sauce suitable for use with FOWL rather like the title BEEF perhaps indicating suitability for use with this type of meat. It could be another name for SICILIAN SAUCE.

50. FRENCH
Most likely a VINEGAR label, it is just possible that this ceramic label was used for FRENCH sauce. There is a silver label for FRENCH VINEGAR hallmarked for 1864.

51. FRUIT
Possibly for FRUIT sauce but the better opinion may be that it was used as a juice label.

52. GAME
As in the case of FOWL this was probably a suitability title.

53. GARLICK
As in the case of ELDER this was a flavoured VINEGAR in constant use from the 1760s onwards. Cloves of GARLICK were used as seasonings and dispensed from a spice pot or jar.

54. GINGER
The long chains on some GINGER labels point to their use on jars. However in Sweden it seems it was dispensed in shredded and chopped form as INGEFARA. Ginger was also used as the basis of a powerful ESSENCE OF GINGER. Mrs Beeton's recipe for GINGER sauce is shown at Fig. 72.

55. GOLDEN TRASSER
This title is a mystery. It does not appear in any of the recipe books mentioned in the Reference Section above.

56. GOOSEBERRY
Most labels of this title being on the large size were used on VINEGAR bottles. It was also a home-made wine which required a similar size label. It was also a delicious sauce but would usually have been dispensed from an unlabelled sauce boat. A recipe for GOOSEBERRY vinegar is illustrated (Fig. 73) and a family recipe for Gooseberrie Chutney (Fig. 74).

57. GRAY
GRAY SAUCE was probably the Army and Navy Store's version of Major Gray's CHUTNEY, derived from experience in India. It has a mango base and was imported in late Victorian times. Alternatively it might, perhaps like PITT, have been a political sauce popularised as it were by a Prime Minister. Such a sauce formed the basis of the political cartoon (illustrated in Fig. 75) published by Gans in January 1831 concerning the preparation of a "Gray-vy-Soup" for the poor using a State Sauce Pan on one of the new fangled stoves, a "curious new invented" (1799) three stove version of which (illustrated with description in Fig. 74) formed a late supplement to Elizabeth Raffald's English Housekeeper. It could take any fuel instead of charcoal, and was an efficient kitchen range, like its successors the Leamington (Fig. 77) and Russell's Herald (Fig. 78). The rich GRAY SAUCE may have been named after Lord Grey.

58. HARVEY
The recipe for this sauce by Frederick Bishop at page

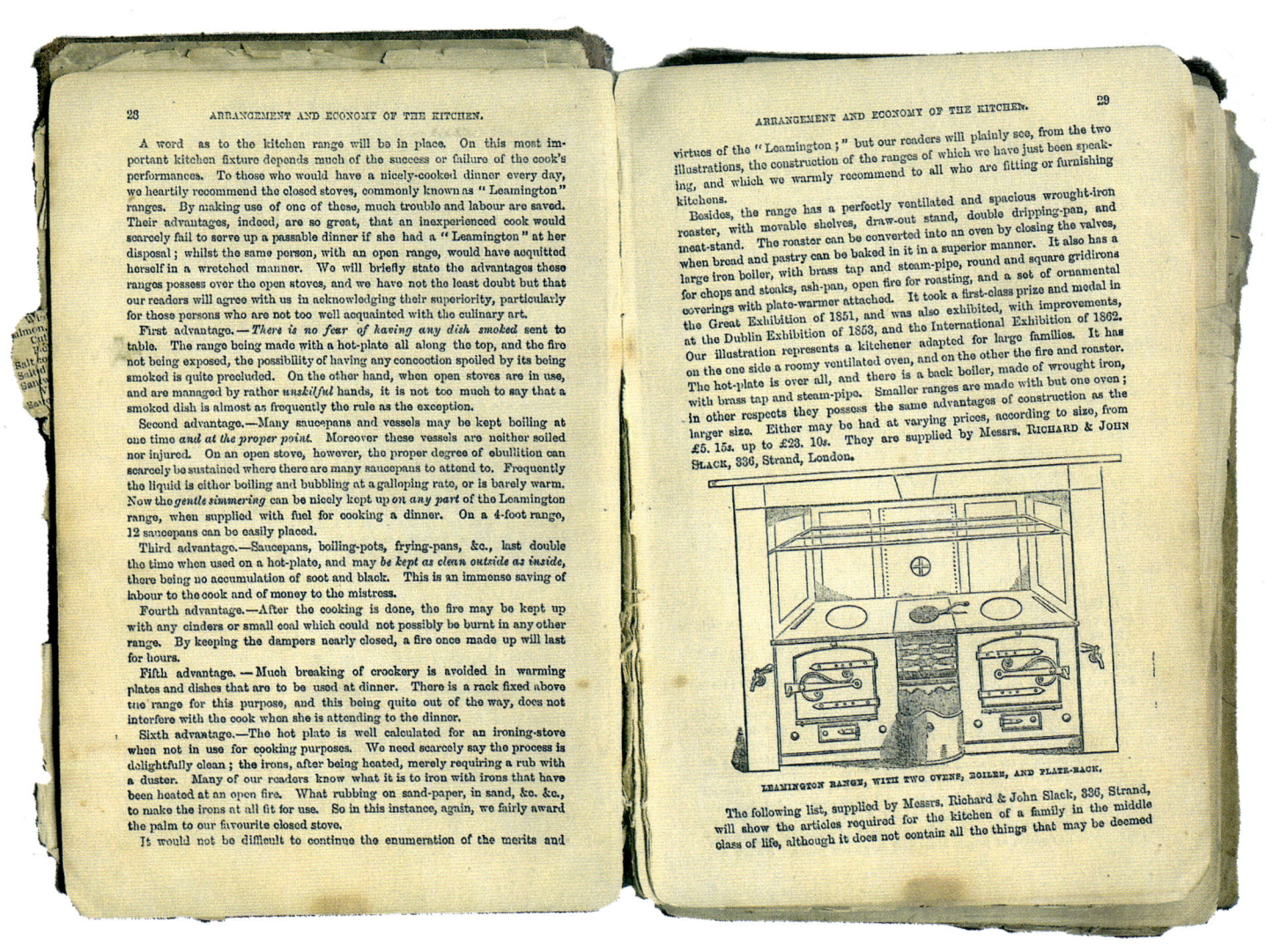

Fig 77. The Leamington Range of 1870

106 is to chop twelve anchovies bones and all very fine; add one ounce of CAYENNE PEPPER, six spoonfuls of SOY, some good WALNUT PICKLE, three heads of GARLIC chopped up small, a quarter of an ounce of cochineal, two heads of SHALLOT chopped up rather large and one gallon of VINEGAR. Let it stand for fourteen days. Then stir it will twice or thrice and pass it through a jelly bag. Repeat this until it is quite clear. Then bottle and tie a bladder over the cork. HARVEY is described by Hannah Glasse in the 1747 edition of her cookbook as HARVEY'S FISH SAUCE. This throws some doubt upon the apocryphal tale of its origin as having been devised by a Mrs. Combers. Her son Captain Charles Combers, born in 1752, was a member of the Quorn hunt. The story goes that when the Captain was on his way to Leicestershire he stopped, as was his wont, to dine at the George at Bedford. Mine host was a Mr. Harvey. The steak served up by Mr Harvey's hostelry needed a little embellishment. So Captain Charles called for a quart bottle of his mother's sauce to be brought in from his saddlebag. It worked very well when mixed with the gravy. Harvey managed to acquire and keep the bottle and used its contents to serve other guests with some success. Later on the Captain let Harvey have a copy of the recipe and Harvey organised its production in what was, in those days, commercial quantities. He advertised it as HARVEY'S SAUCE and by its extensive sale realised quite a large income. It is said that near retirement he sold the recipe for an annuity of £500 per year(10).

59. HENRY

HENRY is a Yorkshire mystery created by James Barber as part of a soy set.

THE RECIPES

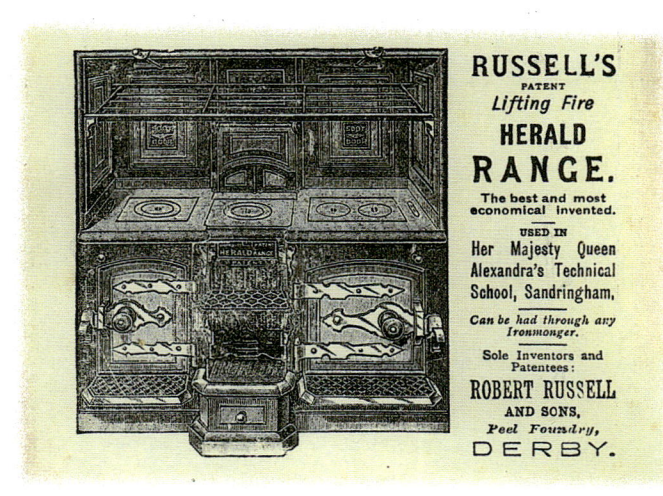

Fig 78. Russell's Patent Lifting Fire Herald range of the 1900s.

Fig 79. Dr Scott's recipe for LEMON PICKLE.

60. HOT
HOT is presumably a spicy sauce or VINEGAR.

61. INGEFARA
INGEFARA is a Swedish title which translates into English as GINGER.

62. JAM
This could stand for JAMAICA VINEGAR or possibly for a fruity flavoured VINEGAR, although there was a JAM sauce.

63. HUILE
This is a French label for oil. Huille de Vanille is not included in the list of sauce titles because it was used as a toilet water and not as an essence since it was part of a set of eight small labels with titles such as Elixir de Spa.

64. IRISH
Undoubtedly a sauce label, IRISH was in a group of three along with KETCHIP and ANCHOVY acquired in Scotland by Mr Alexander Cuthbert(11).

65. KING OF OUDE
OUDE was a popular sauce but KING OF OUDE was something special according to Edward Bradley alias Cuthbert Bede in "Adventures of Mr. Verdant Green, an Oxford Freshman", recording that one Towlinson took into his Oxford College Dining Hall a bottle of the KING OF OUDE's sauce to help him get through his meal. It is interesting to note that Hickson provided no lesser establishment than Harrods with KING OF OUDE at nine pence and one halfpenny per quarter bottle according to their 1895 catalogue.

66. LEMON
The juice of the LEMON was dispensed from a soy bottle as an essence, hence ESSENCE OF LEMON. LEMON PICKLE took a long time in preparation. According to Farley at page 201 it was made out of rinds of two dozen lemons and quartered lemons without the rind. All this was mixed with half a pound of SALT. The mixture was allowed to dry gradually until the juices dried into the peels. They were then put into a well glazed pitcher with an ounce of mace, half an ounce of CLOVES, an ounce of NUTMEG cut into thin slices, four ounces of peeled GARLIC and half a pint of MUSTARD seed. The mouth of the pitcher was secured by a muslin rag. Over the muslin was poured two quarts of boiling white wine VINEGAR. The mixture was allowed to stand and after three months it was bottled. Scott's recipe at page 386 is somewhat different. Take LEMON JUICE and VINEGAR of each three gallons, GINGER one pound, allspice, PEPPER and grated LEMON PEEL of eight ounces, common SALT three pounds and a half, CLOVES and bird PEPPER of each two ounces and mace and NUTMEGS of each one ounce. Having set out the quantities Scott leaves one in suspense as to what to do with them! LEMON PICKLE was retailed by John Burgess in 1788 and Scott's 1826 recipe is illustrated in Fig. 79). LEMON PEEL was also served at table and lemons were used to flavour VINEGAR.

67. LIME
Limes were squeezed to make LIME JUICE for use for flavouring fish. The title was also in use for a cordial.

68. LIMOSIN
This may refer to a KETCHUP of chestnuts and mushrooms à la limousine being derived from the culinary arts of Limoges (12).

THE RECIPES

Fig 80. Raffald's recipe for MUSHROOM Powder.

69. LOBSTER
A recipe for this sauce given by Scott at page 224 advised the melting of some butter in a little milk with a little flour and some LEMON PEEL in it and then the addition of some cream. Then take out the LEMON PEEL and put in some LOBSTER, cut into small pieces, with a little of the spawn; simmer altogether for about ten minutes. It is good with turbot – see the 1864 menu (Fig. 81).

70. MAPLE SYRUP
The label with this title is dated 1987 and presumably adorned a glass vessel containing this well-known syrup.

71. MINT
A sauce comprising VINEGAR with the pounded leaves of the mint plant put in was kept below stairs in a storage jar with a plated identification label such as the oval rococo cartouche shaped example in the Marshall Collection measuring 4.7cm by 3.2cm in Drawer VIII number 115.

72. MIXT
This refers to mixed herbs. The title was engraved on a plated broad rectangular shaped label sold by Christie's South Kensington on the 17th May 1982. It could also, but less likely in the case of this label, refer to a mixture such as a cough mixture.

Fig 81. A menu from the Young Housewife's Daily Assistant, 1864.

Fig 82. PIQUANTE as one of Cre-fydd's condiment sauces in 1864.

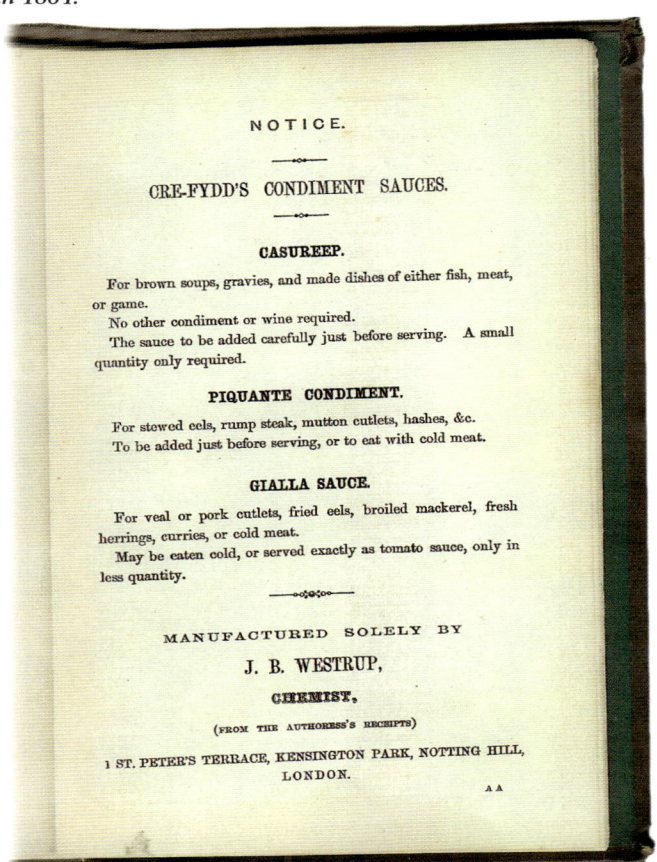

57

THE RECIPES

73. MOGUL
Made in Old Sheffield Plate this 1790s large octagonal label, designed to adorn a jar, was possibly used to indicate a plum conserve of that name.

74. MUSHROOM
MUSHROOM was used in powdered form (see Fig. 80).

75. MUSHROOM KETCHUP
According to Farley at page 201 MUSHROOM KETCHUP was made out of assorted mushrooms allowed to stand for the night and then set in a quick oven for twelve hours and then finally strained through a hair sieve. CLOVES, Jamaica PEPPER, BLACK PEPPER and GINGER were all added together with half a pound of common SALT. It was set on a slow fire and let boil until half of the liquor was wasted away. Scott's recipe at page 323 for MUSHROOM KETCHUP was to take four pounds of mushrooms and sprinkle two pounds of common SALT over them. Then when the juice is drawn out add eight ounces of pimento and one ounce of CLOVES. Boil for a short time and press out the liquor. What remains can be treated agains with SALT – and water for an inferior kind. BLACK PEPPER, mace and GINGER are usually added.

76. NEPAUL
NEPAUL is a particular kind of brownish-red coloured PEPPER when ground. It is not as hot as CAYENNE which is bright red in colour. It was said to be excellent for GAME or FISH. Mr Bruce Jones has noted(12) that the best quality of this finest type of PEPPER came from Nepaul where the peppers were dried on the roofs of houses. It is said to be highly aromatic. Harrod's catalogue for 1895 listed Colonel Skinner's NEPAUL as a sauce. Colonel Skinner also gave his name to a type of CHUTNEY.

Fig 83. Liebig's recipe for a sharp (PIQUANTE) sauce, 1885

THE RECIPES

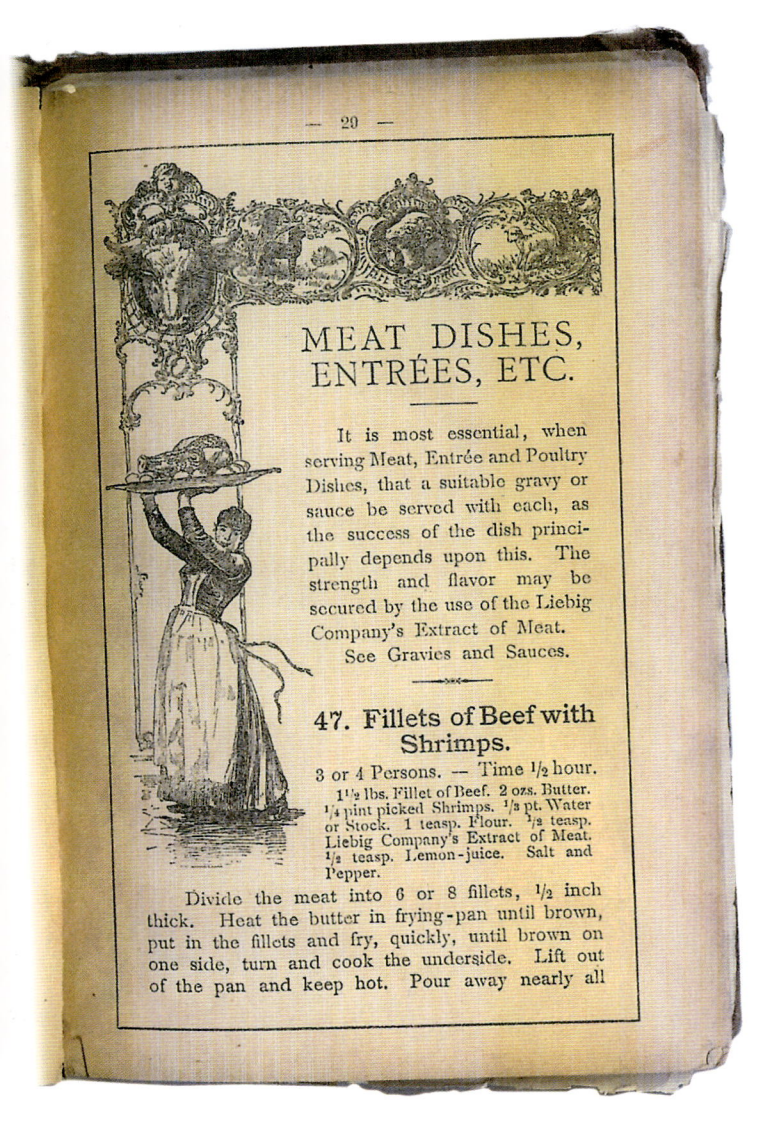

Fig 84. Liebig's introduction to the section on Meat.

77. NIG

NIG has been claimed as a spirit label for Gin spelt backwards in order on moral grounds to delude servants and observers. But no other spirit names have been found in reverse. It may well be, however, that when engraved or pierced on a small label it stands for fennel flavouring which was certainly used, being short for its Latin name often used on spice jars of Nigella Romana. NIG appears engraved on an octagonal double reeded label by Phipps and Robinson dated 1794 in the Cropper Collection in the Victoria and Albert Museum. Significantly the Curator has placed it with other sauce labels. The mistake arose due to a misconception that all sauce labels were small which is far from being the case. Size is relative to bottle size and some spice jars were quite large(13).

78. ORDINAIRE

Being French for "Ordinary", this title probably refers to an unflavoured VINEGAR.

79. OUDE

This sauce is named after the Indian Province from which it is derived. It was, from 1819, known as the Kingdom of Oude. So the story above related about the KING OF OUDE may well be apocryphal or of doubtful authenticity, the reference actually being to the Kingdom of Oude. The sauce was served with cold meats. Being of Indian origin it contained CHILLI peppers to make it hot. Mr. Bruce Jones has given(14) a recipe for home use consisting of 5 onions, 2 ounces of butter, 18 CHILLI peppers, 2 ounces of dried salt fish, half a pint of tomato pulp, juice of one LEMON, once cupful of water and a little SALT. It was still a popular sauce in the Twentieth Century. The Army and Navy Stores retailed it in 1907 at 10d per quarter size bottle.

80. PACKE

Used on a Scottish label by Robert Morton it means SOY in a Chinese dialect(15).

81. PEPPER

There are basically six different types of PEPPER in use during the relevant period, namely BLACK, WHITE, ordinary, CAYENNE, NEPAUL and Jamaica. The differences either relate to colour or to size. Peppers were used for flavouring VINEGARS. PEPPAR, a Swedish title, in pair with INGEFARA (GINGER), stands for PEPPER in English.

82. PINK

John Whittingham's PINK of around 1788 is a broad rectangular reeded PINK VINEGAR bottle label to adorn a bottle on a decanter for VINEGARS.

83. PIQUANTE

Bishop at page 106 gives an interesting recipe for PIQUANTE SAUCE. One puts into a sauce pan a quarter pint of VINEGAR, some allspice, a pinch of PEPPER, a bay leaf and a little thyme. One lets this remain on the fire until reduced to half. Then add two ladlefuls of espagnole and two of stock, and set it on the fire again. When about the consistency of a clear bouilli it is sufficiently done. Put in SALT according to taste. Crefydd had this condiment manufactured by J. B. Westrup, a chemist in Notting Hill, along with according to the advertisement

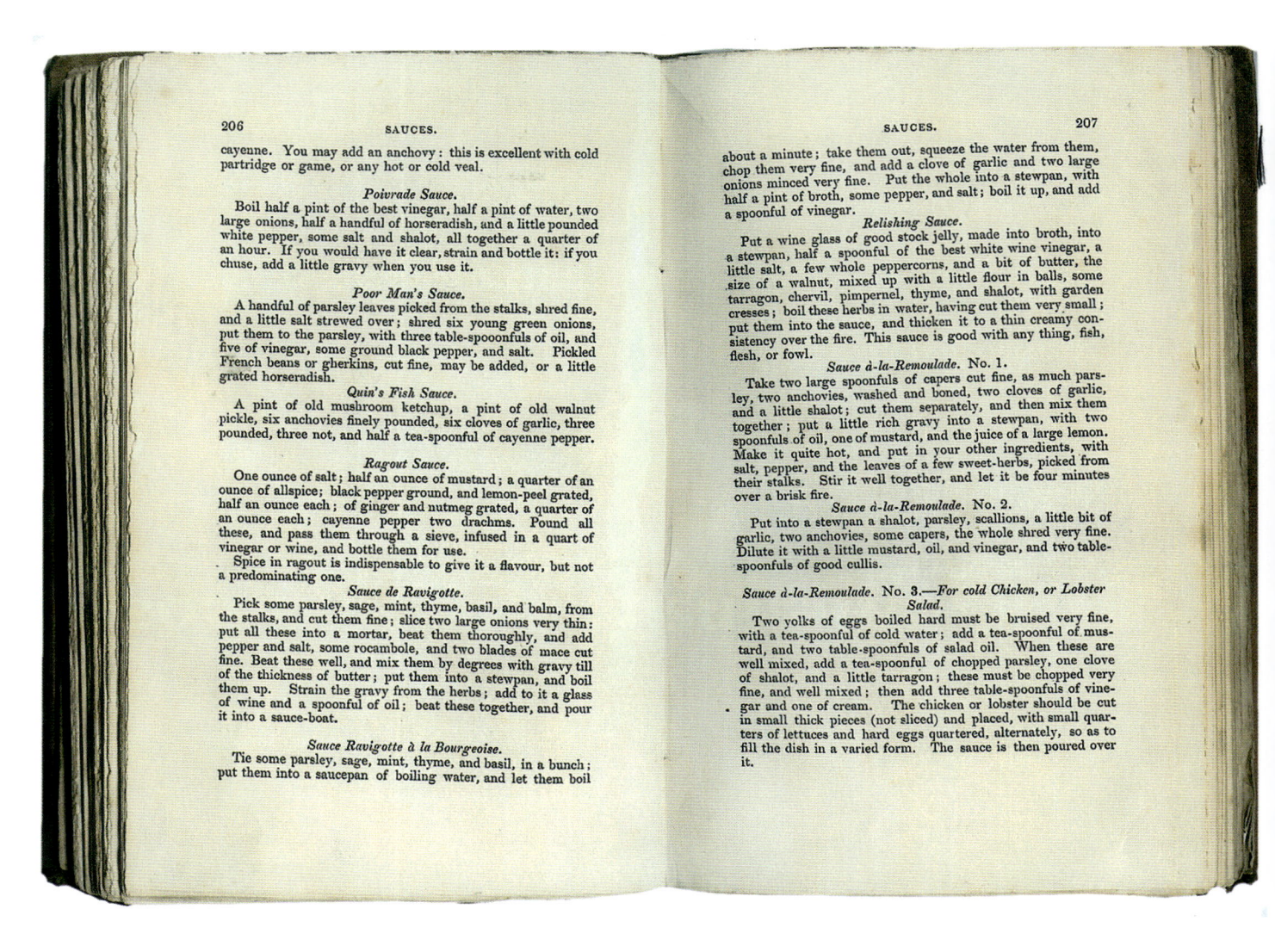

Fig 85. Lady Charlotte's recipes for POIVRADE, QUIN'S, RAVIGOTTE and other sauces (1844).

(illustrated in Fig. 80) casureep and gialla sauce, titles which have not been noted on extant sauce labels observed. It was sometimes referred to as Sharp Sauce (see Liebig's recipe No. 128 at Fig. 83 with introduction at Fig. 84).

84. PONTIFF

Pontiff sauce was based by Henderson at page 118 on VEAL & HAM with sliced onions. A VEAL & HAM label is in the Harvey's Collection in Bristol.

85. POUVRADE

Long before the adoption of the sauce label Carter in "The Compleat City and Country Cook" in 1736 was giving a new recipe for poverade or sauce au poiverade which equates to POUVRADE. It was made with "gravy, ELDER VINEGAR, and SHALLOTS and ONIONS cut small and PEPPER and SALT." One hundred years later Richard Dolby in 1836 gives a recipe for POUVRADE containing various herbs, a dessertspoonful of WHITE PEPPER, a glass of VINEGAR and a small quantity of butter. This was reduced and then two types of meat stock were added(16). Lady Charlote's recipe for Poivrade Sauce is given in Fig. 85.

86. QUIN

Scott and Briggs give insights: take SOY eight pounds, WALNUT CATSUP and MUSHROOM CATSUP of each two gallons, ANCHOVIES eight pounds, CAYENNE PEPPER eight ounces, GARLIC one pound, distilled VINEGAR one gallon, SOY one pound, and all spice eight ounces. No further explanation is given by Scott on page 386. Scott's recipe is shown at Fig. 86 and Lady Charlotte's at Fig. 85. Kenneth Hare adds horseradish as a constituent and asserts that the sauce is

60

THE RECIPES

named after James Quin (1693-1766) the actor and rival of Garrick (17). Some writers attribute the invention of this sauce to the brother of the actor Dr. Henry Quin in 1772 (18). The title was used on labels mainly between 1780 and 1810. Mrs Beeton thought that it was an excellent FISH SAUCE made from WALNUT PICKLE, PORT wine, MUSHROOM KETCHUP, ANCHOVIES, SHALLOTS, SOY and CAYENNE. Quite a powerful combination.

> QUIN'S SAUCE.
> 1. Take soy, eight pounds; walnut katsup, and mushroom katsup, of each, two gallons; anchovies, eight pounds; Cayenne pepper, eight ounces; garlic, one pound.
> 2. Distilled vinegar, one gallon; soy, one pound; allspice, eight ounces.

Fig 86. Scott's recipe for QUIN'S Sauce, 1826.

87. RASPBERRY
This was a flavoured VINEGAR.

88. RAVIGOTTE
This was a piquant French sauce made from SHALLOTS and aromatic herbs. Two recipes for it were given by Lady Charlotte Bury (in Fig. 85).

89. RIEN QUI MANQUE
The title emanates from early-Victorian Birmingham where the engraver was employed by Yapp and Woodward in 1848.

> Shrimp Sauce.
> Wash half a pint of shrimps very clean, and put them into a stew-pan, with a spoonful of anchovy liquor, and half a pound of butter melted thick. Boil it up for five minutes, and squeeze in half a lemon. Toss it up, and pour it into your sauce-boat.
>
> Oyster Sauce.
> When the oysters are opened, preserve the liquor, and strain it through a fine sieve. Wash the oysters very clean, and take off the beards. Put them into a stew-pan, and pour the liquor over them. Then add a large spoonful of anchovy liquor, half a lemon, and two blades of mace, and thicken it with butter rolled in flour. Put in half a pound of butter, and boil it up till the butter is melted. Then take out the mace and lemon, and squeeze the lemon-juice into the sauce. Let it boil, stirring it all the time, and put it into your sauce-boat.

Fig 87. Recipes, taken from the Female Instructor, for sauces to be served from a sauce boat in 1824.

90. RUE
RUE is a herb used in flavouring and would have been dispensed from a spice jar.

91. SAUCE ROYAL
The probability is that this sauce was a favourite of that well known gourmet the Prince Regent (afterwards King George IV). In a well known caricacture by Gillray (illustrated) he is shown with a CHIAN pepper pot on his right and a wide variety of condiments and potions, including Velnop's Vegetable Syrup, on his left, with a Chamberpot holding down unpaid bills (see Fig. 38).

> SOY.
> Seeds of dolichos soja (peas or kidney beans may be used for them), one gallon; boil till soft, and add one gallon of bruised wheat; keep in a warm place for twenty-four hours; then add common salt, one gallon; water, two gallons; put the whole into a stone jar; bung it up for two or three months, shaking it very often, and press out the liquor: the residuum may be treated afresh with water and salt, for soy of an inferior quality.

Fig 88. Scott's recipe for SOY.

92. SHRIMP
Scott suggests at page 224 that SHRIMP SAUCE should be made the same way as for LOBSTER SAUCE. The shrimps should simply be put into plain melted butter. At a dinner in 1754 in London arranged for The Worshipful Company of Scriveners, who were suing it seems The Society of Gentlemen Practisers in the Courts of Law and Equity (the precursor of The Law Society) and a Mr.

> To make SUGAR VINEGAR.
> PUT nine pounds of brown sugar to every six gallons of water, boil it for a quarter of an hour, then put it into a tub lukewarm, put to it a pint of new barm, let it work for four or five days, stir it up three or four times a day, then tun it into a clean barrel iron-hooped, and set it full in the sun; if you make it in February it will be fit for use in August; you may use it for most sorts of pickles, except mushrooms and walnuts.

Fig 89. Raffald's recipe for SUGAR Vinegar

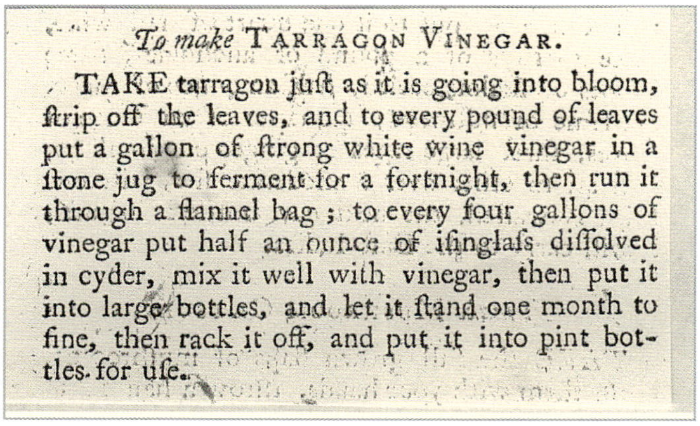

THE RECIPES

> *To make* TARRAGON VINEGAR.
>
> TAKE tarragon juſt as it is going into bloom, ſtrip off the leaves, and to every pound of leaves put a gallon of ſtrong white wine vinegar in a ſtone jug to ferment for a fortnight, then run it through a flannel bag; to every four gallons of vinegar put half an ounce of iſinglaſs diſſolved in cyder, mix it well with vinegar, then put it into large bottles, and let it ſtand one month to fine, then rack it off, and put it into pint bottles for uſe.

Fig 90. Raffald's recipe for TARRAGON VINEGAR.

John Alexander as a representative attorney of the Court of King's Bench about recognition of the requirement to be Free of the Company in order to practice as a scrivener, lobster was served with SHRIMP SAUCE. It was usually served, like Oyster Sauce, from a sauce boat (Fig. 87).

93. SICILIAN
Henderson suggests at page 115 pounding a spoonful of coriander seeds with four CLOVES in a mortar. Then add three quarters of a pint of gravy and a quarter of a pint of essence of ham. Boil up with a half peeled LEMON, three cloves of GARLIC, a sliced head of CELERY, two bay leaves and a little basil. The sauce is for roast FOWL.

94. SOURING
This title is another word for and stands for sorrel.

95. SOY
Dr Scott's recipe of 1926 is illustrated in Fig. 88.

96. SOYER
Perhaps this title stands for soya. It would be nice to think that it stands for Alexis Benoit Soyer's white fish sauce. He was chef at the Reform Club in Pall Mall from 1837 until 1850. His sauce was put on the market in bottled form.

97. SUGAR
Sugar dispensed from a castor would not normally be labelled, so it is likely that the label adorned a decanter from a frame containing VINEGARS. SUGAR VINEGAR was made from mixing six gallons of water with nine pounds of brown sugar, boiling it for a quarter of an hour and then letting it stand (Fig. 89).

98. TARRAGON
Bishop's recipe for TARRAGON SAUCE at page 109 is to put some green tarragon into some second stock and then reduce it gently; strain it off and add some béchamel to the liquor; then add a few finely chopped tarragon leaves; season with SUGAR, SALT and CAYENNE PEPPER. TARRAGON was frequently used to flavour a VINEGAR (Fig. 90).

99. TOMATO
Scott's recipe at page 386 for TOMATOE SAUCE (Fig. 91) is to take a sufficient quantity of love apples, stew them in a little water and then pulp them through a sieve. Then add common SALT, GINGER, CAYENNE PEPPER and VINEGAR; boil, strain and bottle.

100. UNIVERSAL
Frederick Bishop's 1855 recipe at page 109 is to take half a dozen split SHALLOTS, a clove of GARLIC, two bay leaves, basil, thyme, truffles. TARRAGON leaves, half an ounce of bruised MUSTARD seeds, some Seville orange peel, a quarter of an ounce of CLOVES and the same of mace. Double the quantity of long PEPPER and add two ounces of SALT. Pour all these ingredients to infuse in the juice of a LEMON, half a glass of verjuice, four or five spoonfuls of VINEGAR and a pint of white wine. Put them into a jar, cover it as closely as possible and set it on hot ashes for twenty-four hours. At the end of that time let it stand to settle and, when clear, pour it off, strain and bottle. Richard Dolby's recipe of 1836 was the one copied by Bishop, save that Dolby did not split his SHALLOTS, specified "some" bay leaves, and explained that verjuice was the juice of young, unripe and sour grapes. Samuel Pepys attributes the title and recipe to the Duke of York "who gave him a very good sauce" made of "some parsley and a dry toast beat in a mortar

Fig 91. Scott's recipe for TOMATOE SAUCE.

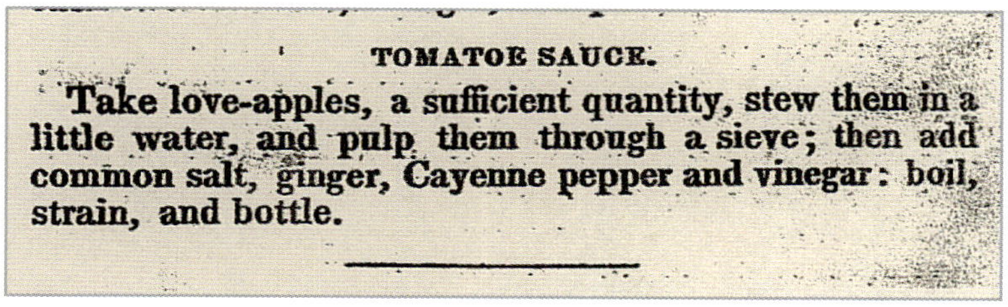

> TOMATOE SAUCE.
>
> Take love-apples, a sufficient quantity, stew them in a little water, and pulp them through a sieve; then add common salt, ginger, Cayenne pepper and vinegar: boil, strain, and bottle.

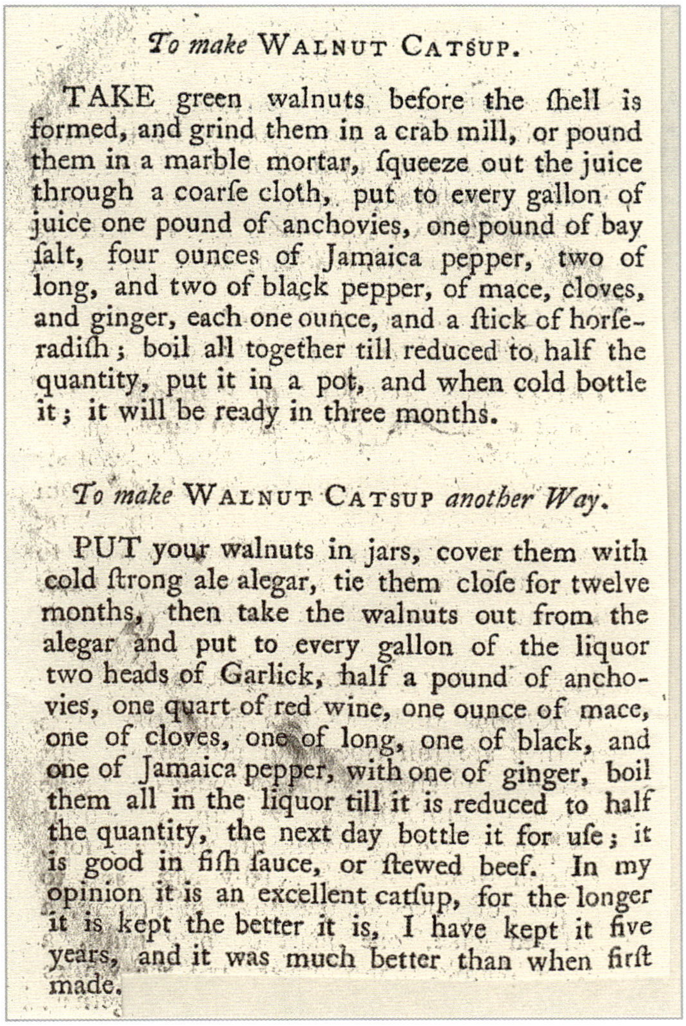

THE RECIPES

> *To make* WALNUT CATSUP.
>
> TAKE green walnuts before the shell is formed, and grind them in a crab mill, or pound them in a marble mortar, squeeze out the juice through a coarse cloth, put to every gallon of juice one pound of anchovies, one pound of bay salt, four ounces of Jamaica pepper, two of long, and two of black pepper, of mace, cloves, and ginger, each one ounce, and a stick of horse-radish; boil all together till reduced to half the quantity, put it in a pot, and when cold bottle it; it will be ready in three months.
>
> *To make* WALNUT CATSUP *another Way*.
>
> PUT your walnuts in jars, cover them with cold strong ale alegar, tie them close for twelve months, then take the walnuts out from the alegar and put to every gallon of the liquor two heads of Garlick, half a pound of anchovies, one quart of red wine, one ounce of mace, one of cloves, one of long, one of black, and one of Jamaica pepper, with one of ginger, boil them all in the liquor till it is reduced to half the quantity, the next day bottle it for use; it is good in fish sauce, or stewed beef. In my opinion it is an excellent catsup, for the longer it is kept the better it is, I have kept it five years, and it was much better than when first made.

Fig 92. Raffald's recipes for WALNUT CATSUP.

together with VINEGAR, SALT, and a little PEPPER", which according to the Duke was "the best UNIVERSAL sauce in the world"(19).

101. VALE OF AYLESBURY
The label with this title is of sauce label small size possibly relating to use with duck. The maker of the label would appear to have been Jane Gallant, who was a smallworker in action between 1760 and 1780 using a maker's mark in script. John Wilkes, Brother John of Aylesbury, might have had some connection with what would have then been a devilish hot sauce!

102. WALNUT
WALNUT PICKLE according to a book published circa 1714 "is good in fish or other savoury sauce" (17). A spoonful of this pickle was the recommended addition. A pair of more or less contemporary pickle spoons are illustrated (Fig. 10) so that one can gage the amount involved. WALNUT KETCHUP was made out of letting walnuts stand in strong ale allegar for a year. They were then removed and into every gallon of the liquor that was made were put two heads of GARLIC, half a pound of ANCHOVIES, a quart of red wine and mace cloves, with PEPPER and GINGER added. This mixture was then boiled until the liquor was reduced to half the quantity. Another method of making it was by taking green walnuts and grinding them in a crab mill or pounding them in a marble mortar. These were then mixed with ANCHOVIES, SALT, PEPPER, mace cloves, GINGER and a stick of horseradish. These were then boiled together and reduced to half the quantity. Another method advocated by Scott at page 323 was to put young walnuts in a press and extract the juice; then to a gallon of juice he would add two pounds of ANCHOVIES, one pound of SHALLOTS, an ounce of CLOVES, an ounce of BLACK PEPPER and a clove of garlic. Boil a little and then bottle. Walnuts were also used to make a good CATSUP (see Fig. 92).

103. WHITE
For a fine WHITE sauce Bishop at page 99 suggests adding to his recipe for CUCUMBER sauce a gill of cream.

104. WOODS
This was a fish sauce popular during the period 1790 to 1830. Labels with this title were made by John Rich (1791), Robert and Samuel Hennell (1804) and Charles Reily and George Storer (1828).

105. WORCESTER
A highly popular sauce, its origins go back to the days of Thomas Hyde (c.1775) and John Rich (1784-5). It became a household name in Victorian times and highly sought after (notwithstanding the emergence of WORCESTERSHIRE sauce from the begining of Queen Victoria's reign), with labels being made, for example, in 1840, 1848, 1858, 1866, 1870, 1876, 1877, 1890, 1894 and 1896.

106. WORCESTERSHIRE
Not to be confused with WORCESTER sauce, it took its name from from the abode of the drug shop of Messrs. Lea and Perrins at 56 Broad Street, Worcester. Lord Sandys brought back the recipe from India and

THE RECIPES

gave it to Mr. Lea, a druggist, to make up for him. He did so. It apparently tasted foul. Having handed over the mixture to His Lordship this prudent man kept a sample and a copy of the recipe, or so the story goes. The sample was stored in a jar kept in the cellar. When at a later date Mr. Perrins was tidying up and proposed to dispose of the jar, he asked Mr. Lea for his agreement. Before assenting to the proposal prudent Mr. Lea tasted the mixture. It was delicious. Ever since then the maturity period has been a closely kept secret. Lea and Perrins ceased to be druggists on becoming from around 1835 successful sauce manufacturers. WORCESTERSHIRE labels have been noted made by James Beebe circa 1837 and Thomas Johnson in 1851.

107. ZEST

Dr William Kitchener (1775-1827) was convinced that eating good food, properly prepared, was the key to healthy living. He experimented in its preparation at home, writing down healthful recipes, with the help of Henry Osborne, cook to Sir Joseph Banks. Kitchener gave rather good lunches. When writing to a friend on 24th February 1827 (three days before Kitchener died from a heart attack) about Mr Cadell's publishing of a new edition of "Apicius Redivivius, or the Cook's Oracle" (first edition was in 1817), William Kitchener added a postscript "I beg your acceptance of some ZEST" (20). So it must have been highly regarded and important. According to an advertisement for it in the back of Kitchener's book ZEST was a "piquante quintessence of Ragout". According to Dr Penzer it was a sauce with a stimulating flavour or a relish. According to the Rev Whitworth it was a sauce with a piquant flavour not unlike Worcestershire sauce. According to Mr Bruce Jones it was a mixture of spices or a mixture of peels from oranges and lemons. One could buy it from Butler's Herb-shop near Henrietta Street in Covent Garden. It was said to keep fresh for any time in any climate.

108. ZOOBDITTY

According to Dr Penzer ZOOBDITTY was a tasty fish sauce and this opinion has much to be said for it. Joobitty means tasty and machli means fish. Mr Robinson, formerly of the Victoria and Albert Museum, thought it might have been derived from "zubdat", a Persian word used in India meaning "cream". Zubdati means creamy. In Volume VI of the Wakelin ledgers where the names of some of the bottle tickets are given there is a reference to ZOOBDITTY . The title was thus in use in the 1770s. It is indeed likely to have been of Indian origin. ZOOBDITY was supplied to the Earl of Chesterfield on the 25th March 1778 to "match 10 labels for OIL, VINEGAR and SOY crewitts" supplied to the Earl in December 1777. Sir Thomas Barlow thinks that the instruction to Wakelin was for ZOOBDITTY – match, i.e. to match an existing label and that this led to the production of ZOOBDITTY MATCH. Hence the existence of a label for ZOOBY. MATCH and the advertisement in the first issue of "The Times" in 1788 for ZOOBDITTY MUTCH offered for sale by John Burgess & Son. The original recipe seems to have involved pounded oysters mixed with either sherry or with claret and port. George Knight produced a ZOOBDITTY label in 1819 and illustrated is one by Alice and George Burrows of 1805 for ZOOBDITTY MATCH. ■

NOTES

(1) See 5 WLJ 159
(2) Feature article, Sunday Times, 9 January 1972
(3) See further articles by Bruce Jones in 6 WLJ 83 and Bill Duprey in 8 WLJ 142
(4) 1 WLJ 95
(5) Jones Murray, New English Dictionary, 1893
(6) 1 WLJ 140
(7) 6 WLJ 278
(8) 1 WLJ 202
(9) 8 WLJ 96
(10) W.C.A. Blew. The Quorn Hunt and its Masters
(11) 1 WLJ 45
(12) As suggested by Bruce Jones in 5 WLJ 159
(13) See further 7 WLJ 223
(14) 5 WLJ 158
(15) 8 WLJ 96
(16) See further 5 WLJ 158
(17) Kenneth Hare, Wine and Food, 1939, p 358; Penzer, The Book of the Wine Label, p130
(18) Lady Ruggles Brise in 3 WLJ 37
(19) R.C. Bignall, Sauce Labels, 3 WLJ 37-39
(20) Sotheby's sale LN 7130, 10. 4. 1997, Lot 370

Photo 1. Alice and George Burrows, 1805. Note the unusual style of chain.

Photo 73. Unmarked labels of the drapery festoon style, showing the larger oil/vinegar labels above and the smaller soy labels below.

THE LABELS

NAME	DATES	LOCATION
CATCHUP	1814	
CHARAC	1814	
SOY	1814	
HARVEY'S SAUCE	1814	
CAYENNE	1814	
KETCHUP	1814	
ANCHOVY	1815	
11. ATKINS, THEODOSIA ANN	**1815**	**LONDON**
ANCHOVY	1815SG	
SOY	1815SG	
CAYENNE	1815SG	
12. BANNISTER, THOMAS	**1829-1836**	**LONDON**
KETCHUP	1834	
13. BARBER, JAMES AND CATTLE, ROBERT	**1808-1813**	**YORK**
HERVY.S	c.1809	
KETCHUP	c.1809	
KYAN	c.1809	
SOY	c.1809	
14. BARBER, JAMES AND WHITWELL, WILLIAM	**1814-1823**	**YORK**
SOY	c.1815	
15. BARBER, JAMES	**1847-1857**	**YORK**
ANCHOVY	c.1850	
CARACHA	c.1850	
HENRY	c.1850	
TARRAGON	c.1850	
CAYENNE	c.1850	
SOY	c.1850	
CHILLI	c.1850	
16 BARKER, SUSANNA	**1778-1793**	**LONDON**
PEP^R. VIN^R.	c.1778 Armorial	
L. PICKLE	c.1778	
CAMP	c.1778	
ELDER	c.1778	
ELDER	c.1778	
ELDER	c.1778	
LEMON	c.1778	
LEMON PICK	c.1778	
SOY	c.1778	
KETCHUP	c.1778	
SOY	c.1778	

NAME	DATES	LOCATION
GARLICK VINEGAR	c.1778	
SOY	c.1778	
TARRAGON	c.1778	
SOY	c.1778	
CORRASH	c.1778	
ANCHOVY	c.1780	
ANCHOVIES	c.1780	
SOY	c.1780	
QUIN	c.1780	
LEMON	c.1780	
KYAN	c.1780	
LEMON	c.1780 Armorial	
CAMP	c.1780 Armorial	
GARLICK VINEGAR	c.1784	
LEMON	1784 SG	
SOY	1784 SG	
ELDER	1784 SG	
TARRAGON	1784 SG	
SOY	c.1784	
GARLICK-VINEG^R	1784/5	
SOY	c.1785	
KETCHUP	c.1785	
KETCHUP	c.1787	
PEP VIN	c.1787	
CHILLI. VINEGAR	c.1789	
SAUCE-ROY	c.1789	
KETCHUP	c.1789	
CAYENNE	c.1790	
C. VINEGAR	c.1790	
CHERre SAUCE	c.1790	
CARRACHE	c.1790	
KYAN	c.1790	
CAYAN	c.1790	
KYAN	c.1790	
INDIA	c.1790	
SOY	c.1790	
ELDER	c.1790	
KETCHUP	c.1790	
CHER SAUCE	1791	
M. CATCHUP	1791	
SOY SAUCE	1791	
CAYENNE	1791	
SOY	1791	
ESSENCE	1791	
CHILLI VINEGAR	c.1792	
CAVICE	1792	
KETCHUP	1792	
SOY	1792	

THE LABELS

NAME	DATES	LOCATION
	CHILLI VIN	1792 Armorial
	CHILLI VIN	1792
	CHILI: VIN	1792
	CAYENNE	1792
	LEMON	1792
	CAYENNE	1793
	FRENCH	1793
	CAYENNE	1793
17. BARKER, ROBERT	1793-1794	LONDON
	FISH SAUCE	1793
	TARRAGON	1793
	KYAN	1793
	LEM PIC	1794
	KETCHUP	1794 Armorial
	TARRAGON	1794
	ELDER	1794
	SOY	1794
	SHALOT	1794
	KYAN	1794
	LEMON. PIC^K	1794
	LEMON PIC	1794
	LEMON PICL	1794
18. BARKER, RICHARD	1808-1815	LONDON
	CAYENNE	1814
19. BARNARD, EDWARD I, EDWARD II, JOHN AND WILLIAM	1829-1846	LONDON
	READING	1829
20. BARNARD, EDWARD II, JOHN AND WILLIAM	1846-1851	LONDON
	HARVEYS SAUCE	1848
21. BARNARD, EDWARD II AND JOHN	1851-1868	LONDON
	ANCHOVY	1864
	CATSUP	1864
	CAYENNE	1864
	CHILI	1864
	CROWN	1864
	HARVEY	1864
22. BARRETT. WILLIAM I	1771-1793	LONDON
	CYAN	c.1782
	HARVEY SAUCE	c.1782

NAME	DATES	LOCATION
23. BASKERVILLE, GEORGE	1775-1794	LONDON
	LEMON	–
	KYAN	1793
24. BATEMAN, HESTER	1761-1790	LONDON
	LEMON PICKLE	c.1770
	APPLE	c.1770
	CAYON	c.1780
	KYAN	c.1780
	LEMON	c.1780
	ELDER	c.1780
	LEMON	c.1780
	SOY	c.1780
	CAYON	c.1780
25. BATEMAN, PETER AND ANNE	1791-1799	LONDON
	CHILLI VINEGAR	–
	TARRAGON VINEGAR	–
	KATSUP	–
	MUSHROOM CATCHUP	–
	CAYAN	1797
	LEM PICKLE	1799
	QUIN SAUCE	1799
26. BATEMAN, PETER, ANNE AND WILLIAM	1800-1805	LONDON
	SOY	1801
	KETCHUP	1801
	KETCHUP	1801
27. BATEMAN, PETER AND WILLIAM	1805-1815	LONDON
	CATCHUP	1805
	CAVICE	1810 One of 24 labels
	HERVEY	1811
	TARRAGON VINEGAR	1812
	ANCHOVY	1813
	CATSUP	1813
	ANCHOVY	1813 Armorial
28. BATEMAN, WILLIAM I	1815-1827	LONDON
	SOY	1820
29. BATEMAN, WILLIAM II AND BALL, DANIEL	1840-1843	LONDON
	CHILLY VINEGAR	1840

THE LABELS

NAME		DATES	LOCATION
30. BEEBE, JAMES LONDON		1811-1837	
	SOY	c.1811	
	READING	1817	
	CATSUP	1817	
	ANCHOVY	1817	
	HARVEY	1817	
	SOY	1817	
	CHILI	1829	
	ESCAVECHI	1829	
	HARVEY	1829	
	TOMATO	c.1837	
	WORCESTERSHIRE	c.1837	
31. BELLINGHAM, SAMUEL		1806	LONDON
	KETCHUP	c.1806	
32. BIDLAKE, RICHARD		1755-1773	EXETER (PLYMOUTH)
	CAYENNE	c.1770	
33. BINLEY, RICHARD		1745-1764	LONDON
	OIL	c.1750	
	VINEGAR	c.1750	
34. BINLEY, MARGARET		1764-1778	LONDON
	PEP^R VINEGAR	c.1764	
	CAYON PEPPER	c.1764	
	KYAN	c.1765	
	ELDER	c.1765	
	GARLICK	c.1765	
	ANCHOVY	c.1770	
	CAYON	c.1770	
	ELDER	c.1770	
	KETCHUP	c.1770	
	SHALOT	c.1770	
	SOY	c.1770	
	ELDER	c.1770	
	SOY	c.1770	
	TARRAGON	c.1770	
	CAYON	c.1775	
	ELDER	c.1775	
	GARLICK	c.1775	
	TARRAGON	c.1775	
	WALNUT	c.1775	
	WAL^T PICKLE	c.1775	
	ELDER	c.1775	
	CARRISH	c.1778	

NAME		DATES	LOCATION
	KAYON	c.1778	
	ELDER	c.1778	
	LEMON	c.1778	
	LIME JUICE	c.1778	
	MUSTARD	c.1778	
	SUGAR	c.1778	
	CAYON	c.1778	
	CUCUMBER	c.1778	
	TARRAGON	c.1778	
35. BLAGDEN, THOMAS		1798-1817	SHEFFIELD
	CAYENNE	1817	
	ANCHOVY	1817	
	KETCHUP	1817	
	SOY	1817	
36. BLANCKENSEE AND SON LTD		1887-1952	BIRMINGHAM
	HARVEY	1902	
37. BOOTH, WILKES		1787-1813	LONDON
	CYAN	c.1790	
38. BOULTON, MATTHEW		1762-1809	BIRMINGHAM
	CARRACHI	c.1780	
	KETCHUP	c.1780	
	TARRAGON	c.1780	
	SOY	c.1780	
39. BOULTON, MATTHEW AND FOTHERGILL, J		1765-1780	BIRMINGHAM
	SOY	1776	
	LEMON PICKLE	1776	
40. BOULTON, MATTHEW PLATE CO		1810-1830	BIRMINGHAM
	TARRAGON	c1820	
	HARVEY	1826	
	SOY	1826	
	CORATCH	1827	
	TARRAGON	1828	
	CHILI	1828	
	CATCHUP	1828	
	OUDE	1828	
	KETCHUP	1828	
	SOY	1828	
41. BOWEN, THOMAS II		1797	LONDON
	KYAN	1797	

THE LABELS

NAME	DATES	LOCATION
SOY	1797	
FISH.S	1797	
KETCHUP	1797	
42. BOWER, FRANCIS	**1835-1853**	**LONDON**
KETCHUP	1853	
43. BOWERS, ROBERT	**1782-1829**	**CHESTER**
LEMON-PICKLE	1791	
44. BOYER, JOHN	**1772-1794**	**LONDON**
ANCHOVY	c.1775	
45. BRITTON, RICHARD	**1812-1842**	**LONDON**
CAYENNE	c.1815	
46. BURROWS, ALICE AND GEORGE	**1807-1818**	**LONDON**
ANCHOVY	1807	
CAMP	1807	
CAVICE	1807	
CHILI VINEGAR	1807	
CORATCH	1807	
HARVEY	1807	
KETCHUP	1807	
PIQUANTE	1807	
QUIN'S SAUCE	1807	
SAUCE ROYAL	1807	
SOY	1807	
TOMATA	1807	
ZOOBDITTY MATCH	1807	
47. BURWASH, WILLIAM AND SIBLEY, RICHARD	**1805-1812**	**LONDON**
CHILI VIN	1808	
LEMON	1808	
MUSH CATSUP	1808	
ANCHOVY	1808	
KYAN	1808	
QUIN	1808	
SOY	1808	
HARVEY	1808	
TARRAGON	1808	
WALT. CATSUP	1808	
CAMP VINR.	1808	
48. CAMERON, ALEXANDER	**1818-1847**	**DUNDEE**
HARVEY SAUCE	c.1840	

NAME	DATES	LOCATION
49. CATTLE, ROBERT AND BARBER, JAMES	**1808-1813**	**YORK**
HERVEY'S	1809	
KETCHUP	1809	
KYAN	1809	
SOY	1809	
50. CHESHIRE, COLEN HEWER	**1865-1927**	**BIRMINGHAM**
WORCESTER	1894	
51. CONSTABLE, WILLIAM	**1806-1820**	**DUNDEE**
ANCHOVIES	c.1810	
KETCHUP	c.1810	
Soy	c.1810	
52. CRESPEL, SEBASTIAN	**1820-1836**	**LONDON**
HARVEY	1820	
CHILI	1824	
OIL	1826	
VINEGAR	1826	
ANCHOVY	1827	
52A. CRESPEL, ANDREW, AND PARKER, THOMAS	**1861-1875**	**LONDON**
ANCHOVY	1861	
CATSUP	1861	
CHILI	1861	
SOY	1863	
HARVEY	1863	
53. CRESWICK, THOMAS, JAMES AND NATHANIEL	**1853**	**BIRMINGHAM**
SOY	1853	
CAYENNE	1853	
54. CRESWICK, JAMES AND NATHANIEL	**1853-1855**	**SHEFFIELD**
CHILI	1853	
ANCHOVY	1853	
HARVEY	1853	
KETCHUP	1853	
SOY	1853	
TARRAGON	1853	
55. CROPLEY, E AND CO	**1819-1824**	**CALCUTTA**
SUGAR	c.1820	

THE LABELS

NAME	DATES	LOCATION
56. CROSSLEY, RICHARD	1782-1816	LONDON
CHILI	1791	
ANCHOVY	1796	
KETCHUP	1796	
ANCHOVY	1816	
KETCHUP	1816	
57. CUNNINGHAM, WILLIAM AND PATRICK	1776-1803	EDINBURGH
CAYENN	c.1797	
58. DANIEL, THOMAS (OR DANIELL)	1775-1778	LONDON
SOY	1777	
KETCHUP	1777	
LEMON	1777	
CAYON	1777	
CAYON	1777	
KIAN	c.1777	
CAYAN	c.1777	
59. DAVENPORT, SAMUEL	1786-1794	LONDON
SOY	c.1790	
60. DAVIES, FREDERICK AND W T WRIGHT See Wright	1864-1866	LONDON
61. EDWARDS, THOMAS	1825-1830	LONDON
ANCHOVY	1824 Armorial	
PEPPERMINT	1825	
62. ELLIOTT, WILLIAM AND STORY, JOSEPH WILLIAM	1809-1815	LONDON
KYAN	1809	
SOY	1810	
KETCHUP	1810	
KYAN	1810	
ANCHOVY	1811	
HERVY	1812	
ANCHOVY	1813	
ANCHOVY	1815	
SOY	1815	
63. ELLIOTT, WILLIAM	1795-1830	LONDON
READING SAUCE	1816	
CHILLY	1816	
LEMON PICKLE	1816	

NAME	DATES	LOCATION
ELDER	1816	
READING	1816	
KYAN	1817	
ANCHOVY	1822	
CHILI	1822	
ANCHOVY	1823	
CATCHUP	1826	
VINEGAR	1827	
KYAN	1827	
CHILI	1828	
CAVICE	1828	
SOY	1828	
KYAN	1828	
64. EMES, JOHN	1796-1808	LONDON
LEMON-PICKLE	1801	
MADEIRA	1803	
CAYON	c.1804	
ANCHOVY	c.1804	
KETCHUP	c.1804	
SOY	c.1804	
KYAN	1807	
65. EMES, REBECCA AND BARNARD, EDWARD	1808-1829	LONDON
CAYENNE	1822	
66. ERSKINE, JAMES	1792-1818	ABERDEEN
CATCHUP	c.1795	
FISH SAUCE	c.1800	
SAUCE A LA MILITAIRE	c.1800	
SAUCE A LA SUISSE	c.1800	
CAMP SAUCE	c.1800	
SAUCE BLANCHE	c.1800	
GOOSE-BERRY	c.1805	
67. FERRIS, GEORGE I	1817-1832	EXETER
SOY	–	
KETCHUP	1822	
68. FLAVELLE, HENRY I	1819-1832	DUBLIN
ANCHOVIE	1833	
CATSUP	1834	
CHILI. V	1834	
69. FOLCKER, GUSTAF	1826	STOCKHOLM
Elf anchovies	1826	
Mushroom ketchup	1826	

THE LABELS

NAME	DATES	LOCATION
70. FOLLIOT, J	1790-1800	MADRAS
OUDE'S SAUCE	c.1790	
71. FRAY, JAMES	1813-1842	DUBLIN
CATSUP	c.1809-1820	
72. F——, C——	1820-1830	JERSEY
KETCHUP	c.1825	
ANCHOVY	1829	
KETCHUP	1829	
73. FULTON, JOSEPH	1838-1860	BRISTOL
Details not known		
74. GALLANT, JANE	1760-1780	LONDON
VALE OF AYLESBURY	c.1780	
75. GARRARD, ROBERT I	1792-1818	LONDON
HARVEY	1806	
SOY	1806	
CAYENNE	1806	
ANCHOVY	1806	
CAYAN	1806	
CAVICHE	1806	
CHILI	1813SG	
CAYENNE	1813SG	
ANCHOVY	1816	
CAYENNE	1816	
KETCHUP	1816	
LEMON	1816	
READING	1817	
CHILLI	1817	
HERVEY	1817	
ANCHOVY	1817	
CAYENNE	1817	
LEMON	1817	
SOY	1818	
CAMP-VINR	1818	
CAMP VIN	1818	
76. GARRARD, ROBERT II	1818-1860	LONDON
CAYENNE	1819	
ELDER	1819	
LEMON	1819	
SOY	1819	
TARRAGON	1819	
WORCESTER	1858	

NAME	DATES	LOCATION
77. GILBERT, JOHN	1876-1877	BIRMINGHAM
Worcester	1876	
78. GLENNY, JOSEPH	1792-1821	LONDON
ANCHOVY	1819	
79. GORDON, HUGH	1770	FORTROSE
CORACK	c.1770	
KETCHUP	c.1770	
VINEGAR	c.1770	
80. GRIERSON, PHILIP	1816-1823	GLASGOW
B	1820	
81. HAMILTON AND INCHES	1880-1910	EDINBURGH
YORKSHIRE	1909	
82. HAMPSON, JOHN AND PRINCE, JOHN	1784-1794	YORK
LEMON	1793/4	
CAYENE. S^c.	1793/4	
83. W. HARWOOD AND CO	1801-1826	SHEFFIELD
READING	1811	
84. HAYNE, JONATHAN	1808-1845	LONDON
Details not known	c.1828	
85. HAYTER, THOMAS	1805-1816	LONDON
ANCHOVIE	1814	
SOY	–	
KETCHUP	–	
ANCHOVY	–	
86. HEMING, THOMAS	1745-1783	LONDON
CARRACHE	c.1765	
87. HENNELL, ROBERT I	1763-1811	LONDON
RED VINEGAR	c.1790	
WHITE VINEGAR	c.1790	
KETCHUP	c.1790	
ANCHOVEY	c.1790	
LEMON PICKLE	c.1790	
ANCHOVIES	1791	
OIL	1791	

THE LABELS

	NAME	DATES	LOCATION
88	**HENNELL, ROBERT I AND SAMUEL**	1802-1811	LONDON
	WOODS FISH SAUCE	1804	
89	**HENNELL, ROBERT II**	1809-1833	LONDON
	FISH-SAUCE	1813	
90	**HENNELL, ROBERT III**	1833-1868	LONDON
	CHILI	1855	
91	**HENNELL, SAMUEL AND TERRY, JOHN**	1814-1816	LONDON
	ANCHOVY	1814	
92	**HOCKLEY, DANIEL**	1810-1819	LONDON
	CAYENNE	1810	
	ELDER	–	
	ANCHOVY	–	
93	**HOLLAND, JOHN II**	1765-1779	LONDON
	KETCHUP	c.1765	
94	**HOLLAND, HENRY**	1850-1864	LONDON
	ANCHOVY	1856	
	CHILLI	1864	
	KETCHUP	1864	
	CHILI	1864	
95	**HOULE, DANIEL JOHN AND CHARLES**	1845-1884	LONDON
	WORCESTER	1870	
96	**HUBBARD, GEORGE THOMAS AND MICHAU, JEAN HENRI**	1896	LONDON
	WORCESTER SAUCE	1896	
97	**HUNT, JOHN SAMUEL AND JOHN MORTIMER (See MORTIMER and HUNT**		
98	**HUNT, JOHN MORTIMER, ROSKELL, ROBERT II AND ROSKELL, ALLAN**	1879-1888	LONDON
	READING	1882	
	HARVEY'S	1882	
99	**HUNTER, WILLIAM II**	1867	LONDON
	ANCHOVY	1867	

	NAME	DATES	LOCATION
100	**HUTTON, EDWARD**	1880-1892	LONDON
	CHILI	1890	
	TAROGON	1890	
	WORCESTER	1890	
	CHUTNEE	1892	
101	**HUTTON, WILLIAM CARR**	1857-1896	LONDON
	CABBAGE	1896	
	CAPTAIN WHITE'S	1896	
	WALNUT	1896	
102.	**HUTTON, WILLIAM AND SONS LIMITED**	1893-1930	BIRMINGHAM
	ANCHOVY	1896	
	HARVEY	1896	
103.	**HYDE, THOMAS I AND II**	1747-1804	LONDON
	CAYON	c.1775	
	WORCESTER	c.1775	
	KETCHUP	c.1775	
	READING	c.1775	
	HARVEY	c.1775	
	LEMON-P	c.1775	
	LEMON	c.1780	
	CARRACHE	c.1780	
	HARVEY	c.1780	
	KETCHUP	c.1780	
	READING	c.1780	
	CARRACHE	c.1780	
	GARLICK	c.1780	
	TARRAGON	c.1780	
	ELDER	c.1780	
	CHILI	c.1785	
	VINEGAR	c.1785	
	CAMP VIN	1800	
	CAVIC SAUCE	1800	
	CHILI VIN	1800	
	HARV.y SAUCE	1800	
	KYAN	1800	
	QUIN-SAUCE	1800	
	TARR.n VIN	1800	
	ZOOB.y MATCH	1800	
104	**HYDE, JAMES**	1774-1799	LONDON
	CAVICE	c.1775	
	KETCHUP	c.1775	
	LEMON	c.1775	
	KETCHUP	c.1775	

THE LABELS

NAME	DATES	LOCATION
KYAN	c.1785	
CYAN	c.1786	
CAMP VIN	c.1790	
L. PICKLE	(3rd Mark)	
CHILLI	(3rd Mark)	
LEMON PICE	c.1790	
LEMON	c.1790	
LEMON	c.1790	
FISH-SAUCE	1795	
SOY	1796	
LEMON	1797 Armorial	
LEMON. PICL	1797	
ELDER	1797	
SOY	1797 Armorial	
CAMP V.	1797	
SOY	1797 Armorial	
CAMP. VIN	1797	
SOY	1798	
BERNIS	1798	
105 HYDE, MARY AND JOHN REILY	1800	LONDON
KETCHUP	1800	
106 JACKSON, JAMES	1805-1832	LONDON
KYAN	c.1805	
107 JENKINSON, THOMAS	1807-1827	LONDON
KYAN	c.1810	
108 JOHNSON, THOMAS	1851	LONDON
WORCESTERSHIRE	1851	
CHILI VINEGAR	1851	
109 JOHNSTON, ALEXANDER II	1760-1785	LONDON
SOY	c.1785	
110 JOHNSTON, JAMES	1840-1873	EDINBURGH
CAVICE	c.1845	
111 JONES, ROBERT II	1796-1800	LONDON
MUSHROOM	c.1796	
112 KAY, CHARLES	1815-1827	LONDON
CAYENNE	1826	
113 KEAY, ROBERT	1791-1800	PERTH
VINEGAR	c.1795	

NAME	DATES	LOCATION
114 KING, ABSTAINANDO	1791-1821	LONDON
KYAN	1805	
115 KIPPAX, ROBERT	1794-1796	SHEFFIELD
ESSENCE ANCHOVIES	1794	
116 KNIGHT, GEORGE	1816-1825	LONDON
CAYENNE	1816	
TARRAGON	1816	
HARVEY	1819	
KYAN	1819	
MOGUL	1819	
NEPAUL	1819	
ZOOBDITTY	1819	
SOY	1820	
READING	1820	
KETCHUP	1820	
CATSUP	1821	
CHILI VIN	1821	
PITTS	1821	
117 KNIGHT, SAMUEL	1810-1827	LONDON
ANCHOVY	1815	
CHILI	1815	
CHILLI-VIN^R.	1816	
HARVEY	1816	
CATCHUP	1816	
ANCHOVY	1816	
READING	1816	
118 KNIGHT, WILLIAM	1819-1846	LONDON
HARVEY	1827	
APPETISSANTE	1829	
MADEIRA	1829	
PITT SAUCE	1830	
GAME	1830	
KYAN	1830	
KETCHUP	1830	
SOY	1830	
LEMON	1833	
CHILI VINEGAR	(NOT KNOWN)	
KETCHUP	1835	
119 LAMBE, JOHN	1765-1796	LONDON
CYAN	c.1780	
LEMON	c.1780	

75

THE LABELS

NAME	DATES	LOCATION
120. LAMBERT, HERBERT CHARLES	1902-1912	LONDON
PEPPER	1910	
HUILE	1908SG	
VINAIGRE	1908SG	
121 LAMBERT, PETER	1804-1816	ABERDEEN
S	c.1810	
122 LANGFORD, JOHN AND SEBILLE, JOHN	1760-1797	LONDON
HARVEY	1772	
SALAD OIL	1772	
123 LANGLANDS, JOHN AND ROBERTSON, JOHN I	1778-1795	NEWCASTLE
READING SAUCE	c.1780	
ANCHOVY	c.1790	
124 LANGLANDS, JOHN II	1795-1804	NEWCASTLE
CHYAN VINEGAR	c.1800	
ESSENCE OF ANCHOVIES	c.1800	
SOY	c.1800	
WALNUT CATCHUP	c.1800	
125. LEWIS, GEORGE SAMUEL AND WRIGHT, JOHN	1812-1824	NEWCASTLE
CATCHUP	c.1812	
ANCHOVY	c.1812	
CAYENNE	c.1821/2	
HARVEY SAUCE	c.1821/2	
ANCHOVY	c.1821/2	
126. GL AND GF (?)	c.1850	NEWCASTLE
SOY	c.1850 Armorial	
127. LINNIT, JOHN AND ATKINSON, WILLIAM	1809-1815	LONDON
CATSUP	1813	
CHILI	1813	
ANCHOVY	1813	
128. LINNIT, JOHN	1815-1841	LONDON
ANCHOVEY	1815	
HARVEY	1815	
129. LINWOOD, MATTHEW II	1793-1821	BIRMINGHAM
ELDER-VINEGAR	1812	
TOMATA	1812	
WALN KET	1817	

NAME	DATES	LOCATION
130. LIVINGSTONE, EDWARD	1790-1825	DUNDEE
ELDER	c.1805	
TARRAGON	c.1805	
131. LOWE, GEORGE	1791-1841	CHESTER
HARVEY SAUCE	1797	
132. LOWE, EDWARD	1800-1810	CHESTER
LEMON	c.1810	
133 MACDONALD, JOHN	1810-1815	EDINBURGH
QUEEN'S SAUCE	1810	
LOBSTER SAUCE	c.1810	
LOBSTER SAUCE	c.1815	
134. MARSHALL, JAMES AND WALTER	1817-1823	EDINBURGH
MUSHROOM CATSUP	c.1820	
135. MARTIN, RICHARD AND HALL, EBENEZER	1854-1891	SHEFFIELD
HARVEY	1887	
136. MCKAY, JAMES	1793-1837	EDINBURGH
CAYENNE PEPPER	c.1805	
ELDER VINEGAR	c.1805	
SOY	c.1805	
SUGAR	c.1810	
SOY	c.1810	
SOY	1815	
KETCHUP	1815	
ANCHOVY	1815	
GINGER	1815	
LOBSTER	1815	
SOY	1815	
SUGAR	c.1835	
CHERRY	1837	
CINAMON	1837	
137 MCKENZIE, JOHN I	1841	INVERNESS
CAYENNE	c.1841	
ANCHOVIE	c.1841	
KETCHUP	c.1841	
SOY	c.1841	
138. MITCHELL, ALEXANDER II	1819-1850	GLASGOW
PIQUANT	1833	

THE LABELS

NAME	DATES	LOCATION
139. MITCHELL, JOHN AND WILLIAM	1834-1851	EDINBURGH
OIL	c.1835	
140. MORLEY, ELIZABETH	1794-1814	LONDON
SOY	c.1794-5	
KYAN	c.1794-5	
KETCHUP	c.1794-5	
CATCHUP	c.1794-5	
CAYANNE	c.1794-5	
CAYENE	c.1794-5	
CHILLI	c.1794-5	
F. SAUCE	c.1794-5	
F^H. SAUCE	c.1794-5	
F^H, SAUCE	c.1794-5	
CORATCH	c.1794-5	
PICKLE	c.1794-5	
TARRAGON	c.1794-5	
SAU^{CE}: ROY^L:	c.1794-5	
MUSHROOM	c.1794-5	
LEMON.PICKLE	c.1794-5	
LEMON-PICKLE	c.1794-5	
OIL	c.1794-5	
SOY	c.1794-5	
C. VINEGAR	c.1794-5	
SOY	c.1794-5	
SOY	c.1794-5	
CHILI VING	c.1794-5	
HARVEY	c.1794-5	
KETCHUP	c.1794-5	
QN. SAUCE	c.1794-5	
CAVICE	c.1794-5	
KYAN	c.1794-5	
SOY	c.1794-5	
KYAN	1796	
ANCHOVY	1798	
SOY	1799	
KYAN	1799	
SOY	1799	
SOY	1810	
141. MORTIMER, JOHN AND HUNT, JOHN SAMUEL	1839-1843	LONDON
BURGUNDY	1840	
142. MORTON, ROBERT	1819-1835	EDINBURGH
PACKE	c.1825	
143. MURRAY, GEORGE	1805-1816	NEWCASTLE
CHILI-VINEGAR	c.1805	
144. NEWLANDS, JAMES AND GRIERSON, PHILIP	1811-1816	EDINBURGH/ GLASGOW
OIL	1813	
145. NICKOLDS, JOHN	1818	LONDON
CAYANNE	c.1818	
146. OLLIVANT, THOMAS	1789-1830	MANCHESTER
FISH SAUCE	c.1790	
147. P——, S——	1987	LONDON
MAPLE SYRUP	1987	
148. PACK, NATHANIEL	1765	LONDON
TARAGON	c.1765	
149. PARSONS, THOMAS	1773-1801	BIRMINGHAM
LEMON	c.1800	
SOY	c.1800	
CHILI	c.1800	
QUIN SAUCE	c.1800	
150. PEARSON, GEORGE	1812-1821	LONDON
CHILLI	1816	
CAYENNE	c.1817	
CHILLI V	c.1817	
ANCHOVY	1821	
151. PECKHAM, JAMES	1830-1847	SOUTH CAROLINA, USA
CHILI	c.1830	
152. PERKINS, JONATHAN I	1800-1810	LONDON
KYAN	c.1805	
BROWN S	c.1805	
DEVONSHIRE	c.1805	
153. PHIPPS, JAMES	1754-1783	LONDON
QUIN	c.1770	
CARRACHIO	c.1770	
WALNUT PICKLE	c.1770	
CAYANNE	—	
KETCHUP	—	
HARVEY	—	
CORATCH	c.1780	

THE LABELS

NAME	DATES	LOCATION
ANCHOVY	c.1780	
LEMON	c.1780	
SOY	c.1783	
ANCHOVY	c.1783	
154. PHIPPS, THOMAS AND ROBINSON, EDWARD	**1783-1811**	**LONDON**
PIQUANTE	c.1783	
KETCHUP	c.1783	
KYAN	c.1783	
CATCHUP	c.1785	
CURRY	c.1785	
KYAN	c.1785	
LEM PICKLE	c.1785	
SAUCE ROY	c.1785	
CHILI	c.1785	
SOY	c.1785	
CAYENNE	c.1785	
CHEROKEE	c.1786	
SOY	c.1786	
KETCHUP	c.1786	
KYAN	–	
KYAN	–	
ANCHOVY	–	
ANCHOVY	–	
LEMON	c.1786	
SOY	c.1786	
LEM PICK	–	
FISH SAUCE	–	
KETCHUP	–	
KETCHUP	–	
LEMON	–	
SOY	c.1790	
ANCHOVY	c.1790	
CHILI	c.1790	
KETCHUP	c.1790	
KYAN	c.1790	
LEMON	c.1790	
SOY	c.1790	
CHILLI	c.1790	
LEMON	c.1790	
SOY	c.1790	
KYAN	c.1790	
HARVEY SAUCE	c.1790	
SAUCE ROYAL	c.1790	
SOYER	c.1790	
TARRAGON	c.1790	
TARRAGON	c.1790	

NAME	DATES	LOCATION
BURGUNDY	c.1790	
CAMP SAUCE	c.1790	
CAYENNE	c.1790	
ELDER	c.1790	
WALNUT PICKLE	c.1790	
SOY	c.1790	
SOY	c.1790	
ANCHOVIE	c.1790	
HARVEY	c.1790	
HARVEY SAUCE	c.1790	
CAYENNE	c.1790	
SOY	c.1790	
CAYAN	c.1790	
CAYENNE	c.1790	
SOY	c.1790	
CAMP	1793	
NIG	1794	
CUCUMBER	1794/6	
LEM. PICKLE	1796 Armorial	
QUIN	1796	
ANCHOVY	1797	
KETCHUP	1797	
QUIN	1797	
KETCHUP	c.1800	
LEMON	c.1800	
LEMON PICKLE	c.1805	
KETCHUP	1809	
LEMON	1809	
LIME JUICE	c.1810 SG	
SOY	c.1810 SG	
ANCHOVY	c.1810 SG	
KETCHUP	c.1810 SG	
CAMP SAUCE	c.1810 SG	
KYAN	c.1810 SG	
PICQUANTE	c.1810	
TARRAGON	c.1810	
LEMON	c.1810	
KYAN	c.1810	
LEMON	1810	
ANCHOVY	1811	
ANCHOVY	1811	
155. PHIPPS, ROBINSON AND PHIPPS	**1811-1816**	**LONDON**
LEMON	1813	
KYAN	1814 SG	
CHILI	1814 SG	
KYAN	1814	

THE LABELS

NAME	DATES	LOCATION	NAME	DATES	LOCATION
CHILLI	1814		157. PIERCY, ROBERT	1757-1795	LONDON
KYAN	c.1815		CAYENNE	1765	
ANCHOVY	c.1815		ELDER	1765	
CAYENNE	c.1815 Armorial		GARLICK	1765	
KETCHUP	c.1815		SOY	1765	
KYAN	c.1815		LEMON	1765	
KETCHUP	c.1815 SG		TARRAGON	1765	
SOY	c.1815		ANCHOVY	1775 SG	
ANCHOVY	c.1815		ELDER	1775 SG	
SOY	c.1815		KETCHUP	1775 SG	
KYAN	c.1815		KYAN	1775 SG	
KYAN	c.1815		SOY	1775 SG	
HARVEY	c.1815		TARRAGON	1775 SG	
ANCHOVY	c.1815		158. PITTS, WILLIAM	1810-1811	LONDON
156. PHIPPS, THOMAS AND JAMES	1816-1823	LONDON	LEMON	1810	
ELDER	c.1816		159. PLUMMER, WILLIAM	1769-1790	
ELDER	c.1816		CATCHUP	1769	
HARVEY	c.1816		ELDER	1769	
KETCHUP	c.1816		GARLICK	1769	
LEMON	c.1816		KYAN	1769	
SOY	c.1816		LEMON	1769	
TARRAGON	c.1816		SOY	1769	
HARVEY	c.1816				
KETCHUP	c.1816SG		160. PLUMMER, MICHAEL	1791-1792	LONDON
LEMON	c.1816		TARAGON	c.1791	
SOY	c.1816				
TARRAGON	c.1816		161. PRICE, CHARLES CLAPTON	1812-1830	LONDON
KYAN	1816		CHILI. VIN[R]	1825 Armorial	
SOY	1816				
LEMON	1816		162. PURTON, FRANCES	1783-1798	LONDON
ELDER	1816		LEMON PICKLE	c.1780	
TARRAGON	1816		LEMON PICKLE	1795	
ANCHOVY	1816		CHILLY VINEGAR	1797	
HARVEY	1816		LEMON PICKLE	1797	
CAYENNE	1816		ANCHOVY	1798	
KETCHUP	1816		CHILLY VINEGAR	1798	
READING	1816				
ANCHOVY	1817		163. RAITE AND SONS	1825	ABERDEEN
SOY	c.1817		HARVEY	c.1825	
ELDER	c.1818				
KYAN	1819		164. RAWLINGS, CHARLES	1817-1829	LONDON
CAYENNE	c.1820		CHILI.VIN	1817	
IMPERIAL	c.1820		SUGAR	1817	
HARVEY	c.1820		SOY	1817	
KYAN	c.1820		ANCHOVY	1818	
ANCHOVY	c.1820		CAYENNE	1818	

THE LABELS

NAME	DATES	LOCATION
KETCHUP	1818	
CATSUP	1818	
SOY	1818	
TARRAGON	1818	
SOY	–	
ANCHOVY	–	
ELDER	1819	
CAYENNE	1819 Armorial	
VINEGAR	1819	
PEPPER	1821	
LEMON	1821	
ESSENCE GINGER	1821	
SOY	1822	
ANCHOVY	1822	
HARVEY	1822	
KETCHUP	1822	
CATCHUP	1822	
LEMON	1822	
SOY	1822SG	
KETCHUP	1822	
CHILI	1823	
CAYENNE	1823	
ESSENCE OF CHILLI	1823	
SOY	1823	
"TWO FIGURED SAUCE LABELS (LARGE SIZE)"	1823	
FISH SA	1824	
FISH. SA^E.	1824	
WALNUT	1824	
HARVEY	1824	
KETCHUP	1824	
CHILI	1824	
VINEGAR	1824	
CAYENNE	1824	
SOY	1824	
SAUCE	1824	
ANCHOVY	1824	
LEMON	1824	
CAYENNE	1825	
CHILI VIN	1825	
A LA RUSSE	1825	
PIQUANTE	1825	
TARRAGON VINEGAR	1825	
GARLIC VINEGAR	1825	
ELDER VINEGAR	1825	
CAMP V	1826 Armorial	
SOY	1826	
CAYENN	1826	

NAME	DATES	LOCATION
ANCHOVY	1826	
Harvey's fish sauce	1827	
ANCHOVY	1827	

165. **RAWLINGS, CHARLES AND SUMMERS, WILLIAM** — 1829-1897 — LONDON

NAME	DATES	LOCATION
REGENT	c.1829SG	
DEVONSHIRE	1829	
SOY	1829	
LEMON	1829	
READING	1829	
CHILI	1830	
SOY	1830	
CATCHUP	1830	
ANCHOVY	1830	
CAYENNE	1830	
CHILI VINEGAR	1830	
CAYENNE	1831	
TARRAGON	1832	
OUDE	1832	
CURRY	1832	
ESCHALOTTE	1832	
REGENT	1832	
HARVEY	1833	
ANCHOVY	1834	
CHILI	1834	
MUSHROOM	1834	
HARVEY	1834	
HARVEY	1834	
CHILI	1835	
CAYANNE	1836	
CHILI	1836	
MOGUL	1836	
KETCHUP	1836	
CHILI VINEGAR	1836	
ANCHOVY	1836	
BURS SCE	1836	
READING	1836	
TARAGON	1837	
CAMP	1837	
OUDE	1837	
V	1838	
HARVEY	1838	
HARVEY	1838	
CAVICE	1838	
KETCHUP	1839	
SOY	1829	
HARVEY	1840	

THE LABELS

NAME	DATES	LOCATION
WORCESR.	1840	
CAYENNE	1840	
KETCHUP	1840	
CHILI	1840	
TARRAGON	1840	
CAYENNE	1840	
B	1840	
ANCHOVY	1840	
TARAGON	1840	
KETCHUP	1840	
CAYENNE	1840	
OUDE	1841	
HARVEY	1841	
CAYENNE	1841	
CATSUP	1841	
CHILLI VINEGAR	1841	
ANCHOVY	1841	
ANCHOVY	1844	
CAYENNE	1844	
CROWN	1844	
CAVICE	1845	
CHILI	1845	
READING	1847	
CHILI VINEGAR	1847	
SOY	1849	
CAYENNE	1849	
CHILI	1849	
CATCHUP	1851	
KETCHUP	1851	
FISH SAUCE	1851	
HARVEY	1852	
ANCHOVY	1854	
READING	1855	
HARVEY	1855	
ANCHOVY	1855	
SOY	1856 SG	
TARRAGON	1858	
CHILI	1858	
SOY	1858	
CAYENNE	1858	
HARVEY	1858	
KETCHUP	1858	
ANCHOVY	1858	
CHILI VINEGAR	1861	
HARVEY	1861	
C	1862	
KAYAN	– Set of 10	
CHILLI	– Set of 10	

NAME	DATES	LOCATION
INDIA SOY	– Set of 10	
HARVEY	1864	

166. **REID, CHRISTIAN KER I AND SONS** — 1819-1884 NEWCASTLE

SOY (?)	–	

167. **REILY, JOHN** — 1800-1826 LONDON

SOY	1800 Armorial	
KETCHUP	1800 Armorial	
KYAN	1800 Armorial	
CAMP	1801	
CARATCH	1801	
CAYENNE	1801	
ANCHOVIE	c.1801-13	
CARRACHE	c.1801-13	
CAYENNE	c.1801-13	
CHILLI	c.1801-13	
FISH SAUCE	c.1801-13	
HARVEY	c.1801-13	
LEMON	c.1801-13	
LEMON PICKLE	c.1801-13	
ANCHOVY	1802	
KETCHUP	1802	
OIL	1802	
QUIN SAUCE	1802	
VINEGAR	1802	
CAYENNE	1803	
ANCHOVY	c.1803-13	
CHILLI VIN.	c.1803-13	
FISH SAUCE	c.1803-13	
ANCHOVY	1804	
SOY	1804	
BURGESS	c.1805-13	
BURMAN SAUCE	c.1805-13	
CAYENNE	c.1805-13	
KETCHUP	c.1805-13	
QUIN	c.1805-13	
QUIN SAUCE	c.1805-13	
TARRAGON	c.1805-13	
HARVEY	c.1805-13	
SOY	c.1805-13	
CAYENNE	1808	
HARVEY	1810	
KETCHUP	1810	
SOY	c.1810-13	
SOY	1810	
CAYENNE	c.1810 SG	

THE LABELS

NAME	DATES	LOCATION
JESSAMINE	c.1810 SG	
HARVEY	c.1810-13	
KETCHUP	c.1810-13	
SOY	c.1810-13	
SOY	c.1810-13	
CAYENNE	1813	
CHILLI	1813	
HARVEY	1813	
KETCHUP	1813	
KETCHUP	1813	
SOY	1813	
ANCHOVY	1814	
CATCHUP	1814	
CAYENNE	1814	
CHILLI	1814	
HARVEY	1814	
CHILLI	1814 SG	
CAYENNE	c.1815	
SOY	c.1815	
READING	1816	
KETCHUP	c.1816 SG	
SOY	c.1816 SG	
CHILLI	1817	
SOY	1817	
CHILLI	1817	
SOY	1818 Armorial	
ANCHOVY	1818 Armorial	
ANCHOVY	1818	
KETCHUP	1818	
SOY	1818	
ANCHOVY	1818	
LEMON	1820	
SOY	1820	
CAYENNE	1820	
HARVEY	1820	
TARRAGON	c.1820	
ANCHOVY	1821	
ANCHOVY	1821	
ANCHOVY	1821 SG	
CHILI	1821	
SOY	1821	
LEMON PICKLE	1821	
CAYENNE	1822 SG	
KETCHUP	1822 SG	
KETCHUP	1822	
CHILI	1822	
OIL	1822	
SOY	c.1822	

NAME	DATES	LOCATION
ANCHOVY	1823	
CAVICE	1823	
CAYENNE	1823	
CHILI	1823	
HARVEY	1823	
LEMON	1823	
READING	1823	
SOY	1823	
SOY	1823	
ANCHOVY	1824	
CHILI	1824	
KETCHUP	1824	
SOY	1824	
ANCHOVY	1825	
ANCHOVY	1825	
CAYENNE	1825	
CAYENNE	1825	
CHILI	1825	
KETCHUP	1825	
LEMON	1825	
READING	c.1825	
ANCHOVY	c.1825	
ANCHOVY	c.1825	
SOY	c.1825	
ANCHOVY	1826	
HARVEY	1826(?)	
LEMON	1826	
168. REILY, MARY ANN AND CHARLES	**1826-1829**	**LONDON**
CAYENNE	1826	
CHILI	1826	
ANCHOVY	1826	
ANCHOVY	1826	
CHILI	c.1826-28	
CAYENNE	c.1826-28	
CATSUP	1826	
KYAN	c.1826-28	
ANCHOVY	c.1826-28	
VINEGAR	1826	
CAYENNE	c.1826-28	
CHILLI	c.1826-28	
CAVICE	c.1826-28	
HARVEY	c.1826-28	
VINEGAR	c.1826-28	
SOY	c.1826-28	
ANCHOVY	c.1826-28	
KETCHUP	c.1826-28	

82

THE LABELS

NAME		DATES	LOCATION
	SOY	1827	
	ANCHOVY	1827	
	CHILLI	1827	
	CHILI	1827	
	SOY	1828	
169. REILY, CHARLES AND STORER, GEORGE		1828-1855	LONDON
	WOOD	1828	
	CAVICE	1828	
	HARVEY	1828	
	ANCHOVY	1829	
	CHILI	c.1830	
	COGNAC	c.1830	
	CAYENNE	c.1830	
	SOY	c.1830	
	ANCHOVY	c.1830	
	FISH-SAUCE	c.1830	
	ESS GINGER	c.1830	
	TARRAGON	c.1830	
	WALNUT PICKLE	c.1830	
	CAYENNE	c.1830	
	CAVICE	c.1830	
	CHILI	c.1830	
	ANCHOVY	c.1837	
	CAYENNE	c.1837	
	CHILI	c.1837	
	READING	c.1837	
	H	1838	
	K	1838	
	R	1838	
	HARVEY	1840SG	
	MADRAS FLAME	1840 Armorial	
	ANCHOVY	c.1840	
	MUSHROOM	1844	
	ANCHOVY	1845	
	KETCHUP	1850	
	CHILI	1855	
170. RENOU, TIMOTHY		1792-1816	LONDON
	KYAN	1814	
	ANCHOVIE	1814	
	KETCHUP	1814	
	WALNUT	1814	
	CORATCH	1816	
	CAYANNE	1816	
	ANCHOVY	1816	
	CATCHUP	1816	

NAME		DATES	LOCATION
	POUVERADE	1816	
	CATSUP	1816	
171. RETTIE AND SON		1810-1847	ABERDEEN
	HARVEY	c.1820	
172. RICH, JOHN		1765-1810	LONDON
	ANCHOVY	–	
	ANCHOVIE	–	
	ESSENCE-OF-KAYAN	–	
	LEMON	–	
	CHILLI	– Armorial	
	KETCHUP	–	
	KAYENNE	–	
	KAYAN	–	
	Worcester	1784/5	
	LEMON	c.1785	
	SOY	c.1785	
	LEMON	c.1785	
	KETCHUP	c.1785	
	ANCHOVIE	c.1785	
	QUIN	c.1785	
	CUCUMBER	c.1789	
	CAVICE	c.1789	
	ELDER	c.1789	
	CATCHUP	c.1789	
	TARRAGON	c.1789	
	KETCHUP	c.1789	
	SOY	c.1789	
	ANCHOVY	c.1789	
	CARRACH	1791	
	CAYENNE PEPPER	1791	
	SOY	1791	
	ANCHOVY	1791	
	GARLIC VINEGAR	1791	
	JAPAN SOY	1791	
	WOODS SAUCE	1791	
	ANCHOVIE	1791	
	LEMON	1791	
	CAY.VIN.^{R}	1791	
	GAR.VIN.^{R}	1791	
	ANCHOVIE	1792	
	KETCHUP	1792	
	CHILLE VINEGAR	1792	
	CAYENNE	1793	
	ANCHOVY	1794	
	ELDER VINEGAR	1794	
	SOY	1794	

83

THE LABELS

NAME	DATES	LOCATION
LEMON	1794	
SOY	1794	
KETCHUP	1796	
SOY	1796	
TARRAGON	1796	
KAYANNE	1800	
CORATCH	1801	
GARLICK	1802	
JUNIPER	1802	
LEMON PIC	1803	
SOY	1804 SG	
ANCHOVIE	1804 SG	
TARRAGON	1805	
SOY	1805	
TARRAGON	1805	
TARRAGON	1806	
LEMON PICK	1808	
LEMON-PICK	1808	
FISH SAUCE	1808	
KETCHUP	1808	
ANCHOVY	1809	
CAYENNE	1809 SG	
SOY	1809 SG	
ANCHOVY	1810	
ANCHOVY	1810	
KETCHUP	1810	
SOY	1810	
173. ROBERTS, SAMUEL II	**1794-1834**	
CAYENNE	c.1830	
174. ROBERTS AND BELK	**1864-1901**	**SHEFFIELD**
READING	1877 G	
WORCESTER	1877 G	
175. ROBERTSON, JAMES	**1800-1825**	**EDINBURGH**
CAYENNE	1814	
176. ROBERTSON, WILLIAM	**1789-1800**	**EDINBURGH**
ANCHOVIE	c.1795	
177. ROBINS, JOHN	**1774-1801**	**LONDON**
CAYAN	1784	
CAYON	1784	
SOY	c.1785	
SOY	1796	
SOY	1796	

NAME	DATES	LOCATION
TARAGON	1798	
CAYENNE	1801	
178. SEAMAN, WILLIAM	**1818-1827**	**LONDON**
WORCESTER	1818	
HARVEY	1827	
179. SECKER, ROBERT	**1863**	**LONDON**
ANCHOVY	1863 Armorial	
CAYENNE	1863 Armorial	
HARVEY	1863 Armorial	
180. SHAW, CHARLES	**1846-1873**	**LONDON**
HARVEY	1869	
181. SIMPSON, WILLIAM	**1825-1855**	**BANFF**
SOY	c.1828	
182. SMILEY, WILLIAM	**1881-1887**	**LONDON**
ANCHOVY	1881	
CHILI	1881	
HARVEY	1881	
KETCHUP	1881	
WORCESTER	1887	
183. SMITH, BENJAMIN II	**1802-1818**	**LONDON**
KYAN	c.1807	
184. SMITH, BENJAMIN II AND JAMES III	**1809**	**LONDON**
KETCHUP	1809 SG	
185. SMITH, GEORGE II AND HAYTER, THOMAS	**1792-1796**	**LONDON**
SOY	c.1792	
ANCHOVY	c.1792	
KETCHUP	c.1792	
186. SMITH, JOHN	**1827-1855**	**DUBLIN**
CHILI	1841	
187. SMITH, SAMUEL WATTON	**1882-1897**	**BIRMINGHAM**
TOBASCO	1893	
188. SMITH, WILLIAM I	**1758-1781**	**LONDON**
SOY	c.1775	

THE LABELS

NAME	DATES	LOCATION
189. SMITH, TATE, HOULT and TATE	1824-1830	SHEFFIELD
CAYENNE	1824	
190. SNATT, JOSIAH	1797-1817	LONDON
QUIN	1797	
P. VINEGAR	1804	
ANCHOVY	1804	
KETCHUP	1806	
ANCHOVY	1806	
KYAN	1807	
KETCHUP	1807	
GARLICK	1809	
MADEIRA	1809	
CATSUP	1813	
191. STORER, GEORGE	1829-1845	LONDON
(see CHARLES REILY)		
192. STORY, JOSEPH WILLIAM	1809-1815	LONDON
(see WILLIAM ELLIOTT)		
193. STORR, PAUL	1800-1838	LONDON
KYAN	1816	
SOY	1816	
LEMON	1816	
ANCHOVY	1818	
CHILI	1818	
HARVEY	1818	
KYAN	1818	
SOY	1818	
TARRAGON	1818	
194. SUMMERS, WILLIAM	1863-1884	LONDON
FRENCH VINEGAR	1864 SG	
SALAD OIL	1864 SG	
HARVEY	1873	
CAYENNE	1879	
195. SUTTON, WILLIAM	1784-1796	LONDON
TARRAGON VINEGAR	c.1784	
196. TAITT, BENJAMIN	1784-1791	DUBLIN
ANCHOVY	–	
CHILI	–	
SOY	–	

NAME	DATES	LOCATION
197. TAYLEUR, JOHN	1775-1801	LONDON
CAYENNE VIN	–	
CUCUMBER VIN	–	
ELDER	–	
SOY	–	
TARRAGON	–	
KETCHUP	–	
CAYENNE	c.1785	
FINE HERBS	c.1785	
KETCHUP	–	
LEMON	–	
GARLICK	–	
TARRAGON	1789	
CAYENNE	1789	
QNS PICKLE	1791	
PORT	1792	
CYAN	1792	
KETCHUP	1792	
GARLICK	1792	
CAYENNE	1793	
CAYENNE	1794 SG	
SOY	1794 SG	
KETCHUP	1794 SG	
SOY	1794	
LEMON	1794	
TARRAGON	1795	
CAYENNE	1795	
SOY	1795	
KETCHUP	1795	
KETCHUP	1795	
CAYENNE	1796	
SOY	1798	
LEMON PICKLE	1798	
SAUCE R	1799	
198. TEARE, JOHN I	1790-1811	DUBLIN
"LABELS"	–	
199. TEARE, JOHN II	1787-1813	DUBLIN
"8 LABELS"	1811	
200. TEARE, JOHN III	1813-1861	DUBLIN
"LABELS"	–	
201. THEOBALDS, WILLIAM AND ATKINSON, ROBERT METCALF	1838-1840	LONDON
CHILI	1838	
CHILI	1840	

THE LABELS

NAME	DATES	LOCATION
202. **TRENDER, JAMES**	1793-1815	LONDON
CAYENNE	1813	
203. **TROBY, JOHN**	1792-1804	LONDON
CAYENNE	1793	
204. **TROBY, WILLIAM BAMFORTH**	1804-1821	LONDON
KETCHUP	1814	
KYAN	1814 Armorial	
205. **TWEEDIE, WALTER**	1768-1786	LONDON
ELDER	c.1780	
206. **T——, H——**	1895	LONDON
A.1	1895	
207. **UNITE, GEORGE**	1832-1861	BIRMINGHAM
HARVEY'S	1840	
TARRAGON VINEGAR	c.1845	
WALNUT CATSUP	c.1845	
READING	c.1845	
CHILI VINEGAR	1847	
TARRAGON VINEGAR	1859	
KETCHUP	1859	
208. **URQUHART, DUNCAN AND HART, NAPTHALI**	1791-1805	LONDON
KIAN	1791	
VINIGAR	1791	
SOY	1791	
209. **VALE, JABEZ**	1813-1828	BIRMINGHAM
ANCHOVY	1827	
210. **VERNON, NATHANIEL**	1802-1808	CHARLESTON, USA
LEMON	c.1805	
211. **WALLIS, THOMAS**	1806	LONDON
LEMON	1806	
SOY	1806	
ELDER	1806	
TERAGON	1806	
212. **WALSH, STEPHEN**	1750-1785	CORK AND DUBLIN
Powerscourt Cruet	c.1750	

NAME	DATES	LOCATION
213. **WALTHER, HERMAN JOHN**	1770	LONDON
TARRAGON	c.1770	
214. **WATSON, JOHN**	1795-1817	SHEFFIELD
HARVEY	1805	
215. **WELSHMAN, JAMES**	1813-1830	BATH, BRISTOL, EXETER and LONDON
KYAN	1816 (London)	
SOY	1816 (London)	
ELDER V^R	1819 (Exeter)	
READING	1819 (Exeter)	
SOY	1819 (Exeter)	
216. **WHITECROSS, WILLIAM**	1824-1840	ABERDEEN
HARVEY	c.1830	
READING	c.1830	
ANCHOVY	c.1830	
SOY	c.1830	
KETCHUP	c.1830	
217. **WHITFORD, SAMUEL AND GEORGE**	1802-1807	LONDON
CAYENNE	1802	
CATSUP	1802	
SAUCE ROYAL	1802	
SOY	1802	
CAYENNE	1802	
TARRAGON	1804	
218. **WHITFORD, SAMUEL II**	1801-1852	LONDON
SOY	1801	
SOY	1801	
SOY	1808	
CAYENNE	1809	
LEMON	1809	
SOY	1810	
ANCHOVY	1811	
ANCHOVY	1811	
CAYENNE	1811	
CYAN	1811	
CAYENNE	1815	
SOY	1815	
READING	1852	

THE LABELS

NAME	DATES	LOCATION
219. WHITTINGHAM, JOHN	1788-1820	LONDON
PINK	c.1788	
QUIN SAUCE	1788	
CORRATCH	1792	
SOY	1801	
TARRAGON VIN.	1810	
SOY	1820	
ANCHOVY	1820	
220. WHITWELL, WILLIAM AND BARBER, JAMES	1814-1823	YORK
(see JAMES BARBER)		
221. WILLIAMSON AND HORTON	1868-1871	LONDON
SOY	1869	
HARVEY	1869	
CATSUP	1869	
WORCESTER	1869	
222. WILLMORE, JOSEPH	1806-1834	BIRMINGHAM
PORT	c.1810	
S	1816	
E.A	1816	
E.S	1818	
C.V	1818	
H	1818	
T	1818	
R (Script)	1818	
G	1819	
CROWN SAUCE	1822	
CUCUMBER V	c.1822	
READING SAUCE	c.1822	
CHILI	1824	
CHILI VINEGAR	1824	
LEMON PICKLE	1824	
UNIVERSAL SAUCE	1824	
CUCUMBER	1825	
KATSHUP	1826	
OUDE SAUCE	1827	
BRIGHTON	1830	
OUDE SAUCE	1834	
CHILLI V	1838	
BRIGHTON	1838	
READING	1841	
223. WILLMORE, JOSEPH AND CO	1845-1856	BIRMINGHAM
FISH	1851	
224. WRIGHT, WILLIAM THOMAS AND DAVIES, FREDERICK	1864-1866	LONDON
WORCESTER	c.1866	
TARRAGON	c.1866	
225. W. GREENER AND CO.	1881	BIRMINGHAM
G	1881	
226. WOOD AND SONS	1850	BIRMINGHAM
BLACK	c.1850	
227. YAPP, JOHN AND WOODWARD, JOHN	1844-1874	BIRMINGHAM
ANCHOVY	1848	
ANCHOVY	1848	
RIEN QUI MANQUE	1848	
WORCESTER	1848	
CHILI VINEGAR	1850	
OIL	1850	
HARVEY	1856	
ANCHOVY	1856	
CHILI	1874	
CAYENNE	1874	
228. YOUNGE, SAMUEL AND CHARLES	1802-1810	SHEFFIELD
CAYENNE	1808	
229. ZIEGLER, ALEXANDER	1782-1795	EDINBURGH
RUE (or RUW)	1782	

Fig 94. *A redrawn original of 1788 taken from Denis Diderot's Encyclopedia, showing a die press for coinage, 1751. The Bateman workshop installed a steam engine around 1770.*

CHAPTER 6

THE MAKERS

THE HEADING DATES given after the maker's name are tentative and represent the maker's very approximate potential sauce label production period. Some overseas makers are included in the list. In Chapter 11 below there is mention of an American soy frame with labels noted in North Carolina. Unfortunately a number of Danish, Dutch, French and Swedish sauce labels are unmarked and separated from their soy frames thus hindering identification.

1. ISAAC AARON 1791-1793

Not much is known about this smallworker whose mark was entered in 1791 recording an address in Duke's Place, London. The attribution is certain (Grimwade 1102).

2. WILLIAM ABDY I 1786-1790

A known maker of wine-coasters and presumably of the occasional soy frame, he occupied premises off Noble Street in the City of London. Abdy also made attractive wine labels. He is the maker of the star designed sauce labels for SOY and CAYAN.

3. GEORGE WILLIAM ADAMS 1840-1881

G.W. Adams, whose family business was watch making, was not surprisingly a Freeman of the Clockmakers' Company. At the age of 30 he married the daughter of William and Mary Chawner at Islington in 1838. Mary (who had been widowed in 1834) took him into partnership in 1840 and then retired (or died) in the same year. Chawners' main productions during the period of his sole partnership (1840-1883) were spoons. However a wide range of table related items in silver were also made by this firm. Their "Canova" pattern dessert service was exhibited at the Great Exhibition of 1851 along with other items of table ware(1). Adams' firm made an OUDE sauce label in 1857 of rectangular shape with cut corners and a double reeded border.

4. STEPHEN ADAMS II 1813-1840

He was the son of Stephan Adams I, a maker of buckles and spoons. Stephen Junior entered his first mark as a plateworker in 1813 with a working address at St. Ann's Lane where his father had worked since 1764. In 1819 he made the QUIN label in the M.V. Brown Collection in the London Museum. He was also a maker of wine labels, usually rectangular and reeded. From 1825 he was working in Islington. He died in 1840.

5. JOSEPH ANGELL 1811-1831

Joseph Angel or Angell was an apprentice of Henry Nutting, but his brother John Angel was apprenticed to William Elliott, the well known sauce label maker in Warwick Lane. His workshop was at 55 Compton Street, Clerkenwell. He first entered his mark as a plateworker in 1811. He made a broad rectangular label for CAYENNE in 1814(2) and a label for Hy SAUCE in 1815. This probably stands for HARVEY'S SAUCE but it could possibly be for HENRY SAUCE. For the wine labels he made in 1816 to 1818 he favoured cast and chased designs using masks (bearded or leopard's), baskets of vine tendrils and bacchanalian figures. What a pity that he did not let this experience escape to his sauce label workbench.

6. JAMES ANSILL and STEPHEN GILBERT 1766-1772

Authority for this firm making sauce labels rests solely on the Wakelin Ledgers which can be perused in the Victoria and Albert Museum. John Wakelin and William Taylor kept "Workmens' Ledgers" showing dealings in sauce labels with other silversmiths. They would appear to have bought in some 76 labels from

THE MAKERS

Ansill and Gilbert and from Margaret Binley during the period 1766-1772. Volume III of the Ledgers contains an entry dated 22nd November 1766 for "6 small crescent soy labels". As they worked for Wakelin they did not have to register their own mark or marks. Stephen in fact had worked for Edward Wakelin from 1750, being apprenticed to him in 1752 and obtaining his Freedom from the Goldsmiths' Company in 1764.

7. JOHN ARNELL 1793

This London goldsmith is said to have worked from 1773 in Little Britain. A double reeded sauce label with rounded ends engraved for CAYENNE has been said to bear his mark and the date of 1793. Perhaps a better attribution might have been to Isaac Aaron.

8. JOSEPH ASH I 1801-1818

This little known smallworker had premises off Butchers' Hall Lane in the City of London. It is perhaps significant that his son was apprenticed to Joseph Biggs who in turn had been apprenticed to Robert Barker, the presumed son of the famous Susanna Barker of Gutter Lane. The attribution is certain (Grimwade 1104).

9. ASTON & SON 1857-1867

This Birmingham firm's mark appears on a CATSUP label of 1860.

10. JAMES ATKINS 1792-1815

In partnership with John Essex in 1791 and on his own from 1792, he specialised in making silver buckles at 12 Well Street, Cripplegate, until his death in 1815. In 1808 he made the KYAN label in the M.V. Brown Collection in the London Museum. He produced a range of designs such as the reeded octagonal (1801), the fretted scroll (1803) and the rectangular initial (1803). It appears that, unlike in the case of his widow Theodosia, he never entered a mark other than as a bucklemaker.

11. THEODOSIA ANN ATKINS 1815

She was the widow of James Atkins and made in 1815 three spectacular narrow long rectangular silver-gilt sauce labels.

12. THOMAS BANNISTER 1829-1836

He was a smallworker with an address at 68 John Street, Fitzroy Square, London.

13. JAMES BARBER and ROBERT CATTLE 1808-1813

John Prince of Hampston and Prince of York fame retired on 6th November 1807 leaving Robert Cattle on his own. On 1st January 1808 Robert announced that he had taken into partnership James Barber who had already "been in the same shop eight years" although he did not go on to explain that seven of these had been as an apprentice. The partnership was dissolved by mutual consent on 1st January 1814, Robert being desirous of taking up an entirely different career. Cattle and Barber produced a set of four sauce labels for HERVEY.S, KETCHUP, KYAN and SOY(3) to adorn the only soy frame they submitted for assay in 1809, of oblong shape, standing on four ball feet. The base is decorated with two bands of gadrooning.

14. JAMES BARBER and WILLIAM WHITWELL 1814-1823

William had for a number of years been an assistant in the firm of Cattle and Barber of York. He made the most of his increased status by marrying in 1816 the eldest daughter of the Governor of York Castle. He fell ill and died in 1823(4). This partnership produced a small rectangular label with rounded ends and double reeded borders engraved for SOY. A York Assay Duty Paid Book, covering the years 1805-1821, discloses that Barber and Whitwell submitted for assay in 1815 a "castor top and label". The firm's headed notepaper shows that they did their own engraving. They submitted several soy frames for assay and presumably made the sauce labels to go with them.

15. JAMES BARBER 1847-1857

After the parting of ways with William North in 1847 James worked on (whilst at the same time pursuing other activities) at 25-26 Coney Street, York, until his death aged 73 in March 1857.

16. SUSANNA BARKER 1778-1793

The first mark of Susanna (sometimes spelt "Susannah") seems to have been entered at Goldsmiths' Hall in London when she was working from 16 Gutter Lane, the premises formerly occupied by Margaret Binley. In the early 1790s it appears that she moved to 29 Gutter Lane – unless the street had been renumbered! She was probably Robert Barker's mother. She was a prolific maker of quality sauce labels. She made the CHILLI VIN and the SAUCE-ROY

THE MAKERS

for John Scofield's combined oil, vinegar and soy frame of 1789 in the Rotch Collection in the Victoria and Albert Museum. It has been said that no one could mount glass better(5). Scofield's workshop at 29 Bell Yard, Temple Bar, was in the area occupied by the glassmakers. His working dates were similar to Susanna's being 1776-1797. Susanna made a label engraved INDIA for Indian soy and in 1793 a label with the unusual title of FRENCH for French vinegar as we know from a label of this title made in Victorian times. Her labels were usually fully marked at from 1790. Her range of designs included ropework, the sunburst, eyes and ovals, the narrow rectangular, feathering and beading, the horseshoe, the eagle, the scroll, the fretted cut-out, the early escutcheon, bright cutting and the top and bottom shell. One of her finest soy labels is crescent-shaped, bright cut, with wrigglework border, engraved for LEMON with a central armorial. Her great skill and flair was recognised by William Beckford of Fonthill who entrusted her to make in 1784 in silver gilt for a silver gilt stand two flavoured vinegar cruet labels for ELDER and TARRAGON and two soy bottle labels for LEMON and SOY to supplement the craftsmanship again of John Scofield(6).

17. ROBERT BARKER 1793-1794

He entered his mark as a smallworker in 1793. In all probability he was the maker of the engraved CAYENNE fancy irregular shaped label with elaborate shell and scroll border in the Cropper Collection in the Victoria and Albert Museum(7). It is certainly one of the most interesting designs displayed. He is also the noted maker of a KETCHUP label engraved on its reverse with a winged horse armorial. He worked from 29 Gutter Lane, and address which clearly links him to Susanna Barker. He obviously also had an aristocratic clientele.

18. RICHARD BARKER 1808-1815

Richard was apprenticed to Charles Chesterman II in 1801 at 62 Fleet Market. What happend after thas is unclear. However a CAYENNE label of unusual design dated 1814 has been attributed to this maker. It is not clear concerning the basis of the attribution made.

19. EDWARD I, EDWARD II, JOHN and WILLIAM BARNARD 1829-1846

This partnership made a label for READING in 1829, the very year Edward Barnard the elder took into partnership his three sons Edward, John and William at Amen Corner, Paternoster Row, the home in London of the firm of Emes and Barnard.

20. EDWARD II, JOHN and WILLIAM BARNARD 1846-1851

Although Edward Barnard I retired in 1842, he remained a partner in the firm until 1846 as security for his investment of £6,000 in the firm. He died in 1855.

21. EDWARD II and JOHN BARNARD 1851-1868

This partnership lasted until the death of Edward II in 1868. The firm of Barnards, whose history goes back to Anthonly Nelme of the 1680s, still exists operating as a subsidiary of Padgett & Braham Limited.

22. WILLIAM BARRETT I 1771-1793

He entered his first mark as a smallworker in 1771 working in premises off Wood Street in the City of London. From 1777 to 1793 he had a shop at 50 Aldersgate Street.

23. GEORGE BASKERVILLE 1775-1794

In 1775 he went into partnership with Thomas Morley and presumably learnt all about label making. It was the expertise of this firm that Elizabeth Morley used after her husband's death in 1794 until 1814. He made a cruet frame in 1793, the same year as a label for LEMON PICKLE(8), which may therefore have adorned that cruet.

24. HESTER BATEMAN 1761-1790

Born around 1708, she married in 1732 John Bateman, a chain maker of limited means but of an educated family. Hester, however, could not it seems from documentary evidence sign her own name. They had six children, John, Letticia, Ann, Peter, William and Jonathan, living in the 1740s in Nixon's Square, Cripplegate, a centre for out-workers being just beyond the law of the City of London. In 1747 they moved to 107 Bunhill Row, a typical Georgian house in a prosperous street where workshops were developed at the rear. Letticia married Richard Clarke in 1754. John Bateman died in 1760, leaving the tools of his trade to Hester as was the custom. She registered her first mark in 1761. For the next thirteen years she organised in exemplary fashion the production of silverware which was sometimes passed on to other silversmiths for

THE MAKERS

retailing. So her mark was often overstamped. Women silversmiths seemed to excel at label making. There was no discrimination. Mrs Agas Harding entered her mark as early as 1513! The list of famous makers of silver includes Louisa Courtauld, Anne Tanqueray, Mary Pantin, Mary Deard, Sarah Holiday, Elizabeth Buteux (later Godfrey), Alice Sheene, Ann Smith, Dorothy Mills, Dorothy Langlands, Mary and Elizabeth Summer, Sara Buttall, Dorothy Sarbitt, Elizabeth Eaton, Dinah Gamon, Ann Robertson, Hanna Northcote, Ann Craig, Elizabeth Goodwin and Elizabeth Aldridge. Thus it was the custom to accept a widow who had worked with her husband for at least seven years as a craftswoman in her own right. Hester was assisted by her sons Peter (from 1761) and Jonathan (from 1769). Hester retired in 1790 and died four years later. She made the kidney shaped CAYON label which is in the London Museum. She organised the making of many frames catering for sauces. It is not known from whom she purchased the bottles. She certainly made good use of technical developments mixed with a sense of style which make her labels outstanding.

25. PETER and ANNE BATEMAN 1791-1799

Peter and Jonathan took over from Hester, and may have made labels for the canoe shaped cruet made by them in 1790, but unfortunately Jonathan died of cancer in 1791 leaving everything to his wife Ann (nee Dowling) who was as able as her mother-in-law in the art and science of organising silversmiths. So Peter and Ann carried on the tradition of Hester at 108 Bunhill Row. A QUIN label bearing their mark dated 1799 is in the Castle Museum in York.

26. PETER, ANN and WILLIAM BATEMAN I 1800-1805

Ann's second son William was taken into partnership in 1800. Then Ann retired in 1805. The Weed Collection had a KYAN label said to be by one of the Bateman family(9).

27. PETER and WILLIAM BATEMAN 1805-1815

Peter probably retired from this partnership in 1815. A number of eight bottle soy frames were made by this partnership. New College, Oxford, is said to possess three such frames each dated 1810, with labels of the same date by Peter and William, affixed by silver wires.

28. WILLIAM BATEMAN I 1815-1827

He took livery of the Goldsmiths' Company in 1816, joined the Court in 1828, and became Prime Warden in 1836. He ran the family business alone until joined by his son William II in 1822 upon completion of his seven years apprenticeship to his father.

29. WILLIAM BATEMAN II and DANIEL BALL 1840-1843

William entered his mark in 1827. He was the great grandson of Hester Bateman. He made a number of wine labels. A sauce label made by this partnership, which manufactured items for Rundall, Bridge and Company, is recorded as being large, rectangular shaped with cut corners, double reeded, and engraved for CHILLY VINEGAR for a tall, narrow necked, wide bottomed Victorian vinegar decanter made in 1840.

30. JAMES BEEBE 1811-1837

He entered his first mark in 1811. From 1827 he worked at 65 Red Lion Street, Clerkenwell. In 1829 he made a label for ESCAVECHI(10). Around 1837 he made some oblong labels engraved for TOMATO sauce and for WORCESTERSHIRE, the new Lea and Perrins sauce. These labels had repouse borders of bold scroll work and are in the Cropper Collection(11). He also made a fine heavy cast pair of labels for HARVEY and CHILI. Quite clearly, therefore, he was a maker of good quality sauce labels with finely worked borders, especially in the use of intricate flower and foliage designs.

31. SAMUEL BELLINGHAM 1806

A KETCHUP label is said to bear his second mark entered as a smallworker in May 1806, when he was working in St. Martins le Grand. The label's inidividuality of appearance is said to reflect his ability as a gold worker.

32. RICHARD BIDLAKE 1755-1773

Sometimes recorded as Birdlake (Jackson) or Bridlake (Simon Hunt, Exeter Museum), it is considered that the better attribution is to Bidlake (Timothy Kent). He was a fine craftsman from Plymouth in Devon. The attribution does, however, seem a little unlikely.

33. RICHARD BINLEY 1745-1764

He was apprenticed to Sandylands Drinkwater, a specialist maker of wine labels. He obtained his freedom in 1739 and was mentioned in the parish

THE MAKERS

records of St. Vedast in 1745. His mark, like Drinkwater's appears to be found only on wine labels suggesting that he too was a specialist. Small labels were not marked at this time. His workshop was near the South-East corner of Gutter Lane. He developed his own style and it is on this ground that a pair of unmarked crescent OIL and VINEGAR decanter bottle labels with feather edging have been attributed to him. It could even be that Richard bought out Sandylands in 1761 when he retired from being Prime Warden of the Goldsmiths' Company and moved into 16 Gutter Lane. No sauce labels are known marked by Sandylands (c.1703-1776). These oil and vinegar frame labels fit exactly around, following the curavture, the large size oil and vinegar frame bottles in use 1720-1760 with pull off silver mounted caps, displayed on a two bottle frame.

34. MARGARET BINLEY 1764-1778

Margaret, thought to be Richard's widow, made labels very like those above attributed to Richard Binley. She also worked from 16 Gutter Lane. In the past her first name has been said to be Mary but this is incorrect. She also seems to have been a specialist maker of silver labels. In 1767 she made sauce labels for Edward Wakelin and John Parker. A silver manufacturer, some of whose records survive in the Kingsteignton Wallpaper Book(12), could have been a maker of sauce labels. He supplied a Mrs. Binley, who could have been Margaret or a relative, on the 12th December 1771 with "5 narrow labels" weighing 20.5 dwt at a cost of 7s 6d. Wine labels usually weighed between 6 and 8 dwt per label. The supply cost of a sauce label was about 1s 6d per label. Unfortunately no rate per ounce was stated in the Book unlike, for example, 7s 2d for sauce boats, 6s 3d for tankards and 5s 6d for a cream pail and ladle, being the charge out rates for Thomas Hemming. A label of hers exists datable to around 1770 entitled KETCHUP but as it carries maker's mark only the date is conjectural. A later label for KAYON is one of a set of four in the collection of Sheffield Museum(13). Starting with the plain shaped design she seems to have promoted, like Richard it is suggested, the use of feathered borders. She was one of the earliest makers of vinegar decanter labels such as those engraved for GARLICK and ELDER to be hung around slightly squarish shaped bottles with lip pourers which were often placed in Old Sheffield Plate vinegar decanter frames of this period. She then developed her famous kidney shaped label and then the shallow crescent such as that for TARRAGON of the 1770s. All her productions were quality labels and mostly of good weight. Where labels were made somewhat lighter than her norm they made up for this by having possibly excessive or at least complex decoration. A crescent shape CAYON, for example, has as a border four rows of differing designs. The latest reference to her work would appear to be in 1778 at 16 Gutter Lane in which year it seems Susanna Barker took over the business as a going concern and maintained the specialism.

35. THOMAS BLAGDEN 1798-1817

In 1798 he was working in Sheffield at Nursery Walk. In 1808 he formed Thomas Blagden & Company

Fig 94. Rare Sheffield Soy sauce Frame with original bottles and labels by Thomas Blagden, 1817.

operating from White Rails at Bridgehouses in Sheffield. The Company sponsored a four bottle soy frame in 1817 (Fig. 94) complete with four fully marked soy labels of that year. It is rare indeed for the original labels to have been kept with their original silver frame. Many soy frames were made of Old Sheffield Plate. However the bottle labels were generally made of silver because it was hardly worth the trouble of plating small labels. Some OSP examples do exist but they are rare. On the other hand OSP wine labels were commonly made, for example by N. Smith & Co in 1810 and by Watson and Bradbury in 1815, as can be seen from the illustrated trade catalogues of the period. Thomas Blagden & Company became Blagden, Hodgson & Company when Thomas Blagden took in Thomas Hodgson, Samuel Kirkby, Joseph Elliott and John Woollen as partners. The firm eventually was taken over by Hawksworth, Eyre and Company in 1833.

36. S. BLANCKENSEE & SON LIMITED 1887-1952

Founded in 1826 and incorporated in 1887, Blankensee's was a large silver and jewellery firm operating out of premises in Great Hampton Street in Birmingham. It reproduced antique silver designs, taking over Nathan and Hayes who were specialists in this area. It was itself taken over after the end of World War II by the Albion Chain Company Limited which then discontinued the silver business.

37. WILKES BOOTH 1787-1813

He carried on, in later times with his son John, a smallworker's business at 8 Albemarle Street. His first mark was entered as a snuffer maker in 1787.

38. MATTHEW BOULTON 1762-1809

He may have been responsible, but this seems rather unlikely, for the production in the early 1770s of the enclosed crescent, a design which is special for sauce labels. If so he may well have copied the design from Heming, whose maker's mark has appeared on it. The authority for the proposition is the marked TARRAGON label in the Dent Collection, the reverse of which was not pictured in his book(14). A date of around 1780 was ascribed to it. Whilst the MB mark observed by Dent was most likely to have been the mark of Margaret Binley, the one design of Richard Binley that she does not appear to have copied is that of the nearly enclosed crescent. In the early Volumes of the Wine Label Journal the mark MB was attributed either to Bock or to Boulton. So Dent would not have had Margaret Binley in mind when making his attribution. Born in 1728, Boulton was in partnership with his father of the same name making buttons from 1749 until his father's death in 1759. In 1762 he studied Sheffield plating, always being interested in innovation. He opened the celebrated Soho Works factory in 1764. He operated under various names. Boulton and Fothergill, famous for their drapery festoon design with riband terminals, made broad open crescent sauce labels for SOY and LEMON PICKLE with big link chains and five bold marks on the reserve for MB, IF, lion passant, date letter capital D and the still crisp Birmingham anchor. From 1780 it was Boulton and Wyatt, from about 1785 it was Boulton and Smith and later on it was Matthew Boulton and Plate Company. He achieved fame in many ways including being both a Fellow of the Royal Society and a Fellow of the Royal Society of Arts. His firm was making blank labels fully marked in Birmingham from 1773 onwards for others to finish off – thus demonstrating the profitability of mass production. He used the die-press process (Fig 93) for producing intricate and pleasing designs. Thus Matthew Boulton and Plate Company made decorative escutcheons for HARVEY and SOY in 1826 of unusual design appropriate for fashionable "Regency style" labels.

39. MATTHEW BOULTON and JOHN FOTHERGILL 1765-1780

During the period 1768-1773, Boulton and Fothergill had their marvellous pieces assayed in Chester with their famous "B&F" arranged in a rectangular punch with a crown mark stamped on either side. Boulton was the promoter of the concept of establishing an assay office in Birmingham. The Bill to authorise this received the Royal Assent on 28th May 1773. Boulton and Fothergill sent in a range of silverware for first assay comprising a parcel weighing 841 oz. Their second parcel contained a "bottle ticket" but as this weighed 10 dwt it was probably a wine label. They made a soy frame in 1776 which might have housed their sauce labels of that date for SOY and LEMON PICKLE.

40. MATTHEW BOULTON & PLATE COMPANY 1810-1830

The company registered its mark after Matthew Boulton's death in 1809. The Company had been formed much earlier. There are accounts extant for the years 1793 and 1805 showing a substantial turnover involving a wide variety of silver articles all manufactured at the Soho Works. Five soy labels were made in 1826, 1827 and 1828.

41. THOMAS BOWEN II 1797

A smallworker, who moved from 19 Albion Buildings and later 48 Lombard Street to 5 Naked Boy Court, Ludgate Hill in 1782, Thomas Bowen made the KYAN spoon in a four soy bottle copper (dressed with leather) frame, the bottles having engraved titles for KYAN, SOY, FISH.S and KETCHUP. The mark used on the slimline spoon fixed to the glass bottle stopper is Grimwade 2692 with its distinctive "T" (See Fig. 116).

42. FRANCIS BOWER 1835-1853

He was a gold worker, his mark being entered on 11th December 1835. He worked at 8 Pollen Street, Hanover Square, London(15).

43. ROBERT BOWERS 1782-1829

Robert Bowers was a working goldsmith member of the Chester Goldsmiths' Company, with a place of business in Eastgate Row, Chester. He is recorded as working closely with George Lowe. His other colleagues in the Company were at this time the Walkers and the last of the Richardsons. He sent 24 labels for assay in 1797 and 36 labels for assay in 1801(16).

44. JOHN BOYER 1772-1794

Like some other label makers, he appeared as a button maker in the Parliamentary Report of 1773. His place of business was in Horseshoe Alley in Middle Moonsfields.

45. RICHARD BRITTON 1812-1842

Presumably he learnt to make labels when apprenticed to George Burrows II from 1st January 1800 to 4th March 1806. Although his principal business was making spoons, he did occasionally produce a label.

46. ALICE and GEORGE BURROWS II 1807-1818

This partnership of mother and son operated at the beginning of the 19th century from 14 Red Lion Street, Clerkenwell, and achieved fame through Mr. Weed's purchase of 13 of their labels at Canterbury including a QUIN'S SAUCE (large size) and ZOOBDITTY MATCH (small size) all dated 1807. They may well have made the frames to go along with these labels since in 1817 they made an oblong 7 bottle soy frame on paw and foliage feet with cherubs masks and foliage decoration.

47. WILLIAM BURWASH AND RICHARD SIBLEY 1805-1812

Richard Sibley was a notable silversmith. Arthur Grimwade's opinion is that his work whether alone or in partnership is of a high standard of design and execution in a restrained key of "Regency taste". Perhaps the labels of 1808 were displayed on two six-bottle soy frames of quality construction.

48. ALEXANDER CAMERON 1818-1847

He was an active Dundee silversmith with premises at 78 High Street Dundee. He had his wares assayed in Newcastle as well as Edinburgh as well as marked in the Burgh. It was compulsory to have goods assayed in Edinburgh after 1835. A crescent shaped HARVEY SAUCE with wide points was assayed in Edinburgh, due to the legislation, and after 1839 because it bears the Victorian duty mark, the punch for which only became available in Edinburgh in 1839, and a thistle but no date letter being a small item.

49. ROBERT CATTLE and JAMES BARBER 1808-1813

The death of George Cattle in 1807 and the retirement in the same year of John Prince led Robert on the 1st January 1808 to take into partnership his former apprentice James Barber who had only just finished his apprenticeship. Their labels were probably not of a very high standard. Three were included in the Sledmere Sale of March 1979 by Sotheby's, purchased originally around 1810 by Sir Mark Masterman-Sykes, the famous bibliophile. They were very ordinary reeded oblongs, somewhat crude in execution.

50. COLIN HEWER CHESHIRE 1865-1927

The Birmingham silversmith was listed in 1878 as a maker of labels, along with ink-stands, muffineers, napkin rings, salts, toast racks, trowels and vinaigrettes(17). He lived in Handsworth, but his workshop was at 3 Northampton Street, Birmingham.

51. WILLIAM CONSTABLE 1806-1820

Constable followed in the tradition and standards set by Edward Livingstone in Dundee, which was an

THE MAKERS

important trading centre and exporter. Jackson's "Trade and Shipping of Dundee" discloses that in 1830 some 37 dozen snuff boxes were shipped to Quebec. Dundee ranked with Edinburgh, Glasgow and Aberdeen as a producer of wine labels, but produced very fine, if not some of the best, sauce labels.

52. SEBASTIAN CRESPEL 1820-1836

He was James Crespel's son, apprenticed to his brother Honorias in 1801 and turned over to Robert Garrard in 1806. He made a neck ring label engraved for "CHILI" in London in 1824 following the example set by Robert Garrard. His workshop was in Haymarket(18) at 11 James Street, but he moved to Leicester Square in 1836.

52A. CRESPEL & PARKER 1861-1875

Andrew (Free in 1846), the son of Sebastian Crespel who died on 25 August 1858, carried on business after his father's death on his own account at 1 James Street, Haymarket, London. In 1861 he took in Thomas Parker as a partner and the firm was styled Crespel & Parker. Crespel died on 10 March 1875. As plate-workers the firm specialised in silver for the dining and tea tables. The 1861 labels have hinged loops.

53. THOMAS, JAMES and NATHANIEL CRESWICK 1853

The firm was founded by Joseph Creswick in about 1777 at West Bar Green, Sheffield. At some time they moved to Queen's Street. In 1810, the partnership consisted of Thomas and James and in 1819, Nathaniel was brought in and the new premises established at Paternoster Row until 1863 when the firm moved to Sycamore Street.

54. JAMES and NATHANIEL CRESWICK 1853-1855

A set of six silver gilt sauce labels beautifully turned out, of fine quality and dated 1853 was produced by the partnership. It is no wonder that this firm won a prize medal at the Great Exhibition of 1851. The 1853 mark, although punched JC with NC, was in fact registered under the partnership of TJ and N Creswick.

55. E. CROPLEY & CO. 1819-1824

The firm of E. Cropley & Co. of Calcutta made between the years 1819 and 1824 two castors with applied rectangular labels with cut corners both engraved for "SUGAR", having gadrooned borders. These are illustrated on Page 11 of Wilkinson's "Indian Colonial Silver" and can be seen in the Victoria & Albert Museum(19). Mr Wilkinson noted these as being uncommon and only applied to castors made by this particular Firm. Usually, Calcutta Silversmiths engraved castors in condiment sets without exception using capital letters with labels for "SALT" (21 recorded by Wilkinson) and for "PEPPER" (24 recorded by Wilkinson) and in one case (by Hamilton & Co.) for "S" "S" "K" and "P" (probably standing for "Sugar" "Salt" "Kyan" and "Pepper").

56. RICHARD CROSSLEY 1782-1816

The RC punch (Grimwade 2288) can easily be confused with that of Robert Clarke (Grimwade 2287) but there are no other candidates! Furthermore, Richard Crossley died in April 1815 (Griwade page 480) so the attribution is dubious unless his widow or successor continued to use his punch in 1816. Crossley was a specialist spoonmaker but his eleventh mark registered in 1812 indicates "plateworker".

57. WILLIAM and PATRICK CUNNINGHAM 1776-1803

These Edinburgh makers utilised an unusual spelling of "CAYENN" on a rectangular label of about 1797 in the Marshall Collection(20). They made spoons, a ewer and basin, cream jugs and Communion cups for Tulliallan, Symington and Dunlop churches.

58. THOMAS DANIEL 1775-1778

Thomas Daniel (or Daniell), son of Jabez Daniel (or Daniell), was one of the earliest makers of soy frame labels. His father Jabez was, like Robert Piercy, apprenticed to Samuel Wood who himself came of a line of specialist caster-makers. Jabez made one of the earliest known soy frames dated 1760 in conjunction with Stephen Walsh who provided silver mounts to the two soy and the two vinegar bottles (illustrated in Fig 110). Unfortunately the silver pepper is missing, replaced by a glass bottle(21). The crest on the frame is identical to the crest on the bottles. At a sale at Christie's on the 14th October 1870 (lot 22) a beautiful small circular four bottle Soy frame made by Thomas and dated 1777 was sold together with four labels, three of those bearing the lion and makers mark matching those on the Soy frame. Certainly his

THE MAKERS

firm was well established. Thomas advertised his London Silver Plate Manufactury at the Silver Lion, 20 Foster Lane (opposite Goldsmith's Hall) as having been "carried on with his late father from upwards of 50 years". Prior to 1781, however, the business had been carried on from 10 Carey Lane from about 1749. The first six listed labels are all square shapes. CAYAN is a beaded oval.

59. SAMUEL DAVENPORT 1786-1794

He seems to have operated as a plateworker from 15 Lime Street London from 1786-1794. Mr Whitworth illustrated his rectangular label with reeded edge for SOY c.1790 in 3 WLJ 115. He went into partnership with Edward Davenport in 1794 and his son was apprenticed to William Seaman in 1809.

60. FREDERICK DAVIES and WILLIAM THOMAS WRIGHT 1864-1866

From premises in Oxford Street, London, they made a variety of items of smallwork in silver mainly for retailers (see Culme page 499 for details where their financial problems are highlighted).

61. THOMAS EDWARDS 1825-1830

Eley's father may have been William Eley of Eley and Fearn fame. He may have been related to C. Eley whose dates are 1826 to 1840 according to Jackson and W. Eley whose dates according to Jackson were 1826 to 1830 and who died in 1841. There was also a J. Eley making silver between 1820 and 1839. A sauce (or perhaps a cordial) label by T. E. entitled PEPPERMINT is in the Cropper Collection dated 1825(22). In 1826, T. E. made an unusual set of four veined vine leaf wine labels. Grimwade attributes T. E. to Thomas Edwards, who, significantly, was apprenticed to John Robins and this would therefore seem to be the better attribution. The famous entwined dolphins (a crest) ANCHOVY label has been attributed to Thomas Eley, but in this work is attributed to Thomas Edwards.

62. WILLIAM ELLIOTT and JOSEPH WILLIAM STORY 1809-1815

William Elliott was probably the son of the William Elliott practising in Warwick Lane in the late 18th Century, operating from premises in Oxford Street from 1805. In 1809 he appears to have gone into partnership with J. W. Story working at 25 Compton Street, Clerkenwell. A number of sauce labels were made eg. a KYAN in 1809 and a pleasing HERVY in 1812 in the Cropper Collection(23). The Cropper Collection also has the exquisite rare shell SOY and ANCHOVY made by Story and Elliott in 1815(24). A wine label is said to bear the Story and Elliott mark and date letter for 1829-30 but this must be inaccurate. William Elliott also practised on his own account, entering two marks alone in 1813 at the same address where he remained until at least the beginning of 1825. The 1813 ANCHOVY label is designed as a shell.

63. WILLIAM ELLIOTT 1795-1830

Two marks were entered for William Eaton in 1813 (WE in oblong punch one with and one without a dot). A Brandy label exists dated 1812, the mark WE in oblong punch with a dot. William Elliott at this time was in partnership with J. W. Story and remained in that partnership certainly until 1815. Perhaps labels attributed to William Elliott may sometimes be properly attributed to William Eaton. Who made the Whisky of 1821 and Gin of 1827? Who made the oval pierced for Port with chased scrolls, borders of leafage, surmounted by a mask in 1814 and the broad rectangular, gadrooned, with shell and foliage corners, pierced for Sparkling Champagne in 1830? The same style, quality and weight is found in sauce labels. There are two beautiful sets of sauce labels dated 1828, each label very heavy with an intricate shell and gadrooned pattern. The Cropper Collection has a fine VINEGAR label dated 1827(25). Eaton appears to have abandoned his oblong punch after September 1828. Elliott's marks appear to have been substantially larger in size to Eaton's marks. Elliott always has a centre pellet. Eaton's pellet after 1824 is at the base. There is, nevertheless, room for confusion and debate on sylistic grounds, but the better attribution as a label maker is to William Elliott (Grimwade 3107) rather than to William Eaton (1812-1830) (Grimwade 3105c).

64. JOHN EMES 1796-1808

John Emes, although in partnership with Henry Chawner (who made wine labels) from 1796, undertook work on his own account with silver labels. His firm was apparently the forerunner of the famous Edward Barnard & Sons. Fig. 92 shows his soy frame of 1804.

THE MAKERS

Fig 95. Boat-shaped soy frame by John Emes, London, 1804, with double-reeded oval labels by John Rich for WOODS SAUCE, GARLIC VINEGAR, JAPAN SOY and CAYENNE PEPPER, for which the silver gilt spoon was used.

65. REBECCA EMES and EDWARD BARNARD 1808-1829

Rebecca was probably the widow of John Emes (see above). Edward had been apprenticed to Charles Wright and subsequently to Thomas Chawner. He became a Liveryman in 1811, having in effect acquired the Emes' business at Amen Corner in 1808 and began to build up a famous firm of platemakers.

66. JAMES ERSKINE 1792-1818

This famous silversmith from Aberdeen was proud of his work. His makers mark was stamped on the face of GOOSE-BERRY which, being small, was probably a sauce label rather than a cordial label. He was responsible for the rare set of five curved plain (as was usual in Scotland) narrow rectangular labels with interesting titles for SAUCE A LA MILITAIRE, SAUCE A LA SUISSE, FISH SAUCE, CAMP SAUCE and SAUCE BLANCHE(26).

67. GEORGE FERRIS 1817-1832

Two labels for "SOY" and "KETCHUP" appeared in Sotheby's catalogues for 1969 and 1970. Ferris sent in a total of 43 wine labels for assay in Exeter in 1817,

THE MAKERS

1818, 1819, 1820, 1822, 1825, 1826 and 1830 (see 6 WLJ 35, Table of Wine Label Production 1783-1876). Curiously, there were two silversmiths working in Fore Street, Exeter with the same name. George Ferris Senior was admitted in 1806 and George Ferris Junior in 1812. Both became Wardens of the Exeter Goldsmiths' Company (see for further details Patrick Gaskell-Taylor's excellent paper reproduced at 6 WLJ 30-49).

68. HENRY FLAVELLE I 1819-1837

He was a jeweller, watchcase maker and engine turner who probably turned his hand to making labels at 17 Leicester Street, Dublin from 1819 to 1837. His son was admitted as a Freeman in 1837 with premises in Eustace Street and was elected Warden from 1843 to 1845 of The Wardens and Company of Goldsmiths of Our City of Dublin (chartered in 1637 under this title). He retired c.1870. To add to the confusion a Henry E. Flavelle I (c.1845 – c.1863) and Henry Flavelle II (c.1843 – c.1847) were silversmiths in D'Olier Street. It is therefore not possible to ascribe the mark HF to any particular silversmith in later years. Labels sometimes carry the retailer's mark of "LAW".

69. GUSTAF FOLCKER

He was the Swedish maker of Elf Anchovies and Mushroom Ketchup in 1826.

70. J. FOLLIOT 1790-1800

Possibly the maker in Madras (or Mauritius) of "Oude's Sauce" (c.1790), which also bears the French 'poinçon de titre' (c.1800), see 9 WLJ 41.

71. JAMES FRAY 1813-1842

He began life as a spoonmaker with premises at 39 Bride Street, Dublin. He was admitted to the Freedom of the Goldsmiths' Company in 1829, being then described as a large plateworker. He was elected Warden in the year 1842. He died in 1843. His mark is a clear and bold IF with no pellet in a rectangular punch with clipped corners as shown on a plate in the Dublin Assay Office. Irish makers of sauce labels are somewhat rare. The attribution of a CATSUP label (27) to Joshua Franklin appears in the Register of the Cropper Collection. It has no date letter but the King's Head is in a shield which was used between 1809 and 1820. It is stamped "WEST" (which presumably is a retailer's mark of Matthew West) as were the examples given in Jackson on Page 614 by James Keeting in 1799 and by James Fray in 1819. The makers mark is very similar to that used by James Fray in 1819 and again 1832 where he is correctly described as "Fray" (see Jackson Page 615), and similar to that on the Shrub label (1801) illustrated in Sotheby's Catalogue (No.51) for 4th March 1971.

72. C.F. 1820-1830

C.F. was a member of the Jersey Guild making silver in the 1820's. He was recorded by Richard Mayne in "Channel Islands Silver" (1985) (at page 52) as "name unknown". Channel Islands silver is comparatively rare. Only 14 lots appeared in the catalogues of Christie's during the four seasons of auction sales 1969-1973. There was apparently no assay office in the islands, so local marks were used without systematic recording. The islands benefited from the Huguenot influx following the Edict of Nantes. Pieces tend to be of good weight and high standard. At the turn of the 18th Century, inspired by this tradition and using the special "J" mark, Jacques Quesnel, Charles William Quesnel, John le Gallais, Thomas De Gruchy, George Helier Hamon, C.J. (name not traced) and C.F. (name not traced) were producing fine silver. Thus, the set of four rare Soy labels made about 1820 by C.F. engraved for KETCHUP, READING, WORCESTER and SOY were weighty and well finished. The standard in Jersey was in fact the same as in England. The Jersey Code of Laws, 1771, prescribes that "Silversmiths shall follow the English standard of alloy and are to put their mark on each piece of their work". C.F. might be the maker of the wine-label for GENEVA illustrated in 4 WLJ 7. There is a long top to the letter F.

73. JOSEPH FULTON 1838-1860

Little is known about this Bristol maker apart from the fact that he made medals and a "soy stand" and so have made soy labels to go with the stand.

74. JANE GALLANT 1760-1780

She was a small worker using a maker's mark in script and possibly the maker of a "Vale of Aylesbury" label in London. The "Vale of Aylesbury" illustrated in 5 WLJ 104 is plated and unmarked.

75. ROBERT GARRARD I 1792-1818

In 1792 he joined up with John Wakelin (having worked with the Wakelins for a time) to form the firm of Wakelin and Garrard still using the premises of 31 Panton Street whose records go back to 1735. In 1793

THE MAKERS

his eldest son (Robert) was born. John died in 1802 and Robert ran the firm on his own account until his death in 1818 when his famous son (with his two brothers James and Sebastian) took over. From a billhead it is apparent that the Wakelins were Royal Goldsmiths – an honour which fell to this famous son also in 1830. Robert Garrard (the Elder) made neck-ring sauce labels engraved LEMON (Lot 276 Christie's 26th July 1972), ANCHOVY, CAYENNE and KETCHUP all in 1816, three similar labels in 1817 and a CAVICHE label in 1806. He also made neck-rings for wine labels Champagne and Hock (1811) – a contrast to his later opulent lion mask of 1816 and his earlier work copying the Bateman style of the crescent enclosing a crest. The first four listed labels undoubtedly form a set.

76. ROBERT GARRARD II 1818-1860
His first mark as a plate worker was entered at the age of 25 in 1818 upon the death of his father. He became Master of the Grocers' Company in 1853 and died in 1881. His firm was appointed Goldsmiths to the King in 1830.

77. JOHN GILBERT 1876-1877
The mark struck on WORCESTER (No 411 in the Marshall Collection) was used from October 1876 to March 1877. In that year John Gilbert incorporated his business with limited liability. This Birmingham silversmith founded a very successful firm of manufacturers.

78. JOSEPH GLENNY 1792-1821
His first incuse mark as a watch case maker was entered on 24th October 1792 with an address at 13 Old Street Square, London. He moved in 1800 to 22 Charles Square, Hoxton and in 1804 to Clerkenwell where he lived at various addresses. From 1804 it was at 20 Red Lion Street, then in 1816 at 6 Badger Yard, 1818 at 23 St John's Square and 1821 at 21 Wynyatt Street. It is possible that he bought in the superb die pressed ANCHOVY sauce label, marked by him in London in 1819, from Mathew Boulton's firm in Birmingham. The design is intricate, such as can only be produced by a die-press. On the other hand the only other sauce label noted with a design which includes vine leaves and bunches of grapes is cast, hallmarked on its face in the manner of Paul Storr, and made by Charles Reily and George Storer in London in 1830. Glenny's design shows at the top, centre, an exotic shell, surrounded by flowers and exotic fruits including pineapples. Below is a vine with bunches of luscious grapes. Some 850 or so makers used incuse makers' marks. It seems that Glenny and perhaps Teare were the only sponsors of sauce labels to do so. Wine label makers using incuse marks include Edward Thomason in Birmingham, John Teare in Dublin and Mark Hinchsliffe in Dumfries. Although categorised in the Registers as a casemaker, Glenny would not have been confined to making watch cases. Famous sauce label makers such as James Atkins and John Rich were shown in the Registers as bucklemakers.

79. HUGH GORDON 1770
The attribution to Fortrose rests on the single key of St Benedict shown on the 18th Century burgh arms being adopted as a town mark. The records of this Royal Burgh were lost when the cellars of the Town Hall were flooded(28). The attribution to Hugh Gordon rests on a directory of 1770, supported by a contemporary map of the Green at Fortrose showing premises marked "silversmith". His labels are illustrated. They have a unique method of attachment using a flexible wire which as it were clips onto the soy bottle. Gordon also made flatware of good quality.

80. PHILIP GRIERSON 1816-1823
It is believed that Philip Grierson, having started off on his own, was in partnership with Luke Frazer Newlands from 1810 to 1816, that Luke went on his own until 1820 when he took in his son James and that Luke retired in 1823. Philip was one of the Petitioners for the Private Act of Parliament setting up the Glasgow Assay Office in 1819.

81. HAMILTON and INCHES 1880-1910
This famous Edinburgh firm entered its first mark in 1880 and further marks in 1884, 1890 and 1899. There was still a demand for sauce labels in the Edwardian era. YORKSHIRE sauce or relish was very popular in 1909 and a label of this date and title made by this firm is in the Marshall Collection(29).

82. HAMPSTON & PRINCE 1784-1794
This York firm made a kidney-shaped label for LEMON c.1784/7 with punched edging. The firm is also known to have made wine labels, for example, those dated 1780 entitled "Champaigne" and "Moselle" which are broad rectangular with cut

THE MAKERS

corners, supported on a kind of menu holder and attached to a ring which has an unusual sort of spring opening which, presumably, clips round the top of a bottle. These wine labels are on display in the Treasury Museum under York Minster.

83. W. HARWOOD & CO 1801-1826

This Sheffield firm with premises in Howard Street first entered its mark in 1801 (Bradbury Page 481 – not recorded in Jackson). A plain narrow rectangular sauce label engraved for "READING" was made by this firm in 1811 bearing full Sheffield marks.

84. JONATHAN HAYNE 1808-1845

He registered a large number of marks of various sizes and had several apprentices and was Prime Warden in 1843. With such a range of output, it is not surprising to find that soy labels were included.

85. THOMAS HAYTER 1805-1816

Thomas Hayter was apprenticed to George Smith at 4 Huggin Lane off Wood Street in the City of London. So it is not surprising to find him in partnership with George Smith II until 1805. In 1816 he took his son George Hayter into partnership. He died in 1840. See also Smith and Hayter, below.

86. THOMAS HEMING 1745-1783

According to his trade card dateable to c.1770 in the Heal Collection he was appointed Goldsmith to His Majesty working from the Kings Arms in Bond Street facing Clifford Street. The trade card illustrates his wares and shows that he made what could be pickle frames. His working dates appear to be 1745 to 1783, starting up near Piccadilly. He was the founder of the famous firm of Messrs Hemming & Co Ltd. In about 1770 he made the attractive CARRACHE label in the Cropper Collection(30). The decoration is particularly fine. He held his appointment as Principal Goldsmith to the King until 1782. This label is of the same quality as his heavy cast design (with his 1745 mark) surmounted by a goat's head and labelled "Claret" (illustrated in 9 WLJ 33). His mark on a silver-gilt wine label is shown at A in 9 WLJ 263, being unregistered (Grimwade 3828).

87. ROBERT HENNELL I 1763-1811

Robert operated from 16 Foster Lane during the years of 1769-1791 and then at 11 Foster Lane. He made much fine silver especially coasters. His single mark mainly used 1773 to 1789 has an ovalish frame. In 1791 he made a six bottle soy frame which was sold as Lot 47 at Christie's on the 12th April 1972. There were six labels with slightly unusual titles including RED VINEGAR but which were unmarked. Five of the labels would appear to be of the early 1790's period.

88. SAMUEL HENNELL and ROBERT HENNELL I 1802-1811

Samuel was born in 1778, the son of Robert Hennell I, and made free by patrimony in 1800. He first entered his mark as third partner to his father and brother David II in 1802 at 11 Foster Lane. Late in 1802 he entered his second mark with his father only, and this partnership made a set of ten sauce labels in 1804, including one for WOODS FISH SAUCE (illustrated in Sotheby's Directory of Silver 1600-1940 at number 1097). An attractive soy frame has been noted marked by Robert and Samuel (1802-1811). This may have carried labels made by them, or five of the set of ten noted elsewhere.

89. ROBERT HENNELL II 1809-1833

This Robert was the son of Robert Hennell I's elder brother John. Having been apprenticed to an engraver (John Houle) he may well have been responsible for much of the fine engraving of this period.

90. ROBERT HENNELL III 1833-1868

This Robert was the son of Robert Hennell II. He took over the business upon his father's retirement in May 1833.

91. SAMUEL HENNELL and JOHN TERRY 1814-1816

Samuel Hennell joined up with John Terry in partnership for just over two years. John Terry, it should be noted, had married one of Samuel's nieces(31). He was a Freeman of the Vintners' Company, his father being an inn-keeper. Terry made silver Livery Medals for the Vintners' Company.

92. DANIEL HOCKLEY 1810-1819

He was born in London in 1788, son of Thomas Hockley of Seven Dials, an oilman. He was apprenticed to John Reily on 25 March 1801 and became a Freeman of the Fishmongers' Company on 7 April 1808. He made quality labels at 9 Brook Street, Holborn, including a CAYENNE neck-ring label in

THE MAKERS

1810. (3 WLJ 37). His wine labels utilised bacchanal designs (pan and satyr) (1817) and lion's mask designs (1817 – see 3 WLJ 43). It seems likely that Charles Rawlings took over his business in 1819. He emigrated to South Africa with the 1820 Settlers and died in Graaf-Reinet in 1835. He is probably the maker of the KYAN label (No. 37 in the Holburne of Menstries Museum in Bath) with find gadrooning c.1810-1817.

93. JOHN HOLLAND II 1765-1779

Holland is a very famous name and the business was clearly associated with the making of wine labels from very early times. John was apprenticed to his father Nicholas. He may have taken over his uncle John's business in 1753. From 1765 to 1779, John Holland was working at 5 Bishopsgate and it is most likely that he was the maker of a KETCHUP label, with wrigglework borders dateable to 1765-70, beautifully designed and executed.

94. HENRY HOLLAND 1850-1864

There may well be continuity of the family connection in that Henry Holland was making small sized sauce labels in the 1850's in the style and manner of the 1790's and 1810's. See, for example, his two oval labels with gadrooned edges for CHILLI and KETCHUP referred to in 1 WLJ 124.

95. DANIEL JOHN and CHARLES HOULE 1845-1884

These two brothers were manufacturing silversmiths operating from 24 Red Lion Street, London. Curiously, they married sisters, Jane and Emma Cranbrook. They made a number of tea and coffee services, tankards, cups and salvers. There would not appear to be any mention of soy frames.

96. GEORGE THOMAS HUBBARD and JEAN HENRI MICHAU 1896

George Thomas Hubbard first registered his GTH mark as a gold worker in 1883. In 1896 he joined up with a manufacturing jeweller, Jean Henri Michau, whose workshop was also at 11 South Crescent, Bedford Square, London. Obviously they included small objects such as sauce labels in their repertoire.

97. JOHN SAMUEL HUNT and JOHN MORTIMER 1839-1843

See Mortimer and Hunt below.

98. JOHN MORTIMER HUNT, ROBERT ROSKELL II and ALLAN ROSKELL 1879-1888

John Samuel Hunt died in May 1865. John Hunt and Robert Roskell continued the firm with a retail outlet in New Bond Street and a factory at 26 Harrison Street. John Hunt died in November 1879, so the firm of Hunt & Roskell was run by the above three gentlemen until Robert's death in 1888. The business was sold to J W Benson in 1889. The Paul Storr tradition is reflected in the quality of the two labels for READING and HARVEYS.

99. WILLIAM HUNTER II 1867

William Hunter II used his father's "manufactory" at 13 Myrtle Street, Hoxton and in 1866 made a silver four-piece tea and coffee set for retailing by Joseph Mayer of Liverpool(32). Perhaps he made a soy frame in the following year to take the ANCHOVY label.

100. EDWARD HUTTON 1880-1892

Edward Hutton entered 53 marks between 3rd March 1880 and 9th January 1891 of various sizes. He belonged to the prosperous firm of William Hutton & Sons (see below) and lived in London. The London showrooms were in 13 Thavies Inn, Holborn at this time. William Hutton & Son became "Sons" in 1880 when Edward joined his elder brothers Herbert and Robert in the partnership. Preston Manor museum has a five bottle soy frame with some cruets with mounts dated London 1879 and five enclosed crescents with wire ring fixings. Two labels are unmarked. Three are by Edward Hutton, including TAROGON marked for 1890 (see 8 WLJ 133 for further details). He made a large die-pressed escutcheon for CHUTNEE in 1892 for use on a pickle jar (See Fig. 39).

101. WILLIAM CARR HUTTON 1857-1896

William Carr Hutton was the son of William Hutton, a plate worker, originally of Birmingham. His father sent him in 1830 to Sheffield to start a plating business there and in 1833 opened up at 35 Pinstone Street. An entry in the Sheffield Directory of that year specifically mentions the production of plated decanter-corks and labels. The business prospered and in 1845 he took over the silver plate works at 27 High Street, Sheffield, the place where possibly Thomas Boulsover had been working in the early 1770's. In 1857 he was formally taken into partnership with his

THE MAKERS

father under the name and style of Wm. Hutton & Son which became "Sons" in 1889 and a limited liability company in 1893. William Carr Hutton had five sons all of whom joined the business. His Sheffield firm made a large WALNUT pickle label in the escutcheon style in 1896 (See Fig. 39). These escutcheon labels may well have been retailed by Liberty's or the Army and Navy store.

102. WILLIAM HUTTON & SONS LIMITED 1893-1930

This firm, incorporated with limited liability in 1893 when it acquired Rupert Favell & Co, was founded in Birmingham by William Hutton in 1800. In 1832, the business was transferred to Sheffield and later on a London branch was opened by his son William Carr Hutton (see below). In 1893, the London branch was moved to 7 Farringdon Road. At this time, the senior partner was Herbert Hutton supported by Ernest Hutton who became the first directors of the company. In 1899, they were joined by Charles Birckman and opened a factory in Harley Street, Birmingham. In 1902, they swallowed up Creswick & Co of Sheffield. Labels marked WH & SS Ld have been assayed in London, Sheffield and Birmingham.

103. THOMAS HYDE I 1747-1804 and THOMAS HYDE II 1769-1789

Thomas Hyde I was the son of James Hyde, a vintner. The Hyde's specialisation in label making can be traced back in a continuous line to the Binleys and to Sandylands Drinkwater. Thomas Hyde I (born in 1725) was apprenticed to John Harvey (see 10 WLJ 48). He took over the premises at 33 Gutter Lane from John Harvey in 1747. His elder son Thomas II (born in 1748) was admitted as a Freeman of the Fishmongers' Company by patrimony on 9 February 1769 and James likewise in 1770. Thomas II used his father's marks. Thomas made a fine set of oval beaded sauce labels c.1785. According to Volume VI of the Wakelin ledgers he made six soy labels in 1777 and supplied them on May 9 for onward sale to the Rev. M. D'Oyly. An oval soy frame bearing a mark similar to Grimwade 2784 was made in 1804 (Christies Lot 15 12.5.71 where it was attributed to one Thomas Holland). Circa 1780 he made a plain crescent KETCHUP.

104. JAMES HYDE 1777-1799

James Hyde seems to have been a prolific maker of labels from 1774 and achieved a fine standard. For example, he made a label dated 1797 and engraved CAMP V (for Camp Vinegar) and in the following year one engraved BERNIS (for Bearnaise Sauce). Wine labels with the pre-1775 lion and his mark are known, so it must have been a second mark that was entered in 1777. In 1797, he made a button shaped SOY label with a single reeded border but with a hand clasping arrow engraved armorial. James worked at 10 and 38 Gutter Lane (directly opposite No 10) and then at 6 Carey Lane from 1796. He died in 1799.

105. MARY HYDE with JOHN REILY 1800

John Reilly took over the business from November 1799 in partnership with Mary Hyde, the widow of James (a brother of Thomas) then at 6 Carey Lane, at its junction with Gutter Lane. It appears that Mary then married John Reily around 1801.

106. JAMES JACKSON 1805-1832

He entered his first mark as a small worker in January 1805 working at 3 Church Road (later 10 Newman Street) St Luke's. It seems likely that he became a specialist watchcase maker.

107. THOMAS JENKINSON 1807-1827

He liked a variety of designs (the kidney 1807, the shallow crescent about 1810, the boar's head and the chase 1824 and the gadrooned rectangular 1827). In about 1810 he is said to have made a KYAN label (a very shallow crescent) with reeded edge (see 3 WLJ 37).

108. THOMAS JOHNSON 1851

He may have been responsible for the oval WORCESTERSHIRE label with reeded edge of 1851 (See 3 WLJ 37/9).

109. ALEXANDER JOHNSTON II 1760-1785

A maker with these initials, whose mark could be that of a maker "not traced" by Grimwade (Mark 3472) entered in 1803, or could be a Dublin silversmith, as there were several Johnstons in the trade, was responsible for the unusual pear-shaped pendant for SOY hung on a neck-ring and illustrated in Weed's "Silver Wine Labels" (Plate VI). A more likely explanation is that the maker was the younger

THE MAKERS

Alexander Johnston as the label is attributable to a date of around 1785.

110. JAMES JOHNSTON 1840-1873
About 1845 he made a broad rectangular label with reeded edge for CAVICE (3 WLJ 37). This Scottish maker seems to have worked only in Edinburgh.

111. ROBERT JONES II 1796-1800
His mother, Elizabeth, ran the business after the death of his father in 1783. They specialised in making salvers and waiters. Robert was also a plate worker having served his apprenticeship with Soloman Hougham. The label noted is in the Marshall Collection.

112. CHARLES KAY 1815-1827
Working in Addle Street, Aldermanbury in 1815 and then in New Street, Blackfriars in 1819, he moved firstly to 11 Addle Hill in 1823, and then to 12 Pump Row, Old Street in 1825 when he made the CAYENNE label. He moved again in 1827 to 14 John's Row(33).

113. ROBERT KEAY 1791-1800
His date of admission entered into the Minute Book of the Perth Hammermen's Incorporation was 1791. He made a number of wine labels (eg. Rum, Sherry, Uisgebeatha and Hollands) and c.1795 a smaller octagonal label engraved for VINEGAR for gracing a vinegar decanter, the name being set in an octagonal engraving.

114. ABSTAINANDO KING 1791-1821
He started his career in 1791 as a snuffer maker in Clerkenwell, moving from 3 Berkely Court near St John's Gate to 10 Berkely Street in 1806 and then to 44 Red Lion Street in 1821(34).

115. ROBERT KIPPAX 1794-1796
It seems that he first registered his mark in 1774 and at the same time registered a separate mark for R. Kippax & Co., operating from High Street, Sheffield. In 1781 he joined up with Nowill carrying on the trade of wholesale cutlers and silversmiths, but it seems that he kept his own mark. Cutlery is known with his own mark and a sauce label ESSENCE ANCHOVIES dated 1794.

116. GEORGE KNIGHT 1816-1825
Little is known about the Knight's except that many of their sauce labels have survived. George entered a mark in 1818 and it is similar in form to that of Samuel entered in 1816, from which it may be deduced that there was some relationship. They both worked from Westmoreland Buildings, Aldersgate Street at this time. In the London Museum there is a CATSUP label made by George in 1821 and in the Cropper Collection a SOY of 1820 (M1944-22). In style they preferred the small rectangular shape with rounded corners, decorated with a double reed. George favoured titles of an unusual kind like ZOOBDITTY and NEPAUL.

117. SAMUEL KNIGHT 1810-1827
Samuel Knight made labels entitled ANCHOVY, KETCHUP, HARVEY and CHILI-VINR. He made the hinged neck ring for CHILI in 1815 (date letter U) which could be confused with the Newcastle mark for 1786 (see 8 WLJ 97).

118. WILLIAM KNIGHT 1810-1846
William seems to have been in partnership with Samuel from 1810 (see the "Shrub" and "Hollands" wine labels in the F.J. Anderson Collection dated 1815). In 1830 William appears to have made the KETCHUP, SOY and KYAN labels referred to in 1 WLJ 154. He entered a mark alone in 1816 and appears to have worked on his own account until 1846-7 (see 2 WLJ 46) at Bartholemew Close until 1827 and then at 7 Westmoreland Buildings where Samuel had gone in 1816. (William Kingdon who used a similar mark was working c.1810). William favoured the boar-hunting design for wine labels. George went in for the lion mask and fretwork.

119. JOHN LAMBE 1765-1796
The son of Edward John Lambe, a goldsmith, he was apprenticed to Ebenezer Coker and whilst making many spoons, from the number and range of registered marks, he was an active plate worker from premises in Fetter Lane.

120. HERBERT CHARLES LAMBERT 1902-1912
Francis Lambert founded in 1803 the firm of Lambert & Rawlings. William Rawlings was his manager. His sons, Francis and George, continued the business. George became Prime Warden. He died in 1901 and his nephews, Herbert and Ernest, took over. The business itself was taken over in 1916. They sent a pair of soup ladles in Louis XIV's style to the Great Exhibition in 1851 and copied antique styles. Perhaps

THE MAKERS

in 1908 they made a reproduction French oil and vinegar frame with appropriate labels for HUILLE and VINAIGRE in parcel-gilt enclosed crescent style (Christies 12.6.80, lot 599).

121. PETER LAMBERT 1804-1816
He worked in Aberdeen from 1804 to around 1816 when he handed over his apprentice Andrew Price to William Jamieson and left, perhaps for Berwick(35).

122. JOHN LANGFORD II and JOHN SEBILLE 1760-1797
These makers of beautiful soy frames and baskets went bankrupt in 1770 but recovered well and became established plate workers. The date of their first mark is uncertain probably because it was entered in the lost register of 1758-1763. Their premises were in St Martin's le Grand. Perhaps the Huguenot flair is derived from Sebille's influence on Langford.

123. JOHN LANGLANDS I and JOHN ROBERTSON I 1778-1795
Langlands and Robertson were goldsmiths, jewellers and plate manufacturers of the Side, Newcastle. The Newcastle Assay Office Ledger shows that "bottle labels" were sent in for assay. Included in the assay list were a "cruet frame" and "a cruet stand".

124. JOHN LANGLANDS II 1795-1804
This Newcastle maker produced a set of three labels c.1800 for CHYAN VINEGAR, ESSENCE OF ANCHOVIES and WALNUT CATCHUP. These titles were in vogue at a much earlier date, so perhaps Phillips' dating is not accurate (lot 145 of sale of Watney Collection on 13 September 1996).

125. GEORGE SAMUEL LEWIS and JOHN WRIGHT 1812-1824
They were jewellers and silversmiths coming from London in 1812 (according to their advertisements) to Dean Street, Newcastle, until 1821 when they moved to 27 Mosely Street. Wright carried on by himself after Lewis retired in March 1824. Their trade card advertised "An elegant assortment of plate and plated goods" (see John Johnson's collection in the Bodleian Library). See further M.A.V. Gill "A Directory of Newcastle Goldsmiths" at page 157.

126. G.L. and G.F. c.1850
Clearly an inaccurate attribution. There is no evidence from assay books that any soy label was sent for assay in Newcastle. The mark is not recorded by Gill. The label is marked "77" and is a mystery. It could possibly have been a badly struck mark for Gowland Bros. (George Hoy and Clement Gowland).

127. JOHN LINNIT and WILLIAM ATKINSON 1809-1815
Linnit and Atkinson entered their mark as goldworkers in partnership in 1809 at 15 Fountain Court in the Strand(36). It is recorded by Grimwade(37) in Section VII relating to Goldworker's Marks 1773-1837. The partnership was responsible for producing good quality gold snuff boxes.

128. JOHN LINNIT 1815-1841
In 1815 John Linnit set up on his own at 9 Craven Buildings in Drury Lane. He and his wife Elizabeth worshipped at St Clement Dane's in the Strand where their first two sons John II and Edward were baptised(38). John Linnit I not surprisingly was known for his production of gold and silver snuff boxes and many other fine items recorded by Culme such as a "silver-gilt mounted oak cup and cover surmounted by a model of the Round Tower" at Windsor Castle made in 1827(39).

129. MATTHEW LINWOOD II 1793-1821
Matthew Linwood, born the eldest son of Matthew Linwood I (1773-1783), was a famous Birmingham maker who was particularly interested in making Sheffield Plate and who entered his mark in this respect at Sheffield in 1808. He made in 1812 a pair of sauce labels entitled TOMATA and ELDER-VINEGAR which are in the M. V. Brown Collection in the London Museum. As early as 1793 he developed the die-struck label which allowed mass production. He made many wine labels during the period 1806-1821. He entered marks in Birmingham in 1801 and 1813 and served as a Guardian of the Birmingham Assay Office in 1811.

130. EDWARD LIVINGSTONE 1790-1825
An apprentice of William Scott, he was the leading silversmith in Dundee at the beginning of the nineteenth century producing a range of items including two beautiful oval soy labels – a rare event in Scotland outside of Edinburgh at this time so far as sauce labels are concerned.

THE MAKERS

131. GEORGE LOWE 1791-1841

George Lowe was very well known as a Chester maker of wine and sauce labels. He made a label bearing the name HARVEY in 1797 (40).

132. EDWARD LOWE 1800-1810

Edward Lowe was a well known Chester maker of wine and sauce labels. About 1810 Edward made a beautiful rectangular shaped label, engraved for LEMON in the style of the 1790's with delicate corner mouldings – a fore-runner of the architectural syle perhaps.

133. JOHN MACDONALD 1810-1815

This Edinburgh plate worker made wine labels of good quality as well as sauce labels with unusual titles. MacDonald is also found spelt McDonald. Lobster sauce was popular north of the border from about 1800. James McKay's label is dated 1815. John MacDonald made two others each small, plain and rectangular, with a two inch chain, one with cut corners. Many Scottish firms of this time are difficult to identify eg. M & R (a firm who made many wine labels now identified as Mitchell & Russell), N & G, D & G, D & P, G & McL and D & M, because only assumptions can be drawn from records of admission in the Minutes of the Hammermen's Incorporation. There is however a QUEEN'S SAUCE label with rubbed Edinburgh marks and makers marks of perhaps "JMD" for John MacDonald., with a date letter for 1810.

134. JAMES and WALTER MARSHALL 1817-1823

Their earliest mention in the Edinburgh directories according to Jackson(41) was 1817. He illustrates their mark on a toddy-ladle for 1816-17(42). Frank was brought into the partnership in 1819 and later (certainly from 1824) the firm became well known as Marshall & Sons with the familiar mark of M&S(43).

135. RICHARD MARTIN and EBENEZER HALL 1854-1891

Plate was made at the Shrewsbury works in Broad Street, part of Sheffield, by the partnership of Richard Martin and Ebenezer Hall.

136. JAMES McKAY 1793-1837

He was admitted in 1793 to the Incorporation of Goldsmiths of the City of Edinburgh and the mark attributed to him by Jackson(44) has been found from 1803 to 1845. Jackson gives examples of this mark for the years 1813, 1817, 1826, 1829, 1830. 1837 and 1844. In 1815 he made a set of four heavy cast full-size scallop shell labels pierced for the titles of SOY, KETCHUP, LOBSTER and ANCHOVY, weighing together 4I ounces having a diameter of one and three quarter inches and each held by 2 inch heavy link chains (Bonhams sale 28th November, 1972 Lot 79). He made in 1837 the CINAMON label which is in the London Museum. Some of his earlier labels, eg. one for SUGAR, carry maker's mark only.

137. JOHN McKENZIE I 1841

According to the Inverness Hammermen's Minute Book John McKenzie was apprenticed in 1833 to John MacRae, an Inverness silversmith who had been admitted in 1826. MacRae specialised in jewellery and watchmaking at 11 High Street(45). No doubt John Mackenzie followed suit. He is a somewhat shadowy figure and the attribution is very much open to question. Another candidate could be James McKenzie of Edinburgh (c.1827-c.1845) although Jackson attributes to him he mark of M^c on a tea-set of 1825(46).

138. ALEXANDER MITCHELL II 1819-1850

His first mark was entered in Glasgow in 1819 and his second in 1822 as a watchmaker and silversmith. He made a sauce label for PIQUANT in Glasgow in 1833.

139. JOHN and WILLIAM MITCHELL 1834-1851

Their mark was entered in Glasgow in 1834 and in Edinburgh about the same time. They made a label for OIL in Edinburgh around 1835.

140. ELIZABETH MORLEY 1794-1814

She seems to have been a prolific maker of good labels both for sauces and for wines entering he first mark in 1794. She was known to Jackson as "E. Morley". Her mark was mistakenly thought by some to belong to one Edward Morley. She made in 1810 a very attractive SOY label. Her address was 7 Westmoreland Buildings and it seems that she was the widow of Thomas Morley and that Samuel Knight took over the business in 1816. No labels of hers have been seen later than 1814. She changed her mark in 1796, 1800, 1808 and 1810. She used at least twelve different styles, namely the two reeded rounded

THE MAKERS

rectangular, the octagonal, the humped octagonal, the domed rectangular, the horse-shoe crescent and the single letter square; the gadrooned rounded rectangular; the bright cut ovals; the crescent the rectangular; the shell and gadrooned rectangular with pointed ends; and the floral octagonal.

141. JOHN MORTIMER and JOHN SAMUEL HUNT 1839-1843

Mortimer and Hunt made in London in 1840 a small label probably for BURGUNDY sauce in matching style with larger wine labels. Paul Storr having retired at the end of 1838, the firm at this time was run by John Samuel Hunt his nephew by marriage, his son John Hunt and Paul Storr's former partner John Mortimer.

142. ROBERT MORTON 1819-1835

This Edinburgh silversmith is probably the maker of a reeded octagonal label with the unusual title of PACKE (8 WLJ 96). A similar style wine label for "Shiraz" has been recorded by this maker (9 WLJ 20). His mark is illustrated in 9 WLJ 16.

143. GEORGE MURRAY 1805-1816

The Newcastle Assay Ledgers show that he produced a significant amount of plate during these eleven years including a "bottle stand", a "castor frame", a "castor stand", a "cruet frame" and a "decanter frame". It is not surprising that he made sauce labels to go with the frame as there is no record of separate bottle label assay(47).

144. JAMES NEWLANDS and PHILIP GRIERSON 1811-1816

Newlands entered his first mark in 1805, was the sixth signatory to the November 1818 Petition for a Glasgow Goldsmith's Company and Assay Office, and worked on until some time in 1819. Grierson entered his first mark in 1810, was in partnership from 1811 to 1816 and then left Glasgow. The plain label for OIL for an oil and vinegar frame was marked in Edinburgh in 1813. Glasgow silversmiths marked their wares in Edinburgh from about 1786 until 1819.

145. JOHN NICKOLDS 1818

Two kidney shaped soy frame labels for CAYENNE and VINEGAR would appear to have been made by this small worker whose two marks were entered in London in September 1818 presumably following the ending of his partnership with Samuel Roberts (1808-1818). Each label is decorated with bright cutting and was presumably made to match similar labels produced much earlier by Susanna Barker.

146. THOMAS OLLIVANT 1789-1830

Thomas Ollivant of Manchester entered his characteristic large lettered TO mark in London as a plate maker on 12th May 1789 (Grimwade 3450). He was a maker of quality silver. He often overstamped Hester Bateman's mark on wine labels with his own.

147. S.P. 1987

Identification of this modern maker (1987) awaits a study of the mark used on MAPLE SYRUP which was reported to the Wine Label Circle but has not been perused.

148. NATHANIAL PACK 1765

An early sauce label engraved for TARAGON with makers mark only, has been attributed to Nathaniel Pack of London. The mark NP (Grimwade 2100) has also been noted on three other sauce labels marked "No 80". The attribution is uncertain, and precise verification of the mark has not been possible.

149. THOMAS PARSONS 1773-1801

He made a set of four soy labels octagonal shaped with double reeded borders preserved in the Birmingham Assay Office and illustrated in Kenneth Crisp Jones' (Ed) "The Silversmiths of Birmingham" at page 15.

150. GEORGE PEARSON 1812-1821

George Pearson, son of John Pearson of Southwark, mathematical instrument maker, was apprenticed on 6 December 1804 to John Reily. His freedom was obtained from the Fishmongers' Company on 13 February 1812. He appears to have made a label for CHILLI in London dated 1816/1817. Grimwade records (page 617) that there is merely one mark as a small worker entered on the 8th May 1817 with an address at 104 Dorset Court in Fleet Street, City of London. The CHILLI V (Frost Collection) was attributed to one "George Purse".

151. JAMES PECKHAM 1830-1847

He was a silversmith working in Columbia, South Carolina, USA.

152. JONATHAN PERKINS I 1800-1810

Jonathan Perkins (born around 1744) entered his first mark as a smallworker in 1772 at Cripplegate. He was a bucklemaker(48) but joined his son in partnership from 1795 to 1800 at 16 Hosier Lane, Smithfield, as plateworkers. From 1800 to 1810 he spent the last years of a long career as a silversmith, during which the KYAN, BROWN S and DEVONSHIRE labels were made.

153. JAMES PHIPPS I 754-1783
James Phipps the Elder, the son of William Phipps of Whitechapel, who originally worked with Robert Collins in Gutter Lane and then with William Bond in Foster Lane made both wine and sauce labels at No. 11 Gutter Lane from about 1767 onwards. Two 1770 vintage labels are for QUIN and WALNUT PICKLE. Three 1780s vintage labels, marked IP, previously ascribed to James Perry, are for CORATCH, ANCHOVY and LEMON.

154. THOMAS PHIPPS and EDWARD ROBINSON 1783-1811
The famous partnership of Thomas Phipps and Edward Robinson (both partners had been apprenticed to James Phipps) made many sauce labels, entering their first mark in 1783 (the year of Edward Robinson's marriage to Ann Phipps) at 40 Gutter Lane (eg. the PICQUANTE label in the Museum of London).

155. PHIPPS, ROBINSON and PHIPPS 1811-1816
The firm called Phipps Robinson & Phipps made a fine pair of small silver-gilt shell labels pierced for CHILI and KYAN in 1814.

156. THOMAS and JAMES PHIPPS 1816-1823
The partnership of Thomas and James Phipps made fine labels eg. the ELDER label in the Cropper Collection dateable to about 1818(49). Thomas Phipps died in 1833.

157. ROBERT PIERCY 1757-1795
He was a specialist cruet frame maker of high quality. Examples of 1763, 1765, 1775 and 1782 have been noted. He was trained by Samuel Wood in the tradition of castor and cruet makers. There are entries in the Wakelin Ledgers showing that he supplied cruets from 1766 onwards. These were accompanied by sauce labels. He made a fine pair of Warwick cruets for the Grocers' Company in 1782 (Christie's New York Sale, 16.4.99, Lot 318).

158. WILLIAMS PITTS 1810-1811
He appears to have worked from about 1784 to beyond the turn of the Century and was the maker of the LEMON label in the Cropper Collection dated 1810(50), at this time (from 1806) being at 14 James Street, Lambeth Marsh.

159. WILLIAM PLUMMER 1769-1790
William Plummer (an apprentice of Edward Aldridge) seems to have worked originally in Foster Lane and then from 47 Gutter Lane for a period of some 34 years from 1757. In 1769 he produced a Soy frame having six bottles with silver collars engraved for ELDER, GARLIC, LEMON, KETCHUP, SOY, and KYAN.

160. MICHAEL PLUMMER 1791-1792
A small TARAGON label marked M.P (Grimwade 2058) may have been made by William Plummer's son Michael who entered his mark in 1791, about this time.

161. CHARLES CLAPTON PRICE 1812-1830
He appears to be the maker of a Regency gadrooned label with top and bottom and side roses in 1825 engraved for CHILI.VIN[R], bought by Mrs Marshall in 1938 for 7 shillings (Marshall Collection, Ashmolean). Engraved on the reverse is a rather splendid Crown or Coronet (see sketch illustration in Fig 98). He was a quality plateworker working in Clerkenwell, having been apprenticed to Cornelius Bland of Aldersgate Street in 1789 and of Bunhill Row from 1790 until his death in 1794. Bland however undertook smallwork as well as platework.

162. FRANCES PURTON 1783-1798
Two LEMON PICKLE labels, an ANCHOVY and a CHILLY VINEGAR were sponsored by the widow of Robert Purton. Their business started in 1772 was that of a small worker at 2 Cary Lane, Foster Lane in the City of London. Sauce label production seems only to have taken place after termination of her short partnership with Thomas Johnson. Three are dated 1798.

163. RAITE & SONS 1825
This Aberdeen firm made a single reeded narrowish rectangular label engraved for HARVEY c.1825.

164. CHARLES RAWLINGS 1817-1829
Charles Rawlings was apprenticed to Edward Coleman, a watch finisher. He was a prolific maker of labels from 12 Well Street, London (which had been the premises

since 1791 of James Atkins and later his widow Theodosia Ann Atkins) from 1817. In 1819 he probably took over Daniel Hockley's business at 9 Brook Street. In the London Museum dated 1822 there is a splendid CATCHUP label. In 1829 he entered into partnership with William Summers and many fine labels were produced, including in 1829 the rare soy label engraved for DEVONSHIRE. William Summers appears to have operated alone from 1863. Charles Rawlings was a great designer of labels. He probably made the HARVEY, ANCHOVY, SOY and KETCHUP labels in the Weed Collection dated 1822 (see 5 WLJ 111) where the maker is said to be Charles Reily but he was not known to have made labels on his own account during the lifetime of his father. Charles Rawlings is said to have introduced the famous vine leaf design for wine labels in about 1824. The design of the Weed Collection of sauce labels mentioned above was utilised to make the wine labels also illustrated at 5 WLJ 111 dated 1829. The latest recorded label of his, a rounded rectangular double reeded for 1827 incised for ANCHOVY, was lot 190 in Phillips sale of 23.2.2001.

165. CHARLES RAWLINGS and WILLIAM SUMMERS 1829-1897

Rawlings had moved to 9 Brook Street, Holborn in 1819 and it is from this address that he began his long partnership with Summers (then aged 25 having gained his freedom in 1826 by patrimony as a goldsmith and jeweller) in April 1829. Some ten years thereafter, they moved to the West End and opened premises at 10 Great Marlborough Street (near Regent Street). Charles died on 9th October 1863, and William on 15th January 1890. William's son Henry Summers carried on the business for seven years and then it was sold by Knight Frank and Rutley(51).

166. CHRISTIAN KER REID and SONS 1819-1884

Newcastle Assay Office records disclose that a "soy label" was submitted for assay by this firm(52) in 1819 but its particulars were not noted.

167. JOHN REILY 1800-1826

John Reily, son of Richard Reily a glazier in Thames Street, was apprenticed to James Hyde on 7 December 1786. He was admitted a Freeman of the Fishmongers' Company on 13 February 1794. John Reily first entered his mark in partnership with James Hyde's widow in 1799 and then on his own account in 1801. He married Mary Hyde in 1801. He took on Daniel Hockley and George Pearson as apprentices. The London Museum has a CAMP sauce label dated 1801 in the Brown Collection. John Reily died in 1826. John Reily was a prolific maker of sauce labels for 25 years. He made the SOY and ANCHOVY for the Royal Yacht "Prince Regent" in 1818-1819, and the bold Regency architectural KETCHUP (illustrated by Stancliffe, p12, fig 13) in 1810.

168. MARY ANN and CHARLES REILY 1826-1829

John Reily's widow, Mary, went into partnership with their son Charles in 1826, and the London Museum has a CAYENNE label of that date.

169. CHARLES REILY and GEORGE STORER 1828-1855

In 1829 Charles appears to have gone into partnership with George Storer who had served his apprenticeship as a watch maker; this partnership made an unusually decorative FISH-SAUCE label not dated but attributable to the 1830 period.

170. TIMOTHY RENOU 1792-1816

A better attribution as a maker of labels with flair is to Timothy Renou rather than to Thomas Roberts (1801-1849), who admittedly was apprenticed to John Roberts (his uncle) (1774-1801). Both makers were basically dinner plate makers. A set of five sauce labels exist dated 1816 and another set exists of three labels dated 1814 assayed in London. The shapes are broad rectangular with engine turned borders. The most unusual design has the label crowned with an engraved leafage motif. Even more unusual is that in the 1816 set (which includes POUVERADE and CORATCH) there is a CAYANNE and an ANCHOVY whereas in the 1814 set there is a KYAN and an ANCHOVIE. Perhaps Renou did not like undertaking repetitive work lacking in originality. These sauce labels match similar style wine labels but the wine labels may be later in date (for example there is a "GIN" by Richard Turner dated 1817). An attribution to Renou is probably better than to Thomas Robbins, based on a comparison of Grimwade 2915 with Grimwade 2904-6.

171. RETTIE and SON 1810-1847

In the earlier part of the Nineteenth Century M. Rettie and Son (mark R&S) traded (in addition to

THE MAKERS

other premises) from 101 Union Street, Aberdeen, from which, according to their trade card of 1824, one could purchase silver plated bottle stands and "cruet, soy, and pickle frames"(53). Bottle stands were also available in fine papier maché with japanning. The partners were Middleton Rettie and his son William Rettie. The firm became M. Rettie and Sons in 1847 when the second son James joined the partnership.

172. JOHN RICH 1765-1810

From 1765 John Rich was a noted maker of labels. His premises were near Whitfield's Chapel, Tottenham Court Road. He made a fine oval beaded ANCHOVY label in 1791. This must be one of the earliest fully marked sauce labels. His earlier labels are marked twice with his own mark, a "JR" in script in a rectangular frame. His maker's mark is generally accompanied by the lion passant. From 1784 a duty mark is included and from 1791 a date letter. His range of designs included the crescent and the kidney with ribbed edging. His later unregistered mark is attributed by Grimwade (with a query) to John Robins (No 3678) but follows the distinctive style of No. 1635. His name appeared in the Parliamentary List in 1773 and some of his wine labels can be dated to circa 1770. He made some wine labels for George III's Coronation Service dated 1794. He died in 1807 but his widow Elizabeth went on disposing of stock for at least three years. His CHILLI in the Marshall Collection (No. 384) has the initials LLB engraved on the reverse.

173. SAMUEL ROBERTS II 1794-1834

Born in 1763, he started up in partnership with George Cadman (died 1823) at Eyre Street, Sheffield, in a factory built for him by his father. Two years later they took in George Ingall (died 1822) and a sleeping partner who later pulled out of the business. Samuel Roberts was a great designer, advocate for Sheffield plate, and inventor. In 1795 his pattern book illustrated some 30 wine labels. In 1824 he book out a patent for dispensing with silver edges on plated wares, which may have accelerated the production of plated labels. In 1826 he brought in Evan Smith, Sidney Roberts and William Sissons to form Roberts, Smith & Co. He retired in 1834 and died 14 years later. About 1830 the firm produced a Sheffield plated sauce label engraved for CAYENNE bearing his famous bell mark which gave its name to the experimental "Bell metal".

174. ROBERTS and BELK 1864-1901

Roberts & Belk were a famous Sheffield firm entering marks in 1867, 1879 and 1892 and making a range of articles, including the gold sauce labels for READING and WORCESTER in 1877.

175. JAMES ROBERTSON 1800-1825

According to Jackson(54) James Robertson's earliest mention is 1804. He may have been the son of William Robertson (c.1789-c.100). In 1814 he made one sauce label for CAYENNE.

176. WILLIAM ROBERTSON 1789-1800

He worked in Edinburgh between c.1789 and c.1800. During this period he made one sauce label entitled ANCHOVIE.

177. JOHN ROBINS 1774-1801

His mark (Grimwade 1623) appears to have been entered in 1774 and there is in the Cropper Collection(55) a label attributed to him engraved for CAYENNE. He worked from 67 Aldersgate Street from 1781 to 1794, and later from 13 Clerkenwell Green.

178. WILLIAM SEAMAN 1818-1827

Sauce labels dated 1818 (WORCESTER) and 1827 (HARVEY) have been recorded as having been made by this maker who was originally a spoonmaker but following a move to 9 Great Sutton Street in 1810 he widened his interests. He moved to 1 New Gloucester Place, Hoxton in 1823.

179. ROBERT SECKER 1863

Robert Secker entered his mark as a goldsmith in London in 1863. The maker's mark RS illustrated on the reverse of ANCHOVY is similar to Culme No. 12647. The three labels he made are in the Victoria and Albert Museum (Fitzhenry Collection) and are crested on the reverse with a basket hilted sword piercing a rectangular object, above a armorial mantling. These labels copied a Regency style and were perhaps made to complete an existing set with sauces liked by the owner. Piercing the titles made the sauce labels more expensive to buy.

180. CHARLES SHAW 1846-1873

He learnt his trade as a working silversmith at 11 Gough Square (1835-1845). He then set up on his own as a small worker at 5 Hind Court, Fleet Street, City of London. He died in December 1873.

THE MAKERS

181. WILLIAM SIMPSON II 1825-1855
William Simpson I made at his premises in High Street, Banff, teaspoons, toddy ladles and vinaigrettes which can be seen respectively in the Royal Scottish Museum, the National Museum of Antiquities and the Glasgow Museum at Kelvingrove. The firm of Simpson and Co was founded around 1855 by his three sons William II, John and Robert. Their workshop was at 43 Low Street. William Simpson I's mark is illustrated on a toddy ladle in the The Silversmiths of Banff(56).

182. WILLIAM SMILEY 1881-1887
His maker's mark has a little central blip beneath. In 1887 he made in London a set of four rectangular labels for ANCHOVEY, CHILLI, HARVEY and KETCHUP. In the same year he made a pair of toilet water labels for "Lavender water" and "Eau de Cologne". All six labels are simple but of good quality.

183. BENJAMIN SMITH II 1802-1818
Benjamin, born in December 1764 in Edgbaston, and his younger brother James began as buckle-makers in the 1780's. Benjamin married firstly, Mary Adams in 1788 at Edgbaston Parish Church and secondly, after her death, Mary Shiers in 1802 at Greenwich. About 1800 Digby Scott provided the capital for Benjamin to set up a firm of London silversmiths specialising in high quality work which opened in 1802 in Lime Kiln Lane (South Street) Greenwich to supply Rundell Bridge & Rundell (the Royal Goldsmiths) with cast labels usually in massive form, such as the famous set of nine which includes Red and White Hermitage, Barsac and Steine(57). Benjamin probably made in 1807 the unmarked clover label for KYAN matching his larger "Sherry" illustrated in the Phillips Catalogue reproduced in 6 WLJ 141.

184. BENJAMIN SMITH II and JAMES SMITH III 1809
These great makers made a fine silver-gilt shell label pierced for KETCHUP in 1809(58). James invented and patented the latchet which led to a partnership with Matthew Boulton. James joined his brother after he had disentangled himself from Boulton's clutches. Benjamin made in 1828 the pair of cast silver-gilt waggon coasters, which decorate the cover of "A Guide to Harvey's Wine Museum"(59), made for the Earl of Hastings as identified by the armorial bearings.

185. GEORGE SMITH II and THOMAS HAYTER 1792-1796
Having been apprenticed to William Aldridge, George Smith II, a smallworker, obtained his freedom in 1758 and Livery in 1771. He then entered nine marks as a bucklemaker, all from 4 Huggin Lane off Wood Street from 1775 to 1789(60). His thirteenth mark was entered on the occasion of his partnership with Thomas Hayter, a plateworker, presumably as part of his retirement planning. See also Thomas Hayter, above.

186. JOHN SMITH 1827-1855
John Smith's mark, with its distinctive punch outline, is illustrated in Jackson(61) for a salt-spoon of 1826-1827. On the CHILI label the maker's mark is accompanied by the head of Queen Victoria (duty mark), Hibernia, the harp crowned and date letter V for 1841-1842.

187. SAMUEL WATTON SMITH 1882-1897
He was one of the proprietors of S. W. Smith & Co. which had taken over George Richmond Collis & Co. He carried on business as a manufacturing silversmith and plater at 57 Cambridge Street, Birmingham. He had a number of outlets and showrooms in the Holborn area of London from time to time.

188. WILLIAM SMITH I 1758-1781
His father was a goldsmith and William finished his apprenticeship in 1749. He entered his first mark as a small worker in 1758. His premises were at 32 Cheapside, City of London, handy for Goldsmiths' Hall. He became a Liveryman in 1751.

189. SMITH, TATE, HOULT and TATE 1824-1830
Smith & Co was formerly G Smith, R Tate, W Nicholson and E Hoult in about 1810 operating from premises at 16 Arundell Street, Sheffield. They were platers as well as silversmiths. G Smith was probably of Nathaniel Smith's family because Nathaniel first registered the open palm of the hand as a plater's mark in 1784. The 1810 registration by the company was of a similar mark. Nicholson must have retired before 1824 when presumably Tate's son was introduced to the firm (still using the STN&H mark) which was taken over by John Watson & Son between 1828 and 1837(61).

190. JOSIAH SNATT 1797-1817
A maker of wine labels also (for example "Tenerife" in

111

1812, "Benedictine" in 1809 and "R" and "H" in 1804) a rectangular label of 1809 with reeded edge for GARLICK is attributed to him (see 3 WLJ 67). He worked from 4 Fan Street Aldersgate from about 1797 to 1817. Certainly he made very fine sauce labels inscribed P. VINEGAR (for Pink Vinegar) and ANCHOVY, hinged to neck rings(62) in 1804 (incorrectly attributed to a "John Saunders"), and probably the CATSUP of 1813 (incorrectly attributed to a "J Salkeld of London") and the QUIN of 1797 in the Marshall Collection (No 496).

191. GEORGE STORER 1829-1845
See Charles Reily.

192. JOSEPH WILLIAM STORY 1809-1815
See William Elliott.

193. PAUL STORR 1800-1838
One of the most renowned makers, Paul Storr, who was apprenticed to Andrew Fogelberg, made sauce labels during the period 1800-1838. This famous maker made a few cruets and a few soy frames (six bottle) certainly between the years 1800 and 1818 from premises at 20 Air Street (until 1807) and then 53 Dean Street during this period. One frame (1800) belongs to Trinity College, Cambridge and according to a College inventory of 1878/9 "there was originally a set of sauce labels for use with this soy frame" (see Penzer's book, page 108). By 1811 and until 1819 he was a partner of Rundell, Bridge and Rundell supplying plates for the Prince Regent. Two frames (1816) are in the Royal Collection "complete with the six labels" (see 1914 Descriptive Inventory Numbers 765 and 1113). Six labels are known of medium size (1818) and three of a larger size (1816), all of good weight and splendid titling. His distinguished sauce labels generally have titles with raised lettering and are marked on their face. In 1819 he set up a business at 18 Harrison Street. Three heavy cast cartouches in the rococo style were made for the French market and stamped with the French import mark on the rim. One is engraved for "Harvey", dated 1835, and illustrated in 7 WLJ 3, and two are pierced for "Ordinaire", dated 1838. They are cast in a sharp curve and have short chains to fit soy bottles. In 1838 he moved his Bond Street outlet to a better location at the corner of Compton Street in partnership with John Mortimer and then retired. He died in 1844.

194. WILLIAM SUMMERS 1863-1884
William Summers gained his freedom in 1826 by patrimony as a goldsmith and jeweller. After his partnership with Charles Rawlings ended he carried on for some twenty years on his own account and in 1864 produced some silver-gilt shell sauce labels, almost exact replicas of those made by Phipps Robinson & Phipps in 1814, entitled SALAD OIL and FRENCH VINEGAR and illustrated in Sotheby's catalogue for 20th February 1975 (Lot 77). William Summers did much to revive in Victorian times styles popular in earlier periods, for example, neo-classical designs and Regency designs inspired by Roman Imperial Art. The increasing popularity of the pickle frame in the later Victorian era coupled with the continuing use of the vinegar decanter meant that the demands for labelling continued after the demand for a wider variety of wine labels had ceased. He died in 1890, the firm being continued by his son Henry until 1897.

195. WILLIAM SUTTON 1784-1796
About 1784 he made a plain eye-shaped label for TARRAGON VINEGAR (3 WLJ 37) operating from his premises at 85, Cheapside in the City of London.

196. BENJAMIN TAITT 1784-1791
His marks were first registered in 1784 under the Act of 1783 with premises at Sherrys Court, Bride Street, Dublin. Information on working dates comes from Street Directories. He was a noted label maker, especially as regards the balloon ascent and the Bacchus astride a barrel wine labels.

197. JOHN TAYLEUR 1775-1801
He appears to have started in Newgate Street in 1775. He was at 14 Red Lion Street from 1780 until 1801 when the workshop was apparently taken over by Alice and George Burrows. His small mark (no pellet) entered in 1776 (Grimwade 1707 Notes) appears on wine and sauce labels and is readily confused with John Thompson's mark (Grimwade 1695), Joseph Taylor's mark (a Birmingham silversmith with a London outlet in Fleet Street) and with some of John Troby's marks (Grimwade 1711 Notes) entered between 1787 and 1800. The Tayleur punch however has a defective top which makes it more easily identifiable. He specialised in making neck-rings, the label itself being plain in decoration and narrow rectangular in shape. Examples are CAYENNE c.1785, FINE HERBES c.1785, QNS PICKLE (for Quin's Pickle) 1791 in the Cropper Collection(63), where it is attributed

to John Thompson (illustrated in Stancliffe, p.2, Fig.13), PORT 1792, CAYENNE 1793, KETCHUP 1795 and SAUCE RL (for Sauce Royal) 1799(64). Other attributions have been made to John Touliet, to John Troby and to Joseph Taylor (1782-1828) who began his career as a watchmaker in Newhall Street, Birmingham but expanded with silversmithing with a retail outlet in London off Fleet Street. He served as a Guardian of the Birmingham Assay Office in 1813. Examples of his sauce labels are said to be in the Birmingham Assay Office. He was a prolific maker of wine labels. On his death Taylor and Perry took over his business.

198. JOHN TEARE I 1790-1811

He was apprenticed to his father, Samuel Teare, a goldsmith in Dublin. He was not admitted to the freedom of the Dublin Goldsmiths' Company. The National Museum of Ireland has at least one of his labels, a wine label for Sherry c.1790 (ref. 95A; 1936).

199. JOHN TEARE II 1787-1813

On 12 September 1811 there is an entry for him in the Account Books of the Dublin Goldsmiths Corporation reading "16 Labels and 8 small do. 5oz 17dwt." It is likely that the small labels were for sauces. 16 labels at 6 dwt each (on the light side) and 8 sauce labels at 3 dwt each (on the light side) would amount to 6 oz in weight. The National Museum of Ireland has at least one of his labels, a wine label for Hock, 1807(65).

200. JOHN TEARE III 1813-1861

Born in 1790, he was a manufacturing jeweller who made many labels, from various locations. In 1827, John Teare became Town Warden at the Assay Office in Goldsmiths Hall in Golden Lane. John Teare was a Warden from 1852 to 1855 and Master from 1855 to 1861 when he went to New York (see 6 WLJ 236). The National Museum of Ireland has at least one of his wine labels, for Madeira c.1820(66).

201. WILLIAM THEOBALDS and ROBERT METCALF ATKINSON 1838-1840

William Theobalds, after a short lived partnership with L St L Bunn (1835-36) joined R M Atkinson in 1838. The partnership was dissolved in 1840. Theobalds was then aged 59 and it looks as if he was trying to find a suitable successor to his business which was operated from 7 Salisbury Court, Fleet Street. He was apparently connected in business with Storr & Mortimer.

202. JAMES TRENDER 1793-1815

James Trender, starting off in the Barbican as a small worker, moved steadily westwards in the City as far as Leather Lane, where he made in 1813 a CAYENNE label (Grimwade 1717).

203. JOHN TROBY 1792-1804.

John Troby was a City of London small worker at Ship Court near the Old Bailey from 1787 to his death in 1804. He made a GARLICK neck-ring label in 1792 (illustrated in 9 WLJ 203) and a CAYENNE label in 1793.

204. WILLIAM BAMFORTH TROBY 1804-1821

William Bamforth Troby, John's son, set up as a large plate worker in the same area in 1812, where in 1814 he made collar or loop labels, engraved for KETCHUP and KYAN, decorated by a top and bottom double reed. Hoops were often made in ivory but are not very common either in silver or plated. KYAN has an armorial engraved upon it contained within a crowned garter which suggests ambassadorial use.

205. WALTER TWEEDIE 1768-1786

He began apparently as a spoonmaker at premises in Holywell Street, Strand but two sizes of a second recorded mark were registered in 1779 as a plate worker. So perhaps he made the extant soy frame c.1780. The attribution is dubious because the mark WT in a rectangular punch outline with rounded ends, stamped twice, is, in both cases, well rubbed.

206. H.T. 1895

It is not practicable to make an appropriate attribution without having sight of the label for A.I. Sauce (1895). Possible candidates include Henry Thornton, Harriet Thomson, Herbert Taylor, Harry Turner, Henry Tracy and Hubert Thornhill. The maker's mark needs to be examined.(67).

207. GEORGE UNITE 1832-1861

Unite from Birmingham was a prolific maker of wine labels. His sauce label output was much more limited – for example TARRAGON VINEGAR c.1845 and 1859, WALNUT CATSUP c.1845, KETCHUP 1859, CHILI VINEGAR 1847 and READING c.1845. He reproduced earlier designs such as Rawlings' simple vine leaf design (of 1824), the very early enclosed crescent design and the more usual rounded rectangular design. His mark

THE MAKERS

has been recorded for 1832, 1834, 1838, 1859 and 1861. His firm continued certainly until 1910.

208. DUNCAN URQUHART and NAPTHALI HART 1791-1805

They were goldsmiths working in Clerkenwell Green who made in 1791 three rectangular labels with raised eyelets entitled VINEGAR, KIAN and SOY (see I WLJ 124). Their main pre-occupation was however with buckles, tea services and other silverware.

209. JABEZ VALE 1813-1828

This Coventry maker, who had his goods assayed in Birmingham, made a broad rectangular label for ANCHOVY in 1827 (3 WLJ 37).

210. NATHANIEL VERNON 1802-1808

An oval soy label with a wrigglework border engraved for LEMON appears to be one of the few recorded sauce labels of American making, in this case by Vernon of Charleston, South Carolina. His name appears in the Directories for 1802 to 1808. The label is lodged in the Winterthur Museum in Delaware.

211. THOMAS WALLIS 1806

He made a rounded oblong cruet stand on ball feet in 1806 with four cut glass condiment bottles engraved for LEMON, SOY, ELDER and TERAGON(68).

212. STEPHEN WALSH 1747-1785

The archives of the Dublin Assay office do not assist in identification of the SW mark of this period which is surrounded by controversy. It is thought that it belongs to Stephen Walsh of Cork who was apprenticed to William Bennett there in 1742. By 1780 he had moved to Dublin but was unsuccessful in petitioning to join the Dublin Goldsmiths' Company in 1781. The SW mark has been found on pieces of plate stamped with the name WALSH, assayed in Dublin for 1747. He was an eminent maker of wine labels and so probably was the maker of sauce labels for the Powerscourt soy frame in 1750 to go with his silver mounted soy bottles of that date.

213. HERMAN JOHN WALTHER 1770

Herman Walther appears as a gold worker in the Parliamentary Report list of 1773. He appears to have entered only one mark as a small worker in 1770. This mark appears on a beautiful and most usually designed fine crescent label engraved for TARRAGON.

214. JOHN WATSON 1795-1817

John Watson's mark I.W. was entered at the Sheffield Assay Office in 1795. It is illustrated in Jackson(69), taken from candelsticks dated 1816 and 1817. A second smaller mark J.W. is also illustrated.

215. JAMES WELSHMAN 1813-1830

He entered his first mark in London as a plateworker in 1813 with an address in Bath. Similar marks to Grimwade 3418 were registered in 1819, 1822 and 1823. He is mentioned in the Bath directories from 1819 – 1830, at 43 Walcot Street until 1825 and from 1825 to 1830 at 23 Kingsmead Terrace, as a working silversmith.

216. WILLIAM WHITECROSS 1824-1840

He was apprenticed to James Erskine in 1800 and probably stayed with him until Erskine's retirement. He then established his own firm at 45 Unicorn Street, Aberdeen.

217. SAMUEL and GEORGE WHITFORD 1802-1807

Samuel and George Whitford of 15 Denmark Court, Strand, made a set of neck-ring labels in 1802 for CATSUP, CAYENNE and SAUCE ROYAL. Their oval soy frame of 1807 is illustrated (Fig. 111).

218. SAMUEL WHITFORD 1801-1852

Samuel carried on making silver on his own account for over forty years from 1807. In the London Museum there is a READING label attributable to him and bearing the date 1852. It seems he died prior to September 1856.

219. JOHN WHITTINGHAM 1788-1820

He entered three marks in 1788 and from the fact that he registered small marks it can be deduced that he made small objects at 13 Staining Lane. In 1810 he made a TARRAGON VIN label and at an earlier dated one for QUIN SAUCE. In 1801 he made a neck-ring label engraved for SOY on a plain curved narrow rectangular shape.

220. WILLIAM WHITWELL and JAMES BARBER 1814-1823

William Whitwell joined James Barber in 1814 until his death in 1823 to prop up the leading firm in York (formerly Hampston and Prince and then Cattle and Barber). Their SOY label for c.1815 is somewhat unimaginative and could even be London trade stock with an over-mark.

THE MAKERS

221. WILLIAMSON & HORTON 1869
John Henry Williamson and John Spinks Horton were in partnership for only some three years between 1868 and 1871 at 1 Upper Gloucester Street Clerkenwell, premises previously occupied from 1854 by John Howes, a silversmith, and subsequently occupied by another short-lived partnership between Frederick Perry and William Frederick Curry, trading as Perry & Curry Silversmiths, which ended in September 1875. Williamson & Horton's small mark (Culme 10510), without full stops, was used on a set of four sauce labels in 1869.

222. JOSEPH WILLMORE 1806-1847
He was a very famous Birmingham Maker producing a wide range of silver objects. Jackson records his mark for 1806, 1818, 1823, 1827, 1831 and 1832(70). Certainly, his name was entered at the Birmingham Assay Office between the years 1803 and 1807(71). In 1827 he made a label with the interesting title of OUDE SAUCE which in fiction Mr Towlinson made famous at Oxford when his fellow undergraduates dubbed him "King of Oude" because of his indiscriminate use of it. In 1822 he made the rare CROWN SAUCE label . In 1818 he produced a script single letter "R" on a squarish single reeded octagonal label, the maker mark being stamped twice. He also produced the gadrooned pair of 1838 for BRIGHTON and CHILLI V. purchased by Mrs Marshall. He was in partnership with Yapp and Woodward (see below) from 1814 to 1845.

223. JOSEPH WILLMORE & CO 1845-1856
Joseph Willmore being possibly the most diverse Birmingham manufacturer formed a company in the 1840's as did his contemporaries. The Mark JWCo is not recorded in Jones or Jackson but can be inspected on the FISH label dated 1851 in the Marshall Collection at the Ashmolean.

224. WILLIAM THOMAS WRIGHT and FREDERICK DAVIES 1864-1866
They made both wine and sauce labels. About 1866 they produced a pair of fretted labels not unlike that of William Summers illustrated on page 15 of Wine Labels, by the Reverend E.W. Whitworth, for WORCESTER and TARRAGON(72).

225. W. GREENER & CO 1881
The reported mark WG and R (worn) with the Birmingham date letters for 1881 is not mentioned in Jones or Jackson. However W. Greener & Co entered W.G. & Co in November 1881 which is thought to be the octagonal punched mark on the label for "G" for GARLICK.

226. WOOD & SONS 1850
The mark W & S in a rectangular punch was entered in Birmingham in January 1849. This is found on a "Black" label (for black pepper) in the Marshall Collection at the Ashmolean, using however lower case letters after the capital B (Drawer II, No. 374) instead of BLACK in Roman Capitals.

227. JOHN YAPP and JOHN WOODWARD 1844-1874
They entered their name in partnership with Joseph Willmore at Birmingham in 1834, but the entry in 1845 omits Joseph Willmore's name. They produced an attractive pair of crescent-shaped labels in 1848 engraved for "WORCESTER" and "ANCHOVY".

228. SAMUEL and CHARLES YOUNGE 1802-1810
John Younge & Co was the name registered in 1779. Later on J.T. Younge & Co, a partnership comprising J.T. Younge, John Allanson, Henry Walker and William Crowder, first registered its mark in 1788, changing its name to John Younge & Sons and then in 1811 to S & C Younge & Co. The two sons were Samuel and Charles. By 1802 William Crowder had left. In 1810 a new partnership deed for a term of eleven years was drawn up, the partners being Samuel and Charles Younge, George Kitchen of Sheffield and Henry Walker of London. The business continued until 1830 in Sheffield and London. Their works were in Union Street, Sheffield. They registered a plater's mark in 1813 incorporating what looks like a bishop's mitre. A MADEIRA label style hexagonal crescent, reeded edge, dated 1828 by Younge & Co was exhibited in the 1973 Sheffield Assay Office Bicentenary Exhibition (No. 72).

229. ALEXANDER ZIEGLER 1782-1795
This Edinburgh maker produced a label for RUW in 1782 which is thought to be a flavoured vinegar label for rue. The text in 1 WLJ 77 (second edition) refers to RUE. The label is illustrated. ■

NOTES

(1) 1851 Great Exhibition Official Catalogue, Class 23, Number 88, illustrated
(2) 3 WLJ 37
(3) 10 WLJ 179
(4) See further Martin Gubbins: "York Assay Office of Silversmiths 1776-1858". The SOY label is illustrated in 6 WLJ 153
(5) See Grimwade: "London Goldsmiths", First Edition, p.653
(6) John Scofield's frame with Susanna Barker's labels can be seen in Brodick Castle, see 9 WLJ 220-237
(7) Reference M 1944 – 536
(8) See 5 WLJ 85
(9) Weed: "Silver Wine Labels", p.62. KYAN was illustrated in Plate VIII, fig.77
(10) See 4 WLJ 129
(11) Reference M 1944 – 538 and 539
(12) See 6 WLJ 155
(13) Reference L 1943 – 473
(14) See Dent: "Wine, Spirit and Sauce Labels", p.14 and illustration on Plate V
(15) See Grimwade p.360 and Culme 3727
(16) See M. Ridgway: "The Chester Duty Books 1784-1840", p.77
(17) Culme, Directory of Gold and Silversmiths, p.83
(18) See 2 WLJ 48
(19) Reference M 1940 – 155 and 155A
(20) Drawer II, No. 379. Has tricusped duty mark for 1797
(21) Powerscourt Sales in Enniskerry, County Wicklow, Ireland, on 24-25th September 1984, lot 176
(22) Reference M 1944 – 407
(23) Reference M 1944 – 61
(24) Reference M 1944 – 577 and 578
(25) Reference M 1944 – 588
(26) SAUCE BLANCHE was sold at Phillips on 15 March 1991
(27) Reference M 1944 – 20
(28) The case for this attribution is set ot in the Author's Occasional Paper on the subject lodged in the National Library of Scotland. For a variety of "key" marks see lots 240 to 242 in Bonham's sale number 31203A, 18th July 2002.
(29) No. 405, Drawer II
(30) Reference M 1944 – 3
(31) See Grimwade, London Goldsmiths, p.544
(32) See Culme, Directory of Gold and Silversmiths, p.247
(33) See Grimwade, op.cit., p.567
(34) See Grimwade, op.cit. p.576
(35) See James, The Goldsmiths of Aberdeen, p.125
(36) See Culme, op.cit., p.298
(37) See Grimwade, op.cit., p.367
(38) See Culme, op.cit., p.298
(39) Ibid., note 5
(40) Weed, p.62
(41) Jackson's Silver and Gold Marks, edited Pickford, 1989, p.563
(42) Ibid., p.551
(43) Ibid., p.505
(44) Ibid., p.551, footnote
(45) See GP Moss and AD Roe, Highland Gold and Silversmiths, 1999
(46) Jackson, op.cit., p.552
(47) See M.A.V. Gill, A Directory of Newcastle Goldsmiths, pp.177-178
(48) Jackson, op.cit., p.396
(49) Reference M 1944 – 122
(50) Reference M 1944 – 252
(51) Culme, op.cit., p.381
(52) Gill, op.cit.
(53) James, op.cit., pp.132-133
(54) Jackson, op.cit., p.562
(55) Reference M 1944 – 586
(56) By the author, Proceedings of the Silver Society, Vol.III, No.1, p.13 at p.16 (27th October 1980)
(57) Lot 139, Christie's Sale on 15th July 1975
(58) Lot 16, Sotheby's Sale on 1st December 1955
(59) Millbrook Press Limited
(60) As researched by Arthur Grimwade, op.cit., p.662
(61) See Bradbury at p.431
(62) His mark is Grimwade 1848. Incorrect attributions were made in Country Life for 3th Sepember 1976 at p.897
(63) Reference M 1944 – 18
(64) Cropper Collection, Reference M 1944 – 19
(65) Museum reference 134 – 1935
(66) Museum reference 155 – 1908
(67) In the Marshall Collection
(68) 10 WLJ 70
(69) Jackson, op.cit., p.443
(70) Jackson, op.cit., pp.355-356
(71) Jackson, op.cit., p.366
(72) See 1 WLJ 124

Photo 3. *A zig-zag bordered crescent label by the famous Hester Bateman, c.1780.*

Photo 72. *English soy labels (testing .925 and .900 respectively, chains .925) exported to The Netherlands, unmarked except for the Dutch control mark (ex Duivenvoorde Castle).*

117

Fig 96. A Newcastle frame by Samuel Thompson II, 1757, with Kidney Shape labels for SOY, KETCHUP, ELDER, and GARLICK, designed with ribbed borders.

CHAPTER 7

THE DESIGNS

7.1 Unmarked sauce labels can be dated according to shape and to design. Shapes and designs can be conveniently classified under a number of headings. A shape is the outline of the label. A design is what is done to the face of the label. Shapes and designs commonly employed during a period of time can be placed in very approximate historical development order as follows:

PERIOD	DESIGN	SHAPE
1750-1770	Plain, feathered or bright-cut	1. Large crescent
1760-1775	Plain	2. Broadly rectangular with shaped sides
1765-1806	Bright-cut with wriggle work, feathered or reeded	3. Eye, navette, shuttle or pointed ends
1765-1780	Plain or feathered	4. Enclosed or nearly enclosed small crescent (1)
1765-1805	Plain, feathered, ribbed, punched or cabled	5. Kidney
1775-1785	Plain or thick double-reeded	6. Small squarish rectangular or postage stamp
1775-1860	Plain, reeded, bright-cut with wrigglework, gadrooned, beaded, cabled, applied cast fancywork or swag and festoon	7. Oval
1775-1850	Plain, reeded, bright-cut with wrigglework, feathered, beaded, rosettes or series of triangles	8. Open crescent including varieties
1760-1785	Feathered	9. Scroll
1783-1810	Fretted	10. Dome
1784-1836	Reeded	11. Rectangular, rounded ends
1785-1786	Bright-cut	12. Urn
1785-1820	Reeded or from 1809 gadrooned sometimes with applied corner shells	13. Broad rectangular
1760-1877	Reeded or if plated beaded	14. Rectangular, cut corners
1788-1789	Engraved	15. Star
1790-1825	Plain or single reeded	16. Narrow rectangular, straight or shaped sides
1790-1791	Engraved	17. Quatre semi-circular
1790-1870	Plain or reeded	18. Collar or hoop

119

THE DESIGNS

PERIOD	DESIGN		SHAPE
1791-1792	Engraved	19.	Canoe
1791-1828	Plain	20.	Attachment to neck-ring
1797-1810	Reeded	21.	Circular, disc or button
1810-1805	Plain	22.	Rectangular, shaped ends
1805-1810	Reeded	23.	Narrow rectangular, cut corners, curved top, bottom and ends
1806-1838	Plain, architectural, fruiting	24.	Basket
1807-1808	Plain	25.	Quatrefoil
1809-1827	Gadrooned or shell and gadrooned	26.	Cushion
1809-1823	Scrolling foliage and grapes	27.	Cherub
1810-1837	Scrolls and shells, thick double reeded	28.	Architectural
1810-1823	Gadrooned or floral and gadrooned	29.	Floreate
1810-1830	Gadrooned	30.	Rectangular
1810-1811	Engraved elaborately	31.	Squashed escutcheon
1813-1815	Chased	32.	Shell
1814-1815	Chased scrolling	33.	Cartouche
1815-1829	Grapes, tendrils and leaves	34.	Vine
1820-1896	Shells and foliage	35.	Escutcheon
1838-1849	Plain	36.	Shaped
1838-1881	Plain or gothic	37.	Initial
1851-1866	Chased	38.	Fretwork
1860-1870	Chased	39.	Shield or heart
1865-1875	Plain	40.	Festoon and drapery

7.2 Some sauce labels bear a maker's (or sponsor's) mark only. Having applied the shape and design test, dating can be refined by reference to the date of entry of a maker's mark and then further refined by reference to the period of currency of a maker's mark. Elizabeth Morley, for example, appears to have used five marks covering the periods 1794-1795, 1796-1800, 1800-1808, 1808-1810 and 1810-1814(2).

7.3 Use is sometimes made of a black composition, not as long-lasting as niello comprised of metallic alloys, for filling in engraved sauce titles to make them stand out and easier to read from a distance. This composition of darkened wax with an applied hardening agent, sometimes called blacking, has been found on sauce labels made by Margaret Binley, John Rich and Robert Keay, for example. As it seems that the majority of labels made by these makers did not have a blacking filling (the traces are not that easy to remove entirely) its use perhaps depended upon the customer's order (and taste) rather than on the silversmith's predilection. It gives no real guide to dating.

7.4 Some familiar wine label styles do not appear to have been used for sauce labels. The cut-out word, the two cupids, the bat and the eastern curios do not appear in the list above. Perhaps there was no call for sauce labels to match these designs on the table. Some styles relating to viticulture, such as the single vine leaf and tendril, were made to match, however incongruously, similar styles of wine labels. The engraved single letter, such as the letter V engraved on a gadrooned edged rectangle, and the cut-out suspended single letters, such as the letters C, H, K, R and S, were made to match albeit on a smaller scale.

7.5 Military wine labels can have a style of their own. For example, the 22nd Regiment of Foot's oak leaf is very individualistic. Wine labels may exhibit regimental insignia rather like a crest above as in the case of the 3rd Battalion of the

THE DESIGNS

Rifle Brigade. Sauce labels were too small to sit comfortably with this kind of attention. Very modest engraving on the front or on the back indicated regimental use(3). It was the oil and vinegar frame or the soy frame which bore the Regimental crest engraved on an applied cartouche.

7.6 The use of script, Gothic, Old English, italic or other fancy lettering is very unusual on sauce labels as part of an overall design concept. Most titles whether for wines or sauces are in Roman capital letters. Anchovy, Anchovie, Elf Anchovies, Caveace, Cayenne(4), Chilli Vin, Fish Sauce, Harvey's Fish Sauce, Mushroom Ketchup, Vinegar, Walnut Pickle and Worcester, for example, have all appeared in script. Two of these titles were produced in Sweden. Four of these titles were produced circa 1803 by John Reily on a set of four narrow rectangular labels perhaps as a special order. VINEGAR also appears in Gothic or Puginesque style writing to fit in with an art nouveau provenance. European countries seem to appreciate the artistic merits of the use of flowing script even if this makes identification difficult from a distance.

7.7 Slip chains rarely appear to have been used on sauce labels. Such chains were designed with a hook at one or both ends to enable the chain easily to be removed from the label to allow unrestricted cleaning around the eyelet. Instead of a chain soldered loops were sometimes used. These date from about the 1750s in the case of wine labels. There is a reference to bottle tickets with soldered loops dated 28th April 1759 in Volume I of the Wakelin ledgers. However no entries for sauce labels can be clearly identified in Volume I.

7.8 Most titles were engraved but some were pierced. This was more expensive. An early mention of piercing is again in Volume I for the 11th May 1749 regarding the supply of two pierced bottle tickets. Each cost a penny more to manufacture than an engraved item and so were more prestigious. Piercing does make a label stand out though not making such a clear statement as a deep engraving filled with niello or with blacking.

7.9 Whilst bottle corks with labels were made for wines and spirits. they do not appear to have been made for vinegar decanters. Glass stoppers were used, which did not lend themselves to marking beyond the use of initials (see "K" in illustration of "Bristol" soy bottle in Fig, 113).

7.10 Economies were made in the use of wine labels on occasions by engraving a wine name on each side of the label so that it could be displayed either way round. This does not seem to have happened in the case of sauce labels. Like wine labels, however, they were sometimes re-used. Reily and Storer's CAYENNE and HARVEY were re-engraved for the spirits NOYAU and COGNAC as spirit labels are often about the same size as sauce labels. John Mackay's ANCHOVY and three other sauce labels in a set of wine label size shells had title plates soft-soldered over the pierced sauce titles engraved for ACID and three other medicinal or toiletry titles. It is believed that these title plates have now been removed and the sauce labels restored to their former glory, although somewhat on the large side for display on a glass container.

7.11 Examples with commentary are now given with regard to each of the shapes with illustrations where possible to assist in recognition.

Style 1, the large crescent, was used on oil and vinegar frame bottles of the 1750s. This is proved by fitting such labels on frame bottles of the period. The curvature exactly matches in the case of a pair engraved for OIL and VINEGAR of this period with feathered borders which are probably the earliest sauce labels known. A smaller pair without decoration engraved for PEPr. VINEGAR and CAYON

Photo 4. Early Crescent Shaped Labels.

THE DESIGNS

PEPPER by Margaret Binley (1764-1778) belong to the later 1760s(5). An unmarked pair engraved for HARVEY (Fig. 9) and WORCESTER belong to the 1770s being intricately decorated with bright cutting and wrigglework. Early sauce labels of this kind can easily be spotted because the silversmiths used large lettering.

7.12 Style 2, the irregular rectangular, was used on early flavoured vinegar bottles, being shaped to fit the vinegar decanter outline. Illustrated are ELDER and GARLICK by Margaret Binley (1764-1778) and an unmarked TERRAGON. The design for its effect relied not on decoration but on the shaping of the outline. The chains are quite heavy and as in Style 1 the lettering is large at this time.

7.13 Style 3, the eye, was designed as a small label for use on the newly introduced soy frame. The early start date for the eye is derived from the evidence of bright cutting and wrigglework as in the example for LEMON PICKLE. The evidence from makers such as James Hyde (from 1774), Susanna Barker (from 1776) and John Rich (from 1784) suggests early use of the eye shape. Dating evidence exists for the years 1784/5, 1792, 1797, 1800 and 1806. Unmarked eye shaped labels carry unusual border designs such as on the example for CHILI V at the turn of the eighteenth century.

7.14 Style 4, the enclosed crescent, appears to be a unique design for early sauce labels. Most are unmarked. They fall into three categories of design. The earliest have no eyelets but a punched hole for the chain (class 1). The next category has small eyelets (class 2) and the third category has larger, decorated eyelets or ears (class 3). The earliest class 1 CAYAN

Photo 5. Irregular Rectangular Shaped Labels.

Photo 6. Eye Shaped Labels

THE DESIGNS

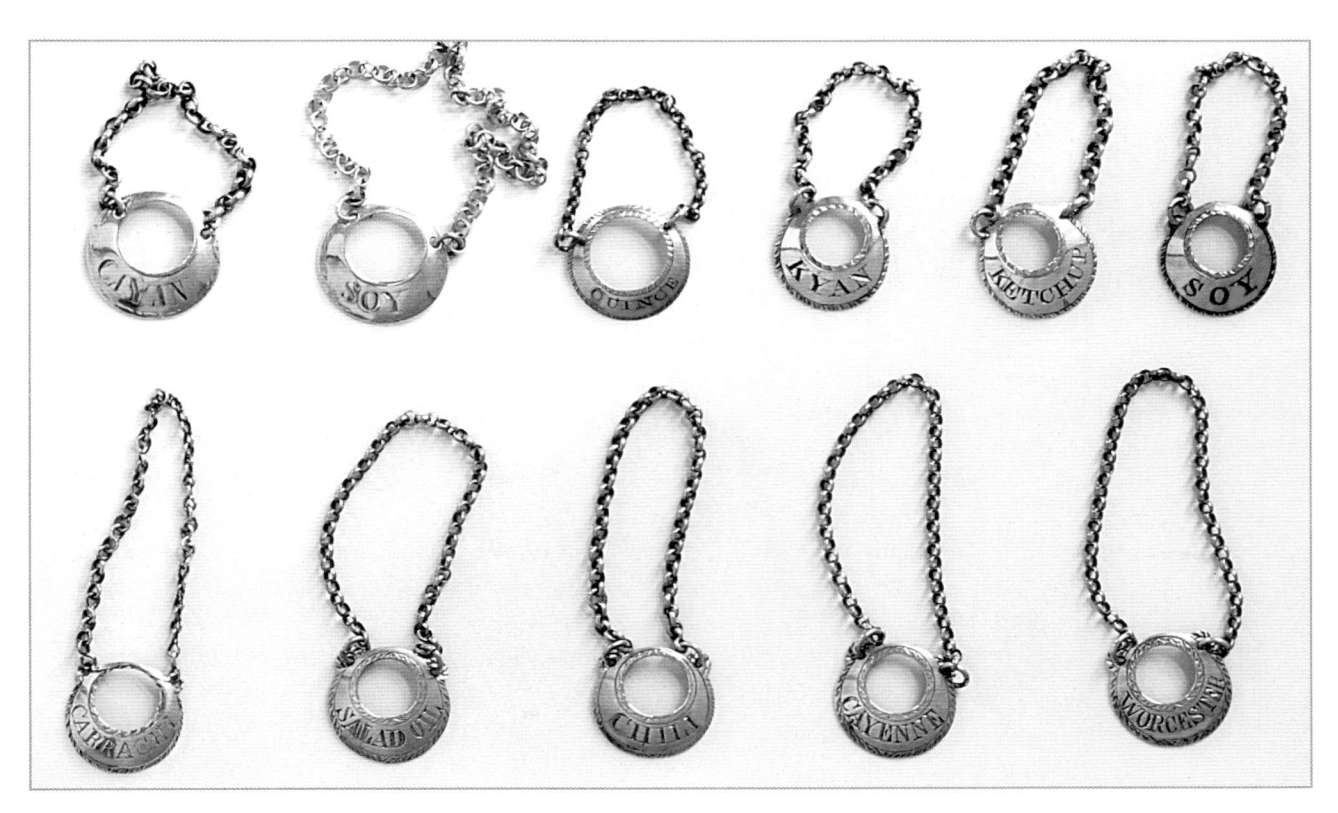

Photo 7. Enclosed Crescent Labels

(illustrated) and SOY have no decoration around the circle. The lettering as might be expected is large and the outer border is of the early cable design. An exception is QUINCE (illustrated). That this is an early label can be gleaned from a comparison with the TARRAGON illustrated by Dent on his plate V which has a maker's mark on it MB which Dent attributed to Matthew Boulton but is most likely to be the mark of Margaret Binley. An unmarked CAYON bearing the Fauconberg and Conyers arms was probably made by Margaret Binley. Documentary evidence concerning the order by the Earl of Holderness suggests a date of 1764-65(6). Thomas Hemming made a CARRACHE label dateable to no later than 1773 and similar to the class 2 CARRACHI label illustrated(7). Similar class 2 labels bear engraved titles for KYAN, SOY and KETCHUP. Class 3 labels have been noted for CHILI, CAYENNE and WORCESTER (illustrated). They are all unmarked. However it is known that Susanna Barker made a label in this style and possibly a set was made by John Langford and John Sebille in 1766(8). A version in ivory is held by the Victoria and Albert Museum in the Cropper Collection. Illustrated (Fig. 36) on later mounted bottles are HARVEY (an original) and TAROGON (a copy made in 1890) belonging to class 3 with wire attachments.

7.15 Style 5, the kidney, was probably introduced by Margaret Binley in about 1765. This is evidenced by her wine labels also made in this style(8). The sauce labels were designed to match. They had however a ribbed (sometimes called "rope") border like the CAYON by Margaret Binley (1764-1778) which is illustrated. Titles used in the 1760s included ELDER, KETCHUP and GARLICK with the larger punch being used and CARRISH, CAYON and ELDER with the smaller punch being used. The style was copied by Susanna Barker for SOY during 1786-1793, by John Rich for ANCHOVY in 1791 and by Rawlings and Summers as late as circa 1830, in each case perhaps to add a new title to a set or to replace a broken or more likely missing one. In the 1770s feathered borders were in vogue and fine examples have been recorded for CAYON by Margaret Binley, for HERVEY by Peter and William Bateman in 1811 and for SOY by James Barber circa 1850. In the 1775s bright cut with wrigglework borders were very much in keeping with the classical revival and examples have been

123

THE DESIGNS

Photo 9. Kidney Shaped Labels

Photo 8. Alexander Cameron Circa 1840

noted by Susanna Barker (1776-1793) for ANCHOVIES, Elizabeth Morley (1794-1810) for SOY and John Nickolds (on his own 1818-c.1840) for CAYENNE. Likewise from the start of this period comes the rare set of six silver-gilt labels by or for Robert Piercy of 1775 with cable designed borders engraved for SOY, ELDER, ANCHOVY, KYAN, KETCHUP and TARRAGON (see Fig. 2). Also during this period of great demand sauce labels were produced in Old Sheffield Plate. Illustrated is a set of three for KYAN, KETCHUP and TARRAGON. Finally come the undecorated labels and the reeded, single or double. CYAN, with large lettering, was made probably at the beginning of William Barrett's career in 1782. CATCHUP, illustrated, unmarked, belongs to the same period. So does another unmarked plain pair for ANCHOVY and CATSUP. So far as the reeded labels are concerned, a pair for ANCHOVY (illustrated) and CATCHUP with double reeding were made in Newcastle between 1812 and 1822 by George Samuel Lewis and John Wright. With a similar provincial flavour a single reeded label for HARVEY SAUCE (illustrated) was produced in Dundee between 1840 and 1847 by Alexander Cameron.

7.16 Style 6, the small squarish rectangle, was introduced in the 1770s. The earliest known datable squares were made in 1777 by Thomas Daniel for a four bottle circular soy frame of that year which stood on claw and ball feet. Three labels survived engraved for LEMON, SOY and KETCHUP. The maker's mark and the lion passant on the labels were identical to the maker's mark and the lion passant on the soy frame. In the early 1780s Susanna Barker made a label of this style for INDIA. Thomas Phipps and Edward Robinson between 1783 and 1792, being the period during which their labels were unmarked, were responsible for the plain WALNUT PICKLE illustrated in Fig. 110. Peter Lambert stamped his maker's mark three times on the single letter "S" for SOY with a single reeded border in the provincial manner which one would expect coming from Aberdeen. It was made between 1804 and 1813. The Marshall Collection in the Ashmolean at Oxford has a set ot almost square reeded "postage stamp" sauce labels. The square was a convenient style for "initial" labels, such as to enable Phipps and Robinson to frame the pierced letter "R" in

THE DESIGNS

Photo 10. Small Squarish Shaped Label

1799(9). A squarish unmarked sauce label with the letter "S" is known, measuring 1.5 by 1 cm(10). One for "M" is illustrated in the Journal which has a long chain for use on a jar of mushroom ketchup perhaps.

7.17 Style 7, the oval, has been popular since 1775. It is yet another of the earliest forms of soy label. One of the earliest labels is for LEMON with large lettering and a feathered edge. James Hyde (1774-1792 for his period of maker's mark only labels) made the attractive KETCHUP, illustrated. The maker's mark is stamped twice, indicating that this was made during the earlier part of this period. Likewise beautifully bright cut with wrigglework is an attractive wide oval (illustrated) for HARVEY SAUCE by Phipps and Robinson. Also shown is a label for WORCESTER by Thomas Hyde (1775-1792 for his period of maker's mark only labels), again stamped twice with the makers mark indicating an early date, this time with beaded decoration. This label is part of a set of four together with HARVEY, KETCHUP and READING. Later on the double reed became a favourite border decoration. Shown is TARRAGON by John Rich in 1796. He also produced a set of five labels in 1791 in the same style for GARLIC VINEGAR, WOODS SAUCE, CAYENNE PEPPER, JAPAN SOY and CARRACH, curved to fit snugly to the bottle shape (see Fig. 95). Exactly the same style, but not so curvaceous, was adopted by Thomas Hyde for a set of four sauces comprising ELDER, CARRACHE, GARLICK and TARRAGON. James Hyde employed a single reed to decorate an early oval CAVICE. This was copied by Rawlings and Summers in Victorian times. Single, double or treble reeded ovals were produced from around the 1780s until about the 1850s by the Hydes, Susanna Barker, John Rich, Rawlings and Summers and Thomas Johnson (1851). Plain ovals were made in much the same period, perhaps starting a little later in the 1790s, by William Robertson, Phipps and Robinson, James McKay, John Watson of Sheffield (1805), Rawlings and Summers and Samuel Whitford (1852). Illustrated is KETCHUP, one of a set with SOY and ANCHOVY, made by George Smith and

Photo 12. Oval Shaped Labels

THE DESIGNS

Thomas Hayter between 1792 and 1796. During the Regency period the shape was used, being decorated with gadrooned borders by makers such as John Reily and Mary and Charles Reily, and copied in Victorian times by Hyans Hougham or Henry Holland in the 1860s. In Victorian times the style was much favoured to support heavy bordering, such as in the case of HARVEY in 1837 with a rope border by Samuel Whitford, MADRAS FLAME in 1840 with a snake border by Rawlings and Summers and CHILI in 1855 with a cable border by Robert Hennell III (illustrated).

Photo 11. Dutch Vinegar Label.

7.18 Style 8, the ordinary crescent, exists in at least six different types:
- (i) With narrow points. In this type there is nearly a full circle inside the crescent between the points. Illustrated are KETCHUP by Thomas and James Phipps in silver-gilt and GARLICK by Thomas Hyde.
- (ii) With medium points. This is the common type. Illustrated are ESSENCE ANCHOVIES by Robert Kippax and SOY by Rawlings and Summers.
- (iii) With wide points. This is an uncommon type sometimes called the shallow crescent. Illustrated are KYAN by George Baskerville and SOY by William Simpson of Banff.
- (iv) With a central cusp or peak or dome. An example of this type made in 1825 by Thomas Edwards has been noted.
- (v) With a central design. An example by Susanna Barker with a cartouche containing an armorial has been noted. Some examples have vacant cartouches which suggest that this was a more popular type that the number of surviving labels would indicate.
- (vi) With a thickened base. This is the gorget type produced in Birmingham by Matthew Boulton and John Fothergill from 1773. Illustrated are SOY and LEMON PICKLE of 1776.

Reeded crescents are rather rare. Thomas Hyde produced the type (i) single reeded illustrated for GARLICK together with KETCHUP and ELDER. Thomas Jenkinson (c.1810) made a type (iii), Thomas Edwards in 1825 a type (iv) and the Vintners' Company have an unmarked label for WALNUT KETCHUP following type (iii). Feathered crescents are also rather rare. The 1750s OIL and VINEGAR labels (type (iii)) have this decoration. So does a 1760s WALNUT (illustrated) of type (ii). Unusual decorations were employed on a number of crescents. The early unmarked HARVEY and WORCESTER labels (Style 1) have a chased ribbon inset along with swags hanging down from the eyelets. Margaret Binley's CUCUMBER (illustrated) has a

Photo 13. Narrow Pointed Crescent Labels.

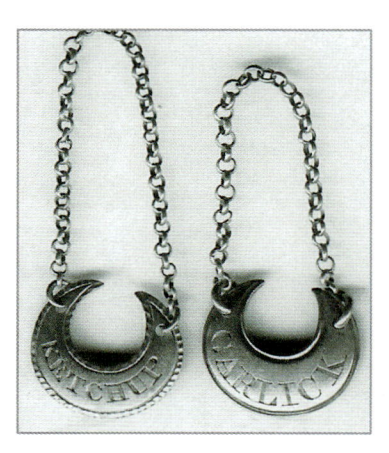

Photo 14. Medium Pointed Crescent Labels.

Photo 15. Wide Pointed Crescent Labels.

THE DESIGNS

Photo 16. Gorget Type Crescent Labels.

rich border of heart-shaped leaves with another border of berries set inside. Herman Walther's TARRAGON of around 1770 (illustrated) has a border of arrow shaped leaves. Benjamin Taitt's ANCHOVY (illustrated), one of a set of three with CHILI and SOY, has a series of interlinked semi-circles. KYAN, unmarked, has a bright-cut border with a delicate band of chasing inside (illustrated). James Phipps decorated one

Photo 17. Old Sheffield Plate Sauce Labels.

Photo 18. Crescent Shaped Labels.

of his early labels for HARVEY (illustrated) with a chain of narrow leaf-like objects with delicate chasing inside. Hester Bateman produced four zig-zag bordered crescents for LEMON, ELDER, SOY and CAYON (see Photo 3) around 1780. Plain crescents were popular throughout the whole period being made by Binley, the Hydes, Rich, Reily, the Batemans, the Burrows, Baskerville, Rawlings and Summers and Yapp and Woodward. In the 1770s it was found that this design lent itself to being reproduced in Old Sheffield Plate. Three examples are illustrated below. They all appear to have beaded edges. The example for LEMON was formerly in the Weed Collection. The beaded design was popular in the 1770s and 1780s. Volume IV of the Wakelin Ledgers records the purchase in 1776 by Mr. Hayes of six beaded labels for his soy frame. Volume VI discloses that

127

THE DESIGNS

Mr. R.H.H.F. Thynne Cartaret was supplied on the 17th September 1777 with beaded soy labels at 3s. 6d. each and 2 larger beaded soy labels at 4s. each. Not long afterwards in January 1778 it seems that the chains of the two larger labels were replaced at a cost of three shillings. One wonders why! According to Volume VII the Hon. Colonel Stewart bought eight beaded soy labels on the 20th May 1779 for 3s. each and Mr. Thomas Fonnereau bought three soy tickets at 3s. each on the 10th February 1780 and a set of beaded soy tickets at 3s. 6d. each on the 26th April of the same year. The Revd. Mr. Weston in 1784 was supplied with four oval beaded soy tickets according to Volume VIII. The price for supplying soy labels in a boxed set of four was 1s. in 1785 and this would have kept the labels in a safe place.

7.19 Style 9, the scroll, is a rare and early design in sauce labels and perhaps was only used where it was desired that the sauce labels should match the wine labels in use at the table. The point is well illustrated by looking at Penzer's Plate 8 in his Book of the Wine Label and contrasting KYAN at the top left with the decanter labels for FINE CHAMPAGNE, VIDONIA, LISBON and WHITE WINE illustrated beneath. Two very early scrolls with feathered edges for LEMON and CAION, unmarked, with large lettering and curvature designed to fit round a soy frame bottle of the 1760s, are illustrated. So also is a Susanna Barker top right bottom left type scroll with bright cut borders enhanced with chasing, for ELDER. The KETCHUP scroll (illustrated) is of the same type but with pierced letters and devoid of decoration relying on the shape for effect. It was made by Charles Rawlings in 1824. The scroll style was also used for plated labels. READING and HARVEY'S (illustrated) are by Hunt and Roskell, 1882.

7.20 Style 10, the dome, is best seen as the fretted domed rectangular. Illustrated is CATCHUP, one of a set of three with ANCHOVY and SOY, bearing maker's mark only I E, which has a distinctive arrow-head serif to the central horizontal bar forming the letter E. The maker is thus unlikely to be John Emes or James Erskine. If indeed it was a London maker who was responsible for this sophisticated label then it could have been John Edlington (1806) not recorded by Grimwade. If it was a maker who used the Chester Assay Office then it could be the same person as the maker of a wine label illustrated at page 107 of Volume 6 of the Wine Label Journal (11), datable to 1785 because of the incuse head, if the mark I F was to be read as I E. The style follows that established for wine labels (12) and the designs is similar to that employed by Hester Bateman of c.1783 (13), Susanna Barker of the same date (14), Samuel Teare of c.1790 (15), J. Keating of c.1795 (16), John Langlands II of the same date (17), Ann Adams of c.1808 (18) and William Constable of c.1810 (19). There were however forms of dome

Photo 19. Early Scroll Labels.

Photo 20. Scroll Shaped Labels.

THE DESIGNS

Photo 21. Dome Shaped Labels.

other than the fretted dome. Timothy Renou used a distinctive border on his labels like a matting, with a domed top on which some sort of fruit was often engraved. Examples made by him in 1814 for KYAN and ANCHOVIE are illustrated. Matting was used by Charles Rawlings in 1819 to form the body of a snake, the head of which neatly fitted into the dome style, as can be seen from the CAYENNE label illustrated. Sebastian Crespel used a dome in connection with a single eyelet suspension design for his ANCHOVY, illustrated, of 1827. The more traditional dome or hump is used by Jonathan Haynes in 1828 for CHILI VINEGAR (illustrated) with a double reeded border.

7.21 Style 11, the rounded end rectangular, is the second most popular style in double reeded form. Single reeding is rare. Treble reeding is sometimes found and some dated examples noted were made in 1796, 1805 and 1819. Judging from the majority of titles used on reeded labels they must have been used to adorn soy

Photo 22. Rounded-end Rectangular Shaped Labels

129

THE DESIGNS

frame bottles. In the 1810s were OIL, KETCHUP and HARVEY; in the 1820s were SOY, FISH SAUCE, ANCHOVY, KETCHUP and TARRAGON; and in the 1830s SOY, CHILLI, ANCHOVY and TARRAGON. This style, however, also catered for the more exotic titles such as NEPAUL, ZOOBDITTY and MOGUL. The style is also found without any decoration at all.

7.22 Style 12, the urn or goblet, is very rare. An urn shaped LEMON label by Phipps and Robinson circa 1785 was reported at page 83 of Volume 10 of the Wine Label Journal as having been sold at Christie's South Kensington on the 13th May 1997. A pair of goblets with festoons has also been noted as sauce labels. The goblet style in wine labels has been illustrated at page 174 of Volume I of the Wine Label Journal.

7.23 Style 13, the broad rectangular, with no cut, rounded or shaped corners, is uncommon and probably in use only between 1800 and 1820. The use of the expression "broad" is simply to distinguish from "narrow". So it does not imply fatness or girth. A gadrooned example with applied corner shells is illustrated in Margaret Holland's "Silver" at page 75. Illustrated are single reeded labels for ANCHOVY and KETCHUP, unmarked. A similar SOY was marked by Elizabeth Morley in 1810. The rare gadrooned ANCHOVY is by Daniel Hockley (1810-1817), the READING is unmarked and the rare beaded ANCHOVY is by John Rich in 1809. CAPSICUM probably hails from Denmark.

7.24 Style 14, the rectangular with cut corners, sometimes referred to as an octagonal, was the most popular style. It was a convenient style for the use of workers in Old Sheffield Plate because the beaded edge could be employed to disguise the plating. An example is shown for CHILLI VINEGAR and other OSP labels have been noted including ELDER and READING and in large size SOY and MOGUL. That the style was in use from early days is proven by the illustrated ELDER using large lettering, niello, and curvature. It is unmarked. KYAN (illustrated) is also of early date, bearing Phipps and Robinson's mark stamped twice, having large lettering, and, it is thought uniquely for this style, having bright cut borders. The common form of double reeding is illustrated by the label for DEVONSHIRE sauce fully marked by Rawlings and Summers. Makers using this popular style and design include Astons, Atkins, Robert Barker (from 1793), Peter, Anne and William Bateman, Bower, Emes and Barnard, CF (an unknown Jersey maker), Flavelle, the Knights, Linnit, McDonald, Phipps and Robinson, Rawlings and Summers, the Reilys, Rich, Shaw, Smith Tate, and Yapp and Woodward to name only a few. Single reeded decoration is uncommon, with a tendency for it to be used by provincial makers such as Joseph Willmore in Birmingham for VINEGAR and Robert Keay in Perth also for VINEGAR (illustrated). Treble reeding was chosen by Robert Barker for his elegant FISH.SAUCE (illustrated) and TARRAGON of 1793 with pierced titling and

Photo 23. Broad Rectangular Shaped Labels

THE DESIGNS

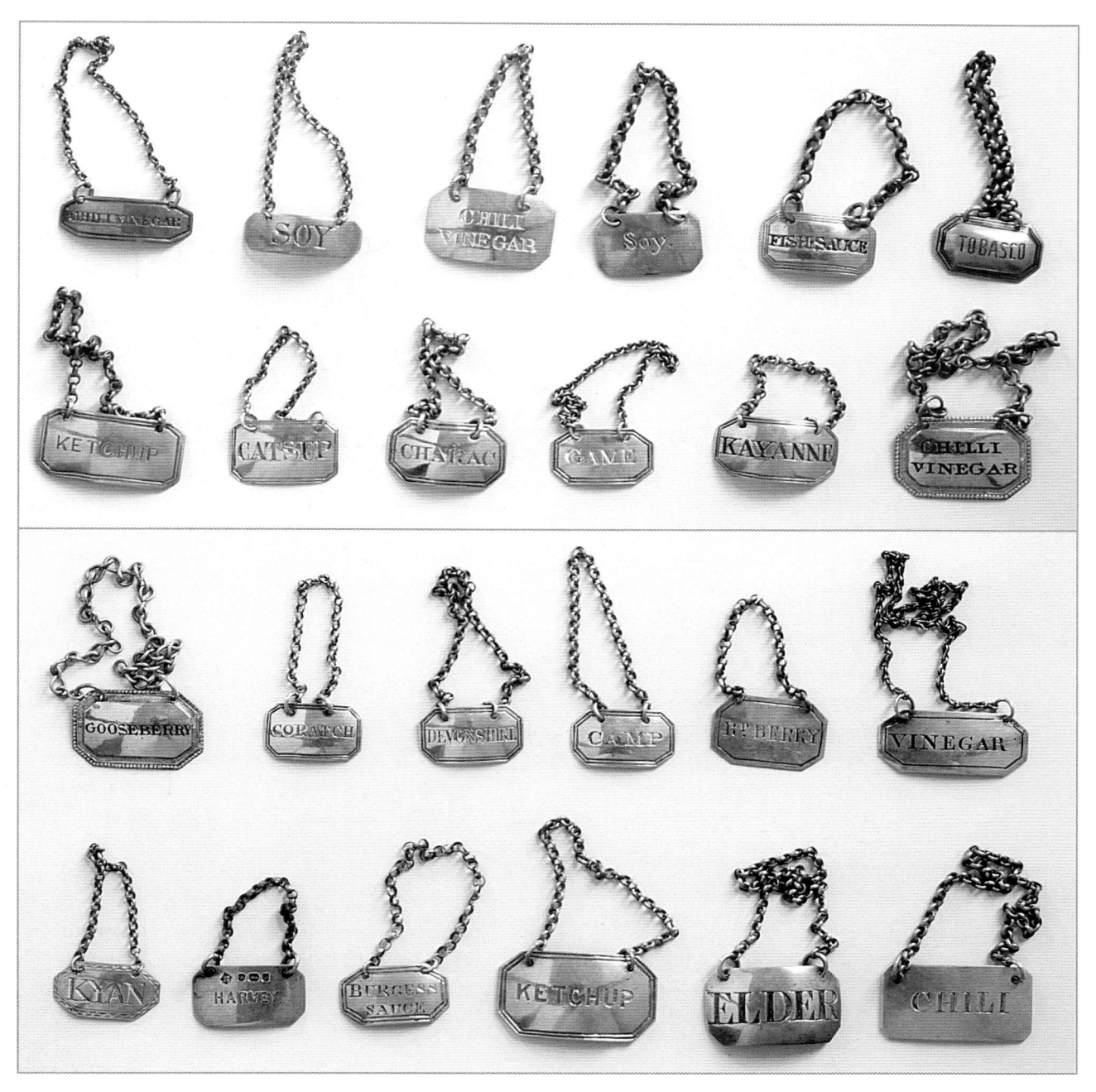

Photo 24. Octagonal Shaped Labels

also by Watton Smith of Birmingham for his TOBASCO of 1893. Piercing was not that popular: out of 115 labels inspected in this style only 5 had pierced titles. The narrow rectangular shape was rarely used in this style: an example for CHILI VINEGAR by George Murray of Newcastle circa 1805 is illustrated. Some labels were just plain and at least six different makers used plainness as an attraction. Richard Martin and Ebenezer Hall of Sheffield went further and had a label for HARVEY (illustrated) assayed on its face for 1887 although curiously the duty mark of Queen Victoria's head is missing. This requirement was not dropped until three years later in 1890.

7.25 Style 15 is the star and rare. Only two are known, both by William Abdy (1786-1790). The star has twelve points. The title is engraved round the top of the circle above a foliate device rather resembling an eagle on the wing. One (illustrated) was for CAYAN and the other

131

THE DESIGNS

Photo 25. Star Shaped Labels.

(illustrated) for SOY. They bear a duty mark, maker's mark and sterling silver mark but no date letter. The lightly decorated leaves are to be contrasted with the heavily decorated points, which perhaps makes the design more of a petalled flower than a heavenly body. Presumably the design was produced to match up with star wine labels in use on decanters.

7.26 Style 16, the narrow rectangular, has straight or shaped sides. It is often slightly curved because of its length. Many of these labels are without decoration. A typical set of eight was illustrated by Lady Ruggles-Brise in "Country Life" for the 19th June 1942 at page 1186. KYAN is early and unmarked, undecorated and with large lettering (not illustrated). CAYON, circa 1775 by Thomas Hyde has an ovolo type unique border; CUCUMBER by John Reily circa 1805 is undecorated but has raised eyelets; SAUCE A LA MILITAIRE and CAMP SAUCE by James Erskine of Aberdeen circa 1800 are undecorated; KIAN by Duncan Urquhart and Napthali Hart is fully marked for 1795 undecorated but with raised eyelets; and CAYENNE (Photo 62) in silver gilt by Theodosia Ann Atkins is fully marked for 1815 with pierced lettering, raised eyelets and a single reeded border. A set of four unmarked labels for CAMP VIN, ANCHOVY, SOY and CAYENNE have a double reeded border. William Smiley made another set of four in 1881 with raised eyelets but no decoration.

7.27 Style 17, the quatre-semi-circle, is illustrated by the set of three labels shown by Major Dent in his "Sauce Labels" for the unusual titles to go with an unusual style of INDIAN SOY, ESSENCE OF ANCHOVY and UNIVERSAL SAUCE.

7.28 Style 18, the collar, refers to a collar or hoop which fits over and around the neck of a soy bottle. Illustrated is READING, one of a pair with SOY, both unmarked. Collars seem to have

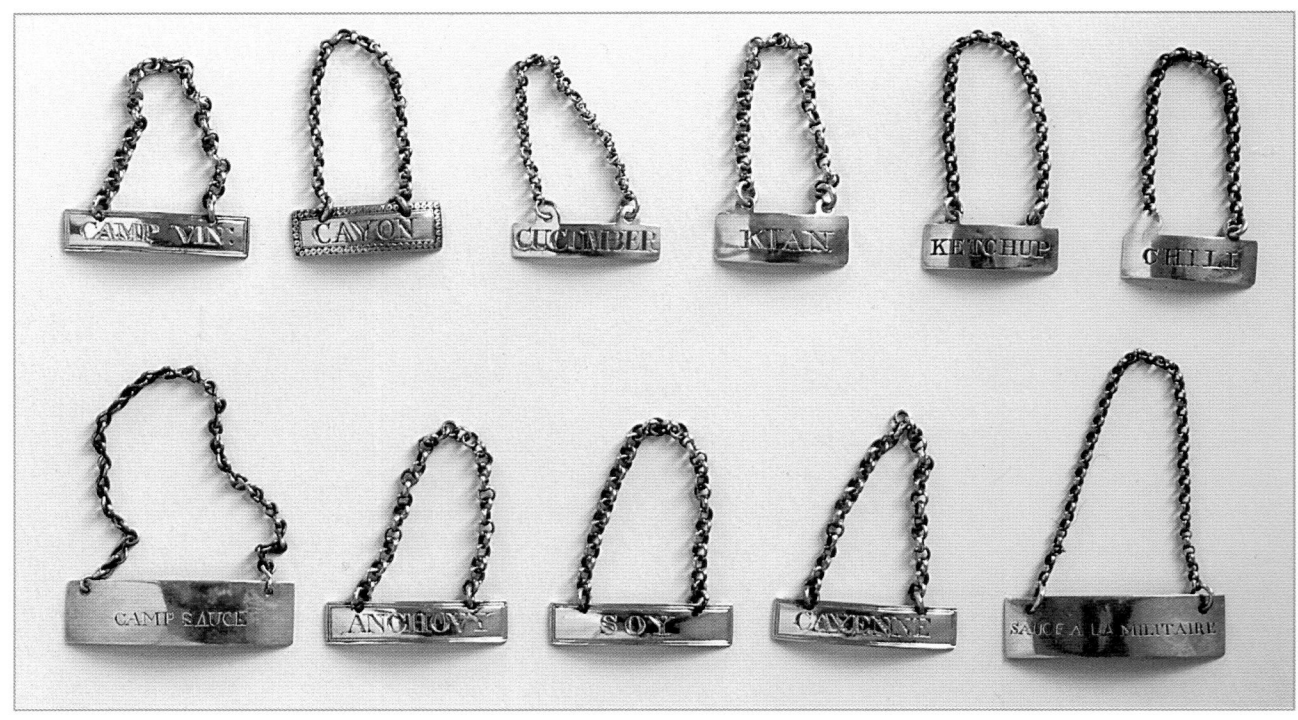

Photo 26. Narrow Rectangular Shaped Labels.

THE DESIGNS

Photo 27. Collar Shaped Labels.

Photo 28. Canoe Shaped Label.

been used between 1790 and 1870. William Summers made small crescents open at the top as bottle collars in the 1870s(20). Troby's ambassadorial KYAN and a plated CAYENNE with a pierced title are also illustrated. There are some collars made from ivory in the Croper collection for ANCHOVY, CATSUP, HARVEY, SOY, WALNUT, WORCESTER and GINGER. These could have been made around 1820 but dating is difficult. A collar label made by Charles Rawlings in 1827 has engraved around it in italic writing HARVEY'S FISH SAUCE.

7.29 Style 19, the canoe, occurs when the points of the crescent are so open and wide apart that the shape of the label looks like a canoe. Robert Bowers of Chester (1787-1814) produced a LEMON PICKLE in this style in 1791 which can be seen in the M.V. Brown Collection. An unmarked pair of similar date engraved for RAVIGITTE and ELDER can also be classified under this style. Illustrated is a double reeded KETCHUP made by a London small-worker Thomas Bannister (1829-1836) in 1834.

7.30 Style 20, the neck-ring attachment, is a style of fixing rather than a shape. It was however very distinctive. There were five different methods of

Photo 29. Neck Ring Labels.

133

THE DESIGNS

attaching a label of whatever style to the silver ring or wire.

(i) Using a hinge. A double reeded rectangle (illustrated) with cut corners engraved for P. VINEGAR was attached in this manner by Josiah Snatt in 1804.

(ii) Suspending by a ring through a single hole drilled at the top of the label. This was the method favoured by Phipps and Robinson for their LEMON and KETCHUP (illustrated) with large letters engraved on a plain rounded rectangular label. It was also used by John Rich in 1784/5 to suspend a bright cut eye shaped label for WORCESTER written in script.

(iii) Soldering a ring on the back of the label at the top with ring attached. This method is a Phipps and Robinson later invention of 1804 to suspend a domed KYAN (illustrated)

(iv) Passing a wire ring through the usual eyelets secured by a twist or by using rings. Illustrated is CORACK, VINEGAR and KETCHUP (Fig. 111) attributed to Hugh Gordon of Fortrose bearing the single key of St Benedict as a Burgh mark. Here rings are inserted into the looped ends of the wire. Rawlings and Summers used this method for SOY and LEMON with cut corners, double reeded, in 1829. The wire clips on to the glass.

(v) Mounting an eyelet on top of the label for permanent attachment to a ring soldered onto the loop. This was the usual method adopted by the great exponents of this branch of label making, namely John Tayleur, Robert Garrard, Samuel Whitford, and Sebastian Crespel. The normal design is to mount an eyelet in the centre above a narrow rectangular style label without decoration. However, John Tayleur also set his eyelet above a dome, sometimes fretted and sometimes solid, and illustrated, for ELDER.

An unusual pear-shaped pendant engraved for SOY is illustrated in Weed's "Silver Wine Labels" at page 59 where the maker's mark is said to be AJ which is said by Grimwade to be of doubtful authenticity. The silver rings are sometimes marked with the lion passant. Examples are known by Rich in 1784/5, Garrard in 1816 and Crespell in 1824. The narrow rectangular labels are usually plain, examples being dated 1791, 1795, 1798, 1799, 1809, 1810, 1815, 1817, 1824 and 1828. However four double reeded examples have been noted for the years 1804, 1820, 1829 and 1837. Thus the neckring was in use mainly between 1784 and 1837 for sauce labels.

7.31 Style 21, the button, was produced in two types, the solid disc by James Hyde and the polo disc having a circular hole in the centre by Robert Garrard the Elder. Hyde's version of 1797 was double reeded, engraved with a sauce title and engraved with an armorial. This matched the wine label button style of 1795 for Shrub, Hollands and Rum (21). An example for LEMON is illustrated, the armorial being a mailed fist clasping a single downward pointed arrow. It is fully marked. Two rings are soldered onto the reverse for attaching the chain. Garrard's version of 1806 is undecorated and engraved for SOY. This matched the wine label polo disc engraved for Rum shown on Penzer's Plate 22 incorrectly there described as a neckring in view of the chain clearly attached. Thus it appears that in both cases this design was produced to match wine labels.

Photo 30. Button Shaped Label.

7.32 Style 22, the shaped-end rectangular, was a style favoured by John Reily and copied from that used for earlier produced wine labels. This may well have been the case in respect of other makers. Illustrated are Frances Purton's LEMON PICKLE circa 1790 with triple reeding, Susanna Barker's FRENCH of 1793 of similar design, James Atkins' SOY with pierced title of 1804,

THE DESIGNS

Photo 31. Shaped-end Rectangular Shaped Labels

Peter and William Bateman's ANCHOVY with vacant cartouche and foliage above a double reeded example of 1813 and Rawlings and Summers' CROWN of 1844 copying an earlier design.

7.33 Style 23, the curved narrow rectangular, is a unique design. It is clearly an early design with feathered edge, the unusual title of CAYENE. being given a full stop and set off with thin lines of reeding. The label is unmarked and probably of provincial origin.

Photo 32. Curved Narrow Rectangular Shaped Label.

7.34 Style 24, the basket, is a convenient way of describing individualistic designs which do not really fall into any particular category. The plain KETCHUP is unmarked. The cast label with pierced title for ESSENCE OF CHILLI is a masterpiece from Charles Rawlings in 1823. William Theobalds and Robert Atkinson made the architectural type basket pierced for CHILI in 1838.

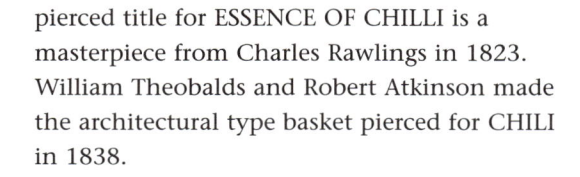

7.35 Style 25, the quatrefoil, or four leaved clover, follows a wine label design pioneered by Benjamin Smith in 1807 for Teneriffe and Hermitage (22) and by Paul Storr in 1808 for Madeira (23). Smith is probably the maker of the unmarked sauce label for KYAN illustrated because Storr appears always to have marked his labels of whatever size.

Photo 34. Quatrefoil Shaped Label.

7.36 Style 26, the cushion, is a plain cushion shape with sauce title engraved or pierced in use in Regency times and the reign of George IV. Thus the edge is heavily decorated with shells and gadrooning. The design was introduced by J.W. Story and William Elliott in 1809 and illustrated are their KYAN of this year and ANCHOVY of 1810. The design was repeated (an example for KYAN in 1827 is shown). Then in 1812 they made a larger, heavier version (24) continued by William Elliott on his own in 1827 for

Photo 33. Basket Shaped Labels.

THE DESIGNS

Photo 35. Cushion Shaped Labels.

VINEGAR and again in 1828 for CHILI, CAVICE, SOY and KYAN (illustrated). The design was copied by Thomas and James Phipps in 1819 for KYAN.

7.37 Style 27, the cherub, was produced in silver-gilt by Digby Scott and Benjamin Smith. The CHILI label reproduced below is unmarked however. The design was copied rather poorly by Charles Rawlings and not in silver-gilt in 1823 for CAYENNE.

Photo 36. Cherub Label.

7.38 Style 28, the architectural, has scrolling raised borders. Illustrated are CAYENNE with pierced title making the maker's mark unreadable and CHILI VINEGAR by Rawlings and Summers dated 1861. In 1810 John Reily made sauce labels for HARVEY, KETCHUP and SOY in an architectural design which had raised borders of scrolls and shells. A similar design has been illustrated for wine labels such as for Sauterne (25) and for Claret (26). This corresponds to John Reily's Hollands label in the M.V. Brown Collection (27). Reily produced HARVEY, KETCHUP, CHILLI and CAYENNE in 1814, LEMON and CATCHUP in 1822 and John McKay CINNAMON and CHERRY in 1837 in similar design.

Photo 37. Architectural Labels.

7.39 Style 29, the floreate, refers to a shape dictated by floral arrangements or foliage. In 1810, for example, William Pitts inserted floral or foliate work in a gadrooned border for LEMON (28). About the same time Edward Lowe of Chester did a similar thing, adding flowers at each

136

THE DESIGNS

corner, also for LEMON. In 1816 John Reily made large sauce labels for READING and other titles using a mixture of flowers and foliage with a top and bottom shell. In 1823 Charles Rawlings used a similar design with flowers centrally placed on each side, adding beading around the title of SOY (29). Several versions of this Regency/George IV design are illustrated. Matthew Boulton's SOY of 1828 follows a similar design of 1826 and is die-pressed. It combines a shell and flower with vine leaves and grapes! The ANCHOVY has a maker's mark too worn to permit of clear identification. It is cast and decorated with vines leaves and grapes! The large CHILI is by William Elliott in 1822 and is die-pressed. The elegant SOY was cast by Paul Storr, marked on its face, and has a raised title by repousse work. It is nearly crescent shaped and enriched with acanthus foliage and shells. Foliage forms part of the border. It mirrors a set of five wine labels for Burgundy, Champagne, Claret, Port and Madeira made by Paul Storr, four in 1816, presented to King Edward VII by the Duke of Roxburgh on 9th November 1900 (30). As these labels were the personal property of a Monarch they do not appear in the Buckingham Palace or Windsor Castle sections of the Royal Inventory prepared by Garrard & Company in 1914. Paul Storr was active in making wine labels for the Royal Grand Service in 1812 and again in 1814. The HARVEY was cast by James Beebe in 1829 and has an applied heavy floral border. Other labels of this kind are for CHILLI and

Photo 38. James Beebe, 1829.

Photo 39. Floreate Labels.

137

THE DESIGNS

Photo 40. Gadrooned Rectangular Shaped Labels.

ESCAVECHI (1829) and TOMATO and WORCESTERSHIRE (c.1840) (31). In 1822 John Reilly and in the early 1830s Charles Reily and George Storer made narrow rectangular floreates pierced for CHILI and FISH-SAUCE respectively (illustrated).

7.40 Style 30, the gadrooned rectangular, usually with rounded ends, was popular during the period 1810 to 1830. Charles Rawlings' SAUCE of 1824 has an uninterrupted gadrooned border. Thomas and James Phipps' CAYENNE has a shell inserted in each side. Charles Rawlings' KETCHUP is a larger size label and the title is set off by beading. Phipps, Robinson and Phipps' KETCHUP has the shell insert. The design was reproduced in 1879 by William Summers for CAYENNE without shell inserts.

7.41 Style 31, the narrow or squashed escutcheon, is a style found on wine labels and copied for use on the soy frame. The sauce labels for CAYENNE and CATSUP (illustrated) are unmarked. They are die pressed and have pierced titles. They are similar to a wine label for Hollands made by Elizabeth Morley in 1810 (32). The HARVEY and ANCHOVY by Hutton and Sons of Sheffield are dated 1896.

7.42 Style 32, the shell, lent itself to the design of sauce labels because a small neat copy of a larger version for a wine label could be made. Illustrated in Chapter 9 are silver-gilt versions with pierced titles for CHILI and KYAN made by Phipps Robinson and Phipps in 1814. William Summers made a pair in 1864 also in silver-gilt, almost identical, for SALAD OIL and FRENCH VINEGAR. Also illustrated is the shell of a marine gastropod by Colen Cheshire of Birmingham made in 1894 engraved for WORCESTER. Inside the shell was a marine species with many legs which glowed in the dark although this would not have been obvious due to the protection offered by the shell. John Mortimer and John Samuel Hunt made some

Photo 41. Narrow Escutcheon Labels.

THE DESIGNS

Photo 42. Shell Labels.

conch shell labels in 1840. Small size labels pierced for BURGUNDY, PORT and HARVEY were produced (33) having a highly rococo effect from the use of the concave side of the tridacna. Recipes exist for BURGUNDY (34) and for PORT sauces, which were popular in Victorian times. Similar style labels in larger size were made for wines. See also the cartouche style (below, Style 33) for rococo labels.

7.43 Style 33, the cartouche, is unusual and is represented by a rococo label in the Cropper collection in the Victoria and Albert Museum made in 1814, probably by Richard Barker who was apprenticed to Charles Chesterman II in 1801. See also the shell style for rococo labels.

7.44 Style 34, the vine, is illustrated by HARVEY with a pierced title, apparently unmarked. The upright vine leaf was made by George Unite around 1845 for TARRAGON VINEGAR and WALNUT CATSUP. Vine leaves, grapes and tendrils have often been incorporated into the design of sauce labels, however incongruously. In 1815 Thomas and James Phipps made sauce labels in a wine label design incorporating vine leaves, grapes and shells. John Langlands and William Robertson made a set of six sauce labels including ANCHOVY and READING SAUCE with repoussé borders of vine leaves and grapes. A similar design was developed by Charles Rawlings in 1822 and 1823 for HARVEY, ANCHOVY, SOY, KETCHUP and ESSENCE OF CHILLI reused by Rawlings and Summers in 1829 for Port and Sherry wine labels. Furthermore in 1826 William Elliott made labels for CATCHUP and other titles engraved on a scroll surmounting a mixture of vine leaves and grapes – a most delightful and unusual design. The vine leaf on its side as shown by Whitworth in his book at page 21 was made by Charles Rawlings in 1824 and had a pierced title for SOY (illustrated). Style 34 was also used for perfume labels.

Photo 43. Vine Leaf Labels.

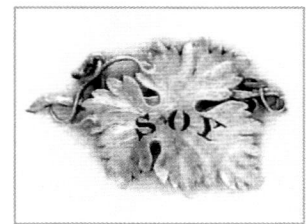

7.45 Style 35, the escutcheon, is simply a smaller version of the same style in wine labels. Makers include Charles Rawlings, Rawlings and Summers, John Reily, Mary and Charles Reily and James and Nathaniel Creswick between the years 1820 and 1853. Illustrated are Reily's

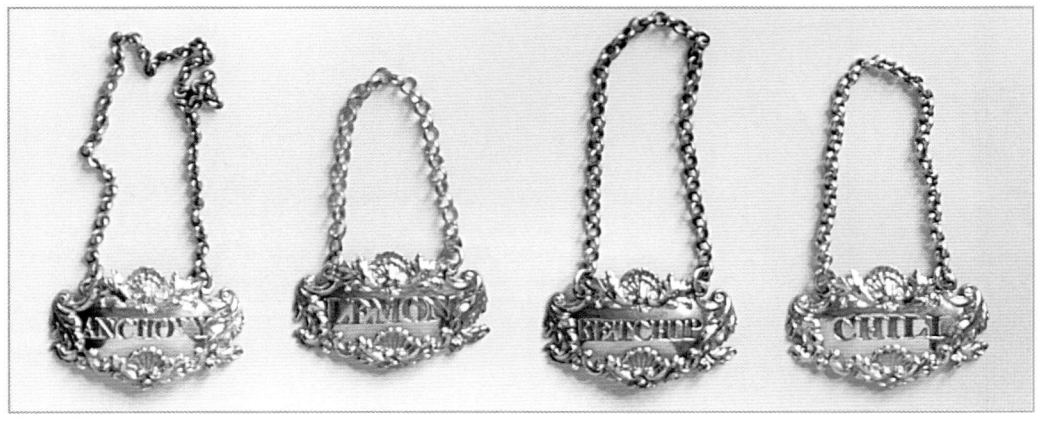

Photo 44. Escutcheon Labels.

139

THE DESIGNS

LEMON and the Reilys' CHILI, KETCHUP and ANCHOVY, all with pierced titles. In the 1890s large labels were made in this style to decorate pickle jars in pickle frames. Examples are for CHUTNEE by Edward Hutton in 1892 and CABBAGE by William Hutton in 1896. Other examples are for CAPTAIN WHITE'S (illustrated, reduced in size) and WALNUT (see Fig. 38).

7.46 Style 36, the shaped, is without decoration, made by Rawlings and Summers reproducing Style 2 in slightly different form and reflecting the design of earlier wine labels. One example for HARVEY was made in 1838. Later examples for SOY and CAYENNE dated 1849 are shown on Dent's Plate V.

7.47 Style 37, the initial, is where the shape of the label follows the outline of the letter, in contrast to the postage stamp style where an initial is engraved or pierced. Illustrated are an example of 1828 by Reily and Storer for K (Kyan) and an example of 1862 by Rawlings and Summers for C (Chilli).

Photo 45. Initial Labels.

Photo 46. Fretwork Labels.

7.48 Style 38, the fretwork, was a popular Victorian design for wine labels and copied for sauces by Rawlings and Summers in 1851 for FISH SAUCE and KETCHUP (illustrated) and by William Thomas Wright and Frederick Davis around 1866 for WORCESTER and TARRAGON.

7.49 Style 39, the shield or heart, is difficult to date because none of the labels observed to fall into

Photo 47. Shield Shaped Labels.

this category are marked and there would not appear to be any wine label comparisons. Shown is CHILI selected from a set of four unmarked labels with WORCESTER, ANCHOVEY and SOY at one time in the Bignell Collection which are of uncertain date and provenance in white metal with the names in niello or blacking (35). The other shields illustrated are continental and probably of Swedish origin having been in the Lind Collection. They are engraved for PEPPAR and INGEFARA.

7.50 Style 40, the drapery festoon, is also difficult to date. Whilst unmarked, these labels (illustrated by ELDER-VIN) have a modern feel about them and do not have genuine armorials.

Photo 48. Drapery Festoon Label.

THE DESIGNS

7.51 The following tests should be conducted to try to arrive at an approximate date with regard to an unmarked sauce label:

TEST 1. First of all one should search for a marked wine label of similar style or failing that having similar decoration or failing that having similar engraving and shape of lettering for the title.

TEST 2. If the first test fails then establish the style of the label by reference to the data given above which should at least indicate a dating bracket.

TEST 3. Then ascertain whether any of the examples given are comparable which may assist in narrowing the bracket.

TEST 4. Finally one should seek a comparison based on size of lettering, the period of any armorial, the period during which the use of the condiment was popular, paying particular attention to the size and weight of the label, and the length of chain if this appears to be original which can be gleaned from the condition of the chain's connecting rings.

TEST 5. The quality of the patina and the standard of workmanship may also be relevant factors to be assessed. ■

NOTES

(1) An entry appears in Volume III of the Wakelin Ledgers, dated 22 November 1766, for "6 small crescent soy cruet labels". Ansill and Gilbert supplied crescent soy labels from 1766 to 1771.
(2) For an appraisal of her marks and designs see 10 WLJ 230. Her five different marks are illustrated at 10 WLJ 234.
(3) Such as for the 88th Regiment of Foot – see para. 8.4 below.
(4) The CAYENNE lable was illustrated in Country Life for 19th June 1942 at p.1187.
(5) Lot 161 (illustrated on p.17 of the Sale Catalogue) Bonham and Brooks Knightsbridge Silver and Wine Related Objects sale, 9th October 2001.
(6) See below para. 8.4.
(7) In the Cropper collection at the V&A Museum.
(8) See Jackson at p.210.
(9) See 10 WLJ 129.
(10) V&A Museum reference M-1223-1944; illustrated by Stancliffe, fig. 59, p.41.
(11) Row B1.
(12) See "Domed Rectangles" 6 WLJ 96 as corrected by 8 WLJ 9.
(13) See Madeira, Row B2, 6 WLJ 104, seventh mark.
(14) See Brandy, Row D2, 6 WLJ 104, but double bright cut border.
(15) See Port, Row A1, 6 WLJ 107, Dublin.
(16) See Vin de Grave, Row A2, 6 WLJ 107.
(17) See White, Row C3, 6 WLJ 107, Newcastle.
(18) See Madeira Row B2, 5 WLJ 107, Exeter.
(19) See Madeira, Row D, 6 WLJ 107, Dundee.
(20) See "Wine Labels", Chapter 2, Part 8, Bottle Collars, Hoops and Neck Rings (in press).
(21) See 5 WLJ 262, B2.
(22) Cropper Collection, V&A Museum reference M 1099-1944.
(23) Ibid. M 621.
(24) Ibid. M 588.
(25) Whitworth, p.36.
(26) Collectors' Guide, December 1974, p.107.
(27) London Museum reference A 15715.
(28) Cropper Collection, V&A reference M252.
(29) This type is illustrated at 5 WLJ 226, B4.
(30) These Paul Storr labels had been given by Queen Victoria to the Duke's father and were once housed in the Butler's pantry in the family seat in Scotland.
(31) Cropper Collection, V&A Museum reference M 538/9.
(32) Illustrated in Dent, Plate II, fig. 5.
(33) BURGUNDY is illustrated at 5 WLJ 112 and described at p. 113.
(34) There is a typical soy label, rectangular with rounded edges, in the MV Brown Collection, London Museum reference A 15921, for BURGUNDY.
(35) The niello or blacking composition stands out proud of the face of the label, which suggests an 1860s date.

Fig 97. Ship's soy decanters with labels for CATSUP and ANCHOVY by Peter and William Bateman, London, 1813.

CHAPTER 8

THE ARMORIALS

8.1 Armorials do not form a separate sauce labels style. Probably they were too small to be considered for design as a whole to represent a crest or another part of a coat of arms such as a shield, or supporters or motto. It follows that an armorial is something added to a style and can occur with any style. When used on sauce labels armorials seem to fall into five different types: for use on a cartouche, engraved on the face, engraved on the reverse, added as a crest and designed as a border.

8.2 Type 1, the cartouche, appeared above Peter and William Bateman's ANCHOVY of 1813 (illustrated). Susanna Barker's CAMP and LEMON of around 1780, which have wrigglework borders, have cartouches containing the letter S beneath a coronet. The oval with a festoon draped over the upper part of the label is an interesting design. Four were sold by Sotheby's in 1993 said by way of provenance to be from the collection of the Earl of Jersey. They were tested and found correct notwithstanding their unusual feel and appearance. These labels were cast and not marked. A date of around 1865 may be attributable. The label of similar design engraved for ELDER VIN (illustrated) was in Mr Weed's collection. The ninth Earl of Jersey died on 9 August 1998 having inherited the Earldom at the age of 13. He was a notable connoisseur and an early collector of Impressionist paintings. He settled in Jersey in 1947 running a successful antiques business (1).

Photo 49. Peter and William Bateman, 1813.

8.3 Type 2, the frontal engraving, is illustrated by James Hyde's LEMON and SOY of 1797 which have engraved beneath the titles an upright cuffed hand clasping a single feathered arrow. Thus just as some owners of wine labels put their crest on the face of their labels, so also did some owners of sauce labels which were certainly not large enough to display a full coat of arms. But just having a crest on view makes identification difficult without more information being available. There are various forms of mailed fists clasping arrows. It is rarely possible to match up a sauce set with a wine set. The cuffed hand on Hyde's LEMON does not match up with that on Sandyland Drinkwater's set of four wine labels in the Cropper Collection in the

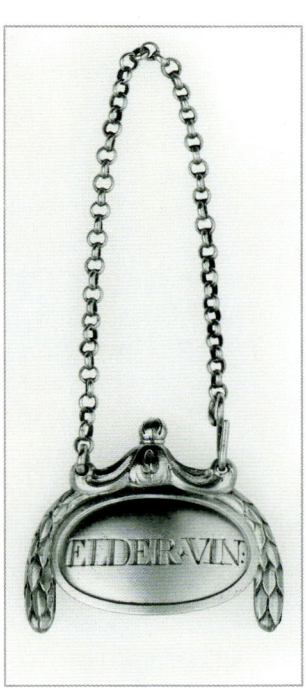

Photo 50. Mr Weed's ELDER·VIN.

Photo 51. James Hyde, 1797

143

THE ARMORIALS

Photo 53. William Bamforth Troby, 1814.

Photo 52. Phipps, Robinson and Phipps, c.1815.

Photo 54. Susanna Barker, 1792.

Victoria and Albert Museum, although is may be related to the same family. No less than seven families have a crest of this kind. The Hales family are considered the most likely candidates for ownership at one time. As to the cost of engraving, William Fraser paid 6d for having his crest engraved in 1780 on six soy labels (2). Also illustrated is Phipps, Robinson and Phipps' CAYENNE showing a lion or a mythical beast over a baron's mantling holding a crusader-like sword. Another lion-like beast over a baron's mantling but this time enclosed by a garter surmounted by a crown, which suggests ambassadorial use is on a collar label engraved for KYAN by William Bamforth Troby in 1814. A typical Susanna Barker product of 1792 of rectangular style with incurved corners engraved for CHILLI VIN displays an armorial comprising a coiled snake pierced with five arrows above a mantling. The sauce label engraved with the number "77th" below the sauce title is said to be made by G.L. and G.F. around 1850. The 77th Regiment of

Foot, later the East Middlesex Regiment, was formed in 1787. This number also appears on wine labels with the Prince of Wales feathers added above the title (3). Perhaps the most celebrated labels are those for Prinny's yacht the "Prince Regent". The ledgers of the Lord Chamberlain contain an entry dated 5 January 1819 which reads "For use of the Royal Yacht – 4 labels with chains and hooks for large cruets and eight small labels with Ditto for SOY". The hooks enabled chains to be temporarily detached to assist in cleaning and are found on better class labels. The Jewel House Book has references to bottle tickets as well as to wine labels which may therefore relate to sauce labels. Both the ledgers and the Jewel Book contain references to bills for engraving names and ciphers on bottle tickets (4). Two of the eight soy labels are known, one for ANCHOVY and one for SOY. Above the title in each case is the Royal Crown and below the title "P anchor R" (see illustration). "P R" stands for the "Prince Regent", the name of the then Royal Yacht ordered in 1814 and launched before but not commissioned until 1820 when the Prince Regent ascended to the throne as King George IV.

Photo 55. Labels for the Royal Yacht, the "Prince Regent," by John Reily, 1818.

144

THE ARMORIALS

For this reason a sovereign's crown is engraved on the labels made by John Reily in 1818/1819. Contemporary engravings of the Prince's arms all contain feathers as shown on a pair of wheel-cut and acid etched glass decanters by Perrin Geddes and Company of Warrington (5). A pair of glass ship's decanters with labels for CATSUP and ANCHOVY, made by Peter and William Bateman in London in 1813, are illustrated (see Fig. 97).

8.4 Type 3, the back engraving, for less exhibitionist owners seeking to protect their property, is represented by Pegasus, the winged horse, on the back of James Hyde's SOY for 1797 and Charles Rawlings' CAMP V for 1826. Robert Seckers' ANCHOVY, CAYENNE and HARVEY of 1863 in the Fitzhenry Collection at the Victoria and Albert Museum show a basket-hilted sword

Fig 98. Sketch of coronet engraved on reverse of Charles Price's CHILLI, VINR.

piercing a rectangular object above a baronial mantling engraved on the reverse of escutcheon style labels with pierced titles. John Reily's SOY, KETCHUP and KYAN of 1800 have a lion above a mantling engraved on the reverse. Some wine labels show the Royal crown and most spectacularly there is a crown (of which a sketch, not to scale, is illustrated – see Fig. 98) engraved on the reverse of Charles Price's CHILI.VINR. in the Marshall Collection. An enclosed crescent style unmarked label for CAYON (possibly by Margaret Binley) with single reeded decoration has engraved on the reverse a baron's coronet above F & C in italics for the Barony of Fauconberg and Conyers, which possibly goes with four kidney-shaped wine labels of the same period by Margaret Binley circa 1765 with this engraving on the reverse, perhaps used by the 4th Earl of Holderness of that family who died in 1778 and who patronised Parker and Wakelin in 1760. "On the reverse of each of Binley's labels is engraved the coronet of a baron, beneath which appears "F&C" (Photo 56). This refers, unmistakably, to the barony of Fauconberg and Conyers which, according to Debrett's, has been in abeyance since 1948. The barony has come down from Walter de Fauconberg of Ryse, summoned to Parliament in 1283 and who

Photo 56. Fauconberg and Conyers Crest.

signed the famous letter of the barons to the Pope in 1301. He died in 1304. On the other side, Sir William Conyers served at Flodden Field and he died in 1524. The barony of Fauconberg was in abeyance between 1491 and 1903, when it was revived by letters patent; but the barony of Conyers continued through various machinations until the 5th Baron Conyers was created Earl of Holderness in 1682. The 4th Earl died in 1778, when the earldom became extinct. This 4th Earl was '…a man of sophisticated taste, accustomed to international life and at one time British ambassador in Venice and subsequently, minister of The Hague. While the Earl enjoyed entertainment and music and was one of the directors of the opera in London…, in about 1760 he ordered new dinner plate from… Parker and Wakelin (who) were among the best London goldsmiths working in the Rococo style after the death of Paul de Lamerie…'(6). Being a patron of the arts, he may well have commissioned items from other silver workers of the time – such as Margaret Binley. The date would be right as Margaret entered her mark in 1764. The barony of Conyers reverted to Amelia, the 4th Earl's daughter, wife of the 5th Duke of Leeds and the titles continued until 1948 when Sackville George

145

THE ARMORIALS

Pelham, 5th Earl of Yarborough, 8th Baron Fauconberg and 14th Baron Conyers died." (7) John Rich's eye-shaped CHILLI in the Marshall Collection has what appears to be a monogram of the initials "LLB" engraved on the back, perhaps for the owner's identification. An otherwise unmarked label for BURGESS SAUCE has "88" engraved on the reverse. Perhaps this was for a Regiment to try and prevent the label from leaving the Mess. The most likely candidate is the 88th Regiment of Foot, formed in 1793 due to the outbreak of war between England and France. Due to the smallness of the label it does not have a crown surmounting a wreath with a harp inside above the figure 88. As it was raised primarily in the Irish Province of Connaught, it became known as the 88th Connaught Rangers. The use of the expression "Ranger" was often indicative of a provincial levy. Early in 1794 the Regiment was on duty in Flanders, followed by postings to the West Indies in a campaign against the French in 1796, to India 1798-1800, to Ceylon 1801, to Egypt 1803 and back to England 1803-6 to repulse the anticipated Napoleonic Invasion in Sussex. The 88th then took part in the Peninsular campaign and the existence of its Regimental mess has been recorded (8). However the Regiment lost some of its silver in 1848 when stationed in the West Indies due to a fire in the Mess. A similar event occurred in 1851 in Nova Scotia, but happily certainly cutlery and two snuff mulls were saved. More silver was lost in Wales in 1892-3 when the Mess was burgled by a private soldier who went so far as to cut up some of the larger pieces of silver to facilitate its removal from the barracks. He was convicted of theft and some of the silver was recovered. The commanding officer organised replacements. It is recorded (9) that he had a four-bottle sauce frame made out of some of the mutilated and non-repairable pieces presumably to accommodate the existing and surviving sauce labels of which BURGESS SAUCE may have been one (10).

8.5 Type 4, the crest above, is represented by Thomas Edward's set of four labels of 1824 each hung from a single eyelet and having a pair of dolphins with tails crossed as a surmount. Susanna Barker's small rectangular shaped triple reeded label engraved for PEPR. VINR. circa 1776 incorporates as a crest displayed above the label a greyhound couchant, gorged and chained (11) (illustrated). Phipps and Robinson's LEM PICKLE of 1796 has a scrolling armorial surmount (12).

8.6 Type 5, the designed in border, allows the snake armorial to be displayed (13). Two examples are illustrated. Charles Rawling's CAYENNE of 1819 has a snake border with the snake almost biting its tail. Reily and Storer's MADRAS FLAME of 1840 with dramatic pierced lettering has a raised snake border with the snake actually eating its tail. An unmarked label for CORRACHE has been noted which also has a snake border.

Photo 58. Charles Rawlings, 1819

Photo 59. Charles Reily and George Storer, 1840.

Photo 57. Susanna Barker, c.1778.

8.7 Many armorials appear on wine labels. The Duguid family in Scotland used the dove with an olive branch in its beak and the motto patientia et spes. The Stanley family as Earls of Derby used the eagle and child. It is likely that other armorials will be noted on sauce labels. These may well include those ordered by the Revd. Carter (in 1771), Henry Scourfield (in 1771) and James Bouchier (in 1776) according to entries in Volume 4 of the Wakelin ledgers. ■

THE ARMORIALS

NOTES

(1) Obituary in "The Times, 14 August 1998, p.23
(2) Wakelin Ledgers, Vol 7, p.216
(3) See further 11 WLJ 6
(4) As researched and reported by Captain Sir Thomas Barlow in 8 WLJ 110
(5) Apollo, March 1999, p23
(6) Country Life, 14 June 1984
(7) Malcolm Harfitt, 10 WLJ 129
(8) See H.F.N. Jourdain and E. Fraser, "The Connaught Rangers", 1924
(9) See R. Perkins, "Military and Naval Silver", 1999
(10) The author is indebted to Mr Bruce Jones for his military research
(11) 1 WLJ 10
(12) 2 WLJ 58
(13) See illustration at 1 WLJ 29 where a wine label of 1813 has a snake border.

Fig 117. Trade card of Antiquarian Cookery Book Sellers.

Fig 99. Beckford's cruet of 1784.

CHAPTER 9

THE GOLD AND SILVER GILT

9.1 GOLD SAUCE LABELS ARE RARE. The only ones known to the author are a pair made by Roberts and Belk of Sheffield in 1877 engraved for WORCESTER and READING being double reeded rectangulars with cut corners measuring 2.5 by 1.5 centimetres. The earliest silver-gilt sauce labels may have been made to adorn in 1767 a small circular five bottle silver-gilt soy frame made in that year by Elizabeth Aldridge (1). However Aldridge has not been recorded as a maker of sauce labels and Grimwade's mark 3530 (2) may not necessarily be that of the widow of Edward Aldridge. The facetted bottles on this frame must surely have had labels at some time because the bottle mounts were not engraved and there were two types of peppers on the frame which would need identifying. One bottle with a pull-off silver cap (marked only with the lion passant) having five large holes in it would have housed black pepper in it; another bottle with a pull-off cap having twelve small holes arranged in two concentric circles would have had cayenne pepper in it. The frame is small, elegant and delicate, designed perhaps for one or two people dining alone. It does not bear an armorial. But then after 1742, when Aldridge was put on trial for allegedly counterfeiting marks, his business may not have been patronised by the nobility. The earliest known extant silver-gilt sauce labels, kidney shape with cable borders, datable to 1775, are attributed to Robert Piercy as they adorned his six-bottle silver-gilt soy frame of that year (illustrated – see fig. 2). He was a specialist castor maker in the tradition of Samuel Wood, to whom he was apprenticed in 1750. In 1765 he made a silver soy stand with names engraved on the bottle mounts for CAYENNE, ELDER, GARLICK, SOY, LEMON and TARRAGON. The 1775 silver-gilt labels were ANCHOVY, KETCHUP, TARRAGON, ELDER, SOY and KYAN, showing perhaps that ANCHOVY had replaced GARLICK and KETCHUP had replaced LEMON as popular sauces in the six-bottle frame over a period of ten years.

9.2 An earlier cruet frame dated 1763 by Robert Piercy is in a Museum collection (3). His mark is often confused with that of Robert Peaston of whom little is known. It is however Piercy who appears in the Wakelin Ledgers as a supplier of castors and cruets. Only a leading cruet frame maker could achieve the "swirling, asymmetric chasing" which "is typical of the costly treatment given to these prominent elements of a dinner service" (4). Samuel Wood indeed learnt his trade from Thomas Bamford to whom he was apprenticed in 1721. Thomas Bamford was himself a specialist castor maker (a set of castors is illustrated – see fig. 10) who learnt his trade from Charles Adam, also a specialist castor maker, to whom he was apprenticed in 1703.

9.3 Piercy's frames of 1763 and 1775 have rococo cartouches engraved with unidentified crests. The silver-gilt labels on his stand of 1775 reflect

149

THE GOLD AND SILVER GILT

the decoration on the frame and so may in all probability have been made by Piercy himself. Other frame makers of this time such as Scofield sub-contracted label-making to specialists like Susanna Barker. Silver-gilt soy frames are not common although quite a few are recorded in the Wakelin Ledgers. References to gilt labels may refer to silver-gilt soy labels as was probably the case of the Duchess of Ancaster's purchase on 9th January 1780 of six cut glass "crewits" (cruets) for £2.10s.0d (i.e. 8s4d. each presumably inclusive of a stand) with six "gilt labells" at 4s. each (5). Likewise George Stainforth might have acquired four gilt labels for 4s. each on 23rd July 1782 (6) and the Hon. Booth Grey purchased a small oval pierced soy stand with four crewits and gilt labels, weighing 8oz 12dwt, for £2.7s.6d. (i.e. 7s. 10d. each inclusive of the stand plus say 4s. each for the silver-gilt labels) (7).

9.4 In April 1781 Wakelins repaired six crewits for John Hagar Esq. including "gilding labells on ditto and furnishing two new stoppers" at a cost of ten shillings (8) which suggests that this refers to labels gilded on the bottles. In January 1783 Wakelins charged General Murray six shillings for "gilding labels on four others", the reference to others being to the supply at 4s. 6d. each of "4 soy crewits with gilt labells" (9). A year or so later in February 1784 the General bought "6 Soy Crewits Gilt Labells" for 4s6d. each and then a month later in March "2 Bottle Labells to match" at 6 shillings each. References to the sale of 2 (10), 4 (11), 6 (12) or 7 (13) soy crewits with gilt labels are not uncommon at the retail price of around 4 shillings per crewit. However Mrs Olier was supplied in 1784 with a single cut glass soy crewit with gilt label for 5 shillings (14).

9.5 The position therefore is not altogether clear by references to the ledgers. However, in 1783 Richard Langley bought from Wakelins "6 Soy Crewitts with silver tops and Gilt Labells" at 9 shillings each. He in fact traded in 11 bottle labels for which he was given credit (15). In his case the labels being replacements were probably indeed silver and gilded.

9.6 William Beckford (1760-1844), the notable silver collector and connoisseur of Fonthill fame (16) acquired a silver-gilt soy frame with labels in 1784. The frame is illustrated in black and white (fig. 99). The glass bottles sit in silver-gilt holders with gadrooned tops. The chains are supported by the bottom of the handles, in the first style of elegance. Beckford was very discriminating in the pieces he commissioned or acquired. He wanted the best of everything. He was as interested in acquiring new silver as he was in buying antique. His earliest acquisitions date back to 1781 when he became of age. On this occasion he seems to have acquired a silver soup tureen with the Beckford heron crest engraved on its cover and a pair of silver candlesticks with the crest put onto the drip pans. The tureen itself was engraved with the arms of Beckford quartering Hamilton on cartouches applied to each side (17). For some items of domestic plate in the neo-classical taste Beckford around this time patronised John Scofield. It was he who made the 1781 candlesticks and another pair in 1791, a snuffer tray in 1793, some tureens and a two-handled cup in 1796. It was only three years after Beckford's 21st birthday that John Scofield made a silver gilt cruet stand mounting two soy bottles and two oil or vinegar bottles. The bottles had contemporary silver-gilt labels by Susanna Barker. The upper side of the base of the cruet was engraved with the Beckford heron crest. Scofield made a similar cruet with eye shaped silver-gilt labels by Susanna Barker in 1789 (18).

9.7 William Thomas Beckford was born on 29th September 1760, probably in London at his father's house in Soho Square. He was the son of a wealthy merchant, Alderman William Beckford, who was twice Lord Mayor of London and who died in 1770. It is said (19) that the son inherited £1 million in cash in 1770 and an income of £100,000 p.a. derived from sugar plantations in Jamaica, developed by earlier members of the Beckford family. Beckford therefore had substantial financial resources. He could afford the best that money could buy, but in making purchases he exhibited a considerably refined taste. He was obsessed with heraldry. The variety of engraved armorials, crests and mottoes found on his silver reflect this interest.

THE GOLD AND SILVER GILT

In 1798 he received a grant of arms incorporating the crest of the Hamilton oak tree as he was related to his family, differenced by a shield charged with the Latimer cross on a two-handled saw along with a new motto "De Dieu Tout". This crest appears in combination with the heron crest on most of Beckford's silver after 1798. In 1810 he obtained an augmented grant of arms whereby they were contained within a double tressure (20).

9.8 Susanna Barker, whose working dates were 1778 to 1793, was therefore given the accolade of being the best label maker during the period May to December 1784 because Beckford would not accept anything less than the best. The silver-gilt cruet set looks like gold and is truly magnificent. It bears no duty mark. The four labels are all the same size notwithstanding the variety in bottle size. Probably Beckford had no direct contact with Susanna Barker at 16 Gutter Lane. At the age of 24 he had not reached his fussiest stage. He probably relied on John Scofield and John Scofield could not take the risk of having anything less than the best if he wanted future commissions from Beckford, who had a reputation of being not only very particular but sometimes very impatient. It is probable that Scofield did not instruct Susanna Barker to make the two soy labels for LEMON and SOY respectively in any different fashion from the two vinegar labels for ELDER and TARRAGON. The labels are heavy silver-gilt with feathered edges and with pierced titles. They carry maker's mark only (21). The usual arrangement was employed whereby the larger vinegar bottles were fitted into the ends of the frame whilst the smaller soy bottles were fitted into smaller containers in the middle of the frame. It is a superb cruet and fully justifies Beckford who commissioned it being called "colourful" (22), "individualistic" (23), a "genius manqué" (24) and a "prodigious virtuoso" (25). John Scofield's work was therefore "unsurpassed in English neo-classical silver for its elegance of design and delicacy of execution" (26).

9.9 Beckford's second daughter, Susan Euphemia, was born in 1786 and married in 1810 the Marquis of Douglas (1767-1854) who became the 10th Duke of Hamilton. In 1827 he built a tower in Bath as a treasure house and study. There is evidence that when Beckford commissioned pieces he indicated his design requirements. Haslett has confirmed that Beckford required "the best, the most highly finished, the most costly" (27). Susanna Barker's well proportioned workmanship and finishing must have come up to Beckford's high standards (28). In fact he liked them so much that he did not put them in the sale by Christie's held on the 9th to the 12th of May 1817, nor did he sell them to the purchaser of Fonthill Abbey, nor did he put them in the two day sale of 1841, when he refurbished the tower in Bath. His daughter and son-in-law presumably took the cruet with them to Hamilton Palace or Brodick Castle, so it was not included in the 1845 sale of what was left in the tower. It is of course possible that the cruet was included in the 1822 sale of Fonthill to John Farquhar and brought back by Beckford in the 1823 sale by Farquhar of Fonthill. It is much more likely that Beckford wanted the cruet for his own use at his home in Bath. The cruet was acquired in 1844 by Susan Euphemia, his younger and favourite daughter, as a bequest (29).

9.10 Silver-gilt was frequently used during the period 1804-1830 to give added embellishment to the opulent style of George IV both during his Regency and his Reign. Benjamin and James Smith made an attractive KETCHUP (illustrated) in the Regency silver-gilt style in 1809. John Rich managed to produce a silver-gilt SOY and CAYENNE in the same year as well as SOY and ANCHOVIE for 1804. A pair (or more) of cast

Photo 60. Benjamin and James Smith, 1809.

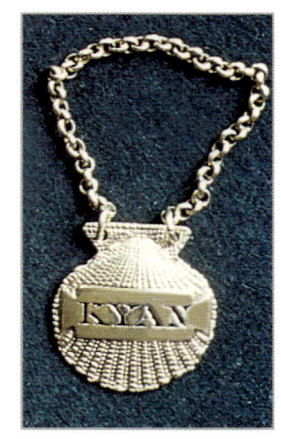

Photo 61. Phipps, Robinson and Phipps, 1814.

151

THE GOLD AND SILVER GILT

Photo 62. Theodosia Ann Atkins, 1815.

Photo 63 and 64. John Reily, 1821-1822

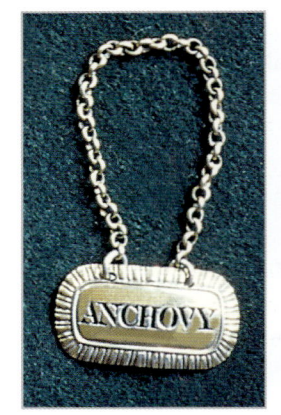

escallop shells with pierced titles for KYAN (illustrated) and CHILI were made by Thomas Phipps, Edward Robinson and James Phipps in 1814. A label for TARRAGON may well also belong to this set. In the following year Theodosia Ann Atkins sponsored three narrow rectangulars (illustrated) with pierced titles for CAYENNE, ANCHOVY and SOY.

9.11 Between 1816 and 1823 Thomas and James Phipps produced a beautiful almost enclosed crescent for KETCHUP like that illustrated, copying a much earlier style either to match existing labels in a set or as a pastiche. John Reily (30) made rounded rectangulars pierced for ANCHOVY (1821) and CAYENNE (1822) with gadrooned borders (illustrated) which were much in vogue at the time. Charles Rawlings also used silver-gilt as shown by an 1822 example with a scroll and shellwork border (31) and an example of around 1829 (he worked with William Summers at this time) for REGENT sauce (32).

9.12 The popular escutcheon shape style was reproduced in Sheffield for the Victorians in 1853 by James and Nathaniel Creswick. Their set of six is illustrated, the titles being pierced for

Photo 65. James and Nathaniel Creswick, 1853

152

THE GOLD AND SILVER GILT

SOY, CHILI, HARVEY, ANCHOVY, TARRAGON and KETCHUP, showing that the popularity of these sauces continued during Victorian times.

9.13 In 1840 Reily and Storer made an oval label for HARVEY in silver-gilt with gadrooned decoration (33). They made more silver-gilt labels to decorate a silver-gilt frame of 1856. William Summers produced excallop shells in silver-gilt (perhaps to match up with those already described) for FRENCH VINEGAR and SALAD OIL as late as 1864. At the turn of the Century an art-nouveau style shallow crescent (illustrated) marked for 1901 and engraved for VINEGAR in the Gothic Puginesque style lettering reminiscent of William Morris was made in silver-gilt as being appropriate for that style. The Normans are said to have adopted the Gothic style following their experiences in Sicily and to have brought it to England. Chippendale was influenced by this style in the Eighteenth Century and A.W.N. Pugin (1812-1852) reformed it into the early Victorian Gothic style. In the late Nineteenth Century it was revived. ∎

Photo 66. Art Nouveau Vinegar

NOTES

(1) Exhibited by Paul Bennett Fine Art at Claridge's Antiques and Fine Art Fair in April 2001.
(2) Arthur G. Grimwade, London Goldsmiths 1697-1837, first edition 1976, p 252.
(3) Victoria and Albert Museum, ref M.6-1968, incorrectly attributed by the Museum to Robert Peaston.
(4) V & A description in Leaflet No. 4 relating to case 13, Dining 1700-1760, in the Silver Galleries.
(5) Volume 7, p157
(6) Volume 7, p154
(7) Volume 7, p164
(8) Volume 7. p168
(9) Volume 8, p47
(10) Volume 8, p198
(11) Volume 7, p178; Volume 8, p47
(12) Volume 7, pp 154, 204, 211 and 251; Volume 8, pp 1, 50 and 71
(13) Volume 8, p69 for Lord George Cavendish
(14) Volume 8, p149
(15) Volume 8, p98
(16) John Millington: William Beckford and his tower, Beckford Tower Trust, 5th edition 1986.
(17) The tureen, with kettle stand and draught excluder essential for Beckford's tea-making, can be seen at Brodick Castle, ref B1, B6 and B9/
(18) In the V & A collection, ref M-46-h-1960; illustrated by Stancliffe in "Bottle Tickets" at p.11.
(19) John Millington, op. cit.
(20) John Millington, op. cit.
(21) John Beecroft, Susanna Barker – Goldsmith, in 5 WLJ 2, June 1971.
(22) John Hayward: Introduction to Beckford and Hamilton Silver from Brodick Castle, Spink & Son Limited 1980.
(23) Michael Snodin and Malcolm Baker, William Beckford's Silver, Burlington magazine, CXXII, November and December 1980.
(24) Hayward, op. cit.
(25) William Haslett, Article on Fonthill, London Magazine, November 1822.
(26) Malcolm Baker, Timothy Schroder and E. Laird Clowes, Brodick Castle Silver Catalogue, National Trust for Scotland.
(27) Haslett, op. cit.
(28) Her quality and versatility can be judged by lookin at the illustrations on page 10 of Volume 5 of the Wine Label Circle Journal.
(29) It was not disposed of in the Hamilton Palace sale of 1882, possibly either because it was not regarded as important enough at that time or because, and this is more likely, it had already been lodged at Brodick castle where it has remained to this day. For further details on Beckford see the author's article "Beckford's Sauce Labels" published in the Wine Label Circle Journal.
(30) John Reily also made in silver-gilt a CAYENNE and JESSAMINE in 1810, a KETCHUP and SOY circa 1816, a LEMON and KETCHUP (1 WLJ 60) and heavily decorated cast ovals for KETCHUP and SOY (illustrated in 3 WLJ 75).
(31) Christie's sale, 5.12.2000, lot 309.
(32) Victoria and Albert Museum, Fitzherbert Collection.
(33) Illustrated in Stancliffe's "Bottle Tickets" at page 12, figure 13.

Fig 100. SALT and PEPPER pots made in India.

Fig 101. A porcelain FRENCH.

Fig 102. An ivory PORT and a bone VINEGAR with bottle coaster for No. 9 Port.

CHAPTER 10

THE NON-SILVER

10.1 Sauce labels made from organic materials, such as tortoiseshell, mother of pearl, paper, parchment, fabric, wood and leather, whilst wine labels are known to have been made from these, have not been noted. Only sauce labels made out of gold, silver, silver-plate, porcelain, enamel, ivory and bone have been recorded. This is not to suggest that such labels do not exist. They perhaps await discovery.

10.2 The setting of such trophies as the claw of a tiger or the tusk of a boar in silver for use to identify condiments would probably not have occurred in the 1850s to Messrs Hamilton and Co. in Calcutta or to Messrs Orr and Co. in Madras (1). That this would be so is partly because of the size and shape of the objects creating particular difficulties for use on the soy frame, partly because success in a hunt or on the polo field was more appropriately celebrated with convidial toasts and partly because in India condiments would appear to have been identified either by silver labels applied to silver containers or by engraved titles on glass containers or on silver containers (2).

10.3 Bone or ivory lends itself to the making of small labels (3). Illustrated in Fig. 102 is a tiny ivory label with soy frame bottle type length of chain entitled PORT perhaps for PORT sauce. If it was for use on a decanter for PORT wine it would have been larger and have made some form of important statement, as is demonstrated by the illustrated bottle coaster for PORT No 9, since port was a significant drink to be revered rather than downgraded. Such a label could have been made in India during the period 1840-1930. Dating evidence for wine labels exists for 1841 (vintage date), 1856 (an engraving), 1857 (an advertisement in India), 1875 (hallmark) and 1929 (an engraving). Ivory and bone would lend themselves to the making of collar neck rings for soy bottles (4). A beautifully engraved sauce label for VINEGAR in bone is illustrated (Fig. 102).

10.4 Mother of pearl lends itself to the production of beautiful designs embellished by gold surrounds or quality chains. Some of these seem to have originated in an been exported from China for use on wine decanters. Designs and uses of armorials suggest an activity in the use of such material as early as 1750-1775. Whilst wood might have been appropriate for use as bin labels in the cellar in the 1870s as evidenced by vintage dates, it seems an unlikely material for use on soy bottles. There would not appear to be any suggestion of the use of parchment labels in connection with condiments. So bottle labelling came at a time when wine labelling using silver was well established. Soy labels simply copied wine labels, even to the extent of showing vine leaves and grapes so that they matched in with the more prominent wine label displays. Enamel was used and a set of four oval shaped soy tickets has been observed(5). Porcelain was also used and a delightful Crown Staffordshire label for FRENCH vinegar is illustrated (fig. 101). ■

NOTES
(1) Tooth and claw wine labels are illustrated on plate 25 of "Bottle Tickets" published by the Victoria and Albert Museum in 1958.
(2) Many PEPPERs and SALTs are illustrated in Wynyard Wilkinson's "Indian Colonial Silver" including significantly a set of four casters at page 69 by Hamilton & Co. engraved for "S", "S", "K" and "P" (reference A.88).
(3) Ivory and bone labels are illustrated on plate 23 of "Bottle Tickets", and see above paras. 7.14 and 7.28.
(4) ELDER and GINGER are also illustrated on plate 23.
(5) Two enamels exist for CANELLE, one crescent-shaped for CANELE (French for CINNAMON) and one for ESTRAGON (French for TARRAGON).

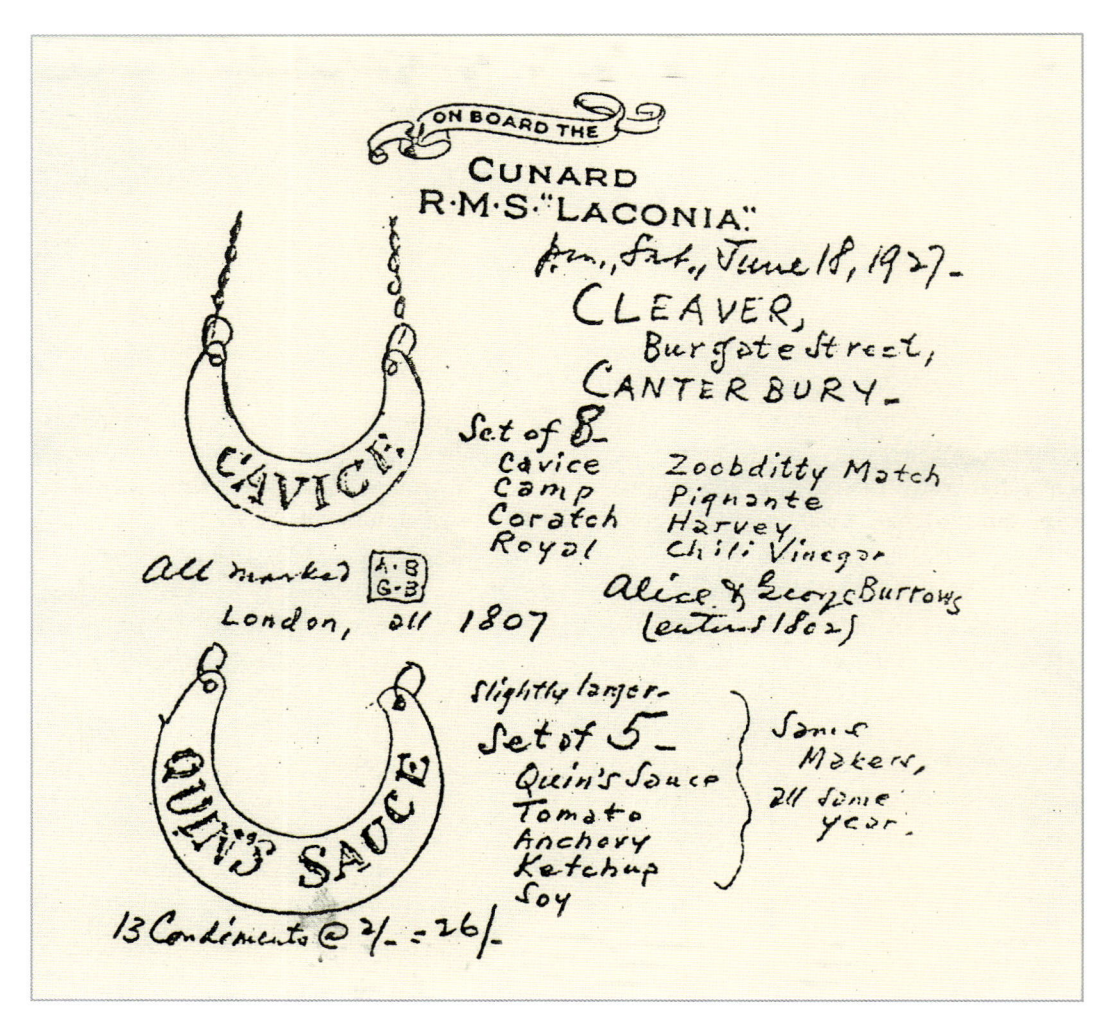

Fig 103. Mr Weed's notes made on the Laconia bound for New York.

CHAPTER 11

THE MARKS AND SETS

11.1 One of the best known sets of sauce labels, formerly in the Weed collection, was said to be of thirteen labels all dated 1807 and all by the same makers. In fact there are two sets. One comprises a larger size set of five labels (Photo 67) for KETCHUP, SOY, ANCHOVY, TOMATA and QUIN'S SAUCE. TOMATA is the correct spelling because this is how the name appears in the recipe books of the time. The smaller size set is of eight labels for CORATCH, PIQUANTE, ZOOBDITTY MATCH, ROYAL, CAMP, CHILI VINEGAR, HARVEY and CAVICE (illustrated in Photo 68 except for CAVICE which was not submitted for sale by the New York Historical

Photo 67. Mr Weed's big set of five.

THE MARKS AND SETS

Photo 68. Mr Weed's little set of eight (one missing).

Society). These labels were all made by Alice and George Burrows in 1807 with date letter capital M and noted up by Mr Weed following his purchase of them from a shop in Canterbury when returning to the USA on board the Cunard Royal Mail Steamship Laconia in 1927 (see illustrated extract from his notes – Fig 103). The blacking filling is worn from SOY, HARVEY and ANCHOVY indicating the popularity of these three sauces.

11.2 Thomas Hyde made a conventional set of single reeded cut corner rectangular labels each some 2.5 cm in length fully marked for London 1800 neatly engraved for HARVEY SAUCE, QUIN-SAUCE, TARRN VIN, ZOOBDITTY MATCH, KYAN, CAVIC SAUCE, CAMP-VIN and CHILI VIN (1). These labels presumably were made for an eight bottle soy frame and indicate what was in vogue at the turn of the century. He also made an interesting set for a four bottle frame with abbreviated titles for MUSHROOM KETP, ELDER VINR, CAYENNE VINR and CAYENNE PEPR (2). The Wakelin ledgers show that sets of sauce labels were ordered more frequently than sets of wine labels because of the use of the frame rather than the wine coaster. Oil and vinegar labels usually came in pairs for a two bottle frame or to go with three coasters in a Warwick cruet, until the development of the specialist vinegar frame (3). A rarity from Robert, David and Samuel Hennell in 1802 is a three bottle frame which is illustrated (Fig. 104).

11.3 Notwithstanding the great and intriguing variety of sauce names slot labels do not appear to have been employed, perhaps due to size, or taste, or the good business sense of silversmiths. On 18 of the 29 occasions when sauce labels appear in the Gentlemen's ledgers sets of five or more labels were sold. Whilst sets of four are often seen one cannot be certain whether or not a label or labels are missing from the set. John Langlands of Newcastle around 1800 made a set of four on hinged neck rings for CHYAN VINEGAR, WALNUT CATCHUP, ESSENCE OF ANCHOVIES and SOY, but there could be more. An emphasis on large sets is seen, however, in the sauce labels bought in from Ansill & Gilbert (4). There is a set of eight in the Ormond Blyth collection (5) which includes KYAN, CAYENNE, KETCHUP, LEMON, READING, WORCESTER RELISH and ZEST. At least two YORKSHIRE RELISH labels have been noted (6). Another set of eight was made in London in 1814 by Samuel Whitford along with the soy frame. As could be

THE MARKS AND SETS

imagined each bottle had a rectangular silver label with ring suspension. There were no rare names and the frame was probably used in Scotland (7). The Earl of Westmorland bought a set of eight from Wakelin's in October 1782 being "8 chaised labels for cut glass crewitts" weighing 6dwts each at a cost of five shillings a label (8). It seems that his Lordship suffered a substantial mark up. So far as sets of six are concerned an interesting example can be cited. A set of six labels for CAYENNE, ANCHOVY, CHILI, CATCHUP, SOY and HARVEY dated 1830 and made by Reilly and Storer have the usual grape and vine pattern but fruit is also included in the design (9). Sets of five have also been made with initials only. Oval shaped labels made circa 1790 have engraved on them B,G,R,M and S. However a set of five made in 1818 by Joseph Willmore in Birmingham were for CV, EA, ES, H and T. He also made a set in 1816 from which S survives. Whilst the first set could stand for Brandy, Gin, Rum, Madeira and Sherry one can think of sauce candidates. The second set mentioned must surely be for CHILI VINEGAR, ESSENCE ANCHOVIES, ESCAVECHI, HARVEY and SOY. Although Tarragon was in earlier times sometimes called Estragon this would not have been the case in 1816 and the recipe books still refer to Escavechi in full rather than Cavechi.

Fig 104. Rare three-bottle soy frame by Robert, David and Samuel Hennell, London, 1802, with labels having shaped corners by John Reily for SOY, TARRAGON and HARVEY.

11.4 Several very large sets comprising ten labels were made but ten bottle frames are rare. Perhaps these were made for six or eight bottle frames allowing some flexibility in the sauces being offered. In the case of unmarked Old Sheffield Plated labels, although kept together, it is not possible to state categorically that they were produced in sets of ten. It is easy to make up sets of look-alikes. A set of ten in plain design has been noted (10) with titles for SHRIMP, LOBSTER, M. KETCHUP, W. KETCHUP, INDIA SOY, LEMON PKLE, READING, CAVICE, HARVEY and ANCHOVIE. This set was probably used in Scotland. Robert and Samuel Hennell in 1804 made a set of ten octagonal sauce labels which included one for WOODS FISH SAUCE (11). Wakelins supplied Sir Henry Gough Bt. in 1783 with a set of ten soy tickets at 3s. each (12), Robert Adams in 1784 with a set of six small square threaded labels at 3s. each (13), the buyer being given credit for four soy tickets handed in, and the Earl of Radnor in 1785 with a boxed set of six soy labels (14).

11.5 With regard to marking, the early type of bottles for oils and vinegars and then for essences and flavourings had pull off silver caps which may or many not bear marks. Whilst duty on silver plate was in force from 1719, under the Act of 1738 (15), entitled an Act for preventing frauds and abuses, mounts, screws or stoppers to glass bottles were exempted under Section 6 both

159

THE MARKS AND SETS

from liability to be assayed and also from payment of duty, as were also chains and "cranes for bottles". So far as silver labels themselves were concerned, they were generally small and not very heavy, although there were exceptions. Silver sauce labels not weighing more than 10 dwts were exempted from marking. This was repealed by an Act of 1790. In the meantime an Act of 1757 repealed the 6d per ounce duty and substituted an annual licence tax to be paid by dealers. In 1784 the duty on silver plate was re-imposed at 6d per ounce payable on an after 1st December 1784. The position on the 1738 exemptions was unclear until 1790 when the Act of that year introduced new provisions. Under Section 3 chains were again exempted from liability to be assayed and from payment of duty. So also under Section 4 were mounts not weighing 10 dwts of silver each, except necks and collars for casters, cruets, or glasses appertaining to any sort of stands or frames. The effect of the exception is to make the specified types of mounts liable whatever their weight.

11.6 Under Section 5 any wares of silver not weighing 5 dwts of silver each were exempted from liability. But once again there was a list of excluded articles from the benefit of Section 5. The list included necks, collars, and tops for casters, cruets, or glasses appertaining to any sort of stands or frames and pieces to garnish stands or frames. It also included bottle tickets. Thus the Inland Revenue was not prepared to forgo what it regarded as lucrative income from widely used labelled cruets. Despite severe penalties there was not always compliance until after the turn of the century, perhaps due to misunderstanding of the legal position. There was also a curious lull in London around 1830 which may have something to do with the availability of punches after the death of King George IV. The problem also arose in 1837 but was solved by use of existing William IV punches or in London a poor edition of Queen Victoria's head (16). In short one should expect silver labels, cruet frames and bottle tops and collars to be fully marked by Assay Offices from 1790.

11.7 With regard to the maker's or sponsor's mark an Act of 1363 required the maker's mark to be set on the maker's work where it was required to be assayed and this requirement is repeated in subsequent Acts, including those relating to Scotland after the Act of Union (17). Where there was no legal obligation for assay there was no obligation to mark and so many sauce labels are unmarked but none the less may well be made of silver. So this accounts for the very high proportion of sauce labels produced before 1790 being unmarked. However cayenne spoons attached to bottle stoppers were often marked and provide dating evidence. Sauce labels being so small are sometimes stamped after 1784 without a date letter. However cusps inserted in the frame of a duty stamp can sometimes help. For example in London cusps inserted at the base and on the left hand side of the duty mark frame denoting that payment of duty has been made at the higher rate of 1s. per ounce instead of 6d. per ounce indicate that the label cannot be earlier than 1797 when the duty was doubled. Maker's marks were usually punched, but the law allowed incuse marks and a few makers distinguished themselves in this way. Joseph Glenny used his incuse mark on an ANCHOVY label with intricate border designs.

Photo 69. Joseph Glenny, 1819

11.8 Surnames stamped on labels in addition to a maker's mark made presumably as a retailer's mark occur rarely, unlike for example on sugar nips, tongs and spoons. "P.ROKER" appears on spoons, "I.GRAY" on nips "ALLEN" on nips and "T.LAW" on tongs. However "WEST" is stamped on James Fray's CATSUP label in the Cropper collection and "LAW" is stamped on John Egar's postage stamp letter M (for Mushroom Ketchup perhaps) bearing the date letter Q for 1812 (18). It was a Dublin Goldsmiths' Company requirement, dating from 1st November 1731,

THE MARKS AND SETS

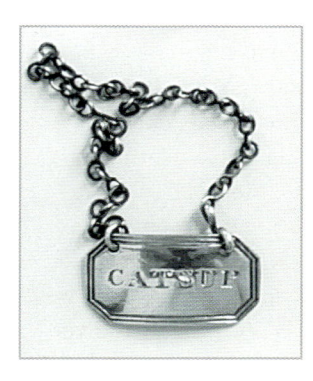

Photo 70. Henry Flavelle, 1834. Stamped "LAW" on reverse.

that a maker had to stamp his maker's mark, comprising his initials, on a label before it was sent to assay. So a maker could not stamp his full name. Thus names on labels such as LAW, WEST and HAMY were added after the label was returned from assay as the name of the retailer as an aide memoire for the next purchase.

11.9 Sauce labels are sometimes hallmarked on their face. Such marking can be either discreet or ostentatious. Paul Storr was possibly the originator of the idea of frontal marking because he was so proud of his work. As a notable silversmith he wished to advertise his creations, being desirous of making a statement of his values by adopting a bold approach. On his SOY of 1816 (Photo 39) the marks are well hidden in the foliate design. His maker's mark appears under the S of SOY and the remaining marks appear under the Y of SOY. However on his CHILI of two years later in 1818 (Photo 71) the marks appear more obviously being more widely positioned. Makers of vine leaf labels 1827-1848 usually arranged for the hallmarks to be hidden in the leaf. Whilst Charles Rawlings appears not to have done so as early as 1824 (Photo 43), he certainly did so on a wine label with William Summers in 1840. Willmore and Elliott each in 1827, Reily and Storer in 1831, Elliott again in 1833 an Unite in 1848 all marked vine leaf labels on the face. Also in the discreet category must be placed the Dutch AZIJN label (Photo 11) where the marks are minute, being located on the band close to each of the eyelets and on one of the eyelets itself. Foreign wine labels are often marked on the face of the label. In the ostentatious category, where the Victorian owner clearly wished it to be made known to his guests that his labels were of appropriate quality and not plated, one must place the READING and HARVEY'S made by Hunt and Roskell in 1882 (Photo 20) and the Harvey made by Martin and Hall of 1887 (Photo 24). Perhaps the idea of demonstrating wealth came from Sheffield where wine label makers (such as Hawksworth, Eyre & Co. in 1840) were adopting a practice, presumably because of public demand, of spreading the marks out across the face of the label above the title. ∎

Photo 71. Paul Storr, 1818.

NOTES

1) This set was sold for £1,900 by Bonhams in 1997; see further 10 WLJ 107.
(2) See an article by W.J. Hollick in 1 WLJ 60.
(3) Very few of these seem to have survived. A set of six unmarked vinegar labels in the Clemson-Young collection were illustrated in 1 WLJ 130, row 8.
(4) From the analysis made by Mr. Bruce Jones and published in WLJ.
(5) See N.M. Penzer's article 1 WLJ 82. Being in a glass case the labels could not be examined.
(6) See 1 WLJ 35.
(7) Sold by Christie's, Edinburgh, 23rd May 1996. The price paid was £1,667 including buyer's premium.
(8) Ledgers, Volume 8, p.52.
(9) See M.E. Paine's article in 1 WLJ 161.
(10) 1 WLJ 64.
(11) See illustration no. 1097 in Sotheby's "Directory of Silver 1600-1940".
(12) Ledgers, Volume 8, p.100.
(13) Ledgers, Volume 8, p.187.
(14) Ledgers, Volume 8, p.241.
(15) 12 GeoII c.26
(16) See the author's article on this subject in 10 WLJ.
(17) For a summary of the legal position in Scotland see the author's article in Proceedings of the Silver Society, Vol. III, p. 13.
(18) See 6 WLJ 239.

Fig 105. Set of three casters by Andrew Fogelberg, London 1774.

CHAPTER 12

THE BOTTLES, CHAINS AND FRAMES

12.1 In the seventeenth century just one sort of oil and one sort of vinegar were dispensed from vinegar bottles or "decanters" self standing on the buffet along with a set of three silver casters dispensing sugar (the tallest), black pepper (largish holes in the cover) and dry mustard (blind cover, no holes). Such a set by Andrew Fogelberg, to whom Paul Storr was apprenticed, made in 1774, is illustrated (see Fig. 105). The "blind" holes for the dry mustard are clearly shown. Other condiments were dispensed from the table: salt from a prime salt on top table, from a secondary salt (such as a bell salt) just below top table and elsewhere from trenchers or cellars; spices from boxes (an example of 1825 is illustrated in Fig. 106); and pickles from china saucers or glass dishes with pickle spoons. With the change in dining habits later in some households to having all the condiments on the table the silversmith invented the frame to hold condiments and to enable them to be passed around the table rather than be bought to an individual diner by a servant from the buffet which tended to slow down the service of the meal and allow the food to get cold. Oil and vinegar frames came into regular use early in the eighteenth century, creating a cruet with two bottles. The glass was lightly cut and the bottles had pull off silver caps. No labels were required as the contents were easily recognisable. However, following George Ravenscroft's patented invention of lead crystal in 1676, its subsequent development under his agreement with the Worshipful Company of Glass Sellers and the introduction of cutting and faceting from Nuremburg and Potsdam in the 1680s and later on from Zechlin and the subsequent development of deep cutting and faceting,

Fig 106. Spice Box, with two compartments, by Claude Odiot, Paris, 1825.

163

THE BOTTLES, CHAINS AND FRAMES

Fig 107. Pickle Dish by John Reily, London, 1801.

especially in London by Georg Kreybich, Christof Piltzen, John Akerman, Thomas Betts and Jerome Johnson (1), bottles containing oil needed to be distinguished from bottles containing vinegar and the sauce label was created. This began, it seems, in the late 1740s. The wooden frame containing a footed pickle dish centre piece, flanked by four glass soy bottles and two glass vinegar bottles, five with pull off glass stoppers and one for (for vinegar) with a glass screw stopper, was in use in Zechlin in the 1740s and exported from the glassworks situated there. The bodies of the glass cruets were clear and so there was no need at that time for labelling. Because of the use of vinegar in them pickles had to be served from glass or ceramic containers and were thus always kept separate from the developed cruet or soy frame. John Reily's pickle dish of 1801 is illustrated which was designed so as to be easily passed around the table. Bottles kept away from the table remained for the most part plain and uninteresting. Not so wine glasses which were brought to table. They had decorated stems. When wine glasses were left on table the decanter came into its own. The 1740s witnessed the introduction of entirely moulded bottles which helped to establish a good shape to fit in circular holders in a frame. Vinegar bottles of lustrous lead-glass were cut into with diamond facets overall, or with slices and bands of roundels, or with diamond facets with flutes, to name only a few designs. The London Tradesman for 1747 contains the statement that glass "scalloping" was "now greatly in vogue". The English technique of shallow, two-dimensional cut motifs was apparently a by-product of mirror bevelling as practised by Kreybich and Piltzen (2). It has been noted that no less than twenty mirror-bevel "grinders" had been registered with the Glass Sellers' Company in 1675 (3). Yet for some reason the glass sellers failed to take the commercial advantage that lead-glass afforded for deep cutting until the late 1740s when this started to become popular for cruet bottles and wine decanters. Just as sauce labels were designed to synchronise with wine labels, so

THE BOTTLES, CHAINS AND FRAMES

sauce bottles were designed to synchronise with wine decanters. Early sauce labels resembled wine labels from the point of view of size, shape and design.

12.2 The two-bottle oil and vinegar frame received the attention between 1700 and 1750 of leading silversmiths such as William Darker, John Edwards, Edward Feline, Charles Kandler, Paul de Lamerie, Peze Pilleau, Benjamin Pyne, Anne Tanqueray, William Townsend, George Wickes and David Willaume. The bottles usually had long necks, originally with pull off silver caps and then with silver handles and beak lids as in the case of Robert Hennell's 1789 cruet which is illustrated (Fig. 108). The glass bottles were either cylindrical or octagonal, with flat, lapidary-cut sides. One could see easily into the main body of the bottles, but the necks were decorated, cut with slightly hollowed diamonds, hexagons or squares. Pointed glass stoppers were a lower cost alternative to silver caps from about 1725. It was not long before the two-bottle oil and

Fig 108. Oval cruet for OIL, VINEGAR, BLACK PEPPER and RED PEPPER with original bottles and mounts marked by Robert Hennell, London, 1789.

THE BOTTLES, CHAINS AND FRAMES

Fig 109. Circular soy frame by Thomas Daniel, 1774, with open crescent labels by Thomas Hyde.

vinegar frame (4) was developed into the three-bottle cruet by the addition of a small pepper (5), then into the five condiment Warwick cruet (6) combining the oil and vinegar bottles with silver sugar, pepper and mustard casters, then into the five bottle cruet (a Newcastle example of 1757 is illustrated – Fig. 96) and finally into the circular soy frame such as that illustrated (Fig. 109) made by Thomas Daniel in 1774 (7). This then quickly developed (8) into the smaller all glass five or six soy or essence bottle circular frame of the 1760s (9). The soup tureen took over from the salt as a centrepiece with the change of dining habits and seating arrangements around the time of the Restoration (1660s and 1670s). French silversmiths created the concept of a "surtout", whereby the tureen in the 1710s was put on a tray and surrounded by salts, casters and oil and vinegar dispensers, as illustrated by Francois Massialot in his "Le Nouveau Cuisinier Royal et Bourgeois". Epergnes, the grand centrepieces, had their own sets of four trencher salts and two cruets designed in to meet the overall design requirements (10). So with the introduction of all-over hollow-diamond cutting from 1743 (11) and its general acceptance by the 1750s (as demonstrated by trade card illustrations of the period) and with the growing choice of condiments, say for example between four or five flavoured vinegars in the 1760s, frame makers started producing stands for larger size vinegar bottles containing GARLIC, ELDER, TARRAGON or CHILI VINEGARS. The leader in the field was probably Jabez Daniel of Carey Lane who had been apprenticed to the great specialist caster maker Samuel Wood. He began around 1749 at the time when the soy frame was beginning to be in demand and took James Mince as his apprentice as early as 1753. Mince appears to have worked in partnership with Jabez from 1766 to 1771, when Jabez took his son Thomas into partnership, until 1774 when Jabez probably retired. Thomas was a

THE BOTTLES, CHAINS AND FRAMES

noted maker of small squarish soy labels to decorate his own designed and made circular soy frames of the 1770s. Their designs were taken up by the Hennells. Thomas' main competitor would have been Margaret Binley producing very often kidney shaped labels for bottles and frames organised by Parker and Wakelin.

12.3 In Ireland Stephen Walsh was, it seems, making sauce labels to adorn bottles on a frame produced by Jabez Daniel as early as 1750 required by the occupiers of Powerscourt near the Wicklow Hills (12), in the style of Thomas Daniel, said to be small squarish, marked SW only, for their dining table, which survived the fire which ruined part of the house. The Powerscourt soy frame of 1750 is illustrated (Fig. 110) showing the pairs of original bottles with mounts by Stephen Walsh. The armorials on the bottle mounts by Walsh match those on the soy frame by Daniel. The frame formed part of the Powerscourt silver auctioned in 1984. Richard Wingfield, created Viscount Powerscourt in 1743, rebuilt Powerscourt ready for entertaining guests by 1750. He died in 1761, the same year as his architect Richard Castle. Extensive dining room silver was purchased in 1750 and surviving pieces included in the sale. These comprised, as well as the Jabez Daniel frame of 1750, several two-handled cups of

Fig 110. Powerscourt soy frame by Jabez Daniel, London, 1750, with four original bottles (the silver pepper and original labels went missing after the fire) mounted with engraved matching crests by Stephen Walsh of Cork and Dublin.

167

THE BOTTLES, CHAINS AND FRAMES

that date and more significantly meat dishes, sauce boats and a splendid epergne, which included provision for pickles, all by John Laughlin of Dublin and all dated 1750. Thomas Daniel in 1776 made a circular soy frame in the Adam classical style with four small essence bottles and four small square shaped labels marked with his maker's mark and the lion passant. With the change to dining à la Russe long tables loaded with food needed two and in certain cases three sets of identical cruets, which varied from three bottles to eight bottles per frame. Thus many cruets were made and survive but not necessarily intact. Bottles and stoppers can be swopped but the stoppers will not fit properly because they were designed to fit only one particular bottle. The wrong bottle may not sit easily in the frame. Sauce labels can be added, not necessarily with their original chains or in their original sets.

12.4 Chains were sometimes damaged and needed repairing. On May 21st 1784 the Revd. Buller was supplied by Wakelins with five "very strong chains to bottle labels" weighing 19.5 dwt. at a cost of 15 shillings. His labels must have been knocked about a bit at the vicarage and he did not wish to suffer further indignity. Volume 6 of the Ledgers also discloses that in 1778 the Earl of Stamford paid two shillings for two soy ticket chains. These were not so strong. The Bishop of Gloucester paid one shilling in May 1782 for a new chain to a soy ticket (13). In 1781 Sir William Molesworth had five soy tickets "done up" and polished at a cost of five shillings (14). The average price for a silver soy label at this time was about three shillings, including the cost of the silver chain. Chains were exempt from hallmarking under Acts of Parliament relating to England, Scotland and Wales. Neck rings and silver wire fastenings occasionally bear a lion passant. Neck collars are usually fully marked. The invention of the slip chain made the cleansing of labels easier. The importance of the chain, if it is the original as evidenced by condition at the

Fig 111. Oval soy frame by Samuel and George Whitford, London, 1807, bearing spring-wire fixing labels for VINEGAR, CORACK and KETCHUP attributed to Hugh Gordon of Fortrose.

168

THE BOTTLES, CHAINS AND FRAMES

eyelet, is in its length, which would be very short for a small, slim line soy or essence bottle, short for a medium sized cruet bottle, medium for a vinegar bottle and long for a pickle jar or storage jar for a stock sauce like ANCHOVY.

12.5 The popularity of silver wires instead of silver chains is difficult to assess. Wires were easier to keep clean. Gilt wires were used to support five square shaped gilt metal labels in 1783 for Sir Thomas Rich (15). Silver wires were used to support nine plain bottle tickets in 1782 for the Earl of Westmoreland (16) and eight threaded square bottle labels also in 1782 for Christopher Langloise (17). Furthermore in 1790 Robert Fellows was supplied with a "jointed wire wine label" (presumably some hinged arrangement) at the surprising cost of ten shillings and six pence (18). Hugh Gordon, it seems, used flexible spring wires to secure his bottle tickets as illustrated on bottles on the frame made by Samuel and George Whitford in 1807 (Fig. 111).

12.6 Eating à la Russe involved wine decanters being left on the table in coasters or slides. So sauce frames had to be as mobile as the

Fig 112. White glass Soy bottles in coasters, gilded for KETCHUP, GARLICK AND SOY.

Fig 113. Buffet four decanter bottle vinegar frame with pouring lips for topping up cruet vinegar bottles.

169

THE BOTTLES, CHAINS AND FRAMES

coasters as passing around gradually became the norm. Sometimes soy decanters were used with coasters, as illustrated (Fig. 112). The titles are for KETCHUP, GARLICK and SOY. Large bottles used for vinegars usually measure about 16cms in height with a circumference of some 22cms. These were topped up from a vinegar decanter standing on the sideboard, the stand usually being of Old Sheffield Plate and containing three or four decanters which had a lip for pouring (see illustration – Fig. 113). The use of larger heavier bottles at table would have caused difficulties in passing round the stand. Medium sized bottles used for relishes usually measure about 14cms in height with a circumference of some 15cms. The small essence bottles measure about 9cms in height with a circumference of some 10cms. It is impossible to be precise but these statistics give an indication. Pickle jars vary in size. Those in a frame presumably stayed on the sideboard. They were distributed at table by dish or small jar. Being fat their labels required longer chains than the norm (see Fig. 39).

12.7 Early glass bottles tend to have the centre of the base hollowed out to enable them to stand up properly, whereas with the development in cutting techiques with the use of steam powered wheels in Regency times bottles often had six or eight pointed stars cut into the thick base. In the 1770s and 1780s soy frames with "Bristol" blue, green or red bottles were much in vogue. As no soy bottle could be regarded as complete without its label the glassmakers reproduced a label by gilding, complete with chain for authenticity. Several different processes were used such as enameling, firing and using two glazes. Gold leaf was used because of its fusion capability. Wakelins supplied in 1774 a "lightly pierced soy-frame with 4 blue crewitts & gold labels" (19). An example of a soy-frame bottle with chains in gilt of rococo design from the London workshop of James Giles (1760-1774) is illustrated by Jane Stancliffe (20). Illustrated here (Fig 113) is a green glass soy bottle with lozenge stopper with the gilt letter K for KYAN or KETCHUP on one side and a gilt leaf on the other. The applied label is an Adam design for

Fig 113. Bristol green soy bottle for KETCHUP.

KETCHUP in an octagonal frame, with a single reed in the style of a silversmith, with added foliage outside the frame below, at each side and above, surmounted by a sauce tureen from whose handles the label is suspended by gilt chains. Red coloured bottles have been observed (21). No enamelled armorial bottles have been spotted but there may have been some on the "Prince Regent" with wide bases for use on board following the precedent for wine set by a ship's decanter engraved with the arms of the Prince of Wales dated circa 1805 which resides in the Pilkington Glass Museum or set by the enameller William Beilby of Gateshead (1760-1774). Titles noted on "Bristol" bottles include ANCHOVY, SOY, KETCHUP, KAYON, OIL and MUSTARD. Unmarked "Bristol" bottles with 1793 silver

THE BOTTLES, CHAINS AND FRAMES

mounts had fused plate labels for ANCHOVIES, KETCHUP, RED VINEGAR and WHITE VINEGAR (22).

12.8 Stands for bottles with applied labelling either by gilding or by glass engraving were seldom made of silver. A papier-maché stand with metal bottle holders and handle painted black and decorated with a single red stripe throughout is illustrated (Fig 115) containing three "Bristol" blue glass bottles showing off large gilt labels for SOY, KYAN and KETCHUP. The labels are oval in shape, with broad gilt borders of interlinked circles. They are suspended from a single point by a gilt chain. The lozenge-shaped stoppers have a gilt twelve-petalled flower surrounded by a gilt wavy line on both faces. Also illustrated (Fig 116) is a long boat-shaped stand, for four bottles engraved with soy titles for KETCHUP, FISH.S, KYAN and SOY, made of leather with metal supports including a handle which can be demounted by unscrewing a securing nut. The titles LEMON, TERAGON, SOY and ELDER were engraved on bottles standing in a rounded oblong four bottle silver cruet stand on ball feet made by Thomas Wallis in 1806 (23). Of similar design, engraved with a family crest on its base, is a cruet marked by Robert Cattle and James Barber in York dated 1809. As this is the only recorded soy frame assayed by this partnership during the years from 1808 to 1813, it seems likely that their four known soy labels for HERVEY.S, KETCHUP, KYAN or SOY go with it. Interestingly the successor firm of Barber and

Fig 115. Bristol blue three bottle soy frame.

Whitwell had at least five soy frames assayed between 1814 and 1823 in York. A pewter frame houses five bottles with labels for PEPPER, MUSHROOM, OIL, VINEGAR and SOY in an American Museum (24). Wooden cruet frames were made by a turner, George Hutchinson, of The Amberley Trout in Snow Hill in the City of London, according to his trade card of 1762 (25).

12.9 The six bottle cruet was probably the most popular in the 1770s. The Wakelin Ledgers reveal a few exceptions. Mrs Inge, for example,

171

THE BOTTLES, CHAINS AND FRAMES

bought a five bottle cruet for her crescent shaped soy labels in 1771 and Sir John Nelthorpe, the Revd. Carter, Mr. James Bourchier and (probably) the Earl of Scarborough chose four bottle frames between 1771 and 1780. All the other customers appear to have chosen six bottle frames weighing between 7oz 2dwt for the Revd. Doyly up to 12oz 10dwt for Sir Robert Clayton. The cost of soy frames can be culled from the Wakelin Ledgers. An oval pierced frame for the Duchess of Ancaster weighing 10 ounces cost £2.15s 0d. for the silver and £2.10s.0d. for making it in 1780. A similar but smaller frame for the Hon. Booth Grey in the same year weighing 8 ounces 12dwt. cost £2.7s.6d for the silver and £2.10s.0d. for making it plus 2 shillings for engraving a cipher on it.

12.10 A trade card (26) of George Maydwell (one hopes he lived up to his name – he was indeed elected a Fellow of the Royal Society of Arts in 1759) and Richard Windle, engraved by Robert Clee between 1750 and 1756, who were glass-cutters working at the cut glass warehouse adjacent to the King's Arms, Norfolk Street, off the Strand in London, shows "Essence Bottles" and "Cruet Frames". Clee also engraved silver. Parker and Wakelin paid him up to £345 per annum for engraving silver between 1769 and

Fig 116. Copper and leather soy frame by Thomas Bowen II, London 1797, with four bottles engraved for KETCHUP, FISH·S, KYAN (with silver-gilt cayenne spoon) and SOY.

THE BOTTLES, CHAINS AND FRAMES

his death in 1773 (27). He worked also for Thomas Heming and probably engraved his trade card (28) disclosing that it was his practice to sell "up-to-the-minute productions" (29). Decanters were not mentioned save that in a vignette at the bottom right of the card a man is shown grinding the base of a hollow-diamond cut decanter on a circular horizontal disc operated by the workman's left hand. Maydwell and Windle's trade cards in the Heal Collection also show a hand-driven glass cutting wheel (30). Heming did make soy labels and was a well respected maker of silver mounts for cut glass (31). The glass makers seem to have congregated near Fleet Street and the Strand at this time. Silversmiths would have bought in glass from Weatherly Crowther (c.1755), Colebran Hancock (1762), William Parker (1760s) and John Jacob (c.1763). Parker ran the Glass Warehouse at 69 Fleet Street (32). Glass-works were conveniently situated at the Savoy and less conveniently at Henley. Others were situated at Vauxhall and near to London Bridge. ■

NOTES

(1) See Andy McConnell, "The First English Cut-Glass circa 1700-1745", Antique Collecting, Vol.36, No.9.
(2) As explained by McConnell, op. cit.
(3) See further McConnell, op. cit.
(4) The earliest example noted, by Benjamin Pyne, is dated 1704.
(5) The earliest example noted, by Paul de Lamarie, is dated 1714, similar to another of his dated 1725. Whilst the necks of the bottles were cut in hollow diamonds, the bodies were plain. A similar frame by Thomas Daniel dated 1776 has been noted (The Silver Collection Limited), so the style lasted for some time.
(6) The earliest example noted, by Anthony Nelme, is dated 1715 (bottles not original). The Victoria and Albert Museum has a Warwick cruet dated 1729.
(7) The earliest example noted, by Jabez Daniel, is dated 1750.
(8) A circular frame by Jabez Daniel and James Mince dated 1771 had two oil and vinegar bottles with silver pull off caps and three glass casters with silver mounts.
(9) A good example would be Elizabeth Aldridge's circular frame of 1767, in which the five small soy bottles with pull off caps nestled against a central carrying handle with a star shaped bottom moulding. The bottles were cut with large strawberry diamonds. Thomas Daniel in 1776 made a circular frame for six soy bottles.
(10) Such grand centre pieces can be seen in the Hermitage Museum in St. Petersburg.
(11) See above, para 1.4
(12) Powerscourt Sale, 24-25th September 1984, by Christie's on the premises.
(13) Wakelin Ledges, Volume 7, p118. P.C. Crespigny paid a similar amount in 1784, idem, p77.
(14) Idem, p239.
(15) Wakelin Ledgers, Volume 8, p11.
(16) Idem, pp 34 and 52.
(17) Idem, p54.
(18) Idem, p219.
(19) Idem, Volume 5: supplied at a cost of £2.18s.0d.
(20) In "Bottle Tickets" at p.8. A green shoulder decanter with a spire stopper of circa 1770 probably by the Whyte Fryars Glasshouse and decorated in gilt in the workshop of James Giles is illustrated by Andy McConnell in his article on the British Decanter, "Antique Collecting", June 1999, p.28.
(21) By R.G. Bignall, see 2 WLJ 18.
(22) Stephen Helliwell, "Understanding Antique Silver Plate," illustration, p.54.
(23) 10 WLJ 69-70
(24) John McKnitt Alexander Museum in North Carolina, USA, ref: A87.22d – J. Henry McGill bequest.
(25) Country Life, 10 December 1948, p1211.
(26) Hilary Young, "An eighteenth century London glass-cutter's trade card", Apollo, Vol CXL VII, No 432 (new series), February 1998, p41.
(27) Idem, p45.
(28) Idem, fig.7, p46.
(29) Apollo, op.cit. p45.
(30) Illustrated by McConnell, op. cit.
(31) Idem, p46, note 35.
(32) See A. Werner, Journal of the Glass Association, 1985. Thomas Betts was also a well-known glassworker, with premises at the King's Arms Glass Shop in the 1740s.

ILLUSTRATIONS

References are to figured illustrations

1. The Circle's Presidential Badge was designed by Mark Fitzpatrick, a student who won an open competition, and produced by C. J. Vander Limited.
2. Rare Silver-Gilt Soy Frame complete with all six original labels by Robert Piercy, London, 1775.
3. Part of Elizabeth Smith's Preface of 1737. Clinging muslin dresses from France replaced the huge hoops and wide skirts, which were confined to Court occasions at St James's Palace from 1790 until Queen Charlotte's death in 1818.
4. Elizabeth Raffald's Title Page, 1799.
5. 1782 Portrait of Elizabeth Raffald.
6. Elizabeth Raffald's Dedication to her Mistress.
7. Extracts from Mrs Beeton's Cookery Book, 1910 Edition.
8. Oil and Vinegar frame by William Darker, London, 1720, with labels circa 1750 probably by Richard Binley.
9. Single Diamond Cut Vinegar Bottle circa 1760, with pull off cap and label for HARVEY, one of a pair with WORCESTER.
10. A pair of rat-tailed Pickle Spoons by Isaac Davenport, London, 1698.
11. Set of casters by Thomas Bamford I, London, 1720.
12. Pair of salt cellars by Ebenezer Oliphant, Edinburgh, 1742.
13. Mustard pots by Thomas Daniel, London, 1776 (with mustard spoon) and by William Carr Hutton, Sheffield, 1894 (in silver-gilt).
14. Spice box, with three compartments, and in the centre a pull-out nutmeg grater, by André Martin, Marseilles, 1758-1763.
15. The Royal Kitchen at Windsor Castle circa 1855.
16. Mrs Beeton's sweetmeats and displays of fresh fruits, 1910.
17. Advertisement for Mr Keen's Mustard, 1870.
18. Eliza Smith's Preface. It took her a long time to collect all her recipes.
19. Eliza Smith's Kitchen in 1737.
20. Eliza Smith's Title Page in 1737.
21. Eliza Smith's Buffet layout for Supper, 1737.
22. Eliza Smith's Buffet layout for a First Course, 1737.
23. Eliza Smith's Buffet layout for a Second Course, 1737.
24. William Henderson's Title Page in c.1797.
25. William Henderson's Kitchen in c.1797.
26. Henderson's Table Plans for a Small Company, c.1797.
27. Henderson's First Course for a Dinner Party, c.1797.
28. Henderson's Second Course for a Dinner Party, c.1797.
29. Henderson's Instructions for Suppers, c.1797.
30. Hannah Glasse's Title Page, 1774.
31. First Course Table layout by Elizabeth Raffald 1799.
32. Second Course Table layout by Elizabeth Raffald 1799.
33. Portrait of John Farley, 1804.
34. John Farley's Title Page, 1804.
35. John Farley's Bills of Fare for August and September.
36. Eliza Smith's Bills of Fare for April until September.
37. Old and new crescent soy labels for HARVEY and TAROGON displayed at Preston Manor, Brighton.
38. Gillray's view of a user of SAUCE ROYAL and CHIAN pepper.
39. Pickle Frame with jars labelled for CHUTNEE by Edward Hutton and WALNUT by William Carr Hutton.
40. Elizabeth Smith's first recipe of 1737.
41. Richard Bradley's Title Page 1727.
42. Raffald's autographed opening of Chapter I of her 1799 edition.
43. Farley's autographed conclusion of his Preface in 1804.
44. William Scott's Title Page of 1826.
45. Mrs Scott at work in 1826.
46. Bishop's Frontispiece showing a kitchen in 1855.
47. Frederick Bishop's Title Page of 1855.
48. Bishop's view of the art of carving in 1855.
49. Insull's joints, 1824.
50. Insull's cuts, 1824.
51. Insull's instructions on carving, 1824.
52. 1910 Preface to Mrs Beeton's Cookery Books.
53. Frontispiece to Mrs Beeton's 1910 Edition.
54. Pickles and Vinegar advertisment, 1910.
55. 1910 Table Arrangements for folded napkins.
56. Robert Kemp Philp's inspiration for his recipes.
57. A1, Tomato Chutney and Tomato Catsup advertisements.
58. Preface to Mrs Beeton's The Englishwoman's Cookery Book.
59. Taken from "The Female Instructor" of 1824, the Bride.
60. Bishop's Bridal Breakfast à la fourchette.
61. Recipe for preparing John Dory with ANCHOVY sauce, 1870.
62. Poetical recipe from Sydney Smith (1741-1845).

63   The opening pages of Bishop on Sauces, 1855.
64   Recipes for CATSUP from Raffald's Experienced English Housekeeper, p. 339.
65   Cherokee Chiefs bring their sauce to England.
66   Lady Charlote Bury's 1844 recipes for CAVECHI.
67   Mrs Beeton's 1870 recipe for Mango CHETNEY.
68   Premier Household Recipe Book's recipes for pickles and CHUTNEY (1930s).
69   Lady Charlotte Bury's Preface and recipe for DEVONSHIRE sauce (1844).
70   Lady Charlotte Bury's General Rules for a Good Dinner in 1844.
71   Elizabeth Raffald's recipe for ELDER Flower Vinegar (1799).
72   Mrs Beeton's 1910 recipe for GINGER sauce.
73   Raffald's recipe for GOOSEBERRY Vinegar.
74   Family Recipe for GOOESBERRIE Chutney.
75   1831 cartoon published by S. Gans showing the Prime Minister's cronies enjoying the fine rich soup in the State Sauce Pan to the detriment of John Bull, a figure invented in 1712 to represent all that could be regarded as basically British.
76   The new fangled stove of 1779 used for the preparation of sauces taken from Raffald.
77   The Leamington range of 1870.
78   Russell's Patent Lifting Fire Herald range of the 1900s, used at Queen Alexandra's Technical School at Sandringham.
79   Dr. Scott's recipe for LEMON PICKLE.
80   Raffald's recipe for MUSHROOM Powder.
81   A menu from the Young's Housewife's Daily Assistant, 1864.
82   PIQUANTE as one of Cre-Fydd's condiment sauces in 1864.
83   Liebig's recipe for a sharp (or PIQUANTE) sauce, 1885.
84   Liebig's introduction to the section on Meat, Entrée and poultry dishes, 1885.
85   Lady Charlotte's recipes for POIVRADE ,QUIN'S, RAVIGOTTE and other sauces, 1844.
86   Scott's recipe for QUIN'S sauce, 1826.
87   Recipes, taken from the Female Instructor, for sauces to be served from a sauce boat in 1824.
88   Scott's recipe for SOY.
89   Raffald's recipe for SUGAR Vinegar.
90   Raffald's recipe for TARRAGON VINEGAR.
91   Scott's recipe for TOMATOE SAUCE.
92   Raffald's recipes for WALNUT CATSUP.
93   A redrawn original of 1788 taken from Denis Diderot's Encyclopedia, showing a die press for coinage.
94   Rare Sheffield Soy Frame with original bottles and labels by Thomas Blagden, 1817.
95   Boat shaped soy frame by John Emes, London, 1804, with double-reeded oval labels by John Rich for WOODS SAUCE, GARLIC VINEGAR, JAPAN SOY and CAYENNE PEPPER, for which the silver-gilt spoon was used.
96   A Newcastle frame by Samuel Thompson II, in 1757, with kidney shaped labels for SOY, KETCHUP, ELDER and GARLICK.
97   Ship's soy decanters with labels for CATSUP and ANCHOVY by Peter and William Bateman, London, 1813.
98   Sketch drawing (not to scale) of coronet engraved on reverse of Charles Price's CHILI.VINR.
99   Beckford's cruet of 1784.
100 SALT and PEPPER pots made in India.
101 A porcelain FRENCH.
102 An ivory PORT and a bone VINEGAR with bottle coaster for No. 9 Port.
103 Mr Weed's notes made on the Laconia bound for New York.
104 Rare three-bottle soy frame by Robert, David and Samuel Hennell, London, 1802, with labels having shaped corners by John Reily for SOY, TARRAGON and HARVEY.
105 Set of three casters by Andew Fogelberg, London, 1774.
106 Spice Box, with two compartments, by Claude Odiot, Paris, 1825.
107 Pickle Dish by John Reily, London, 1801.
108 Oval cruet for OIL, VINEGAR, BLACK PEPPER and RED PEPPER, with original bottles and mounts marked by Robert Hennell, London, 1789.
109 Circular soy frame by Thomas Daniel, London, 1774, with open crescent labels by Thomas Hyde.
110 Powerscourt soy frame by Jabez Daniel, London, 1750, with four original bottles (silver pepper and original labels lost after the fire) mounted with engraved matching crests by Stephen Walsh of Cork and Dublin.
111 Oval soy frame by Samuel and George Whitford, London, 1807, bearing spring-wire fixing labels for VINEGAR, CORACK and KETCHUP attributed to Hugh Gordon of Fortrose.
112 White glass soy bottles in coaster, gilded for KETCHUP, GARLICK and SOY.
113 Buffet four decanter bottle vinegar frame, with pouring lips for topping up cruet vinegar bottles.
114 Bristol green soy bottle for KETCHUP.
115 Bristol blue three bottle soy frame.
116 Copper and leather soy frame by Thomas Bowen II, London, 1797, with four bottles engraved for KETCHUP, FISH.S, KYAN (with silver gilt cayenne spoon) and SOY.
117 Trade card of Antiquarian Cookery Book Sellers.

INDEX

References are to paragraph numbers.
Chapters 3, 4, 5 and 6, being arranged
in alphabetical order, are not indexed.

Abdy, William 7.25
Aberdeen 7.16, 7.26
Adam, Charles 9.2
Adams, Ann 7.20
Adams, Robert 11.4
Akerman, John 12.1
Aldridge, Elizabeth 1.5, 9.1
Amsterdam, 1.4
Ansill and Gilbert 1.15, 1.18, 1.20, 11.3
Apicius, Marcus 2.1, 2.2
Architectural 7.38
Argyles, 1.9
Armisted 1.15
Armorials 8.1
   Border 8.6
   Cartouche 8.2
   Crest 8.5
   Front engraving 8.3
   Rear engraving 8.4
Assay 11.5, 11.6
Astons 7.24

Bamford, Thomas 1.2, 9.2
Baniel, WB 1.13
Banff 7.18
Bannister, Thomas 7.29
Barker, Richard 7.43
Barker, Susanna 7.13-7.18, 8.2-8.5, 9.3, 9.8, 9.9
Barrett, William 7.15
Baskerville 7.18
Basket 7.34
Bateman, Hester 7.18, 7.20
Bateman, Peter and William 7.15, 7.24, 7.32, 8.2
Bedford, William 9.6-9.9
Beebe, James 7.39
Beeton, Isabella 2.10, 2.16, 12.1
Beilby, William 12.7

Bellasize 1.15
Bennett 1.15
Benyon 1.17
Betts, Thomas 12.1
Bignall Collection 7.49
Birmingham 7.24, 11.3
Binley, Margaret 1.18, 1.20, 7.3, 7.11, 7.12, 7.14, 7.15, 7.18, 8.4, 12.2
Bishop, Frederick 2.15
Black composition 7.3
Bolton, Lord 1.8
Bone 10.1
Borders
   Arrows 7.18
   Bead 7.15, 7.18, 7.27
   Bright cut 7.11
   Cable 7.15, 7.17
   Cherub 7.37
   Feather 7.11, 7.14
   Festoon 8.2
   Flower heads 7.18
   Foliate 7.21, 7.39
   Fretwork 7.48
   Frond 7.20
   Fruits 7.34
   Gadroon 7.23, 7.40
   Greek 7.13
   Leaves 7.35
   Matting 7.20
   Reed, triple 7.32
   Scalloped 7.18
   Scrolling 7.34, 7.38
   Shaped 7.12
   Shell 7.42
   Shells 7.21
   Shells and foliage 7.38, 7.41, 7.44, 7.45
   Shells and gadroon 7.36, 7.40
   Snake 7.20, 8.6
   Splayed 7.13, 7.14, 7.15

   Viticulture 7.39, 7.44
   Wavy line 7.11
   Wrigglework 7.11, 7.15, 7.19
   Zig-zag 7.18
Bottle tickets 1.14
Bottles
   Eight ounce 2.9
   Four ounce 2.9
   Two ounce 2.9
Boulton, Matthew 1.2, 7.14, 7.39
Bourchier, James 1.15, 8.7, 12.9
Bowen, Thomas 12.8
Bower 7.24
Bowers, Robert 7.29
Bradley, Richard 2.4
Bradley's fish sauce 2.4
Bristol glass 1.8, 12.8
Brown Collection 7.29, 7.38
Buffet 1.9, 1.10
Buller 12.4
Burgess, John 1.17, 1.20
Burrows, Alice and George 1.17, 7.18, 11.1
Bury, Charlotte 2.15
Button 7.31

Cambridge University 2.4
Cameron, Alexander 7.15
Campbell 2.5
Canoe 7.29
Caps, pull off 1,5
Caracciola, Domenico 2.3
Carracioli, Francesco 2.3
Carter 2.4, 8.7, 12.9
Cartouche 7.43
Carving 2.15
Cattle and Barber 12.8
Chains 12.4
   Slip 7.7
Chardin 1.16

INDEX

Cherub 7.37
Cheshire, Charles 7.42
Chester 7.18, 7.29, 7.39
Chesterman, Charles 7.43
Clayton, Robert 12.9
Clee, Robert 12.10
Coasters, soy 12.6
Collar 7.28
Collinger 1.10
Condiments 2.17
Constables, William 7.20
Conyers, Sir William 8.4
Cork labels 7.9
Coronet 8.2
Courses 1.10
Cre-fydd 2.17
Crescent
   Enclosed 7.14
   Large 7.11
   Ordinary 7.18
Crespel, Sebastian 7.20, 7.30
Creswick, James and Nathaniel 7.45, 9.12
Cropper Collection 7.14
Crown 8.4
Crown Staffordshire 10.4
Cruet 1.3
Curved labels 1.1
Cushion 7.36

Daniel, Jabez 12.2, 12.3
Daniel, Thomas 1.2
Darker, William 1.1, 12.2
Dating by
   Tests 7.51
   Title 1.23
Davenport, Isaac
Decanters
   Green 1.4
   Shaft and globe 1.4
   Soy 1.5
   Vinegar 1.3, 1.5, 12.6
Dent Collection 7.11, 7.27, 7.46
Designs 7.1
Copycat 7.4
Dessert 1.9
Devil Tavern 2.4
Documentary evidence 1.1, 1.14
   Notebooks 1.17
Dome 7.20

Doncaster 2.11
Double-sided 7.10
Dove 8.7
Doyly 12.9
Drapery festoon 7.50
Dressings 1.11
Drinkwater, Sandylands 8.3
Duke of
   Ancaster 9.3, 12.9
   Devonshire 2.15
   Hamilton 9.9
   Leeds 8.4
   Newcastle 2.8
   Roxburgh 7.39
Dutch East India Company 1.6
Dutch label 11.9
Duty marks 11.5, 11.6, 11.7

Earl of
   Bedford 1.2
   Chesterfield 1.17
   Derby 8.7
   Holderness 7.14, 8.4
   Jersey 8.2
   Lincoln 1.15
   Louth 1.15
   Radnor 11.4
   Scarborough 12.9
   Stamford 12.4
   Warwick 1.3
   Westmoreland 11.3, 12.5
   Yarborough 8.4
Earliest labels 1.1
Edinburgh 7.17
Edington, John 7.20
Edwards, John 2.1
Edwards, Thomas 7.18
Eighty-eight 8.4
Eley, Thomas 8.5
Elliott, William 7.36, 7.39, 7.44, 11.9
Enamel 1.1, 10.1, 10.4
Epergne 1.9, 1.13
   Labels 1.22, 2.9
Erskine, James 7.26
Escutcheon
   Ordinary 7.45
   Squashed 7.41
Essences 2.14
Evans, Thomas 7.18
Eye 7.13

Fane, Henry 1.15
Fane, John 1.15
Farley, John 1.11, 2.12
Fauconberg and Conyers 7.14, 8.4
Fellows, Robert 12.5
FitzHenry Collection 8.4
Flavelle, Henry 7.24
Flavourings 2.9, 2.10
Floral displays 1.13
Floreate 7.39
Fogelberg, Andrew 1.12
Fonthill Abbey 9.6, 9.9
Fortrose 7.30
Frame – see Stand
Fraser, William 8.3
French cooking 2.5
Fretwork 7.38

Garrard, Robert 7.30, 7.31
Garter 8.3
Giles, James 12.3
Gillray, James 1.16
Ginger jars 1.22
Glass
   Bases 12.7
   Blue 1.8, 12.7
   Crystal 1.3
   Cutting 1.3, 12.7
   Flutes 1.5
   Green 12.7
   Grooves 1.5
   Opaque 1.2
   Prisms 1.5
   Red 12.7
Glass makers
   Crowther, Weatherly 12.10
   Hancock, Colebran 12.10
   Jacob, John 12.10
   Parker, William 12.10
Glass sellers 12.1
Glass works 12.10
Glasse, Hannah 1.11, 1.19, 2.5, 2.6
Glenny, Joseph 11.7
Gloucester, Bishop of 12.4
Gold 9.1
Gordon, Hugh 7.30
Gough, Henry 11.4
Grand entertainments 2.11
Gravies 1.7

INDEX

Grey, Booth 9.3, 12.9
Grimwade, 7.20

Hagar, John 9.4
Hales, 8.3
Hamilton and Co 10.2
Hammick's and Buller 1.15
Hamy 11.8
Hand clasping arrow 8.3
Hawksworth, Eyre 11.9
Hayes, Jonathan 7.20
Heart 7.49
Hemming, Thomas 7.14, 12.10
Henderson, William 1.10, 1.11
Hennell, Robert 7.17, 12.2
Hennell, Robert and Samuel 12.2
Hennell, Robert, David and Samuel 11.2
Herbs – see Spices
Heron 9.6
Hockley, Daniel 7.23
Holland, Margaret 7.23
Hopkins 1.15
Hunt and Roskell 7.19, 11.9
Hutton, Edward 1.13, 1.22, 7.41, 7.45
Hutton, William 1.2, 1.22, 7.45
Hyde, James 7.13, 7.17, 7.31, 8.3, 8.4
Hyde, Thomas 7.17, 7.18, 7.26, 11.2

Incuse marks 11.7
India 1.8, 10.2, 10.3
Inge 12.9
Initial 7.47
Insull, Elizabeth 2.15
Ireland 7.18, 7.20, 7.24
Ivory 10.1, 10.3

Jenkinson, Thomas 7.18
Johnson, Jerome 1.4, 12.1
Johnson, Thomas 7.17

Keating, J 7.20
Keay, Robert 7.3
Keen 1.9
Kidney 7.15
Kippax, Robert 7.18
Kitchiner, William 2.9, 2.12
Knight 7.24
Kreybich, Georg 12.1

Laconier, RMS 1.17, 11.1
Lamb 1.9
Lambert, Peter 7.16
Lamerie, Paul de 8.4
Langford and Sebile 7.14
Langlands, John 7.20, 11.3
Langlands and Robertson 7.44
Langley, Richard 9.5
Langloise, Christopher 12.5
Law 11.8
Lea and Perrins 1.20
Letheutier 1.15
Lettering
    Fancy 3.6
    Pierced 7.8
    Size 1.1
Lewes, White Hart 2.8
Lewis and Wright 7.15
Lind Collection 7.49
Linnit 7.24
Loops, soldered 7.7
Lowe, Edward 7.39

Maker's mark 7.2
Manchester 2.11
Marshall Collection 1.17, 7.16, 8.4
Martin and Hall 7.24, 11.9
Maydwell and Windle 12.10
McDonald 7.24
McKay, James 7.17, 7.38
Menus 1.9, 1.10, 1.11, 2.6, 2.17
Metallic alloys 7.3
Military 7.5
Mince, James 12.2
Molesworth, William 12.4
Morley, Elizabeth 7.2, 7.15, 7.23, 7.41
Morris, William 9.13
Mortimer and Hunt 7.42
Mother-of-pearl 10.4
Murray 7.24, 9.4
Mustard
    Dry 1.2, 1.9
    Wet 1.2, 1.9

Neck-ring 7.30
Nelme, Anthony 1.3
Nelthorpe, John 12.9
Newcastle 7.24
New College Oxford 1.8
Nickolds, John 7.15

Niello 7.3
Nott, John 2.4

Odiot, Claude 12.1
Oil 1.1, 1.3
Old Sheffield Plate 7.15, 7.18, 7.24, 11.4, 12.6
Olier 9.4
Oliphant, Ebenezer 1.2
Organic materials 10.1
Ormond Blyth Collection 11.3
Orr and Co 10.2
Oval 7.17

Parker, William 12.10
Parker and Wakelin 8.4, 12.2, 12.10
Patent 1.3
Peaston, Robert 9.2
Pegasus 8.4
Pembroke, Lady 1.1
Penzer 7.19, 7.31
Perth 7.24
Philp, RK 2.16
Phipps, James 7.18
Phipps and Robinson 7.16, 7.17, 7.22, 7.24, 7.30, 7.40, 8.5
Phipps, Robinson and Phipps 7.42, 8.3, 9.10
Phipps, Thomas and James 7.18, 7.36, 7.40, 7.44, 9.11
Pickle 2.3
    Dishes 1.9
    Jars 1.2, 1.13, 1.22, 12.6
    Saucers 2.3
    Spoons 1.2
Piercy, Robert 1.5, 1.14, 1.19, 9.1, 9.3
Piltzen, Christof 12.1
Pitts, William 7.39
Porcelain 1.7, 10.1, 10.4
Powerscourt 1.5, 12.3
Preston Manor 1.13
Price, Charles 8.4
"Prince Regent" 8.3, 12.7
Pugin 7.6, 9.13
Purton, Frances 7.32
Pyne, Benjamin 1.3

Quatrefoil 7.35
Quatre-semi-circle 7.27

INDEX

Raffald, Elizabeth 2.11
Ravenscroft, George 1.3, 12.1
Rawlings, Charles 7.19, 7.20, 7.28, 7.34, 7.37, 7.39, 7.40, 7.44, 7.45, 8.4, 8.6, 9.11, 11.9
Rawlings and Summers 7.15, 7.17, 7.18, 7.24, 7.30, 7.32, 7.38, 7.42, 7.45, 7.46, 7.47, 11.9
Rectangular
    Broad 7.23
    Curved narrow 7.33
    Cut-cornered 7.24
    Gadrooned 7.40
    Irregular 7.12
    Narrow 7.26
    Rounded-end 7.21
    Shaped end 7.32
    Small squarish 7.16
    Victorian irregular 7.46
Reily, John 2.3 7.17, 7.24, 7.26, 7.31, 7.38, 7.39, 7.45, 8.3, 8.4, 9.11
Reily, Mary and Charles 7.17, 7.45
Reily and Storer 7.47, 8.6, 9.13, 11.3
Renou, Timothy 7.20
Retailer's marks 11.8
Rich, John 7.3, 7.13, 7.15, 7.17, 7.23, 7.24, 7.30, 8.4, 9.10
Rich, Thomas 12.5
Roberts and Belk 9.1
Roberts, William 7.17
Rochefoucauld, François de la 1.9
Rooy, Anthony de 1.4
Rowlandson 1.9
Royal Yacht 8.3
Ruby 1.15
Ruggles-Brise 7.26

Salomon-grundy 2.7
Salt 1.2
Sauce boat 1.7, 2.3
Sauce box 2.9
Saucer 1.2
Scofield 9.3, 9.6
Scotland 1.21
Scott, William 2.14
Scott and Smith 7.37
Scourfield, Henry 1.15, 8.7
Scroll 7.19
Secker, Robert 8.4
Seeds 2.10

Seventy-seven 8.3
Shapes 7.1
Shaw 7.24
Shield 7.49
Ship's soy decanters 8.3
Simpson, William 7.18
Size 1.14, 2.3, 7.12
Slip chains 7.7, 12.4
Slot labels 11.3
Smiley, William 7.26
Smith, Benjamin 7.35
Smith, Elizabeth 1.10, 2.2, 2.3
Smith, James 9.10
Smith and Hayter 7.17
Smith Tate 7.24
Snatt, Josiah 7.30
Spices 1.6, 1.8, 2.7, 2.10, 2.16
Sponsor's mark 7.2
St. Clouet 2.8
Stainforth, George 9.3
Stancliffe, Jane 12.7
Stands
    Eight bottle 1.5, 1.18
    Five bottle 1.1, 1.5, 1.8
    Four bottle 1.3, 1.5, 1.8, 1.18
    Leather 12.8
    Pairs of 1.8
    Papier mache 12.8
    Pewter 12.8
    Six bottle 1.5, 1.8, 1.18
    Ten bottle 1.2, 11.4
    Three bottle 1.3, 1.5, 1.8
    Two bottle 1.1, 1.5, 7.11
    Wooden 12.8
Stock sauces 2.3, 2.6, 2.11
Storr, Paul 7.35, 7.39
Story and Elliott 7.36
Style
    A la Francaise 1.9
    A la Russe 1.9
    Sauce labels 7.1
    Wine labels 7.4
Summers, William 7.28, 7.40, 7.42, 9.11, 9.13
Sweden 7.6
Sweetmeats 1.9

Table arrangements 2.18
Tayleur, John 7.30
Teare, Benjamin 7.18

Theobalds and Atkinson 7.34
Thompson, Samuel 12.2
Tongue, Samuel 7.20
Trinity House 1.24
Troby, WB 7.28, 8.3

Unite, George 7.44, 11.9
Unmarked labels 7.1
Urn 7.22
Urquhart and Hart 7.26

Vauxhall Gardens 2.1
Verral, William 2.8
Vine 7.44
Vinegar 1.1, 1.3, 1.8, 1.16
Vinegar decanter 12.6
Vintners' Company 7.18

Wakelin, Edward 1.1, 1.4, 1.15, 1.20, 7.7, 9.2, 9.3, 9.4, 9.5, 11.2, 11.3, 12.4, 12.7, 12.9
Wallis, Thomas 12.8
Walsh, Stephen 1.14, 12.3
Walther, Hermann 7.18
Warburton, Elizabeth 2.11
Warwick cruet 1.1, 1.2, 1.3, 12.2
Watson, John 7.17
Wax 7.3
Weed Collection 1.17, 7.18, 7.19, 11.1
West 11.8
Westrup, JB 2.17
Whitford, Samuel 7.17, 7.30, 11.3
Whitworth 7.44
Williams 1.15
Willmore, Joseph 7.24, 11.3, 11.9
Windsor Castle 1.9
Wingfield, Richard 12.3
Wires 12.5
Wood, Samuel 9.1, 9.2, 12.2
Woodforde, Parson 1.11
Wright and Davis 7.48

Yapp and Woodward 7.18, 7.24

Zechlin 12.1

179